No-Win War

The Paradox of US-Pakistan Relations
in Afghanistan's Shadow

T0345827

No-Win War

The Paradox of US-Pakistan Relations in Afghanistan's Shadow

Zahid Hussain

OXFORD
UNIVERSITY PRESS

OXFORD
UNIVERSITY PRESS

Oxford University Press is a department of the University of Oxford.
It furthers the University's objective of excellence in research, scholarship,
and education by publishing worldwide. Oxford is a registered trade mark of
Oxford University Press in the UK and in certain other countries

Published in Pakistan by
Oxford University Press
No. 38, Sector 15, Korangi Industrial Area,
PO Box 8214, Karachi-74900, Pakistan

First Edition published in 2021

ISBN 978-0-19-070419-3

Second Impression 2021

Typeset in Adobe Garamond Pro
Printed on 68gsm Century Pearl Shade

Printed by Mas Printers, Karachi

Acknowledgements
Cover Image: © PRESSLAB / Shutterstock

Contents

Acknowledgements

I am hugely indebted to all the people who agreed to interviews and provided valuable information that helped shape this book. I am particularly thankful to Pakistani civil and military officials who have been very generous with their time and candidly shared their experience and perspective of the events that marked the post-9/11 US–Pakistan relations. I have also benefitted hugely from my interaction with American and Afghan officials and experts that have helped make this book objective.

I started working on this book during my term as a Pakistan scholar at Woodrow Wilson International Center for Scholars, Washington D.C. (2010-2011). My initial research was on Pakistan's tribal areas and regional security but subsequent developments in Pakistan and the expanding US war in Afghanistan encouraged me to widen the scope of the book.

I am thankful to the Fellowship Fund for Pakistan, for sponsoring my stay at the Center. I owe special thanks to Robert Hathaway, former Director Asia Center at the Woodrow Wilson International Center and William Milam for their encouragement and support.

I have hugely benefitted from my experience as a journalist covering Pakistan and Afghanistan for *The Times* London, *The Wall Street Journal*, and the *Newsweek* for almost three decades. My reporting of various events in Pakistan and Afghanistan forms a significant part of this book.

Moreover, I am extremely grateful to Kathy Gannon and Francoise Chipaux, who encouraged me at every stage of my work. Special thanks to Riaz Mohammad Khan, Maleeha Lodhi, Sherry Rehman, Salman Bashir, and Jalil Abbas Jilani for their valuable input. Many thanks to Afsheen Ahmed for her help with editing and fact-checking.

I owe a huge debt of gratitude to all my friends in and out of journalism who helped me accomplish this book in different ways.

Special thanks to Rehana Hakim, Farrah Durrani, Zeeshan Afzal Khan, Zeba Sathar, and Arifa Noor.

Many thanks to Gulrukhsar Mujahid at Oxford University Press who gave the book its final shape.

It has also been love encouragement of my daughter Maria and son Adnan that made this book possible.

Introduction

Two months after al-Qaeda had struck the US with the deadliest terrorist attack ever on its soil, President Pervez Musharraf stood with President George W. Bush at New York's Hotel Waldorf Astoria on 10 November 2001 for a joint press conference. 'Pakistan's efforts against terror are benefitting the entire world and linking Pakistan more closely with the world,' President George W. Bush remarked looking at Pakistan's military leader. 'I've authorized a lifting of sanctions and over $1 billion in US support. I will also back debt relief for Pakistan.'[1]

Visibly pleased with the US president's effusive compliment President Musharraf saw the dawn of a new era of relationship between Pakistan and the US. 'Pakistan will hope for a very sustainable and longstanding, futuristic relationship developing between Pakistan and the United States; a relationship which we always have had in the past,' he responded.[2]

The events of 9/11 and return to America's embrace had catapulted Pakistan back on world stage. It was almost a return of 1979 when the Soviet invasion ended the decade long estrangement between the two erstwhile allies and brought them together to help Afghan 'mujahideen' fight the occupation forces. Pakistan was then seen as the linchpin in the West's battle against the communist bloc.

The CIA and ISI collaborated in conducting the biggest covert war ever in history that forced the Soviet forces to leave Afghanistan. The collapse of the Soviet Union and end of the Cold War in 1990 also gave birth to a new world order. Pakistan was no more as important for the US, which had emerged as the world's sole superpower. This marked yet another period of separation between the two Cold War era partners causing a deep sense of betrayal in Pakistan. For the next ten years, Pakistan suffered banishment. But 9/11 changed the world. America was attacked by a global terrorist group with its leadership based in Afghanistan. Within hours of the devastation, the Bush administration had declared war against al-Qaeda and its host in Afghanistan. It was another war in Afghanistan that became the pivot around which the new US–Pakistan partnership was built. The circumstances of the two unisons were, however, very different.

While there was a strong convergence of interest that had bound the two nations in a strategic relationship in the 1980s, the alliance that emerged after 9/11 was more out of expediency and compulsion. It was often described as a 'shotgun marriage'. Although it was projected as a strategic partnership, in reality, it had been a transactional relationship from the outset. The two countries had pursued divergent agendas in Afghanistan in the 1990s. Pakistan's backing for the Taliban regime was the major source of tension between Washington and Islamabad. But it all changed after the 9/11 terrorist attacks on America.

While for the US, Pakistan's support was critical to its war against al-Qaeda and the Taliban in Afghanistan, the new partnership brought an end to Pakistan's international isolation. The removal of multiple sanctions revived the flow of US financial and military aid to Pakistan.

The post-9/11 US–Pakistan partnership, however, remained paradoxical and full of ironies. Despite Pakistan's reservation over the installation of Northern Alliance-led administration in Kabul after the fall of the Taliban regime in November 2001, the cooperation between Washington and Islamabad against al-Qaeda remained extremely effective. Several top al-Qaeda leaders were captured in Pakistan in the joint CIA and ISI operations. Yet that cooperation was missing when it came to taking action against the Taliban leadership residing in Pakistan's border regions.

The US didn't have any understanding of the country when it went to war in Afghanistan to punish the perpetrators of the 9/11 terrorist attacks. The ouster of the Taliban regime was not much of a problem for the mightiest military power on earth. For Washington, the Taliban had been defeated as the Bush administration diverted its focus on the other theatre of war—Iraq.

American officials didn't even ask Islamabad to act against the Taliban leadership then; for them the conservative Islamic movement had become history. Meanwhile, the sanctuaries in Pakistan and support from their allies among Pakistani Islamic groups helped the Taliban reorganise. Within a few years, the Taliban had turned into a formidable resistance force challenging the occupation forces.

Perhaps the biggest mistake the Bush administration had made was to ally the US with a particular Afghan faction and warlords. That reinforced the perception of it being part of the Afghan civil war. The decision to exclude the reconcilable Taliban from the political process would come back to haunt the US with the rise of insurgency. Many senior Taliban leaders who were willing to become part of the mainstream, instead suffered persecution and many of them were sent to Guantánamo.[3]

Washington ignored Pakistan's repeated plea for the installation of a broad-based and more representative post-Taliban administration in Kabul.[4] Exclusion of reconcilable elements of the ousted regime fuelled Pashtun alienation feeding into the Taliban insurgency. By 2005, the insurgency had spread to vast areas in eastern and southern Afghanistan that had traditionally been a Taliban stronghold.

That was the beginning of what Robert L. Grenier would later describe as the second American–Afghan war.[5] The insurgency became widespread with the Taliban establishing parallel administration in the areas under their influence. It was an unwinnable war but there was no realisation in Washington about the deteriorating battlefield situation.

Meanwhile, the growing Indian influence in Afghanistan became a major source of tension between Kabul and Islamabad. What was then widely perceived as a rapidly diminishing commitment by the West to the Afghan war, has also intensified Pakistan's battle with India for supremacy of influence in Afghanistan. The resolution of the Afghan war became deeply entangled in the prolonged rivalry between Islamabad and New Delhi. The Pakistani military establishment viewed the expanding Indian presence in its 'backyard' as a serious threat to the country's own security.

Afghanistan's strategic partnership agreement with India in October 2011, involving New Delhi in the training of Afghan security forces, had reinforced Pakistan's apprehension. It was the first time Kabul had signed such a pact with another country.[6] The expanding Indian presence in Afghanistan had compounded Islamabad's fears of being encircled.

A major worry for Pakistan, therefore, was how to defend both its eastern and western borders as India and Afghanistan became increasingly close. Some of Pakistan's security concerns were legitimate, but the fears of encirclement verged on paranoia. It also resulted in Pakistan's continuing patronage of some Afghan Taliban factions, such as the Haqqani network, which it considered a vital tool for countering Indian influence, even at the risk of Islamabad's relationship with Washington.

For Pakistan, the network remained a useful hedge against an uncertain outcome in Afghanistan. The deep reluctance to take action against the Haqqani network was a reflection of Pakistan's narrow security concerns. Former President Pervez Musharraf later admitted that Pakistani backed the insurgents against the Kabul government because according to him President Hamid Karzai helped India 'to stab Pakistan'.

Increasing US tilt towards India had added to Islamabad's worries that may also be one of the reasons for the Pakistani security agencies for not acting against the Taliban safe havens on its soil and not fully cooperate with the coalition forces. The struggle for influence had also escalated into a wider regional conflict, with Afghanistan becoming the centre of a new 'Great Game' with Pakistan, India, and Iran vying for influence in the strife-torn country. After taking over in 2008, President Obama had declared Afghanistan a 'good war'. He deployed thousands of additional troops in Afghanistan in an effort to achieve military victory. His administration did not have any clear exit plan. His biggest blunder, perhaps, was to give an 18-month deadline for the US troops to complete their counterinsurgency objectives. That deadline reinforced the confidence of the Taliban that the time was with them. 'You have the watches. We have the time', a Taliban commander was quoted as saying.[7]

There was a major difference of views between the US and Pakistani military leadership over America's counterinsurgency strategy in Afghanistan. Pakistan consistently argued that reconciliation with the Taliban was the only way out of the Afghan conflict. But for the US military commanders, even the mention of reconciliation was an anathema. They believed that a military victory was possible. Predictably, the surge in the number of US troops and counterinsurgency strategy failed to contain the Taliban insurgency that had by then spread to a large part of the country.

The confusion in the Obama administration's approach to the Afghan war was also reflected in its AfPak policy, lumping Pakistan with Afghanistan in the new regional strategy. Looking at Pakistan through the Afghan prism was not acceptable to Islamabad. The AfPak strategy also posed a paradox for the Obama administration; it didn't offer any sure way forward or an exit plan. The term was soon dropped.

In its second term, the Obama administration did open up to the idea of reconciliation. But talks with the Taliban remained a non-starter; it didn't go beyond a few informal contacts. There was still no clear strategy to take the process forward. The opening of the Taliban office in Doha in 2013, however, marked a significant breakthrough.

In mid-2014, President Obama declared that he was ready to open a 'new chapter' by transferring the complete security responsibility to the Afghan administration. He gave a new timeframe for the total withdrawal of American forces from Afghanistan by 2016. It was clear that Obama's 'good war' had already gone bad.

Worsening US–Pak relations had also seriously affected America's war efforts in Afghanistan. A series of incidents in 2011 had brought an already uneasy alliance to a breaking point. The Raymond Davis episode in January 2011 exposed the CIA's secret network operating in Pakistan. The scandal had revealed the widening trust gap between the two allies. The crisis was resolved with both sides taking a step back, but the damage was done.[8]

The unilateral raid by the US Special Forces on Osama bin Laden's compound in Abbottabad on 2 May 2011 further strained the relations between Washington and Islamabad. The US action on Pakistani soil was seen as a national humiliation. The very fact that the world's most wanted terrorist was living in a garrison town close to the Pakistan Military Academy had put Pakistan in a very embarrassing position. Pakistan faced questions whether it was just an intelligence failure or was there anything more to the presence of the al-Qaeda leader in a high security zone.[9]

But the most serious blow to the alliance came on 29 November 2011 when US air force jets bombed a Pakistani border post at Salala in Bajaur tribal region, killing several soldiers. It was an inflection point in the rocky relationship. The Obama administration's reluctance to even offer an apology for the killing of soldiers of an allied country made things worse.[10]

For seven months, Pakistan closed down the vital ground supply line to the NATO forces in Afghanistan. The stalemate was finally broken after Secretary of State Hillary Clinton said 'sorry'. But the cracks in the alliance had become irreparable. The Salala incident led to a resetting of the relationship; now there was not even a pretense of a strategic alignment.[11]

There was nothing much left in the partnership wrecked by allegations of 'double game' and 'deceit'. Almost all US military aid to Pakistan had been stopped and only a trickle of civilian assistance continued. Yet a complete rupture was not a choice for either side. Pakistan was still critical for the US to extricate itself from its longest war.

While the illusion of any strategic convergence has been absent for long, the mutual interest in ending the Afghan war kept the relations alive. Even during the worst crisis, the line of communication between Washington and Islamabad remained open. Backchannel contacts worked to resolve crises on various occasions.

As the war in Afghanistan got messier, there was growing realisation in Washington that the only way out of the Afghan quagmire was a negotiated political settlement. It could only be possible through direct talks with the Taliban. After a long period of indecisiveness, Washington finally took the first concrete step towards a structured peace process in early 2018 when President Donald Trump appointed Zalmay Khalilzad as point-man for peace talks with the Taliban.

A naturalized American citizen of Afghan origin, Khalilzad was the most appropriate person for the job. It was much easier for him to communicate with the insurgents. An old Afghan hand, he was a member of the American delegation at the Bonn Conference in November 2001 that put together the post-Taliban administration in Kabul. He had later served as American ambassador to Afghanistan.

Taliban also responded positively to Washington's talks offer. Even though the Taliban were not willing to talk to the Kabul government; the group never had any problem talking to the US. The problem was on Washington's side. The insurgents appeared much more confident following their battlefield successes and growing international recognition. The timely release of Mullah Abdul Ghani Baradar—a founding member of the Taliban movement—from detention in Pakistan gave the Taliban a huge boost.

Mullah Baradar led the Taliban delegation in the gruelling peace negotiation. His pragmatic approach was one of the most important factors in the success of the talks that produced the historic 29 February 2020 peace accord raising the prospect of ending America's longest war.

Pakistan's role in facilitating the peace talks was critical. The Doha accord was seen as a vindication of Pakistan's long-standing position that there was no military solution to the Afghan war. Pakistan might not have total control over the Taliban leadership, but it had enough clout to nudge them to come to the negotiating table. Pakistan would also play a significant role in fixing the problems arising during the Doha negotiations.

The success of the Doha talks helped improve Pakistan's relations with Washington, but their relations remained transitory. The changing regional geopolitics has created a new alignment of forces. The growing strategic alliance between the US and India and the China–Pakistan axis reflects the emerging geopolitics. Indeed, the

US–Taliban peace deal has brought the withdrawal of American forces closer, yet peace in Afghanistan remains elusive.

This book tells the story of two decades of US–Pakistan relations that emerged in the aftermath of the 9/11 terrorist attacks on the US. It's perhaps the most complex and the oddest of relationships. The two were supposed to be allies but were also regarded as adversaries. It's the story about critical cooperation between the two countries in the so-called 'war on terror' as well as the 'cloak and dagger game' between their intelligence agencies. It's also a story of America's unwinnable war in Afghanistan and the resurgence of the Taliban. The following pages also cover the impact of Pakistan's alliance with the US on the country's domestic politics and civil-military relations. The two-decade war in Afghanistan has had devastating effects on Pakistan, turning the country into a battleground for militants. This book probes what the US war on terror meant for Pakistan and the region.

I have covered Pakistan and Afghanistan for various national and international publications for almost three decades. After 9/11, I have closely followed the war in Afghanistan and Pakistan's battle against militancy. I have travelled many times to Waziristan and other former tribal regions to report on the military operation against militants.

I have written extensively on post-9/11 US–Pakistan relations. Direct interactions with senior Pakistani and American officials have provided me unique insight into the perspective of both sides on the complex alliance. I have also been meeting senior Afghan government officials and representatives of other factions during my visit to Afghanistan and at various international forums.

I also had the opportunity of interviewing key characters involved in policy decision at the highest level including the former president, Pervez Musharraf (who I have interviewed several times in and outside power) and former Afghan president, Hamid Karzai. I also had several sessions with the former Pakistan army chief, General Ashfaq Parvez Kayani during his tenure as COAS and after his retirement.

This book is also a sequel to my previous publications—*Frontline Pakistan: The Struggle with Militant Islam* (2007) and *The Scorpion's Tail: The Relentless Rise of Islamic Militancy in Pakistan and How it Threatens America* (2011).

1 | History Starts Today!

George Tenet, Director CIA, waited anxiously for his Pakistani counterpart, Lt. Gen. Mahmud Ahmed, DG ISI. It was just two days after 11 September 2001, when the US was shaken by the worst terrorist attacks on its soil.

The atmosphere at the CIA headquarters at Langley that day was grim—completely different from just a few days earlier when General Mahmud had visited Langley. 'General, we need your support,' said Tenet, clasping the General's hands. 'We completely depend on you.'[1]

The two then sat down to discuss the future plan of action. With the footprint of the terrorist attack leading to Osama bin Laden and with al-Qaeda now based in Afghanistan, US military action seemed inevitable and imminent. With its deep involvement with the Afghan Taliban regime, the ISI was the only agency that had ground knowledge of Afghanistan. For any action in that country, the CIA needed close ISI cooperation. General Mahmud promised every support, on behalf of Pakistan, at the Langley meeting that day. The details were to be discussed later.

There was a distinct—and positive—change in tenor. Just a few days ago, on 9 September 2001, General Mahmud had a tense encounter with Tenet and other CIA officials on Pakistan's support for the Taliban regime in Afghanistan. He had vigorously defended his country's relations with the radical Islamic regime and told CIA officials that Mullah Mohammed Omar, known as the supreme leader of the Taliban, was a pious and religious person, not a man of violence.[2]

The discussion at Langley on 9 September had mainly revolved around the al-Qaeda and terrorism coming out of Afghanistan. Tension had further increased with the assassination, also on 9 September, of Ahmad Shah Massoud, the leader of the rebel Afghan Northern

Alliance. Two Arab suicide bombers, masquerading as television journalists, blew themselves up during an interview with the most powerful anti-Taliban commander. Al-Qaeda and the ISI were blamed for the attack.[3]

Tenet recalled that he 'tried to press' Mahmud to do something about Taliban support for bin Laden but stated that Mahmud was 'immovable when it came to the Taliban and the al-Qaeda.'[4] The ISI chief had then argued that recognition of the Taliban regime by the US could help in getting bin Laden expelled from Afghanistan. However, for the US, recognition of the Taliban regime was out of the question. But George Tenet had got quite excited by the General's indication that getting bin Laden, was a possibility.

The CIA chief later said that General Mahmud's sole suggestion was that the US should try bribing key Taliban officials to get them to turn over bin Laden. However, 'even then he made it clear that neither he nor his service, would have anything to do with the effort, not even to the extent of advising the agency whom it might approach.'[5]

One of the architects of the 1999 coup that saw the return of military rule in Pakistan, General Mahmud, was the second most powerful member of the junta after President General Pervez Musharraf. Notwithstanding strained relations between Washington and Islamabad, General Mahmud had developed a good working relationship with George Tenet. He was given VVIP protocol when he arrived in Washington in the first week of September 2001—his second visit within one year.

After the end of his official visit, General Mahmud was due to fly back home but was stranded in Washington because of the closure of air space following the terrorist attacks. His presence in the country made it convenient for the Bush administration to deliver the message on what it wanted Pakistan to do.

Before his meeting at Langley on 13 September, General Mahmud had met with the US Deputy Secretary of State, Richard Armitage, for the second time in 24 hours. Richard Armitage was curt and emphatic in his message on what the Bush administration expected from the

ISI chief. General Mahmud and other Pakistani officials listened to him quietly as Armitage read out a list of US demands.[6]

A burly man and former wrestler, Armitage, normally had a reputation of being a level-headed person. But the terrorist attack on the US a day earlier had changed everything in Washington. He did not mince his words: 'What I am going to ask you is not negotiable—it is black and white.' He paused to see the Pakistani spymaster's reaction. Armitage was echoing the words of his president: 'You're either with us or against us.'[7]

General Mahmud got the message. He took no time in promising Pakistan's full cooperation with the US plan of action. But he did not sound fully convinced about the possible military action against the Taliban regime in Afghanistan. He tried to talk about the history of US–Pakistan relations.[8]

Armitage snapped at him, saying that he knew the history very well. 'General, we're talking about the future, and for you, and for us, history starts today!'[9] That was the end of the meeting. General Mahmud was glum as he was being driven to Langley. For the US, history may have started after 9/11, but for Pakistanis, reverting to America's embrace was a return to history. General Pervez Musharraf was in Karachi when he got news of the terrorist attacks in New York and Washington. He immediately called the US ambassador, Wendy Chamberlin, to offer his condolences. 'We are with the people and the government of the United States,' the General assured the ambassador. She told him that Osama bin Laden and the Taliban were involved. 'It is too early to assume that,' Musharraf replied. 'Don't ever say it again. There is no tolerance of this in the United States,' Ms Chamberlin snapped. Musharraf understood the sentiment—and the message.[10]

Collin Powell, the US Secretary of State, was equally blunt in his message when he called General Musharraf on 12 September. 'The American people would not understand if Pakistan was not in this fight with the United States,' the former top American military commander told the Pakistani military leader. General Musharraf took it as a 'blatant ultimatum.'[11] He assured Colin Powell of Pakistan's unconditional support to the US. There was no conversation between them on the specifics.

What the Bush administration needed Pakistan to do was later specified in a list of seven demands conveyed to Musharraf by Wendy Chamberlin. The list included cutting off all supplies to the Taliban regime, sharing all intelligence information about the Taliban and al-Qaeda operation in Afghanistan with the US, and providing US forces logistic support.[12]

Except for two demands—blanket access to Pakistani airspace and permission to use airbases—the military government acceded to all other US demands. Pakistan, however, allowed US air force jets to fly through an allocated air corridor and handed over three bases—two in western Balochistan and one in Sindh province—as US forces readied for the invasion of Afghanistan.

Pakistan's quick acquiescence to the demands surprised even the US officials, who had expected the military rulers to do some hard bargaining. While Pakistan's support was critical for the US military action in Afghanistan, US officials had believed that getting Pakistan's military government to extend unqualified support would not be easy.[13]

There was a reason for this pessimism. The relations between the two countries had been in the deep-freeze for the past decade after the US clamped multiple sanctions against Pakistan for developing a nuclear weapon. More sanctions came after Pakistan conducted nuclear tests in 1998 in response to India's tests. Pakistan was further punished after the 1999 military takeover.[14]

From being a close ally in the 1980s, Pakistan had become a pariah nation. The US had walked out of the region after the Soviet forces pulled out of Afghanistan in 1989. Months later, Washington slapped sanctions on Pakistan for its nuclear weapons programme. The sanctions had hurt military-to-military relations the most, which had been the pivot of the decades-long relationship between the two countries. It was seen as a great betrayal by Pakistan, the erstwhile partner, who had together with the US, fought the biggest covert war against the Soviet occupation of Afghanistan. The divide had further widened with Pakistan's support for the Taliban regime in Afghanistan. The conservative Islamic militia had grown out of the civil war among various Mujahideen groups in Afghanistan that ensued after the fall of the Najibullah government that had, in the past, been supported by the erstwhile Soviet Union in 1992.

It was in mid-1993, when some three-dozen Taliban (students) got together at Kashke Nakud, near Kandahar, in southwestern Afghanistan, to voice their concerns over the lawlessness in the country.[15] Taliban is a Pashtu word, meaning students of a religious school or madrasa. The group, led by a former Mujahideen commander, Mullah Mohammed Omar (who had lost one eye in the war against the Soviet forces), took upon themselves the task of cleaning up their region of corrupt Mujahideen commanders.

Within three years, the militia had swept most of the country and took over the control of the capital, Kabul, in 1996. Initially, many US diplomats in Islamabad and State Department officials, worried about the growing lawlessness in Afghanistan, believed that the Taliban could play a useful role in restoring a strong and centralised government to Afghanistan. This view was also shared privately by many relief organisations, who were frustrated by the fruitless negotiations of the UN Special Mission. They saw in the Taliban, with all their prejudices, a peculiarly Afghan solution to the problem which had defied international peacemakers for many years.

The meteoric rise of the Taliban movement owed much to the backing of Islamabad and help from Pakistani Islamic parties. When the Islamic Emirate of Afghanistan began their rule in September 1996, after the fall of Kabul, they controlled approximately 90 per cent of the country. The Northern Alliance was formed in late 1996 as a counterforce to the Taliban, comprised mostly Tajiks, Uzbeks, and Hazaras, and controlled parts of the country in the northeast.

Although Islamabad had lost much leverage with the Taliban, it continued to support the conservative Islamic administration for geostrategic, *not* ideological reasons. The fear of the Opposition Afghan forces, supported by India and Iran, taking over the country, was the major reason for Pakistan to help prop up the Pashtun-dominated militia.

Over the years, Afghanistan had been turned into al-Qaeda's capital and became known as the epicentre of global terrorism. 'How to take out bin Laden?' had been a major challenge for successive US administrations. The issue had become more urgent after al-Qaeda was blamed for the attack on the USS Cole, a US Navy guided missile destroyer in Aden, Yemen in 2000, and the bombing of US embassies in East Africa in 1998. Washington needed Pakistan's help in taking bin Laden out of Afghanistan.

In January 2000, General Musharraf had promised senior US officials that he would meet with the Taliban supreme leader, Mullah Omar, and press him on the matter of expelling bin Laden. But the visit never materialised.[16] In March 2000, President Bill Clinton made a few hours stopover in Islamabad on his way back from India. During his brief one-on-one meeting, Clinton asked General Musharraf for help regarding bin Laden and linked Pakistan's help with getting rid of the al-Qaeda chief with the improvement of relations between the two countries. Again in May 2000, President Clinton reminded Musharraf to carry out his promise to visit Afghanistan and convince Mullah Omar to get rid of bin Laden.[17]

In June 2000, George Tenet, Director CIA, travelled to Pakistan with the same message. However, Musharraf could not visit Afghanistan because of clear indications that Mullah Omar would not respond positively to any suggestion to extradite bin Laden.[18] Islamabad seemed to be losing whatever clout it may have once had, on the Islamic fundamentalist regime. Mullah Omar was not prepared to listen to his patrons anymore. In early 2001, he had snubbed Musharraf's Interior Minister, Moinuddin Haider, who sought the extradition of leaders of a Pakistani sectarian group who had taken refuge in Afghanistan. However, the worst snub came in March 2001, when Mullah Omar rejected Pakistan's request not to obliterate the statues of Buddha in Bamiyan. Despite international outrage and even dissent within their own ranks, hard-line Taliban extremists systematically destroyed Afghanistan's pre-Islamic heritage.[19]

The tentacles of the al-Qaeda terrorist network had also extended into Pakistan, where it had strong allies among the Islamic militants. The country became home to a thriving community of foreign jihadists, many of whom were veterans of the anti-Soviet Afghan war and had stayed on there for the simple reason that they could not return to their countries of origin for fear of persecution. The jihadist culture provided them with a safe haven in Pakistan. But the events of 9/11 had changed the world. Rarely had the world witnessed such unanimous international unity supporting what President Bush had described as, the 'war on terror,' and the invasion of Afghanistan. A UN Security Council resolution bound all nations to support US action.

General Musharraf had realised, within hours of the 9/11 terrorist attacks that America would accept nothing short of complete compliance from his government on the US war plans. He had a clear idea by then of the consequence of resisting America's demands. He was apprehensive that the Pakistani military could be completely destroyed in a confrontation with the world's greatest superpower. His other fear was that the country's weak economy could not withstand international sanctions. His greatest concern, however, was US forces using Indian bases in case of Pakistan's refusal to cooperate.[20]

Pakistan and the US were back together after a decade of estrangement that had followed after a close partnership, bringing about the downfall of the Soviet Union. However, this time around, it was a shotgun marriage, unlike the consensual one in the 1980s.

Pakistan's policy volte-face after 9/11 was more of an expediency and not driven by any strategic convergence. Ironies abounded in the new relationship. After having spent the past seven years helping the Taliban, Pakistan was required to help the US to dislodge the Islamic fundamentalist government that was seen by Pakistan's military establishment as critical to Pakistan's security. Pakistan's vast cache of intelligence information on Afghanistan was seen as crucial, by the US, for taking military action against the Taliban and al-Qaeda.

Musharraf saw that for Pakistan, it was 1979 all over again; a reference to the start of the Soviet–Afghan war that led to billions of dollars in aid for Pakistan. 'We should offer up help,' said Musharraf, 'and, mark my words, we will receive a clean bill of health.'[21] But the turnaround would not be easy.

A major challenge for General Musharraf was to take the nation into confidence about the decision to support America in its war in Afghanistan. He expressed his concern about the domestic fallout to the US ambassador during his long meeting with Wendy Chamberlin on 15 September. 'These decisions are not very easy and we need understanding from the United States and also support from them, so that I can take the nation along with me in our fight against terrorism,' General Musharraf recalled telling her.[22]

It was the most difficult moment for the military strongman when, in an address to the nation on 19 September 2001, he tried to explain why he had decided to side with the US in the 'war on terror.' His tone was defensive as he told his countrymen how hard he had tried to defend the Taliban against all odds. He justified his decision to support the US, saying it was done to save the country's strategic assets, safeguard the cause of Kashmir, and prevent Pakistan from being declared a terrorist state.

'Pakistan is facing a very critical time. And I would say, after 1971, this is the most critical period in the nation's life. And at this point, our decisions will go [have] far-reaching and decisive results. On the one hand, if we make any mistake, they can culminate in very bad ends. And on the other hand, if we make the right decisions, they would be very fruitful for us. The bad results can put into danger our very existence.'[23]

'Our main concerns are, they can be hurt and harmed. And it can also devastate our main power, our main cause, Kashmir. And the fruitful results in our favour can be [good], we can emerge as a powerful nation and our problems can be solved.'

The speech was aimed at defusing domestic opposition and to assure the public that by sacrificing the Taliban, he had protected Pakistan's vital interests.[24]

General Musharraf was, perhaps, more concerned about the reaction within the military. He had a tough time convincing his generals of, once again, getting into a partnership with the US. The divide was tangible in the corps commanders' meeting. The atmosphere in the conference room at the GHQ was tense. At least four commanders, including the Vice Chief of Army Staff General Muzaffar Usmani, were opposed to abandoning the Taliban.[25]

Some commanders agreed that Pakistan didn't have any other option but to comply with US demands. Others kept quiet. After the meeting, the dissenters gathered in Usmani's room. This raised Musharraf's suspicion that something was cooking. General Mahmud was still in the US. When he returned, he too joined the dissenting camp. He argued completely opposite to what he had agreed to in Washington.[26] Musharraf had to walk a very difficult tightrope.

A strong argument in support of change of policy direction was that the US would obliterate Pakistan if it did not cooperate. India had already offered logistical support and use of all their military facilities to the US. India had even cleared its airbase at Farkhor, near Dushanbe in Tajikistan, close to the Afghan border, for American forces to operate from. The fear of an American–Indian alliance that could lead to Pakistan being declared a terrorist state finally swung the decision.[27]

Nevertheless, antipathy towards the US ran deep in Pakistan. It was the beginning of an extremely uneasy relationship. There was a deep distrust of the US. The general view was that 'we can't trust them.' That is how the new phase of the US–Pakistan partnership began. It was seen as a good opportunity to join the international community, but there was also a vote of caution.[28]

With the prevalent scepticism among his top commanders, it was not easy for Musharraf to extend unqualified support to the US in its war against the Taliban. He was desperate to somehow stop the US invasion of Afghanistan and knew that was only possible if Mullah Omar could be persuaded to hand over Osama bin Laden to the US.

With that end in view, General Musharraf sent General Mahmud to Kandahar to speak to Mullah Omar and wrote a letter to him in which he warned the Taliban leader about the seriousness of the situation. The ISI chief was on good terms with the founder of the Taliban movement whom he had met several times. Musharraf wanted Aziz Khan, Pakistan's former ambassador to Afghanistan, to accompany the ISI chief to the meeting in Kandahar. Apparently, the president wanted a foreign ministry official to be present at the meeting.[29]

General Mahmud, curiously, was reluctant to have anyone else present in the meeting. He insisted on meeting the Taliban supreme leader alone. Aziz Khan travelled with the Pakistani delegation to Kandahar but was kept out of the meeting.[30] Although General Mahmud reported back to General Musharraf and the Americans that there had been some progress in the talks, there was no independent verification of what had really transpired in the meeting.

General Mahmud said he told Mullah Omar that 'It's the well-being of 26 million Afghan citizens against one foreign visitor, bin Laden. This is what you're forfeiting if you don't do what the Americans want.' The General was confident that he had made some headway.[31] But as it turned out, he had not. 'Being a Muslim, I would never give any advice to [the] Taliban that could bring destruction to them,' he was later reported as saying in an interview.

A few days later, General Mahmud sent a delegation of Pakistani clerics to talk to Mullah Omar. Interestingly, the delegation comprised hard-line pro-Taliban clerics headed by Mufti Nizamuddin Shamzai, who later issued a *fatwa* (religious edict) for jihad against the American forces. He would also lead violent protests against the Musharraf government for supporting the US-led war against the Taliban. With their hard-line views, those clerics could hardly be expected to persuade the Taliban leader to do something they themselves didn't believe in. Some officials even suggested that the delegation had told Mullah Omar to remain steadfast and not to succumb to US pressure.[32]

It seemed that the impact of 9/11 was lost on Mullah Omar. 'It was God's punishment against injustices against Muslims,' Mullah Omar had declared. General Musharraf later said that negotiating with

Mullah Omar was more difficult than one could imagine. 'It was like banging one's head against a wall,' General Musharraf would later write in his memoir *In the Line of Fire.* 'We told him that his country would be devastated but he didn't understand.'[33]

It was not only the Pakistani generals who were trying to find a way out. Robert Grenier, the CIA station chief in Islamabad, was in constant touch with some senior Taliban leaders in an attempt to persuade them to surrender bin Laden. Interestingly, some of them were given satellite phones by the CIA to maintain contact with Grenier. Most of the top Taliban commanders wanted to get rid of the al-Qaeda leader, but they could not prevail on Mullah Omar to do so. The CIA also tried to induce revolt against Mullah Omar, but it was not so easy.[34]

While Mullah Omar would not agree to the US demand to hand over bin Laden, he was willing to explore other options. He called a meeting of the Afghan religious elite to find a way out. For him, it would be all right if bin Laden left Afghanistan of his own volition, but categorically stated that al-Qaeda could not be forced out. Mullah Omar called a Pakistani journalist, Rahimullah Yusufzai, in the midst of an imminent US invasion, to discuss if there was any other option. Chechen leaders, he said, had agreed to receive bin Laden; 'how can we send him there?' he asked Yusufzai. He went quiet when told that the Chechen leader had already been deposed by Russian forces.[35]

As Pakistan's desperate diplomatic efforts failed to make Mullah Omar change his mind, the 7 October 2001 deadline imposed by President Bush was getting close. By the end of September, US forces were making final preparations to launch an attack on Afghanistan. They had already acquired three airbases in Pakistan close to Afghanistan and set up a command post at the air force base in Jacobabad, in the southern Sindh province.

The American military build-up and the presence of US troops in Pakistan had fuelled public anger. Thousands of people, largely supporters of radical Islamic groups, took to the streets across the country. Violence also broke out in northwest Pakistan. Thousands of Pakistanis crossed over the border to join the Taliban forces.

It was not easy for General Musharraf to deliver on what the US was demanding, with so many in the top army command having strong reservations over the new alignment. A new policy needed a new team. In a surprise move on 7 October 2001, he relieved four lieutenant generals, including the vice chief of army staff, General Usmani.

Musharraf wanted to remove General Mahmud from the ISI and offered to elevate him to the post of chairman of the Joint Chiefs of Staff Committee, which he refused. General Mahmud was one of the strongest voices against abandoning the Taliban with whom he had developed a close affinity as head of the ISI. He could not be trusted with the new policy.[36]

Musharraf went to Mahmud's house with his wife. There, he got an earful from Mahmud's wife. 'You owe your power because of my husband,' she shouted. That was the end of a long friendship.[37] After retirement, General Mahmud turned to a fundamentalist version of Islam. He grew a long beard and joined the Tablighi Jamaat (Society of Preachers) which is an Islamic missionary movement that focuses on exhorting Muslims to return to practising their religion as it was practised during the lifetime of Prophet Muhammad (PBUH), particularly in matters of ritual, dress, and personal behaviour. It has been deemed as one of the most influential religious movements in twentieth-century Islam. Mahmud 'rediscovered' religion mid-career, though socially he appeared moderate. He was extremely well-read and would often quote Clausewitz, Bertrand Russell, and Aristotle during his interaction with American officials.

His political views, though, were religiously inspired. He also had a reputation of being a 'closet Islamist' and a strong proponent of a 'jihadist' foreign policy. Support for militant groups increased during his tenure as ISI chief. General Mahmud never appeared on any public forum post-retirement. One of the architects of the 1999 military coup, he opted for a low-profile and started working on his favourite project—a book on the 1965 war.

Within a few weeks of 11 September, Musharraf had swept aside five of his top thirteen generals. 'The critical element of strategy are timing, space, and strength,' he told me in January 2002, adding, 'No democratically elected government could have moved so quickly.'

The changes coincided with the launching of the joint US–British military operation in Afghanistan and were seen as a part of General Musharraf's plan to appoint to key positions those officers who would support his policy shift. The shakeup in the army high command changed the entire composition of the junta, which had ruled the country since seizing power in October 1999. The top brass now bore a totally new image, seemingly tailored to the requirements of the new situation, with Pakistan trying to cut its umbilical cord with the Taliban. With no peer, Musharraf could now operate much more freely.

The change in the military's high command got tacit approval from the Bush administration. '… his [General Mahmud's] departure seemed to us a further signal that general Musharraf was trying to make it clear, in word and deed, that the last 10 years of Pakistan policy regarding Afghanistan had been somewhat of a waste, and he was going in a new direction,' said Deputy Secretary of State, Richard Armitage.[38]

The changes in the military hierarchy did not resolve all the problems. Many senior officers harboured strong anti-American sentiments and obviously resented Pakistan fighting what they described as 'America's dirty war'. It was going to be very difficult for them to break their associations and change their opinions.

General Musharraf had decided to appoint Lt. Gen. Ehsan ul Haq as ISI chief even before sacking General Mahmud. A Pashtun from the troubled northwestern province, General Haq had earlier served as head of Military Intelligence. Given his strong intelligence background, he was a logical choice to head the organisation that was to play a pivotal role in the US's war on terror in the region.

Unlike his predecessor, General Haq did not come with any ideological baggage. He was one of those commanders who had fully endorsed General Musharraf's decision to support the US. It was not an emotional matter for him to abandon support for the Taliban. His secular outlook and pro-Western tilt made it easier for US officials to deal with him. His rise to the coveted position was, however, resented by some senior officers, particularly among those who had served in the ISI under General Mahmud.

With its growing role in the US's war on terror, the ISI and its chief had become much more powerful. The ISI assumed much greater importance, not only because of its new-found role in the US-led war on terror, but also because of its expanding role in domestic politics. One of the new ISI chief's first jobs was to revamp the agency and to weed out those officers who had a long association with Islamic militants. The move was seen as one of the most significant shifts emerging from Musharraf's decision to align his country with the US.

Though the changes in the military hierarchy had placed General Musharraf firmly in the driving seat, his position still remained quite tenuous. The Afghan war had already spilled into Pakistan. Musharraf had hoped for a quick end to the war, but that would not happen. He continued to face a strong challenge from the country's powerful Islamic groups who were up in arms against his pro-US policy.

Despite the renewed alignment with the US, there was still a huge wall of distrust between the two countries. While Pakistan was important for the US forces for logistic support, there was no coordination between the two countries on war strategy. The CIA and US Special Forces conducted the war with the help and support of the Northern Alliance—with who it had maintained close ties in the past—and with anti-Taliban Afghan warlords. Pakistan was not even informed about the Tora Bora operation that took place in the cave complex of Tora Bora, in the White Mountains near the Khyber Pass in eastern Afghanistan, close to the Pakistan border, from 6–17 December 2001.[39] The US claimed that al-Qaeda had its headquarters there and that it was bin Laden's location at the time. The objective was to capture or kill Osama bin Laden.

It was only on 18 December 2001, after the Tora Bora operation was over, that General Tommy Franks, who was the US General leading the attack on the Taliban in Afghanistan (and who later oversaw the

2003 US invasion of Iraq), called Pakistan to deploy its forces on the borders. But it was too late by then as thousands of al-Qaeda operatives and Taliban had already entered the Pakistani tribal areas. Some Generals were furious about keeping Pakistan in the dark about the action that brought war inside Pakistan. 'It was a deliberate move by America,' General Shahid Aziz, who was appointed to the position of COAS, was quoted as saying after his retirement.[40]

As it turned out, the US and Northern Alliance forces didn't face much resistance from the Taliban and took control of the capital, Kabul, without much difficulty. Realising that they could not fight the US forces, Taliban fighters had just retreated with their weapons. They melted away to their villages, knowing that they always had the opportunity to regroup. Many crossed over the border to Pakistan where they found refuge among the Pashtun population.

The Taliban regime had withdrawn but the Islamic movement was not really defeated. There was little realisation at the time that America would be fighting its longest war without ever winning it. It also marked the beginning of a new relationship between the US and Pakistan that could well be described as 'frenemy'.

2 | The Original Sin

A continent away from the Afghan battlefield, in the scenic and historic sprawling Hotel Petersberg, near Bonn, Germany, the UN special envoy to Afghanistan, Lakhdar Brahimi, and the US representative, James Dobbins, shuttled among various Afghan squabbling groups at the International Conference on Afghanistan being held there, to get them to agree on a transitional government in Kabul.[1]

By the end of November 2001, the Northern Alliance forces, backed by US troops and air support, had entered Kabul, upstaging and changing the balance of power over other anti-Taliban groups, who were mainly operating from foreign capitals. Operation Enduring Freedom, the official name used by the US government for what was termed the 'Global War on Terrorism', had begun.

The Northern Alliance was a loose coalition of four anti-Taliban factions seeking to topple the rule of the Taliban in Afghanistan. It comprised an ethnically and religiously disparate group of rebel movements fighting a defensive war against the Taliban. Initially it included mostly Tajiks, but by 2000, leaders of other ethnic groups had joined the Northern Alliance.

Aside from the Pashtuns, the Alliance primarily comprised three non-Pashtun ethnic groups—Tajiks, Uzbeks, and Hazaras—who had long fought one another during the civil war years in the 1990s. Within the group themselves, there was an asymmetry of power, with the Jamiat-e-Islami in a dominant role. Even within the Jamiat-e-Islami, the military wing of the Shura-yi Nizar (Supervisory Council of North) had the upper hand. Wheels within wheels!

With only a small number of its troops on the ground at the time, the US was heavily dependent on the Northern Alliance. The Taliban offered no resistance to the invading forces. Intensive US bombing had made it easier for the Northern Alliance's forces to enter the capital. However, the prospect of the Northern Alliance—dominated by factions loyal to the Afghan commander, Ahmad Shah Massoud, who was assassinated on 9 September 2001 (just two days before 9/11)—replacing the Taliban regime, evoked concern among other groups.

There was a general consensus that it would be presumptuous to take the Northern Alliance's takeover of Kabul as a fait accompli before a political agreement could be agreed on. More worrisome were the indications that the loosely connected Northern Alliance was reluctant to share power with other Afghan factions. Pakistan was particularly apprehensive about Kabul falling under the control of forces hostile to it. That hostility had its roots in the Afghan civil war in the 1990s when Pakistan had backed the Taliban. The Northern Alliance had close links with both Iran and India.

Ahmad Shah Massoud and Abdul Rashid Dostum, two former archenemies, created the United Front (Northern Alliance) in September 1996, against the Taliban that were preparing offensives against remaining areas under the control of Massoud and those under control of Dostum. The CIA had established contacts with the Alliance led by Massoud, before 9/11, in a move to counter the Taliban. That connection paid off for the Alliance when the US invaded Afghanistan.

General Pervez Musharraf conveyed his apprehension to President George Bush when the two leaders met in New York in November 2001. The US invasion of Afghanistan was already underway by then. Musharraf had two major concerns: to avoid needless collateral damage, the war should be short and targeted; and there should be a friendly post-operation political dispensation in Afghanistan. He suggested working with what he called the 'moderate Taliban.'

Musharraf argued that the moderate Taliban were willing to bring about a change in their policies and it should be accepted in the post-war political arrangement in Kabul. He repeatedly sought assurances from the US administration that the Northern Alliance, which had a strong anti-Pakistan bias and close ties with India, would not be permitted to enter Kabul.[2]

Bush assured Musharraf on 10 November that the Northern Alliance forces would stay out of Kabul. He also agreed to put in place a representative government in Kabul and declare it a demilitarised city. Getting Bush to agree to his request was seen as a major diplomatic success for Musharraf.[3] Not for long though.

The very next day after this assurance, the Northern Alliance triumphantly entered Kabul to the utter embarrassment of President Bush who had asked them to stay out of the Afghan capital. But it was not possible for the US military to prevent the Northern Alliance from entering Kabul. Musharraf was greatly disappointed.[4]

Dobbins arrived in Islamabad the same day that the Northern Alliance entered Kabul and what he heard over there reflected outrage over the development. The Pakistanis made it clear that they would be hostile to any government headed by the Northern Alliance. He heard the same concerns in his meeting with Peshawar-based Afghan factions. A Northern Alliance government replacing Taliban would fuel anger among the Pashtuns on both sides of the border, Pakistani officials told the US envoy.[5]

Pakistan's hostility to a Northern Alliance domination in Afghanistan stemmed from the group's historical links with India. General Musharraf conveyed his fear to the US Ambassador to Pakistan, Wendy Chamberlin, that a Northern Alliance-run Afghanistan would align with Indian interests and threaten Pakistan. Washington viewed Musharraf's concern as a continuing soft corner for the Taliban. Chamberlin reminded Musharraf of his post-9/11 announcement that Pakistan would cut support to the Taliban. It was a black and white situation as far as the Bush administration was concerned.[6]

Musharraf was not bothered with what happened to Mullah Omar and some of his extremist commanders, but he wanted the US and the international community to accept the rest of the Taliban movement as a stakeholder in Afghanistan's future. He told the US ambassador that he would like the post-Taliban government in Afghanistan to not only be Pashtun-dominated, but also to not be 'anti-Pakistan.' He later told Colin Powell that it would be wrong to brand every Taliban an extremist, adding that there were many moderate elements within the Taliban movement willing to accept the new reality.[7]

In a desperate attempt to prevent complete destruction of the Taliban, Musharraf sent his newly appointed ISI chief, General Ehsan ul Haq, to Washington. Accompanied by Saudi Foreign Minister, Prince Saud Al Faisal, General Ehsan carried a four-page letter from Musharraf to President Bush that proposed another effort to resolve the Afghan conflict through negotiations with Taliban leaders willing to cooperate against the al-Qaeda.[8]

British Prime Minister, Tony Blair, was also supportive of Pakistan's proposal. However, the US was adamant that the war would continue until the Taliban surrendered unconditionally or were annihilated.[9] For the Bush administration, the Taliban were beyond the pale because of their association with Osama bin Laden; even dissident Taliban groups were not acceptable.

With the US having decided against deploying a large number of ground troops in Afghanistan, there was concern that the Northern Alliance would replace the Taliban before a political agreement could be reached. But Washington was reluctant to step in and intervene at the time.

It was not just Pakistan, which had reservations about the Northern Alliance being entrenched in Kabul. At the UN, Francesc Vendrell, a veteran diplomat and negotiator, who was appointed in January 2000 as the Secretary General's Personal Representative for Afghanistan, suggested that the UN Security Council adopt a resolution stating that conquest of territory by military force was not an acceptable basis for a future distribution of power in Afghanistan. A new asymmetry was in place with the Northern Alliance having established its control in Kabul. It was emphasised by Francesc Vendrell that any delay in the installation of an interim government in Kabul, comprising other Afghan factions as well, could be damaging.[10]

Finally, the UN and the US woke up to the urgency of installing an interim set-up. Bonn was chosen as the venue for a conference expected to last up to two weeks, arranged by the UN, of varied anti-Taliban Afghan factions to decide on a plan for governing the country and to restore stability after more than twenty years of vicious, nearly nonstop fighting.

Bringing together squabbling Afghan factions was never easy. The only common point among them was opposition to the Taliban. On 25 November 2001, representatives of various Afghan factions and delegates of neighbouring countries who were attending as observers, started to convene in a secluded hilltop hotel near Bonn.

In an unexpected move, the UN, sidelining Francesc Vendrell, appointed Lakhdar Brahimi in his stead—just before the Bonn Conference. Brahimi, a former Algerian foreign minister, had earlier served as the UN special representative (1997–1999) for Afghanistan, but had resigned in 1999, frustrated by the UN's inability to manage the conflict between Taliban and other warring factions. He returned to his former position after Operation Enduring Freedom in late 2001. He was reputed to be a tough-minded realist who respected and understood power dynamics. It was assumed that he would figure out which players were in charge on the ground and how best to meet their minimum demands. It was apparent that the Americans preferred Brahimi.

James Dobbins, a career diplomat, represented the US at the Bonn Conference. Dobbins had a 37-year long career with the State Department and had held key positions in Washington. He served as the US ambassador to the European Community and had negotiating experience in Somalia, Haiti, Bosnia, and Kosovo.[11] Dobbins knew the value of understanding and, where necessary, 'reining in' the position of US security agencies before beginning negotiations. He came with no prior experience of the region, particularly Afghanistan. He received only general guidance on what he was expected to do. There was no clear strategy in place. The only thing he was told to do was to make the transition process fast.[12]

The situation was quite chaotic in Washington regarding a clear policy on Afghanistan. There was no single coordinating authority in the interagency below the cabinet level. So, Dobbins set about the task of determining the US position on Afghanistan, acting on the basis of very general guidance that he received from Secretary of State, Collin Powell, and other senior officials in the Bush administration.[13]

Among those working with Dobbins on the Afghanistan policy was Zalmay Khalilzad, a US citizen of Afghan origin. He was probably the only one in the team who had an understanding about the country. A short-term US position envisaged the formation of a broad-based, moderate Afghan regime that would reassure its neighbours and assist in stamping out residual terrorism. Given Afghanistan's history of resistance to foreign occupation, one of the US objectives was to keep a minimal military footprint. Yet in later years, this historical lesson was completely forgotten. The foreign presence got bigger and bigger, reinforcing the view of Afghanistan being an occupied country.

Getting deeply polarized Afghan groups, warlords, chieftains, and power brokers—divided along ethnic and tribal lines—to agree on any power-sharing arrangement was an enormous challenge. The Northern Alliance, who had established effective control over 50 per cent of Afghan territory after the fall of the Taliban regime, was reluctant to cede its domination and enter a coalition with other smaller groups. It was also important to bring on board the neighbouring countries to make the transition process more credible. Besides Pakistan, Russia and Iran were particularly critical for the future of Afghanistan.

Despite their overt adversarial relations, Washington and Tehran shared common interests in Afghanistan. Iran tacitly supported the US invasion for removal of the radical Sunni Islamic regime of the Taliban with which it had hostile relations. During the civil war, Iran had actively supported the Northern Alliance. The ouster of the Taliban by US forces and the Northern Alliance gaining control of Kabul was politically advantageous to Iran's regional interests.

Dobbins sought to leverage the mutual US–Iran interests in the negotiations. He wanted to use Tehran's influence over the Northern

Alliance as well as other anti-Taliban factions operating in exile in different world capitals. Iran also appeared keen to cooperate on the issue. But there was a problem in communicating directly with Tehran.

The two countries did not have diplomatic relations and had limited dialogue. All communication was supposed to be channelled through Swiss embassies in either capital. Acknowledging the importance of Iran's assistance, Secretary of State, Colin Powell, allowed Dobbins to interact with the Iranian delegation directly, setting aside the existing protocol.

Brahimi and Dobbins combined this leverage, in tandem with pressure from Russia,[14] to overcome some of the most difficult challenges associated with a power-sharing arrangement. Perhaps equally important was the limited nature of US objectives at Bonn. Dobbins was not operating under a mandate to build a 'US-style democracy' for Afghanistan.

For Pakistan, the growing Iranian role was not favourable to its interests. The two countries have had clashing interests in Afghanistan for long. The divide became sharper under the Taliban regime that was propped up by Pakistan. For Tehran, the rise of a Sunni fundamentalist regime, which had also been recognised by its arch rivals—Saudi Arabia and the UAE—was a threat to its interest in the region. Although Iran had remained in contact with the Taliban regime, it actively supported the Tajik-dominated Northern Alliance.

Tension between the Taliban regime and Iran had heightened after the militia overran Mazar-e-Sharif in 1999 and arrested more than a dozen Iranian diplomats and other officials based in the city, at the time under the control of warlord Rashid Dostum. The incident brought the two neighbours to the brink of war, with Iran deploying thousands of troops along its borders with Afghanistan. The situation was defused after Pakistan mediated the release of Iranians. Continuing Iranian support for the anti-Taliban forces remained a sticking point in the relations between Tehran and Islamabad.

With various national interests at play, the US focused their significant influence on trying to overcome the biggest negotiating hurdles at

Bonn. This was essential to reach necessary compromises and achieve consensus among the four Afghan groups at the negotiating table. Because of its longstanding support, some US officials, including the then American ambassador to Delhi, Robert Blackwell, also favoured the inclusion of India in the Bonn negotiation process.

Diplomatic power—much of it in the form of Dobbins's experience and teamwork with Brahimi—was also a key factor in reaching an agreement. Dobbin's mandate was to minimise the US footprint and structure an agreement that would give Afghans the opportunity to build a stable government over some years. Given Afghanistan's history of fierce resistance to outside influence, it was understood at Bonn that 'overreaching' might doom the project to failure.

After failing to convince the US to include the moderate Taliban in the conference, Pakistan lost interest in the Bonn Conference. Islamabad sent a mid-level foreign ministry official to represent it in the conclave.[15] Clearly it didn't have any influence among the anti-Taliban groups who were invited there.

Despite being a strategic partner of the US in the so-called 'war on terror' and providing critical logistic support to the US forces in Afghanistan, Islamabad felt sidelined in the decision-making process about the future of Afghanistan, which was bound to have major repercussions on Pakistan's own stability and national security. This oversight would cast its shadow over relations between Islamabad–Washington, and Islamabad–Kabul in the coming years.

The Northern Alliance and its various factions sent a team comprising ethnic Tajiks, Uzbeks, Hazaras, and Pashtuns. Its delegation was led by Interior Minister Younus Qanooni, a Tajik and a relatively junior member of the Northern Alliance. The official leader of the Northern Alliance, former President Burhanuddin Rabbani, refused to attend the conference.[16]

Rabbani had returned to Kabul and moved back into the presidential palace after Northern Alliance captured the city earlier in the month. He was insistent that any talks on the future of Afghanistan should take place inside Afghanistan. He categorically stated that there could be no decision taken on a new Afghan government in Bonn. But despite his opposition, the Northern Alliance delegation stayed on.[17]

Another important Afghan group invited to the conference was the Rome group comprising the supporters of former Afghan King, Zahir Shah, who once had a sizeable influence in Afghanistan's Pashtun belt. But his absence from Afghanistan, for more than two decades, had eroded whatever little influence the group was left with. The Cyprus and Peshawar groups came to the conference with their own agenda; they were not there to reach a peace settlement, but to agree on a road map consisting of various stages that would culminate with the holding of general elections in the country targeted for mid-June 2004. Qanooni was more conciliatory than Rabbani. He assured other Afghan delegates that the Northern Alliance did not want to have a monopoly on power and that he was willing to discuss a power-sharing formula.[18] But the gap was too wide to bridge.

The domination of the Northern Alliance was too apparent. It was obvious that the US did not have much leverage to get a consensus.

The Northern Alliance and Rome group had eleven delegates each, compared to five each from the Cyprus and the Peshawar groups. It was clear from an early stage that while the Northern Alliance would get most of the seats in the transitional administration, it was decided to leave the post of chairman to the Rome group. In this sense, each group was a winner even though the Northern Alliance and Rome group, were in a far stronger position. While the Rome group was selected as a counterbalance and to represent Western interests, the Northern Alliance was the winner the against Taliban, while the two smaller groups were selected, arguably, to please Iran and Pakistan.

After much discussion and heated arguments over who would be nominated for cabinet posts in the interim administration, the delegates finally came to an agreement, calling for a 29-member interim administration.[19] The Northern Alliance received about half of the posts in the interim cabinet, and members of the Rome group were named to eight positions.[20] Given the correlation of forces and with US approval, the Northern Alliance ended up with plum jobs in the new dispensation, starting with the ministries of defence and interior. Zalmay Khalilzad, who was part of the US delegation, was instrumental in getting the deal done.

Iranians, who had been deeply involved in the Afghan civil war, had more influence on the Afghan groups, including the Cyprus and Rome groups. Mohammad Javad Zarif, a charismatic senior member of the Iranian foreign ministry, led the Iranian delegation. A US-educated university professor, he later became Iran's foreign minister and led his country's negotiations on Iran's nuclear deal with the US and other members of the P5 countries.

Zarif was the busiest person in the conference room. He would move from one delegation to another, arguing and reasoning with them. He seemed to have a lot of influence with the delegates. After the vote was over and the delegates finally agreed on the structure of the interim government, Zarif was pleased with himself. He would later gloat over the success of his efforts at getting the contentious delegates to agree.[21]

Zarif wanted Dobbins to acknowledge his contribution in getting the job done. After twenty years of animosity, the two countries had found a common agenda in Afghanistan; they were both opposed to the Taliban and al-Qaeda. However, the prospect of Tehran and Washington working together in Afghanistan ended abruptly after President Bush's speech where he described Iran, along with North Korea, as an axis of evil. Subsequently, Iran provided sanctuary to al-Qaeda fugitives, including Osama bin Laden's son and other members of his family.[22]

Although the position of president was reserved for a Pashtun from the former King's group, the Bonn Conference virtually legitimised the Northern Alliance's control over the interim administration. It was also made clear to all four factional groups at the conference that they would all be part of a new government in Kabul. Hence, they had an incentive to ensure that the peace agreement was finalised.

Hamid Karzai was nominated to head the administration as president. A Pashtun from the powerful Populzai tribe, Karzai, who had served as deputy foreign minister in the first Mujahideen government led by Sibghatullah Mojaddedi in 1992, was not present in Bonn. Karzai became the main choice for the US after another prominent Pashtun commander, Abdul Haq, was killed on 26 October 2001 by the Taliban in eastern Afghanistan.

While the Taliban were ousted in quick succession from most of Afghanistan's cities, there were still pockets of resistance in parts of western Afghanistan, particularly Kandahar, where Mullah Omar and other senior Taliban leaders were based. Karzai was negotiating terms of withdrawal from the region with emissaries of Mullah Omar.

Pakistan, too, had put its weight behind the Pashtun Karzai to head the interim government hoping that he could bring some ethnic balance in the Northern Alliance-dominated administration. In October 2001, during a meeting in Turkey, Lt. Gen. Ehsan ul Haq, had suggested to Dobbins that Karzai should be named the head of the Afghan government.[23] The ISI had also helped Karzai to get into Afghanistan.

Karzai and his family had lived in Pakistan's western city of Quetta for a very long time after they fled from Afghanistan during the Soviet invasion. However, he was never comfortable with the ISI who he accused of killing his father. It was an uneasy relationship with the Pakistan military establishment who, Karzai believed, had stopped the Taliban from appointing him as Afghanistan's permanent representative to the UN.

I remember meeting Karzai in Islamabad in early 1996 when the Taliban were sweeping across Afghanistan. He was then a great supporter of the Taliban and was convinced that they were not interested in running the government and would invite Zahir Shah, the former king, to take over.[24] But it was not to be. Later, Karzai turned against the Taliban. His contacts with the CIA had been quite deep. Unlike other former Mujahideen leaders, representing Afghan factions assembled at Bonn, Karzai did not have any military backing of his own.

Not surprisingly, during the six weeks preceding his installation, the Northern Alliance leaders had commandeered the positions of governor and chief of police in most of the country's provinces.[25]

Ironic that the very people who had destroyed Kabul in the early 1990s, and whose rapaciousness and ill governance had facilitated the Taliban takeover in 1996, were back at the helm.

The participants in Bonn pledged to withdraw all military units from Kabul and from other areas. An international peacekeeping force, organised by the UN, was to provide security in Kabul. The International Security Assistance Force (ISAF) was mandated to carry out a process of Demobilization, Disarmament, and Reintegration. But that never happened.[26]

No serious effort was made by the US to force the Northern Alliance to comply with the decision of the Bonn Conference to withdraw from Kabul, let alone from other areas. It became a tragi-comic affair in which the Northern Alliance forces handed in their oldest weapons to the Ministry of Defence, at the time headed by none other than Marshal Fahim, the most powerful of the Northern Alliance warlords.

The Bush administration continued its financial and military support to the warlords. The security of Karzai was in the hands of Northern Alliance. The US also warned the interim president that any attempt to remove officials appointed by the Northern Alliance could meet with resistance. The mandate of the ISAF was limited to Kabul, making it difficult to disarm the private militias of the warlords.[27]

It was evident that the main concern of the US and UN at Bonn was to fill the military vacuum that was created in Afghanistan with a new, friendly, and weak regime. The decision on who could attend, which factional elites should be excluded, and how they should be accommodated was made in the first place by the UN.

The Bonn Agreement, passed on 5 December 2001, was the initial series of agreements intended to recreate the State of Afghanistan following the US invasion of Afghanistan post-9/11. It was only meant to serve short-term US policy interests. Khalilzad and the Northern Alliance hijacked the conference as both parties decided on the outcome. For instance, according to Barnett Rubin, who was a UN advisor to the conference, 'Hamid Karzai was handpicked and imposed on others.' Much like previous Afghan elite settlements,

international coercion shaped the process and led to a formal
agreement, which would be undermined by marginalised factions
and interest groups.[28]

Despite the attempt at ethnic inclusiveness, the group assembled in
Bonn did *not* represent the people of Afghanistan, either directly or
indirectly. The conference exposed the ethnic fault lines. The divide
was apparent within the group's participation in the conference.
The groups in Northern Alliance, including one under Abd al-Rabb
al-Rasul Sayyaf, had no ethnic or tribal base of support in the
heartland of the Pashtuns. That raised questions about the extent of
the Bonn success as is often claimed.

The absence of the Taliban, whose main support base was in Pashtun-
dominated areas in southern and central Afghanistan, had left a big
void in the ethnic balance in the new dispensation in Afghanistan.
There was a strong view that if moderate Taliban had been included
in the Bonn negotiations, the insurgency that developed in later years
could have been minimised.

Robert Grenier, CIA station chief in Islamabad, also felt strongly that
a seizure of Kabul by the Tajiks and Uzbeks would make an eventual
political settlement with the Pashtuns far more difficult. Even after the
start of the US invasion Robert Grenier was in contact with some of
the top Taliban leaders, trying to split the group.[29] Meanwhile, Karzai
too was negotiating safe passage for the Taliban commanders after the
fall of Kandahar became imminent.

Years later when the insurgency started spreading in Afghanistan,
Lakhdar Brahimi, one of the architects of the Bonn Agreement,
bitterly regretted the absence of the Taliban at the November 2001
Bonn Conference, declaring, *that was the original sin,*[30] vindicating
what Francesc Vendrell (and others, including Musharraf) had
prophesied at the very beginning; that the installation of an interim
government in Kabul, without taking on board other Afghan factions
as well, could be damaging. Which it was, undoubtedly.

However, Lakhdar Brahimi went on to say that he also accepted that
the Bonn Agreement would probably not have been possible had

the Taliban been at the table. The US objective was the expulsion of the Taliban from Afghanistan so that al-Qaeda could be pursued and destroyed.[31]

Dobbins and Brahimi were not required to broker an agreement that ensured long-term stability of the region—particularly with regards to Pakistan. President Musharraf had promised to cut ties with the Taliban, and the Bonn negotiations proceeded under the assumption that Pakistan would fulfil its obligation.

There was no pressure from the Afghan factions at Bonn to accommodate the Taliban or to consider any role for the militia in the future of Afghanistan—they were deemed defeated. 'For US and participants at the Bonn Conference, the Taliban were history,' and not coming back. Yet in reality, the Taliban had not surrendered and never accepted defeat—they were determined to fight another day.

The biggest failure of the Bonn Conference was to leave out the discussion on the nature of the State in Afghanistan. The Loya Jirga that was held a few months later just put a stamp on the decisions taken at the Bonn Conference. The 2004 Afghan constitution established a strong unitary state that was part of the post-Bonn peace process. This then became a contest between the Western-educated Karzai network and the former Northern Alliance network. The consequence of this was a further exacerbation of ethnic and patronage linkages in the Afghan polity.

Pakistan was not happy with the installation in Kabul of the new Northern Alliance-led administration that it considered hostile to its interests. It was a bitter pill for Musharraf's military-led government to swallow. The Northern Alliance's close ties with India had made Pakistan wary of the new administrative arrangement in Kabul, replacing Islamabad's erstwhile ally—the Taliban. While the Pakistani military establishment was eager to reassert its influence in Kabul, it was not possible in the new power equation that emerged in the post-Taliban Afghanistan.

Pakistan's support for the conservative Taliban Islamic regime had not been based on any ideological consideration. It was based on purely geostrategic reasons, aimed at asserting Pakistan's influence over Afghanistan through a Pashtun movement. The main objective was to get strategic depth vis-à-vis India and isolate Iran. Pakistan's military strategists believed that a Pashtun-dominated friendly government in Afghanistan could provide strategic advantage in the country against its arch-rival, India, with whom it had long been locked in a bitter conflict over Kashmir.[32]

The attainment of this 'strategic depth' had been a key element in Pakistan's Afghan policy since the 1980s. The main objective of Pakistan's policy had been to establish a friendly or pliant government in Afghanistan, using ethnic and religious connections.[33] Throughout the war against the Soviet forces, Pakistan-backed radical Pashtun Mujahideen commanders like Gulbuddin Hekmatyar. The decision to support the Pashtun-dominated Taliban was driven by the same consideration.[34]

But the support for a radical Islamic regime in Afghanistan had its own perils for Pakistan. The Taliban rule turned the war-ravaged country into a conduit for training aspiring militants across the world. The tentacles of the al-Qaeda terrorist network extended into Pakistan, where it had strong allies among the ISI-trained Islamic militants. The Taliban also created a nexus with militant groups operating in Kashmir. In fact, the Taliban had established strategic depth in Pakistan.

The Taliban enjoyed significant support in Pakistan's northwestern province and the semi-autonomous tribal region bordering Afghanistan. The anger against US invasion was palpable in the Pashtun areas with thousands of volunteers crossing the border to join the battle. Many were killed as the Taliban resistance collapsed.

Pakistani intelligence agencies maintained some degree of cooperation with the Taliban elements fleeing the fighting, supporting them, and even encouraging them to revive activities in Afghanistan. They carefully created 'conditions of deniability for their activities.' For the US, the main enemy was al-Qaeda, and Pakistan did provide cooperation in chasing the al-Qaeda militants crossing the border. However, there was no pressure on Pakistan to act against the Taliban. Quite a few Taliban leaders shifted to Pakistan and moved around freely. They had a strong support base among Pakistani militant groups.

Although the Taliban had lost a lot of support because of their oppressive practices during their governance in Afghanistan, their exclusion from the political process attracted support from those Pashtuns who believed that their interests were not adequately represented in the post-Bonn power structure. This fuelled the insurgency. It soon turned into a Pashtun war on both sides of the Pak–Afghan border. As a consequence, Afghanistan would once again be 'struggling with its old demons of internal strife' that would get the US into the longest war it had ever fought.

3 | The Fall and Rise of the Taliban

On the night of 13 November 2001, as the US-backed Northern Alliance forces were closing in on Kabul, Hamid Karzai received a call from Tayyab Agha, head of Mullah Omar's staff. Karzai was launched inside Afghanistan by the CIA sometime in October 2001 to mobilise a Pashtun revolt against the Taliban in the south.

While paying his respects to the Populzai chief, Tayyab Agha enquired about Karzai's future plans. He was probing possible peace options as the collapse of the Taliban regime seemed imminent.[1] The Taliban leadership trusted Karzai since he was a Pashtun. Karzai promised to consider granting safe passage to the Taliban fighters and leaders who were willing to lay down arms and settle in their villages. Tayyib said he would respond to the offer after consulting with Mullah Omar.

Once the US air bombardment began in early October 2001, the Taliban were ousted in quick succession from most of Afghanistan's cities. They pulled out from the capital, Kabul, within hours of the Northern Alliance forces entering the city. They put up no resistance. But the situation in the south was quite different. Kandahar, where Mullah Omar had resided, was the actual seat of power of the so-called Islamic Emirate.

Most Afghan Taliban leaders and military commanders were Pashtuns from the southern provinces. The Pashtuns—who straddle Pakistan's northern and western provinces and Afghanistan and constitute more than 40 per cent of the Afghan population—were the dominant political force prior to the US invasion of Afghanistan. Being a Pashtun himself and belonging to the powerful Populzai clan of the Durrani tribe, made it easier for Karzai to communicate with the Taliban leaders. While operating secretly near Kandahar, Karzai established contact with some of the Taliban cabinet members while the war was still ongoing.

Meanwhile, some other senior Taliban leaders were in direct contact with Robert Grenier, the CIA station chief in Islamabad. Some of them used satellite phones provided by the CIA. From the Taliban side, the main interlocutor was Mullah Jalil, a former deputy foreign minister. There were some others like Mullah Akhtar Usmani who met the CIA station chief after the US invasion had started. Grenier hoped that he could split the Islamic Emirate militia by weaving out some of the key leaders from Mullah Omar.[2]

At one point, even Mullah Abdul Ghani Baradar, co-founder of the Taliban movement in Afghanistan, and the second-in-command of the Taliban, reportedly approached the US through an emissary. The purpose was probably to see if war could be avoided.[3] Being a Populzai as well, Baradar probably felt more at ease dealing with a person from his own tribe. The communication, however, went cold when no clear response was received from the Americans.[4]

In the first week of December 2001, a high-level Taliban delegation arrived at Karzai's hideout in northern Kandahar with a letter from Mullah Omar which stated that the Taliban leader had given his cabinet the authority to decide about Afghanistan's future. The meeting was arranged through Mullah Naqibullah, a former Afghan Mujahideen commander, who had maintained a good relationship with Karzai for years. Notwithstanding political differences, tribal connections remained critically important in Afghanistan.

After several rounds of meetings, the Taliban cabinet ministers agreed to surrender to Mullah Naqibullah. Some high-level Taliban members, such as the minister of defense and top commanders, were among those who surrendered to Karzai in the first week of December. In addition to the city of Kandahar, the agreement provided for the Taliban to surrender the surrounding Kandahar province, the province of Helmand to the west, and Zabul to the northeast.[5] As a result of the surrender, the control of the Taliban was reduced to a few pockets in the north, and the still unsettled mountainous areas in the east.

Under the agreement, the Taliban abandoned the city—Kandahar—where the Taliban movement had originated and that was its stronghold. In a sense, the relinquishing of Kandahar signaled the end of the Taliban control of the country. Had the Taliban forces decided to make a last stand in Kandahar, it would have created a major problem for the US forces and their local allies. There were not enough Pashtuns to fight against the Taliban.

Karzai came very close to an agreement with the Taliban that would have allowed Mullah Omar to remain in Kandahar and to 'live in dignity.' Addressing a press conference in Islamabad, Mullah Abdul Salam Zaeef, the Islamic Emirate/Taliban's Afghan Ambassador to Pakistan, revealed that a surrender agreement had been reached to save civilian lives. Zaeef said that Mullah Omar would be allowed to live in Kandahar under the protection of Mullah Naqibullah.[6]

Mullah Zaeef was one of the founders of the Taliban movement and was considered very close to Mullah Omar. A tall, thin man with a long wavy beard, he had held key ministerial positions in Kabul before his posting to Islamabad. His daily press briefings after 9/11 in Islamabad, provided the international media with information about the Taliban position. Pakistan had not severed diplomatic relations with the Islamic Emirate even after the US invasion of Afghanistan on the advice of Bush administration, which wanted Islamabad to keep a line of communication open with the Taliban regime.[7]

'The Taliban are finished as a political force,' said Mullah Zaeef, adding, 'I think we should go home.'[8] The development came as the Afghan factions at the International Conference on Afghanistan held in Bonn, Germany, in December 2001, reached an agreement on the interim government setup in Afghanistan with Karzai as president. Mullah Zaeef chose to remain in Islamabad for a while even after the fall of the Taliban regime, acting as the militia's spokesman to the annoyance of Washington.

He ignored repeated warnings by Pakistan's military regime, now fully in the US camp, to leave Pakistan.[9] He was later, forcibly, pushed into Afghanistan by the ISI where he was arrested by US forces and sent to Guantánamo. He remained in custody till 2005 and would never forgive Pakistan for the treatment meted out to him.

A deal with the Taliban leadership would have ended the war much quicker and could even have possibly brought reconcilable elements of the Taliban into the new power arrangement. But that never happened. As the negotiations reached final stages, the US intervened and stopped Karzai from making any deal with the Taliban leadership. The Bush administration's woeful lack of knowledge about the complex Afghan political and tribal dynamics prevented it from appreciating Karzai's early efforts to win the war by negotiation.

The US's desire for revenge ended any possibility of a peace deal. Secretary of Defense, Donald Rumsfeld, said on 1 December 2001, that he wouldn't let Taliban leader, Mullah Omar 'live in dignity' in Afghanistan and that the military campaign would continue. He rejected any negotiated end to the situation.[10] The Americans wanted the Taliban supreme leader to first publicly disassociate his group from al-Qaeda and hand over Arab commanders. Ari Fleischer, the White House spokesperson, said that Washington felt that Mullah Omar remained 'a combatant against the United States and other nations.'[11] For Washington, every Taliban was a terrorist.

It seemed improbable that the terms of the deal would be acceptable to Mullah Omar. It was also not clear whether Mullah Omar would have agreed to stay under protection. He had already left Kandahar before the city fell to the US and their Afghan allies. Taliban fighters melted into the population or took sanctuary across the border in Pakistan among their Pashtun brethren. Kandahar fell on 7 December 2001, and even though the US forces and their allies tried to block the routes, nearly 2000 Taliban fighters crossed over to Pakistan. Most of the leadership had survived the offensive and moved to Pakistan.

In that initial displacement period, senior leaders were fragmented and disunited over what they should do. The shock and trauma of the fall of their regime had paralysed the leadership. The organisation had crumbled. There was no structure with which to regroup and revive. While some were determined to fight, others were more inclined towards exploring negotiated political options.[12] Their isolation had increased as their support among the Afghan people declined. In the first eighteen months after being ousted from power, the Islamic movement faced the danger of fracturing. Some elements even broke away to form their own factions.[13] Occasional statements and threats from senior leaders condemning the occupation, found little response among the Afghans.

There was a good reason for this. Towards the end of its rule, the Taliban had lost a significant mass support base with its regressive social policies, which included forcing women to wear burqas, banning music and television, and implementing harsh criminal punishments for petty offenses. Initially, Afghans at large seemed content and hoped for a better future under the new order, headed by Karzai, and installed by the occupation army. A new political paradigm was in play and the Taliban did not hold much appeal for the war-weary Afghan population. There was no serious effort to organise a resistance.[14]

For the Taliban generally, however, the events leading to the US invasion of Afghanistan began fraying the group's ties with al-Qaeda. Many mid-level Taliban commanders blamed bin Laden and the 9/11 attacks for the US assault on Afghanistan. There was clearly no love lost among Taliban leaders for Arab fighters and the al-Qaeda, who they held responsible for Afghanistan's plight. The Taliban and al-Qaeda leadership largely cut off contact after their retreat across the border into Pakistan, with the exception of the militant faction operating in eastern Afghanistan.[15]

With Kandahar under siege, Osama bin Laden and his Arab fighters fled to eastern Afghanistan from where they crossed over to Pakistan's tribal areas—the Federally Administered Tribal Areas (FATA). The region was a stronghold of Jalaluddin Haqqani, one of the most powerful Afghan militant leaders heading the Haqqani network, a guerrilla insurgent group, who had joined the Taliban towards the end of the conservative Islamic Emirate regime. Haqqani wielded considerable influence on both sides of the Pak–Afghan border.

A former anti-Soviet resistance commander, Jalaluddin Haqqani was known for his ruthless effectiveness as a fighter. During the war against the Soviet occupation of Afghanistan, he had also developed strong ties with the CIA and ISI. He was once described as 'goodness personified' by Charlie Wilson, the US congressman who helped to fund CIA support for the Afghan resistance.[16] President Ronald Reagan had declared Jalaluddin Haqqani to be a 'freedom fighter.' A stout man with a long, bushy beard he was distinguished by his huge turban.

He was strongly influenced by the radical political Islamic views espoused by the Muslim Brotherhood, as were so many of the Mujahideen leaders at that time. Jalaluddin, who belonged to the Zadran Pashtun tribe that inhabits the 'greater Paktia' region of eastern Afghanistan, comprising Khost, Paktia, and Paktika provinces, had emerged as one of the most powerful Mujahideen commanders in the 10-year-long anti-Soviet war in the 1980s. Fluent in Arabic, he became close to bin Laden during the anti-Soviet war, and the relationship between the two strengthened during the Taliban rule in Afghanistan, from 1996 to 2001.[17]

During this period, he served as minister for the frontier region, and in late September 2001, just before the US invasion of Afghanistan, Mullah Omar appointed Jalaluddin Haqqani as the commander-in-chief of Taliban forces. After the ouster of the Taliban regime by the US and its allies, he moved to North Waziristan in FATA and regrouped his militant force. He wielded influence, not only as a militant commander, but also as a spiritual leader. His family had established a number of madrasas in North Waziristan; the largest among them was Manba'-al-uloom (source of knowledge), located just outside the city of Miranshah, the administrative headquarter of North Waziristan.

The Haqqani network's links with the al-Qaeda, and its influence on both sides of the border, made the network the most formidable militant force. Jalaluddin Haqqani was also seen as relatively moderate among the Afghan rebels, who had built their movement on Islamic fundamentalism and strict adherence to conservative Pashtun culture. Given the influence of the Haqqanis in the region, the US wanted to weave the group out of both al-Qaeda and Taliban. Washington sought ISI support in this endeavour. General Ehsan ul Haq sent his men to meet Haqqani with the message from US officials.

Jalaluddin Haqqani refused the offer and told Pakistani officials that he would fight against the US forces as he did against the Soviet invaders.[18] But the CIA continued its efforts to prise the group away from the Taliban. In late 2002, US soldiers arrested Ibrahim Haqqani, brother of Jalaluddin, in eastern Afghanistan on a tip-off by rival tribesmen, pre-empting the CIA's efforts to establish contact with the Haqqani network.

There was some indication at the time that the Haqqanis had shown some willingness to negotiate with President Hamid Karzai's new coalition government. CIA officers had even held talks with Ibrahim Haqqani and made plans to meet with Jalaluddin in person in Dubai at the end of 2002. However, the capture of a key member of the group ended the possibility of any reconciliation with the Haqqanis that would haunt the US forces for the next two decades.[19] Although the US released Ibrahim after nine months, his detention effectively dashed the CIA's hopes of meeting with Jalaluddin, or of striking a broader strategic agreement with the Haqqanis. Instead, the group turned into its most fierce opponent.

It took more than two years for the Taliban to recover and rebuild its structure. The fall of the Taliban regime and the absence of governance by the new US-installed dispensation, had led to a complete breakdown of law and order in eastern Afghanistan. It had brought back the rule of rogue warlords. The Taliban and their family members who had laid down arms and had moved back to their villages, and tribal elders, were targeted by the newly installed interim administration.[20]

It was déjà vu, a return to the early 1990s situation that had originally led to the rise of the Taliban militia. The victims, of the new source of abuse, started contacting the Taliban leadership that had started regrouping in Quetta. In early 2002, Taliban propaganda reappeared in Afghanistan, in the form of leaflets and letters left or dropped at homes and school buildings. Civilian deaths caused by US air raids added to the support for the Taliban. The growing perception of foreign occupation fuelled public anger.

In June 2003, a 10-member Taliban leadership Shura council was formed and given the responsibility to formulate a political and military strategy for the resistance. Led by Mullah Omar, the council, later known as the Quetta Shura, mostly comprised the old guard that had formed the core of the former Taliban regime.[21] The Quetta Shura won implicit support from the Pakistani security establishment, which was deeply concerned by the unfriendly government in Kabul (which, in turn, accused Pakistan of supporting the Taliban). Later, as the insurgency picked up, the number of Shura members was increased to 33.

In that early period of revival, the Taliban leadership had not yet fully developed a clear political or military strategy and merely reacted to circumstances. The period from 2003 to 2005 was a turning point as the Taliban consolidated their organisational structure and expanded their activities. It was also the time when Afghanistan enacted its new constitution with a highly centralised presidential form of government. Public support for the new political dispensation began eroding as security remained weak, and reports of fraud and corruption increased.

Scores of madrasas in Pakistan's western Balochistan province, close to the borders, became the main recruitment centres for Taliban insurgents in Afghanistan. They were run by the Jamiat Ulema-e-Islam (JUI), one of Pakistan's most powerful Islamic political parties, which had also been a part of the alliance that controlled the Balochistan provincial government from 2002 to 2007. The seminaries not only provided the Taliban with ideological training, but also extended material help.[22] The Taliban also began an organised recruitment effort in the madrasas in Khyber Pakhtunkhwa and in Karachi.

Pashtunabad, a congested slum district in the provincial capital, Quetta, had a large concentration of former Taliban activists. A stronghold of radical Islamic groups, it looked more like a Kandahar neighbourhood under the former Taliban regime, and several former

Taliban leaders were believed to have taken refuge there. But it was Chaman, a dusty border town in Balochistan province, that became the main base for resurgent Taliban fighting against the US and Afghan troops.

Many Pakistani provincial ministers and members of parliament belonging to the ruling alliance in Balochistan became actively involved with the Afghan rebels using the region as their base. Some of the seminaries run by the alliance leaders were used as a conduit for weapons supply to the Afghan rebels. The same seminaries from where Taliban forces were initially raised, once again became the centre for producing a new generation of Islamic warriors. Not only were the madrasas harbouring and aiding existing Afghan warriors, but they were also creating new ones. More than 8,000 new pupils had enrolled in the seminaries in the border areas alone since the fall of the Taliban when I visited the area in 2005. There was a constant stream of new entrants and it was difficult to find accommodation for the newcomers.[23]

Afghan refugee camps set up during the Afghan resistance war against the Soviet occupation in the 1980s spread across Balochistan and in northern Pakistan too and they became the centre of Taliban recruitment. They provided shelter to the fighters and, in some areas, they also served as training camps. Pakistani security authorities looked the other way, even if they were not directly helping them.

Most of the Afghan Taliban leaders fleeing from Afghanistan with their families settled in various cities of Pakistan, mainly in Quetta and Peshawar, where many of them had stayed during the 1980s when they fled the Soviet occupation. They had no problem in assimilating with the local Pashtun population.

But it was in Karachi, Pakistan's biggest city and financial hub, where some senior leaders chose to establish their residence. Gulshan-e-Iqbal, a middle-class neighbourhood in Karachi, was where at least three top leaders had chosen to stay; this included Mullah Mohammad Akhtar Mansour, the former aviation minister in the Taliban administration, Mullah Abdul Ghani Baradar, the co-founder of the Taliban and deputy to Mullah Omar, and Agha Jan Motasim, a former Taliban finance minister.[24] All of them were members of the Quetta Shura. The group owned several properties in the city.

Contrary to widespread belief, Mullah Omar never left Afghanistan after the fall of the Taliban regime. He reportedly lived and died in a village in Afghanistan's Zabul province, located close to an American military facility. Both US and Afghan officials had claimed that after fleeing from Kandahar in December 2001, Omar had crossed into Pakistan and was guiding the group from Quetta.

When I interviewed former Afghan President Hamid Karzai in 2004, he gave me an address in Quetta where he claimed Mullah Omar was residing under the protection of Pakistan's intelligence agencies—a revelation that incited strong reactions from Pakistani authorities. Later on, I found out that the address belonged to the owner of a grocery shop.[25]

Even during the Afghan resistance war against the former USSR, and unlike other Mujahideen commanders, Mullah Omar would not travel to Pakistan. The only time he reportedly visited Quetta was when he needed surgery for his eye after being injured in a battle. What is intriguing is that despite him staying away from day-to-day operations of the group, it was Mullah Omar's name that kept the Taliban united and the insurgency alive.

While in hiding, Mullah Omar was cut off from the rest of the insurgency. His deputy, Mullah Baradar, conducted the day-to-day matters of the organisation, and because of his proximity to the supreme leader, he wielded enormous influence within the movement. Both hailed from the same district in Uruzgan and were childhood friends. Baradar's background as a frontline commander and his political acumen allowed him to bridge Taliban's traditional divide between the military and political leadership. In the process, he became a major binding factor in the insurgency.

Meanwhile, the Taliban's resurgence was also aided by a strategic mistake made by the US in tacitly helping to empower former strongmen and warlords, which reprised old ethnic and tribal tensions. The alienation was greatest in the eastern and southern parts of the country populated by Pashtuns, who felt politically sidelined and targeted by the coalition forces and the new authorities in Kabul.[26]

These regions were the bastion of the ousted Taliban regime, and in a repeat of 1994 when the Taliban restored order amid criminal activity and fighting in southern Afghanistan, the local population started contacting the Taliban.[27] People willingly gave shelter to the insurgents. It was a dramatic change from the period after its fall in 2001 when the Taliban could not find any haven in the community. The insurgents later began to get a foothold in the north as well, exploiting the divisions among various power groups within the new Afghan government.

Success spurred momentum for the Taliban in the entire country. As the resentment against foreign occupation forces grew, the Taliban's influence increased. Indiscriminate killings and arrests of innocent people by the government added to the alienation and anger felt by local communities. Growing numbers of women and children were also being killed in air attacks. 'Each bombing and killing of civilians added to our support base,' a senior Taliban commander told me in an interview given in 2006 in a Pakistani border region. Police brutality turned even those who had initially supported the new Afghan administration, towards the Taliban.

After regrouping in Pakistan and strengthening its support base at home in Afghanistan, the Taliban leadership set out to establish a shadow government appointing district chiefs and provincial governors. They also revived their legal system in the areas under their influence. In 2003, the Afghan Taliban established roaming courts, expanding their outreach to areas under the militia's control. These courts settled local disputes and even criminal cases. The enforcement of their justice system was an indicator of the diminishing writ of the Kabul government. In many areas, the Taliban justice system outperformed the official system.

Members of the Quetta Shura were assigned specific responsibilities in the regional command structure. The individual commanders re-established their contact networks. The operations carried out by the Taliban up to 2003 comprised relatively small and targeted attacks. There were very few instances of any large-scale attacks on coalition forces during this period.[28] But, by summer 2006, the Taliban had developed its military and political strategy with an ambition to establish territorial control, particularly in southern Afghanistan. There was a serious attempt to force the international community and coalition forces to review their policy in Afghanistan by escalating attacks.[29]

The new tactics were to carry out frontal attacks on the western forces, unleash a massive increase in suicide bombings, utilise Improvised Explosive Devices, and wage an aggressive public relations campaign. The full-scale attacks were not very successful and resulted in heavy civilian casualties. Nevertheless, the spectacular acts of violence and the growing insurgency in the south and southeast, propelled the Taliban propaganda message that western forces and the Afghan administration were unable to provide security for the local population.

The growing use of suicide bombings dramatically increased the level of violence. Initially, most of the suicide bombers were either Pakistanis or Afghans living in Pakistan. But later on, more local Afghans started signing up. Suicide bombings became a weapon of choice for the insurgents, generating fear and projecting greater capacity than was the actual case.[30]

But the escalating civilian casualties also produced a backlash against the Taliban among the local population. This led to a heated debate within the Taliban leadership over the effectiveness, as well as religious legitimacy, of suicide attacks. That led to the landmark declaration in 2009 by the Taliban military council that suicide bombing was not a legitimate tactic, although sporadic suicide attacks continued to be carried out by some insurgent factions. The Taliban started focusing more on winning over the local population as violence increased in 2008 and 2009.

This was also the time that President Barack Obama took office and embarked on an ambitious multiple-level programme that shifted US attention from the war in Iraq back to Afghanistan. Despite the surge in US forces—the numbers moved toward 100,000 by the end of 2009—the security situation deteriorated all over the country. Particularly in the south and in the southeast, insurgent attacks hit an all-time high, as did the number of casualties among Afghan and Western soldiers. The north also saw a significant rise of Taliban influence during that period.

A report by the US military to the US Congress in 2010 estimated that 48 districts, out of the 92 surveyed, were supportive of the Taliban. According to an estimate by the Afghan intelligence agency, some 1700 Taliban field commanders controlled anywhere between 10,000 to 30,000 fighters. More than 6200 Afghan and coalition soldiers were killed or wounded in roadside bomb attacks during this period.

The increasing influence of the Taliban in the north was the most significant development. The insurgents made important gains in the northern provinces—in particular, Kunduz, Baghlan, Badghis, and Faryab—where active Taliban or associated groups operated. Turning their focus on the north helped the Taliban show that the movement was not confined to only the Pashtun region in eastern and southern Afghanistan. The Taliban reportedly also made significant inroads among the Uzbek and Tajik communities as well.

Despite these successes, thinking within the Afghan Taliban concerning the future of Afghanistan remained obscure. This, perhaps, was an outcome of the fracture within the group. Although Mullah Omar enjoyed the absolute loyalty of the leadership council, his influence seems to have waned over the years with the growing radicalisation of a new generation of field commanders. Most of them had been teenagers during the Taliban rule in Afghanistan, but they now formed the core of resistance.[31]

Being out of the field for so long—and, mistakenly, believed to be operating from the Pakistani side of the border—seems to have turned Mullah Omar into more of a symbolic figurehead. While the core leadership had formed strong administrative structures, the exact composition of, and details surrounding the operational command remained opaque.

Field commanders act somewhat autonomously, with little control by the central leadership council. Some reports suggested that the young and more radicalised commanders and lower ranks had even started questioning the decisions of Mullah Omar. But his position as supreme leader was not likely to be challenged publicly. Quetta Shura administrative leadership structure had evolved over the years. The regional Peshawar and Miranshah Shuras also operated under the Quetta council.[32]

While the overall leadership still resided with Mullah Omar, the head of the local Shura was responsible for guiding day-to-day operations. Committees under the provincial Shura, however, carried out many administrative functions. The relationship between various Taliban committees based in Pakistan and the field commanders in Afghanistan was complex. It was quite evident that the insurgency on the ground was less organised and that decision-making was often left to individual commanders.

Unlike the top administrative structure, the hierarchy in the field was less clear. The Taliban may have been united under one banner, but the group was comprised of various factions. How deep the divisions within the Taliban really went was not at all clear. There are conflicting views about the state of unity within the insurgency. While one view suggests that the Taliban was an amorphous collection of groups and factions, other analysts portrayed the Taliban as a monolithic and organised resistance movement.

Arguably, the Haqqani network was the most powerful faction within the Taliban movement. Sirajuddin Haqqani had effectively taken over the command of the network as his father, Jalaluddin, was sidelined because of prolonged illness. In his early thirties, the younger Haqqani had earned a reputation of being the fiercest insurgent commander. His radical worldview was shaped by his personal ties with al-Qaeda and international jihadist groups, in contrast to other members of the Taliban Leadership Council who did not share al-Qaeda's global agenda.[33]

Sirajuddin headed the Miranshah Shura and had a seat in the leadership council in Quetta. The Haqqani network, which operated from Pakistan's North Waziristan tribal region, emerged as the most lethal insurgent group fighting coalition forces in the eastern Afghan provinces of Khost, Paktia, and Paktika. It had also been involved in some spectacular attacks inside Kabul. The network wielded significant influence and power among the Afghan, as well as among the Pakistani militant groups. Mullah Omar's absence from the scene had weakened his authority and the arrests and killing of some of the most powerful members of the Shura's leadership had further strengthened Haqqani's role in the insurgency.

Sirajuddin Haqqani had made his mark by extending his area of operation. He represented a new generation of Taliban commanders, who were more aggressive and more ruthless. He extended the network's activities in Afghanistan, beyond Khost, Paktia, and Paktika provinces, to the Ghazni, Logar, Wardak, and Kabul provinces and provided support to Taliban networks in Kunar, Nangarhar, Helmand, and Kandahar provinces. His faction also drew many new recruits from among the militants in Pakistan, Uzbekistan, Chechnya, Turkey, and Middle Eastern countries.[34]

Sirajuddin quickly eclipsed his father in power and influence and rivalled more senior leaders for the overall leadership of the Taliban. In many ways, he was smarter and more respected than many of them, and the strong connections he had formed with top al-Qaeda leaders made him the most dangerous militant commander, not only in the FATA but also in Afghanistan.

Some senior Pakistani security officials believed that he wielded much greater influence in Afghanistan than even Mullah Omar. The US Army also identified Sirajuddin as the primary threat to security in eastern Afghanistan. Under him, the Haqqani network became increasingly violent and was responsible for more and more complex attacks inside Afghanistan. Sirajuddin claimed responsibility for a series of suicide attacks around Kabul and for the failed assassination attempt on President Hamid Karzai at an Independence Day parade in the capital in 2002. 'Yes, I organised those attacks,' Sirajuddin said

later, adding, 'But I had help from a serving Afghan military general.'
The US placed a $200,000 bounty on his head.[35]

The Haqqanis were also important to the Pakistani security agencies
due to their influence over other tribal militants, particularly in North
Waziristan, since so many of them had fought under Jalaluddin
Haqqani's command in the fight against the Soviets. Islamabad
believed that by dealing with the Haqqanis it could exercise influence
over other militant groups.

For these reasons, the military had no interest in a confrontation
with the Haqqanis, which was to become a source of increasing
tension between the US and Pakistan as the insurgency escalated out
of control. For Pakistani authorities, the Haqqani network remained
a useful hedge against an uncertain outcome in Afghanistan. The
deep reluctance to take action against the network was a reflection of
Pakistan's worries about the fallout from an eventual withdrawal of
western forces from Afghanistan.

However, despite increasing US pressure, Pakistani military authorities
largely turned their backs on the activities of the Haqqani network.
Western intelligence experts claimed that the ISI had maintained
links with Sirajuddin Haqqani, considering him a strategic asset for
maintaining a degree of influence in Afghanistan and to counter
Indian influence. In fact, the ISI stepped up its covert support for
the Taliban, particularly the Haqqani network, as insurgency in
Afghanistan escalated in 2005.

Pakistan's major objective in supporting the insurgents was to
undermine the Karzai government. Pakistani security agencies had
accused the US-backed Kabul administration of allowing India to use
Afghan territory for alleged subversive activities in Pakistan's border
areas. For a long time, Pakistan had accused India of using its consulate
offices in Afghanistan's border cities for espionage and of stirring up
separatist insurgency in Pakistan's western province of Balochistan.
Many of the Baloch insurgency's leaders operated from sanctuaries in
Afghanistan, causing tension between Islamabad and Kabul.

What was widely perceived as a rapidly diminishing commitment of the US to Afghanistan, because of its focus shifting to Iraq, had also intensified Pakistan's long-standing struggle with India for supremacy of influence in Afghanistan. The Pakistani military establishment viewed the expanding Indian presence in its 'backyard' as a serious threat to their country's own security. Since 2001, India had moved aggressively—and successfully—to expand its political and economic influence in Afghanistan. India's interest in Afghanistan was not just to help rebuild the war-torn country, but also to counter Pakistan's ambition to gain influence there.[36]

Pakistan was upset when President Bush, during his visit to New Delhi on 3 March 2006, hailed India as an emerging power and awarded it an unprecedented civilian nuclear technology deal.[37] The next day, on his short stopover in Islamabad, Bush lectured President Musharraf on getting tougher with the Taliban and vague promises of future military technological assistance.[38] Although Pakistan remained central to US security interests in the region, this raw deal raised further scepticism in the Pakistani military about America's long-term commitment to their country.

Islamabad's anxiety over the expanding influence of its arch-enemy on the country's western borders, therefore, was to be expected. That apprehension resulted in Pakistan's continuing patronage of some Afghan Taliban factions, such as the Haqqani network, which it considered a vital tool for countering Indian influence, even at the risk of Islamabad's strategic relationship with Washington. The struggle for influence took a more vicious turn when the Haqqani network carried out attacks on Indian installations and Indian nationals, working on various development projects in Afghanistan.[39]

'Karzai had helped India stab Pakistan in the back,' General Musharraf stated later, justifying his government's policy of supporting the Taliban fighting against coalition forces. 'In President Karzai's times, yes, indeed, he was damaging Pakistan and therefore we were working against his interest. Obviously we had to protect our own interest,' Musharraf said.[40] The relations between Islamabad and Kabul had hit a new low with the growing Taliban insurgency.

Pakistan's patronage of the Afghan Taliban, and particularly of the Haqqani network, became a convenient rationale for the government in Kabul to permit sanctuaries for Pakistani insurgents on Afghan soil. This tit-for-tat policy had made it impossible for the two countries, both allied to the US, to work together. Their age-old legacy of using proxies against each other had disastrous consequences for regional security.

Pakistan was also wary of what it perceived as a US tilt towards India and, therefore, saw no strategic advantage in eliminating Taliban safe havens on its territory, or in acting in full cooperation with the coalition forces. The devastating attacks launched by the Haqqani network seemed aimed at sending a clear message that Islamabad, not Delhi, held the key to stability in Afghanistan. Pakistan was not going to fully commit to fighting Afghan insurgents until its own insecurities towards India were addressed.

President Musharraf had never reconciled with the Northern Alliance government in Kabul led by President Karzai. He had nothing but contempt for the Afghan leader and called him 'third rate.' Once a senior aide suggested to Musharraf that he mend fences with Karzai and invite him to Islamabad. 'I will not invite him. He is nobody. Bush is my friend,' Musharraf retorted.[41] His arrogance was one of the major reasons for the widening gulf between Kabul and Islamabad.

The worsening hostility between Islamabad and Kabul had caused a major problem for the US in the war against insurgents in Afghanistan. Sensing the need for a patch-up between the two leaders, President Bush invited them to the White House after the UN General Assembly session in September 2006. While driving to the White House, General Mahmud Durrani handed Musharraf a one-page outline provided by the US officials on how Bush wanted to proceed. It suggested that the US President, after his remarks, would invite the two guests to speak. 'I don't agree with it,' Musharraf snapped.[42] But he did not have any choice.

President Bush had already received Musharraf and Karzai separately, a few days ago. But the tension was palpable when the two leaders arrived for the dinner meeting at White House on 26 September 2006. The two stood glumly in the Rose Garden with President Bush. While General Musharraf stood at the right side of Bush, Karzai stood a safe distance away on his left. The two didn't even shake hands, making their estrangement quite obvious.[43]

At the dinner table, Bush sat in the middle with Musharraf and Karzai on either side. Also present were the Pakistan and Afghan ambassadors. After Bush's remarks, Musharraf started speaking. Ignoring all diplomatic norms, he blasted Karzai, accusing him of all the problems in Afghanistan. It was extremely ugly. Karzai sat there quietly, listening to Musharraf's harangue. Each blamed the other for the resurgence of the Taliban in Afghanistan.

After trading accusations, Karzai took out a copy of the agreement, which a Pakistani military commander had signed with the Pakistani Taliban in South Waziristan that supported the jihad inside Afghanistan. Karzai viewed it as a pact to cede control to the Taliban. 'You cannot train a snake to bite someone else,' Karzai said. Musharraf did not have any riposte. Bush sided mostly with Karzai. That further upset Musharraf.[44] The major reason for Musharraf's aggressive tone was alleged Indian expansion in Afghanistan.[45]

The 2006 White House meeting failed to bridge the divide between the Pakistani and Afghan leaders. While Karzai was not willing to accept Pakistan's demand to reduce Indian presence in Afghanistan, Pakistan's support for the Taliban would not cease. The proxy war in Afghanistan took an even more violent turn in 2008 when a devastating car bomb attack on the Indian embassy, allegedly carried out by the Haqqani network, killed more than 50 people. The Taliban had expanded their influence to a larger part of Afghanistan, further widening the gulf between Pakistan and the US.

Weeks before his visit to Washington on 5 September, Musharraf had approved signing a truce with the militants in North Waziristan. The Waziristan Accord, as it was known, put an end to all army operations in the territory, and troops were pulled back from the security checkpoints to their barracks.[46] The government not only released all militants captured by the military but agreed to pay compensation to those killed during fighting, effectively legitimising their activities.

To help sell the deal to Washington, Musharraf took General Ali Jan Orakzai, the governor of the North-West Frontier Province (now Khyber Pakhtunkhwa), who was also responsible for tribal territories, to the Oval Office. In his presentation to President Bush, Orakzai advocated a strategy that would rely even more heavily on ceasefires and said that striking deals with the Taliban inside Afghanistan would allow US forces to withdraw from Afghanistan within seven years.[47]

Bush supported the deal, claiming that it would not create safe havens for the Taliban and could even offer 'alternatives to violence and terror,' but he added, 'You know we are watching this very carefully, obviously.' Musharraf had approved the controversial deal despite the warning from some of his senior generals that it would carry serious consequences for the country's internal security.

In the months after the Waziristan Accord was signed, cross-border incursions from the tribal areas into Afghanistan rose by 300 per cent. In the spring of 2006, the Taliban had launched an offensive in southern Afghanistan, increasing suicide bombings six-fold and the US and NATO casualty rates by 45 per cent. In November 2006, Lt. Gen. Karl Eikenberry, head of US forces in Afghanistan, warned that the number of Taliban attacks out of North Waziristan had tripled since the deal was signed.[48]

4 | The Great Escape

It was late 2002, almost a year since Osama bin Laden escaped into the Pakistani tribal region when he came close to detection. The van he was travelling in, to go to the northern mountainous district of Swat, was stopped by a police officer for a traffic violation. Bin Laden had shaved his long trademark beard and was hardly recognisable. A lanky man, dressed in local attire, travelling with a family, did not arouse any suspicion in the police officer.[1]

Bin Laden moved to Martung, a small scenic village in the Shangla district of Swat Valley, ensconced amid high mountains, with the family of his two couriers who hailed from that area. The village is a quiet collection of mud houses scattered along a hillside, surrounded by terraced fields.[2] Its district, Shangla, was a stronghold of Pakistani Taliban insurgents. Though raised in Kuwait the two courier brothers—Abrar and Ibrahim Said Ahmad—had maintained some connections with their home village. Their father was a strictly religious Muslim who had migrated from Martung to Kuwait around 50 years ago, where he came in contact with al-Qaeda.[3]

Martung's inhabitants had no inkling about the man living in the village with the two brothers; he was only known to them as 'Miskeen Baba.' Bin Laden would seldom venture out of the house and it was in this village that bin Laden was reunited with his baby daughter, Safiyah, and his third wife, Amal Ahmad Abdul Fatah al-Sadah, a twenty-year-old Yemeni.[4] His health had deteriorated but he was still very much in charge of the al-Qaeda that had scattered after the US invasion of Afghanistan. His deputy, an Egyptian, Ayman al-Zawahiri, managed operational matters. Bin Laden would occasionally receive some visitors, but otherwise, his links with the outside world were through the two couriers.[5]

Before moving to Martung, bin Laden had stayed in Waziristan and the Bajaur tribal region of FATA in northwestern Pakistan. During his early period in Pakistan, bin Laden also briefly went across the border to the Afghan province of Kunar, and was helped by supporters of one of the most infamous Afghani warlords, Gulbuddin Hekmatyar.[6] He travelled with a very small entourage to avoid being tracked.

Bin Laden first entered Pakistan around mid-2002 after fleeing the US bombardment of the Tora Bora caves in December 2001 in eastern Afghanistan. He and his close aides had already made plans to make Pakistan their new base in anticipation of the US invasion of Afghanistan following 9/11. Hundreds of al-Qaeda operatives, including many senior leaders of the group, had managed to escape the hunt, travelling through treacherous routes. Another wave of fugitives had entered Pakistan in March 2002, during the allied force's Operation Anaconda against al-Qaeda's positions in the eastern Shah-i-Kot Mountains. Many others followed in the next several weeks.[7]

There were not enough US troops to cover all possible escape routes. In early December 2001, there were only 1300 US troops in Afghanistan, spread over seventeen areas. The Pakistan Army had entered the autonomous tribal areas only once before—in 1973—to put down a revolt.[8] They were now having serious problems sealing the long, treacherous, and porous 2430 km (1510 miles) Durand Line border between Afghanistan and Pakistan—the outcome of an agreement in 1893 between Sir Mortimer Durand, a secretary of the British Indian government, and Abdur Rahman Khan, the Afghan emir.

General Musharraf had spent two weeks negotiating with the FATA tribal chieftains before they finally agreed to the army deployment to the Afghan border in late 2001. By that time, hundreds of al-Qaeda fighters had already escaped into Pakistan, including many senior leaders. Many of them made their escape bribing Afghan warlords.

Al-Qaeda had more than 3000 activists in Afghanistan before the US invasion; most were Arabs, others came from more than a dozen Islamic countries. The 1500-mile porous border with Pakistan was a major exit point for the fleeing militants. Many used Pakistan as a transit point to the Gulf countries and Iran. Among the top al-Qaeda leadership, only Mohammed Atef, commander of military operations, had been killed in a US airstrike in Afghanistan in November 2001; surprisingly, given the ferocity of the hunt, almost the entire leadership of the group was still intact.[9]

The network that al-Qaeda had built among Pakistani militant groups helped the fugitives find safe haven, not only in the lawless tribal regions, but also in major Pakistani cities. These associate groups provided al-Qaeda with logistical support, safe houses, false documentation, and—in some cases—manpower. Al-Qaeda's nexus with Pakistani jihadi groups was strengthened when thousands of Pakistani militants who had received ideological and military training at al-Qaeda's camps, returned home.[10] The evidence of the close connection between Pakistani militants with al-Qaeda emerged when several Pakistani militants were among those killed in a US cruise missile attack in 1998 on an al-Qaeda training camp in the Afghan province of Khost. Ayman al-Zawahiri was al-Qaeda's principal contact with the Pakistani jihadist community.

Al-Qaeda had decentralised its activities, as US and Pakistani intelligence agencies trailed them; many started scattering again, travelling back and forth. Karachi, Pakistan's financial and industrial heartland, with a population of more than 20 million, became a sanctuary for senior al-Qaeda leaders. The masterminds of the 9/11 terrorist attacks—Khalid Sheikh Mohammed, known in intelligence circles as KSM, and Ramzi bin al-Shibh—made their base in the city, with the help of a vast network of homegrown jihadists.

In some cases, they also appeared to have received help from their sympathisers in Pakistani intelligence agencies and the police. During 2002 and 2003, Karachi had virtually turned into a terror capital. Islamic militants carried out more than half a dozen terrorist attacks in the city, targeting western nationals and US assets; all of them carried al-Qaeda imprints.[11]

Bin Laden, too, stayed in the city for a while, where he narrowly escaped capture by Pakistani security agencies and the FBI. He had ignored the risks and gone to Karachi to spend time with his youngest wife, Amal, who was staying with Khalid Sheikh Mohammed's (KSM) family. Another purpose of bin Laden's visit was to discuss future terror projects with other senior members of al-Qaeda.[12]

Some weeks after bin Laden's arrival in the village of Martung, KSM came to see him. He had travelled under the alias 'Hafeez.' Accompanied by his wife and seven children, he stayed there for two weeks. The couriers were known to KSM who, in fact, had introduced them to bin Laden. The meeting showed that the coordination among senior al-Qaeda leaders was still intact, despite the hunt for them.[13]

From Shangla, KSM went to see Zawahiri in the Shakai district of South Waziristan that had become another base for al-Qaeda. The 5000-square kilometer swathe was the largest of the seven tribal agencies on Pakistan's western border with Afghanistan.[14] The treacherous, inhospitable mountainous region, which had been used by the American CIA and the Pakistani ISI in the 1980s as a base for their covert operations against the Soviet occupation forces in Afghanistan, had been turned by al-Qaeda-linked militants into a base for the battle against their erstwhile patrons. Some of the Arab fighters chose to stay on, after the end of the anti-Soviet war in 1990, while some had married into local tribes and so were not seen as 'aliens' by the residents. Many al-Qaeda leaders escaping the US bombing raids in Afghanistan ended up in Waziristan. It was widely suspected that bin Laden and al-Zawahiri were also among them. A few months before the 9/11 attacks, during an interview with an Arab TV journalist, a close aide of Osama's hinted of their fleeing to Waziristan in an event of war in Afghanistan.

For more than a year, al-Qaeda fugitives had moved freely, turning the border area into a new base for their operations. Clusters of mud compounds in a valley surrounded by rugged mountains served as the world's largest al-Qaeda command and control centre. Several training camps were operated with the support of sympathetic tribesmen, mostly around Wana and Shakai. The militants had also established a sophisticated propaganda factory equipped with CD burners.[15] The clampdown was inevitable. Scores of militants were captured or killed by Pakistani security forces as they tried to move to other parts of Pakistan or to other countries from the tribal areas. Many others were captured by the tribesmen and sold to the CIA for a hefty bounty ranging from $3000 to $25,000. Most of these detainees later landed in the notorious American prison at Guantánamo Bay.

General Ehsan ul Haq, DG ISI, was very concerned about al-Qaeda's growing activities in the tribal areas. He was receiving alarming reports from ISI agents on ground.[16] He was one of the few officers, in the senior hierarchy, who knew the region well. He had served as the brigade commander in Kohat and later as corps commander Peshawar before getting the new assignment. The Americans seemed quite pleased with his appointment; they felt he was a man they could work with. CIA Director, George Tenet, found him to be a good partner.

General Ehsan, however, had a serious problem with the army GHQ; they did not believe, or were in a state of denial, about al-Qaeda reorganising in the tribal areas. General Yousuf Khan, Vice Chief of Army Staff, and Lt. Gen. Shahid Aziz, Chief of General Staff, dismissed the information as alarmist. General Ali Muhammad Jan Orakzai, the commander of Pakistani forces in the area containing Waziristan, dismissed the reports of al-Qaeda's resurgence. General Orakzai considered the American and ISI warnings about al-Qaeda to be mere 'guesswork,' saying that his soldiers had 'found nothing'. There was speculation that he deliberately ignored the large presence of foreigners since he feared that action against them would spark a tribal uprising.[17]

This sharp difference of perspective between the ISI and GHQ over the seriousness of the problem was a boon for al-Qaeda, as this uncertainty provided them an opportunity to continue their activities with impunity in the tribal areas. There was still a huge distrust of the US among senior commanders despite General Musharraf's new alignment with Washington. General Musharraf's problem was that he would get confused with the conflicting views he was receiving from the GHQ and from the ISI.

Curiously, a few years after his retirement, General Shahid Aziz came out with a scathing criticism of Musharraf's decision to support the US war in Afghanistan and abandoning the Taliban. General Aziz joined the militants fighting the US forces in Afghanistan, where he was reportedly killed in a drone strike.

However, after the events of the night of 25 June 2002, when several Pakistani army commandos were killed in a clash with Arab fighters, the reality of al-Qaeda's presence in the territories could no longer be denied. The troops had surrounded a compound in Kazha Punga village in South Waziristan after receiving reports of the presence of some key al-Qaeda operatives there. The planned ambush turned into a disaster after nearly 35 militants escaped, killing 10 commandos.

Musharraf said the operation was a turning point 'because it highlighted the magnitude of and seriousness of the threat.'[18] The incident made clear that the foreign fighters had substantial local support and was a stark indication of the growing power of al-Qaeda in Waziristan. The Kazha Punga incident also convinced Musharraf of the need to create a fast-reacting force to counter al-Qaeda threat, but a number of problems hampered Pakistani military's operations.

A small number of US Special Forces were allowed to accompany Pakistani forces on a number of raids in the tribal areas in 2002 and early 2003, and these raids were extremely controversial within the Pakistani military. Although Pakistani officials publicly denied the presence of Americans on these incursions, local tribesmen had no trouble spotting them and vigorously protested.[19] The military feared that a full-scale tribal rebellion would break out, therefore, under pressure from Musharraf, the Bush administration decided in 2003 to pull out its Special Forces from the territory.

General Ehsan, in the meantime, assured the US of ISI's full cooperation, while cautioning them to respect his country's sovereignty. He took the CIA operatives to Waziristan to show them that Pakistan was completely on board, but also delivered a clear message that the CIA must not try to create a network of its own. 'We need to build an atmosphere of trust and any secret parallel network will not be tolerated.' Despite the warning, CIA tried to act separately. 'We didn't want to embarrass them. But we knew what they were doing,' said General Ehsan.[20] The Americans wanted the ISI to build its own counterterrorism force, but General Musharraf shot down the suggestion. However, a year later, Pakistan raised a special force under army command.

Just months after the influx of al-Qaeda activists into Pakistan, US and Pakistani security agencies got their first major success when, in a joint operation, they captured one of the most wanted al-Qaeda members. On 28 March 2002, scores of FBI agents and members of Pakistani security forces stormed a two-storey modest house in Faisal colony, a middle-class neighbourhood in Faisalabad, one of Pakistan's largest industrial towns.

One person was shot dead and one other was badly wounded. After a thorough check, agents finally established the identity of the wounded man lying on the floor in a pool of blood. He was the man they wanted to catch: Abu Zubaydah, a Saudi citizen. After his condition stabilised, he was flown to US military headquarters at Bagram in Afghanistan, for interrogation.[21] Abu Zubaydah, also known as Zayn al-Abidin Mohammed Husayn, had long been considered a key member of al-Qaeda's inner circle. Since the death of Mohammed Atef, he had moved up the organisation's hierarchy. He was responsible for training thousands of Islamic militants in al-Qaeda's training camps in eastern Afghanistan. He had also been in operational control of the attack on the USS Cole in October 2000. His arrest came as a gold mine of information to the investigators and led to the arrest of many al-Qaeda operatives in the West.

The operation had been organised and conducted by the FBI and CIA, who had been given a free hand by Pakistan's military government. The raid was conducted after electronic surveillance by US agents detected satellite phone calls from Afghanistan, which pinpointed the location of one of al-Qaeda's two top operatives.[22] The Americans kept the information top-secret and only President Musharraf and General Ehsan were kept in the picture.[23] The operation in Faisalabad was followed by subsequent raids in Lahore, the main city of Punjab, which netted more than 60 suspected terrorists, including 29 foreigners, mostly Arabs and Afghans. That was the first major success in the hunt for al-Qaeda operatives who had fled from Afghanistan.

Abu Zubaydah had developed strong connections with Pakistani Islamic militant groups. The house he was occupying in Faisalabad, belonged to a member of Lashkar-e-Taiba (LeT). The fact that LeT had strong connections with Wahabi Saudi clerics may also be one of the reasons for the strengthening of its bond with al-Qaeda. The capture of Abu Zubaydah came as a serious blow to al-Qaeda, but the network nevertheless continued to operate in Pakistan with the help of new recruits from among Pakistani militants.[24]

On the first anniversary of the 9/11 terrorist attacks, on 11 September 2002, a joint ISI–FBI operation in Karachi nabbed another key al-Qaeda leader, Ramzi bin al-Shibh, one of the masterminds of the 9/11 attacks. He was arrested in a raid on a newly constructed, half-empty, five-storey apartment building, in an upscale neighbourhood of the city that served as an al-Qaeda safe house. The place was under surveillance for weeks after a lead from the CIA.[25]

Interception of a satellite phone conversation between al-Qaeda leaders reinforced suspicions about some important operative residing in one of the apartments. The capture of Ramzi was certainly the biggest success in the war against al-Qaeda since the arrest of Abu Zubaydah earlier in March. A roommate in Hamburg, Germany, of Mohammed Atta, the ringleader of the 9/11 plot, Ramzi had played a vital role in organising 9/11. From his base in Germany, he handled the logistic and financial arrangements for the hijack team.[26]

Ramzi, who called himself the head of al-Qaeda's military wing, had worked closely with KSM and spent much of the spring of 2001 in Afghanistan and Pakistan, helping to move the hijackers as they passed through Karachi. He also reported directly to bin Laden about the preparations for the attack in an al-Qaeda facility, known as 'Compound Six,' near Kandahar.

Ramzi had moved to Karachi from Afghanistan soon after the fall of the Taliban regime and tried to regroup al-Qaeda. Just a week before his capture, the Arab television station, *Al Jazeera,* had broadcast an interview in which Ramzi and KSM claimed to have masterminded the 9/11 attacks. Pakistani investigators believed that US intelligence might have tracked down Ramzi by intercepting his conversation with *Al-Jazeera's* London bureau chief, Yosri Fouda, who had interviewed him in Karachi.

After his meeting with Zawahiri in Shakai in South Waziristan, KSM stopped over in Kohat where he stayed with a Major Adeel in the army garrison.[27] That was indicative of the formidable support network the al-Qaeda had developed in Pakistan. KSM had received huge support from his extended family members living in Balochistan and Karachi. Many of them had been active in Pakistani Islamic militant groups: his nephew, Musaad Aruchi, also known as Abdul Karim Mehboob, was a critical cog in al-Qaeda's operations in Pakistan and in other countries.

KSM had been directly involved in planning several terrorist attacks inside Pakistan after 9/11. It was he who, in February 2002, beheaded Daniel Pearl, the *Wall Street Journal* reporter.[28] A Pakistani militant group had kidnapped the American journalist from Karachi and handed him over to KSM. Later that year, KSM, along with Ramzi, had given an interview to a London-based Arabic magazine in Karachi, boasting about his role in masterminding the 9/11 attacks. While bin Laden and Zawahiri restricted their movements, KSM moved around freely.

Both the ISI and the CIA had been on KSM's trail for months. In early 2003, while he was travelling northwest, ISI agents tracked him to a hotel in Peshawar and intercepted his calls. But he left before the raid. The ISI had also been pursuing KSM's couriers, eavesdropping on their calls. They detected the calls to Kohat where KSM had stayed for a few days on the way back from Shakai. It was clear that both the ISI and the CIA were closing in on one of the 'most wanted' terrorists in the world.

Just before dawn on 2 February 2003, CIA and ISI agents broke into a small house in a prosperous neighbourhood in Rawalpindi, not far from the army GHQ. The house belonged to a doctor who had worked with the World Health Organisation, and it had been frequented by KSM. The doctor's wife was an active member of the Jamaat-e-Islami, perhaps Pakistan's most powerful Islamic party, and which also had close links with al-Qaeda. It was their nephew, a Major in the Pakistan Army, with whom KSM had stayed in the Kohat garrison a few weeks earlier.

A few minutes later, the Pakistani security officials dragged KSM out of his bed. He had reportedly taken sleeping pills that night. In another room, the security agents found a long-bearded Arab man who was later identified as Ahmad al Hasawi, one of the key members of al-Qaeda's inner core who had also arranged finances for the 9/11 attacks. The capture of KSM was the biggest feat for the CIA and ISI who had been working very closely in the hunt for al-Qaeda fugitives.[29]

The tip-off about KSM's presence apparently came from a CIA informer who also happened to be closely related to an al-Qaeda leader. Pakistani security agencies were not informed about the identity of the target when called by the CIA for the raid.[30] The security agents gleaned a treasure trove of information from Hasawi's laptop about the group's support base. Perhaps the most important piece of evidence recovered from KSM were three letters from bin Laden; one of them was to his son, Hamza, that seemed to have been given to KSM during his visit to Shangla a few weeks ago.

Bin Laden heard the news of KSM's arrest on *Al Jazeera*. The news jolted al-Qaeda and three days later, accompanied by the brothers Ibrahim and Abrar, bin Laden left Martung village in Shangla district where the group had lived for six to eight months. Throughout the stay, 'the tall Arab' did not mix with the couriers' families. It was during this time that Amal got pregnant again.[31]

Bin Laden moved to a rented house in Haripur, about 35 km south of Abbottabad, with the two courier brothers and his wife Amal. The two-storey house, in the Naseem Town area, is described as being spacious, with three bedrooms and a lawn. Later, they were joined by bin Laden's second wife, Siham Sabar, a Saudi national known locally as Sharifa, her son, Khalid bin Laden, and two other bin

Laden daughters—Sumayya and Mariam—both in their early 20s. The group stayed here for almost two years, during which Amal gave birth twice. The children were delivered at a local clinic.[32]

In Haripur, neither bin Laden nor his couriers would use mobile phones. Instead, they would travel to Peshawar, 150 km away, or Rawalpindi, a distance of 65 km, to make phone calls from public call offices. They watched *Al Jazeera* via satellite dish. No 'guests' ever visited the men during that time. While in Haripur, however, bin Laden was already planning his next move.[33]

Intriguingly, the ISI could not detect the world's most hunted man, living in such a crowded neighbourhood in a small town. It was one of the most prominent houses in the middle-class neighbourhood. Any intelligence agency worth its salt should have been able to infiltrate into the bin Laden support network. In a place like Haripur— with a close-knit community—missing bin Laden who lived there with a large family, raises many questions, particularly when many top-ranking al-Qaeda leaders, including KSM, were apprehended in areas not far from the town.

With new high-tech equipment and better human intelligence in place, al-Qaeda operatives living in Pakistani cities became more vulnerable to capture. The CIA had developed extensive intelligence assets and used money to buy information. It was in thickly populated towns, rather than the lawless tribal areas, that the US and the Pakistani intelligence apprehended some big fish. Bin Laden, though, remained elusive.

With the arrest of KSM, al-Qaeda's operation was dealt a serious blow. Pakistan's intelligence agents made a significant breakthrough with subsequent high profile arrests. The wave of arrests and intelligence discoveries in Pakistan in mid-2004 revealed a network of operatives connected to the past al-Qaeda operations and aligned with the imprisoned masterminds of the 9/11 attacks.

More importantly, the material gleaned from the computers seized during the raids offers a rare insight into al-Qaeda's network. But it was hard to completely dismantle the loosely connected and highly mobile groups. The information received from the captured men led to the capture of another key al-Qaeda operative in 2005.

On 24 June 2003, President Bush and President Musharraf jointly announced at Camp David that the al-Qaeda network had been dismantled and many of its chief operators captured.[34] But the claim appeared to be premature. Despite these successes, the terrorist network was still very active in Pakistan.

Three months later, *Al-Jazeera* aired a new video of bin Laden walking through mountainous terrain with al-Zawahiri.[35] In an audiotape accompanying the video footage, the men warned of the real battle to come. The terrain where the video was filmed led to fresh speculation about his whereabouts. Intelligence agencies believed it could be between the Pakistani Bajaur agency and Kunar, across the border in Afghanistan. The video was taken months ago.

In July 2004, Pakistani intelligence services received yet another indication about al-Qaeda having established a strong network in Pakistan. The information extracted from some newly captured al-Qaeda operatives, including its communication chief, Naeem Noor Mohammed Khan, had provided the clearest idea about bin Laden's possible presence in the tribal area. A young Pakistani engineer, with an upper middle-class background, Naeem, was the key connection between bin Laden's inner circle in Pakistan and al-Qaeda operatives around the world.[36]

The information gleaned from Naeem's computer, provided an unparalleled insight into al-Qaeda's inner workings. It revealed al-Qaeda's plans for fresh terrorist attacks against the USA and Britain; specific targets included Heathrow airport in London, and top financial institutions in the USA.

Naeem had other important tasks as well. He handled operative reports and recommendations and together with his own observations, sent them via courier to the terrorist leadership. He had made at least five trips to Britain over the previous six years. He also collected intelligence to plan terrorist attacks on important installations in

Britain. Naeem's arrest, and his interrogation, helped in breaking al-Qaeda's cell in Britain, led by Dhiren Barot, alias Essa al-Hindi.[37]

The capture of the man who worked as bin Laden's backchannel exposed an intricate web of al-Qaeda contacts in Pakistan, Britain, and the US. Information received during his interrogation helped not only break al-Qaeda's cell in Britain, but also in tracking down Ahmed Khalfan Ghailani, a Tanzanian national indicted for murder, in connection with the 1998 bombings of US embassies in East Africa. He had a $25 million prize on his head.

Abu Faraj al-Libbi, a Libyan national, had been working as the head of al-Qaeda's external operations after the capture of KSM in February 2003, and was the key link with the Pakistani militants. Al-Libbi's name surfaced after he was identified as the mastermind behind failed assassination attempts on Musharraf in December 2003. He had been on the list of the six 'most wanted' men in a Pakistani poster campaign for his involvement in a series of terrorist actions. Al-Libbi was captured by the ISI in a dramatic raid on 2 May 2005, while he was being driven on a motorbike in Mardan, a town in the North-West Frontier Province (now Khyber Pakhtunkhwa).

After a series of arrests of high profile operatives, al-Qaeda had minimised the use of electronic communications and largely relied on manual messaging. However, that also made them more vulnerable. Intelligence agents tracked down al-Libbi after arresting a messenger. Al-Libbi's arrest led to some startling revelations about his contacts across eight countries. He was certainly a very important man in the global terrorist network. It was suspected that al-Libbi had been in contact with bin Laden or Zawahiri.

The ISI kept picking up chatter indicating Zawahiri's presence in South Waziristan, but he would always slip away before Pakistani security agencies could get to him. Ayman al-Zawahiri kept travelling between the Pakistani tribal areas and Afghanistan. He was believed to be in South Waziristan when Pakistani security forces launched an offensive against the militants in the second week of March 2004. The army suffered heavy casualties in twelve days of bloody fighting.

Scores of foreign fighters, fighting alongside local militants, forced the Pakistani troops to retreat. Pashtun paramilitary soldiers deserted the government forces in droves as the offensive against al-Qaeda and their tribal supporters descended into chaos. Those who belonged to the local tribes had refused to fire on their brethren. Some of them, perhaps, had also been inspired by a videotape recorded by Zawahiri in which he had called Musharraf a traitor and urged Pakistani troops to disobey the order. 'Fight the supporters of the devil,' he exhorted.

The tape also reinforced the suspicion that the al-Qaeda's number two had been hiding in the border areas protected by sympathetic tribesmen. The videotape caused serious embarrassment to Musharraf who, just a few days before, had claimed that his forces had encircled 'a high-value target.' He tried to play down al-Zawahiri's ranting. 'Zawahiri is on the run. For heaven's sake, it is just one tape. Let's not get excited,' he told an American TV network.

Pakistan Army commandos came very close to seizing al-Zawahiri in mid-2004, when they raided an al-Qaeda safe house in South Waziristan. The vast mud compound was used as the group's hidden command centre. A huge cache of weapons, radios, and sophisticated electronic equipment, including a video-editing machine, was found buried underground. Pakistani intelligence officials believed Zawahiri had used the place, but he had apparently fled days before the raid.

With bin Laden's deteriorating health condition and security concerns making it more difficult for him to maintain contact with al-Qaeda members, Zawahiri was running the network. He had become the face of al-Qaeda with his audio and video messages being used for propagation of the group's message. As Pakistani forces intensified the offensive in South Waziristan, Zawahiri moved between Bajaur tribal areas, in FATA, and across the border to Afghanistan's Kunar province.

Damadola village in the Bajaur tribal region, well north of Waziristan, had also become a hotbed of extremism. Nestled among high peaks, Damadola, which lies just five miles from Afghanistan, was suspected to be a hideout of Zawahiri. It was an ideal base for militants and the stronghold of a pro-Taliban militant group. The Pakistan Army had never set foot there.

Shin Kot, a small village just south of Damadola, had hosted al-Qaeda's headquarters in the winter of 2005–6, and the area featured an elaborate network of mountain caves that served as al-Qaeda's nerve centre. Pakistani security officials believed that Zawahiri constantly moved through the 40-kilometer square area along the border. He was known to have regularly visited the Damadola area, and some believed he had even married a local girl.[38]

In the early morning hours of 13 January 2006, several CIA Predator drones struck a mud-walled compound in Damadola village. The strike on Damadola was apparently launched after the CIA received ground intelligence that Zawahiri and other senior al-Qaeda operatives were invited to an Eid al Adha feast to be held there. Reports suggest that CIA may have waited too long for confirmation of his presence and decided to strike when the al-Qaeda leader had already left the place.[39]

Unlike the protocol followed prior to this strike, Pakistani authorities were not consulted and were informed of the pending attack less than an hour before it occurred. Dozens of people were killed in the most devastating CIA drone strike. Pakistani security officials claimed that at least four al-Qaeda operatives were among the dead, though they were never identified, as their supporters took away the bodies within hours of the attack. The strike sent a shockwave across the country, greatly fuelling anti-American sentiment.

On 15 January 2006, thousands of people in Karachi joined a protest against the Damadola attack in one of the largest anti-American rallies since Pakistan joined the war on terror in 2001. A highly charged crowd chanted 'Death to America!' and 'Stop bombing innocent people!', organised by rightwing Islamic groups, the rally badly shook the government.

Once again, the Pakistan government tried to cover up the CIA's role in the attack, insisting that it was carried out by its own security services, but mounting public outrage forced the government to backtrack. The foreign ministry condemned the raid and lodged a formal protest to the US ambassador, Ryan Crocker, over the loss of innocent lives. But, at the same time, Musharraf also warned people not to harbour militants. 'If we keep sheltering foreign terrorists here … our future will not be good,' he said in a speech broadcasted on state television. There was no public comment from US officials on the incident.

In a video message released a couple of weeks later, on 30 January 2006, Zawahiri came out with a stinging tirade against the US and Pakistani governments for killing innocent people. Sporting his trademark white robes and white turban, the al-Qaeda second-in-command vowed to avenge the deaths.[40]

Meanwhile, in 2005, bin Laden moved to his newly constructed hideout known as 'Waziristan House,' close to the Pakistan Military Academy in Abbottabad, and 65 kilometers from Islamabad. Construction began in August 2004 on a two-storey structure, custom-built with walls as high as 18 ft in some places. The building was completed in just one year. In August 2005, the group moved to the newly constructed house. Abrar and Ibrahim took their families over there first, with bin Laden and his family following soon after.[41]

The brothers posed as businessmen, purchasing the land under a false identity (Abrar posed as 'Muhammad Arshad,' and his brother was known as 'Tariq Khan'). The story they gave out was that they fled the tribal area as a result of a family feud—and this was the reason for the high walls and isolation of the residents from their neighbours.[42]

Life in Waziristan House was kept strictly private. The brothers had utility companies install four separate meters for electricity and natural gas respectively, in an apparent attempt to ensure that none of the meters showed an excessive amount of activity, betraying the true number of residents. They used their alias—Muhammad Arshad and Tariq Khan—for the installation of meters. Abrar and Ibrahim saw to the procurement of food and provisions. There was seldom any other contact with the outside world. The brothers were the only people to leave the compound to interact with the community. They would regularly offer their prayers in the local mosque.

Bin Laden reportedly suffered from various ailments, particularly in his kidneys, but there is no evidence to suggest a doctor ever visited him and he almost certainly never left the compound.

Bin Laden's children, apparently, lived extremely regimented and secluded lives. Khairiyyah Sabar, a 61-year-old Saudi national and bin Laden's first wife, joined the group just three months before the US raid, having spent eight years between 2002 and 2010 in detention in Iran. There was strong evidence to suggest that bin Laden had monetary problems.[43]

It is also believed that bin Laden was actively planning al-Qaeda's future operations. While he had cut off personal contact with other al-Qaeda operatives following the capture of KSM in 2003, he remained in communication with them although there was no internet or telephone connection in Waziristan House. The two brothers helped bin Laden release videos and communicate with other al-Qaeda leaders. While bin Laden was seen as the mastermind and inspiration of the organisation, he now had a much less active day-to-day role.

Zawahiri, meanwhile, had long been viewed as al-Qaeda's chief ideologue and operational commander. He was also considered the more radical of the two. Through statements and books, Zawahiri attacked Iran, Egypt's Muslim Brotherhood, Hezbollah, Hamas, and other radical Islamists that bin Laden preferred to keep under a broader jihadist umbrella.

Over the years, bin Laden's role had become increasingly marginalised. There were also reports of growing differences between the two leaders over al-Qaeda's strategy. Tensions between bin Laden and Zawahiri reportedly sharpened around 2005 after the US-led invasion of Iraq prompted the creation of a new affiliate group, al-Qaeda in Iraq, led by a Jordanian named Abu Musab al Zarqawi.[44]

The Iraqi affiliate had unleashed a brutal campaign against Shiites in Iraq, including attacks on Shiite mosques, which undermined al-Qaeda's efforts to win over the local population. While bin Laden and much of the al-Qaeda leadership distanced themselves from Zarqawi's tactics, Zawahiri acknowledged the 'heresy' of the Shiites and gently admonished Zarqawi. There were also other issues on which bin Laden and Zawahiri did not agree, but there had not been a parting of the ways.

The presence of al-Qaeda in Pakistan had thinned because of a series of high profile captures, and also because many al-Qaeda members had shifted to new venues of jihad, particularly to Iraq, following its occupation by US forces. Pakistan's growing crackdown on al-Qaeda's command structure, forced them to adapt, breeding new and homegrown militant Islamic threats in Pakistan that the security forces found harder to uproot.

5 | Not-So-Invisible War

President Pervez Musharraf's political fortunes took a downturn after his fatal decision on 10 March 2007 to sack the Chief Justice of Pakistan. Musharraf's unprecedented action against the country's top judge triggered nationwide protests by lawyers that soon turned into a mass anti-government movement. For the first time, Musharraf appeared vulnerable. Both rightwing religious groups and liberals had united in support of the sacked chief justice.

Musharraf's position became more untenable after he ordered his troops to raid the Lal Masjid in Islamabad in July 2007. The incident turned Pakistan into a new battleground for the militants. A wave of suicide bombings hit Pakistani cities with the military as the prime target of militant attacks. The military had been completely bogged down in Waziristan where three years of a military campaign against al-Qaeda-backed militants had produced little results. Hundreds of soldiers had been killed in a war that seemed to have no end.

The Bush administration had been nervously watching as al-Qaeda rebuilt its infrastructure along the border between Afghanistan and Pakistan, often with the help of local sympathisers. The relationship between al-Qaeda and local insurgents had been strengthened by a common antipathy towards the pro-West Musharraf government. The groups shared resources and training facilities, and sometimes even planned attacks together.

Musharraf had become more dependent on Washington as he battled for political survival. Growing political uncertainty in Pakistan had caused huge concerns in Washington and London. The worries had increased as Musharraf's five-year term as president neared completion. Fearful of a rightwing Islamist backlash, the US and Britain sought to bring together pro-West moderate political forces in Pakistan—an alliance between General Musharraf and the Pakistan

Peoples Party (PPP) led by Benazir Bhutto—to safeguard their interests in the region.

In the summer of 2007, a plan took shape during discussions in Islamabad, Washington, and London. The goal was to give Pakistan a government with more democratic legitimacy than the regime led by General Musharraf, without opening the door to forces that could be a threat to Pakistan's alliance with the US in the aftermath of the 9/11 attacks.

Reaching this goal involved a number of steps: Musharraf was to win re-election as President in the fall, arrange for Benazir Bhutto to return from exile, and step down from his position as head of the military. Finally, in parliamentary elections scheduled for January 2008, the forces led by Benazir Bhutto and parties loyal to Musharraf would win a majority, allowing the two to pursue a pro-American, anti-extremist Islamic agenda.

After many long and late-night talks on the telephone, the two leaders finally reached an agreement. Condoleezza Rice and her deputy, Richard Boucher, were also active behind the scenes in Washington pushing the two leaders to firm up the deal.

On 5 October 2007, Musharraf signed the National Reconciliation Ordinance (NRO), giving amnesty to Benazir and other political leaders. The Ordinance came a day before Musharraf faced the crucial presidential poll. In return, Benazir and the PPP agreed not to boycott the Presidential election.

On 6 October 2007, Musharraf won the parliamentary election for President. However, the Supreme Court ruled that no winner could be officially proclaimed until it finished deciding on whether it was legal for Musharraf to run for President while remaining the COAS. Fearing that the Supreme Court would not ratify his re-election, Musharraf imposed a state of emergency in the country on 3 November, citing sanctions by the Court and religious extremism, prevalent in the country. This action, described as Musharraf's second martial law, triggered a massive backlash in the country as well as widespread international condemnation.

Musharraf's desperate measure threatened to derail the US-backed plan for a new power-sharing arrangement in Pakistan. In a strongly-worded statement, Rice called for the immediate lifting of the emergency. The 3 November action almost sealed Musharraf's fate and for the first time, there was a realisation in Washington that the situation was fast becoming untenable for the military ruler.

The development gave a new twist to the political situation in Pakistan. Benazir was briefly put under house detention as she tried to hold a rally in Islamabad and Lahore. In mid-November, President Bush dispatched deputy secretary of state, John Negroponte, to Pakistan to put the derailed reconciliation process back on track. Washington also wanted Musharraf to end the emergency immediately and take off his uniform before the parliamentary elections. The pressure worked, as Musharraf agreed to end the emergency, give up his position as chief of army staff, and become a civilian president.

On 3 December 2007, Musharraf handed over the army command to General Ashfaq Parvez Kayani, bringing an end to his 46-year-long military career. General Kayani had the reputation of a hard-working officer who rose rapidly through military ranks. Son of an army soldier, he received his commission in the Pakistan Army in 1971. General Kayani was known as a man of few words and kept a low profile until he was appointed ISI chief in 2004.

A graduate of the elite command school in Kansas in the US, General Kayani was almost everything his American partners could want: a deep-thinking, thorough professional military man who ascended through the ranks by his own merits, and who was convinced that the armed forces should stay out of politics.

The assassination of Benazir Bhutto on 27 December 2007, a few weeks before the polls, deepened the crisis, which had gripped the country for the past one year. Initial investigation showed that the assassination was clearly the hallmark of al-Qaeda-linked militants. The authenticity of the investigation was, however, questioned by Benazir's supporters who suspected a deeper conspiracy behind the assassination.

For Washington, there was no better partner in the war against terrorism than the Pakistanis. The turmoil generated by Benazir's assassination had only deepened cooperation to protect mutual interests. White House, Intelligence and Defence Department officials held a series of meetings to discuss US's options if the crisis deepened, including the possibility of covert action involving Special Forces.

The parliamentary elections held in February 2008 swept into power the PPP that was then led by Asif Ali Zardari.

The die had already been cast against Musharraf, but he was not prepared to concede. Concurrently, serious doubts also emerged in Washington about the tenability of Musharraf's presidency. The Bush administration conveyed its concern to its ally through Richard Boucher, who had also played a key role in brokering a power-sharing deal between Musharraf and Benazir. The message was clear: Musharraf should work out his exit plan.[1]

Musharraf resisted the US pressure, telling the American officials that he was indispensable and could weather the crisis. The army had also been the main source of his power for the past eight years. He tried to convince himself and his allies that the army leadership would stand by him, but the writing on the wall was clear. When the crunch came, even his loyalists in the army were not there to protect him.

The new military leadership had become increasingly wary of criticism for protecting an unpopular leader. The situation became more embarrassing for the military after Musharraf was threatened with impeachment if he did not resign. General Kayani conveyed the concern of his commanders about the impossibility of continuing with the standoff situation, to his former chief.

General Kayani's decision to keep the army out of the fray finally compelled Musharraf to step down. He made it clear that Musharraf could no longer rely on the army's support. But it was also the promise of indemnity negotiated by the US that paved the way for Musharraf's exit. In a cable sent to Washington, Anne Patterson reported that Zardari had told her on 23 August that he was committed to giving indemnity to Musharraf.[2]

In a long and emotional televised speech on 18 August 2008, Musharraf announced his resignation. He was assured a safe and honourable exit in a deal brokered by the military leadership who would not allow their former commander to go through the humiliation of impeachment. General Kayani also ensured that the outgoing president was given a guard of honor by the armed forces.

Musharraf's resignation drew a muted reaction from the Bush administration. It was partly the result of Washington having come to terms with the fact, months ago, that it would have to pursue its strategy in Pakistan without Musharraf. One major concern of Washington was who would succeed the man who remained a staunch ally of the US in the region.

Zardari had indicated to US officials his intention to take up the top job himself, long before Musharraf's exit. He found a good ally in Anne Patterson. Zardari had convinced the US ambassador that it would be better for the country, and the US, that instead of pulling the strings from outside, he should lead from the front. Although officially the US had remained neutral in the electoral contest to succeed Musharraf, it was apparent that Zardari had the blessing of the Bush administration. He became the accidental beneficiary of the reconciliation (NRO) deal between Musharraf and Benazir, brokered by the US.

Meanwhile, President Bush had decided to step up action in the tribal territories and, in July 2008, he passed a secret order authorising raids inside Pakistan without the prior approval of Islamabad. US Special Forces were permitted to carry out ground assaults on Pakistan soil to kill or capture al-Qaeda operatives.[3]

The order clearly illustrated a lack of faith in Pakistan's ability to combat the militants, and probably also reflected suspicions that the Pakistani intelligence agencies were not fully trustworthy. The civilian, PPP-led, government that came to power after the February 2008 elections, was considered too weak to control the powerful military that effectively controlled national security and foreign policy despite return to democracy. However, the civilian government was evidently eager to show its support for the US.

Just months after he was sworn in as Prime Minister in 2008, Yousaf Raza Gillani assured US Ambassador, Anne Patterson, that he 'didn't care' if drone strikes were launched in the tribal areas as long as the 'right people' were targeted. 'We'll protest in the National Assembly and then ignore it,' Gillani said nonchalantly.[4]

President Zardari was even more forthright in his endorsement of CIA drone strikes that had turned into an explosive political issue in Pakistan, provoking widespread public anger. 'Kill the seniors. Collateral damage worries you Americans. It doesn't worry me,' he reportedly told a senior US official. He had given the CIA 'license to strike' if it had actionable intelligence.[5] The US administration would not acknowledge the actions.

CIA drone strikes had, in fact, been a feature of the US war in Pakistan since 2004. The Pakistani military had not only acquiesced, even the ISI actively cooperated in determining the targets.[6] As the Predator raids escalated, they became a permanent feature of life for people in the borderland. It became a mere formality for Pakistan to protest, but with the increase in frequency, even that pretense of outrage disappeared. Pakistan had maintained a policy of plausible deniability.[7]

By maintaining secrecy, US administration officials believed they could avoid any controversy over its use. Successive US administrations refused to answer any questions about the drone operation in Pakistan in any open forum, though off the record, they would rave about its invisibility and the hearty support they received from Pakistani authorities.[8]

US security officials had often accused Pakistani intelligence agents of alerting militants in advance of strikes.[9] The political unrest that had been roiling the country was also a strong factor in the administration's decision to ignore Islamabad. Previously, it had been agreed that the CIA would carry out action inside Pakistani borders only after consultation with the ISI. But this policy changed. When the CIA carried out a Predator missile attack in 2008 without first informing the ISI, the Pakistani ambassador in Washington, General

Mahmud Ali Durrani, went to meet the CIA chief, Michael Hayden, at Langley.[10]

'What's happening?' Durrani enquired. Hayden informed him about the secret order passed by President Bush that allowed the CIA to operate unilaterally. Hayden was particularly unhappy with the ISI's continued support for the Haqqani network operating from North Waziristan. He narrated instances where the insurgents were informed before the attack, allowing them to escape. Hayden also conveyed to the ambassador the decision to escalate drone strikes without first consulting Pakistan.[11] The distrust between the CIA and the ISI had further widened.

Weeks after Durrani returned to take up his new posting as National Security Advisor to Prime Minister Gillani in mid-2008, Admiral Mike Mullen, Chairman Joint Chiefs of Staff Committee, and Stephen Kappes, Deputy-Director CIA, travelled to Islamabad to complain about the difficulties in the 'coordination process' in the drone strike programme. It was an extremely tense atmosphere in the meeting held at the Prime Minister House, as the two US officials presented strong evidence alleging ISI's close connection with the Haqqani network.

'The militants are tipped off about the drone strikes whenever we share information with the ISI,' they told the prime minister. Then Mullen suddenly turned to Lt. Gen. Nadeem Taj, the ISI chief, who was sitting next to Durrani. 'You are a criminal organisation,' he shouted, wagging his finger at General Taj. Stunned by the remark, the ISI chief tried to explain that being an intelligence agency, the ISI did maintain contacts with the insurgent group but denied charges of actively supporting it. 'We are an intelligence organisation and we do have our informers with the insurgents crossing into Afghanistan, but we are not supporting them,' General Taj told Durrani after the meeting.[12]

There was a growing US concern over the Haqqani network's audacious attacks in the Afghan capital and rising casualties of the coalition forces. The footprints of the devastating truck bombing at the Indian embassy in Kabul in July 2008, that killed dozens of people, were traced to the group's base in North Waziristan. Sirajuddin Haqqani later confided to a Pakistani journalist that the attack was carried out by his group.[13] US officials were furious over the connection and Pakistan's persistent denial.

Following that testy meeting, Durrani flew to Washington to meet his counterpart, Stephen Headley, for further talks. The Haqqani network issue again dominated the discussion. 'It's also your responsibility to intercept those crossing the border. Kill them even if they are our people,' Durrani told Headley. Durrani's assurance may have calmed down the situation but failed to remove the suspicion about the alleged 'double game' by Pakistan's premier intelligence agency. A major problem was that we were never straight. That was the main reason for distrust,' Durrani admitted.[14]

The Americans were still not willing to share information about the targets for drone strikes. The complicated and cumbersome process in getting clearance from the Pakistani military authorities was also a major factor in the US administration's decision to bypass the ISI. Previously, the protocol was that the US would inform the ISI after spotting the target. ISI, in turn, would forward the information to the GHQ, who would convey the message to the Peshawar Corps Commander.

The whole process was not only time consuming, but also allowed the elements within the agency to alert the insurgents, particularly if they belonged to the Haqqanis. The CIA was furious when, on a few occasions, the target disappeared. Steve Kappes complained that sometimes it took up to four days to get a response from Pakistani military officials handling the matter.

The Americans were particularly unhappy with General Taj and wanted him removed. General Taj was appointed to the post only a year earlier, towards the end of General Musharraf's government. He had replaced General Kayani as DG ISI, after Kayani was appointed the COAS. General Taj had served Musharraf in various capacities, including as head of Military Intelligence (MI), for almost a decade but seemed to have little control over the agency. His position had also become untenable with the fall of General Musharraf and the installation of a new civilian government. Prime Minister Gillani had no objection to his removal.[15]

Several months after Bush's new order, in August and September 2008, US forces entered Pakistan's tribal areas on two occasions in order to raid suspected Taliban and al-Qaeda sanctuaries. On 3 September, about two-dozen US Navy SEALs dismounted from two helicopters at Angoradda, a village in South Waziristan, and raided three houses late at night in search of militants. They spent several hours on the ground and killed about twenty people, who they suspected of being al-Qaeda operatives.[16] The validity of that claim was later called into doubt when it was revealed that most of the victims were women and children and belonged to one family.

The intrusion provoked an intense reaction from the Pakistani military, which fired at the helicopters and warned of retaliation if any more such operations were carried out. In a strongly-worded statement, COAS General Kayani warned that Pakistan would not allow foreign troops on its soil and that the country's sovereignty and integrity would be defended at all costs.[17]

A few days later, on 19 September 2008, General Kayani flew out to meet Admiral Mike Mullen on the aircraft carrier, USS Abraham Lincoln, which was then patrolling the waters south of India and Pakistan, and gave him the toughest possible warning against any future intrusion. General Kayani was accompanied by DGMO, Lt. Gen. Ahmed Shuja Pasha. It was Mike Mullen's first interaction with General Pasha, who was appointed to the ISI some weeks later. Pakistan had apparently bowed to US pressure and named a new spy chief amid allegations that elements within the ISI had been playing a 'double game.'[18]

As DGMO, General Pasha had led the Pakistani Army's campaign against Islamic militants in the lawless northwest of the country. He was serving with the UN Peace Force when he was appointed to the coveted position in 2007 as the military faced a serious challenge from an escalating insurgency sweeping northern Pakistan. He was scheduled to retire but was instead promoted, indicating the degree of trust General Kayani reposed in him.[19]

A short sturdy man in his early 50s, General Pasha had a mixed reputation in the army. He was reputed to be blunt in his views in meetings, unlike other senior officers. But some found him to be an 'extremely complex person' who would always take a 'controversial position to be important.'[20] However, General Kayani trusted him and appointed him as DG ISI.

In fact, General Kayani had continued to be deeply involved in ISI matters even after becoming COAS. 'He never came out of the ISI mindset,' a senior ISI officer told me. 'Kayani would meet heads of various ISI departments almost every day. S branch, responsible for covert operations, remained completely under Kayani.'[21]

The change was part of a much broader shakeup of the Pakistan Army's high command and the ISI, as General Kayani sought to assert his control over the institution. In less than a year since he became the army chief, two other senior ISI officers, both two-star Generals in charge of Counter Intelligence and Internal Political Affairs—Asif Akhtar and Nusrat Naeem—were removed.[22] Both were suspected by the US of having links with some militant factions. Kayani and Pasha installed their own generals in critical positions.

Maj. Gen. Zaheerul Islam, considered close to General Kayani, was appointed as head of Counter Intelligence. He later became ISI chief, succeeding General Pasha in 2012. General Taj was given charge of an important corps that meant he remained a part of the critical decision-making body.

Pasha was well-regarded at the Pentagon.[23] He had attended all six of Kayani's meetings with Admiral Mike Mullen. In these, and other meetings with US interlocutors, he and Kayani had described and defended their approach to the war against the Taliban. Despite differences over the US decision to conduct unilateral action and choice of targets, the cooperation between the CIA and ISI continued. Pakistan's tacit approval of the drone programme had been a poorly kept national security secret. 'We don't admit it in public, but Predators have proved very effective in eliminating al-Qaeda operatives,' a senior ISI officer working on counterterrorism told me. 'Precision strikes rarely cause collateral damage.'[24]

Pilotless aircraft had been used by the US against the militant sanctuaries along the border with Afghanistan from the very early stages of the US war on terror in the region. The CIA was permitted to operate the lethal Predators under presidential authority promulgated after the 9/11 attacks. Shortly after the attacks, Bush also signed a presidential order that allowed the CIA to write a set of highly classified rules describing which individuals could be killed by CIA officers. They had given the CIA counterterrorism officials in the field, a free hand to decide much more quickly when to fire. Such killings were defined as self-defense in a global war against al-Qaeda.

The drone's primary mission had been to supply real-time intelligence, surveillance, and reconnaissance, but they had proved highly successful as a battlefield weapon as well. They were extremely effective, especially in killing individuals and small groups of people. The Predators were fuelled, serviced, and armed by CIA technicians in Afghanistan, or in some cases, in bases in Pakistan, but they were flown by CIA operatives in the US.[25]

In September 2001, as part of a deal, Pakistan had provided the US access to some military bases and helped establish facilities including Intermediate Staging Bases at Jacobabad, Pasni, Dalbandin, and Shamsi. It also allowed the basing of Predators at some of those facilities. Jacobabad was the main base used where some 50 aircraft and 2000 coalition military personnel were located. The bases were completely under the control of Americans where Pakistani officials had limited access.

Even top Pakistani military officials did not have much knowledge about the activities of US forces on those bases. Though the airstrips were strictly for logistic support to US forces in Afghanistan, they were also used for combat purposes, and the Pakistani Army was completely barred from going inside these bases.

The CIA had secretly used the Shamsi airbase, originally built by Arab sheikhs for falconry expeditions in the southwestern province of Balochistan in southern Pakistan, to launch the Predator drones to observe and attack al-Qaeda and Taliban militants on the Pakistani side of the border. The strip, which is about 30 miles from the Afghan border, allowed US forces to launch a drone within minutes of receiving actionable intelligence, as well as allowing them to attack targets further afield.

It was known that US Special Forces had used the Shamsi airbase during the invasion of Afghanistan in 2001, but the Pakistan government only declared it publicly in 2006 that the Americans had left Shamsi base and two other airbases. But it was later revealed that the CIA had routinely used the Shamsi base till 2011 for carrying out drone strikes in Pakistani tribal areas, allegedly killing not only several top Taliban and al-Qaeda targets, but also many civilians. While the Pakistan military guarded the outer perimeter, the airfield itself was under the control of US forces.[26]

Shamsi lies in a sparsely populated area close to Afghanistan's southern province of Helmand. That would put the Predators, which have a range of more than 2000 miles and can fly for 29 hours, in a position to reach militants in Balochistan, southern Afghanistan, and in Pakistan's northern tribal areas. The airstrip was too short for most aircraft, but was big enough for Predators and ideally located, as there were few civilians in the surrounding area to witness the drones coming and going.

US Marine Special Forces were also briefly based at Shamsi. However, in January 2002, a US Marine KC130 tanker aircraft crashed close to its runway, killing seven Marines on board.[27] In July 2006, the Pakistan government declared that the US was no longer using Shamsi, Pasni, and Jacobabad bases, although they were at its disposal in an emergency.

The deployment of foreign troops and Pakistan being used for the invasion of Afghanistan was an extremely sensitive political issue in Pakistan. For that reason, Musharraf rejected a proposal from US officials in 2002, to allow Special Operations Forces a base in the tribal areas. Instead, a small number of Navy SEAL units were allowed to accompany Pakistani forces on raids in the tribal areas in 2002 and 2003.

The arrangement did not last long as the presence of even a small number of foreign troops provoked an intense reaction from the tribesmen, causing huge embarrassment for the Pakistani military. This had also caused friction between Islamabad and Washington.

The CIA carried out its first Predator drone strike in Pakistan on 17 June 2004, when it targeted Nek Mohammed, a top Taliban militant commander, near Wana, the main town in South Waziristan. Nek Mohammed, who had led the resistance against the Pakistani forces, was hit when he was talking on a satellite phone to a BBC correspondent. The attack had come after several days of surveillance. The Hellfire missile had pierced through a mud wall surrounding the compound where Nek Mohammed sat with his supporters. He was killed a few days after his men attacked a Pakistan Army post, killing several soldiers.

It was evident that the attack was carried out with the cooperation of Pakistan's military-led government. Pakistani security officials denied any US involvement, claiming the strike was carried out by their forces. There was complete silence over the incident from US officials. The rules of engagement were very clear at that time: while surveillance flights were allowed, strikes could not be carried out without Islamabad's approval. The strike against Nek Mohammed was owned by the Pakistan government and did not provoke any controversy.

Less than a year later on 14 May 2005, the CIA struck again. This time the target was Haithem al Yemeni. A senior al-Qaeda operative from Yemen, he was seen as a potential successor to Abu Faraj al-Libbi, al-Qaeda's number three who had been captured a few months earlier from the northwestern town of Mardan with the help of information provided by the US.

Al-Libbi, who was a Libyan national, had worked as head of al-Qaeda's external operations after the capture of KSM and was the key link with Pakistani militants. Haithem al Yemeni was the first senior al-Qaeda member who was targeted by a CIA drone inside Pakistan. His death drew very little attention in Pakistan.

It was on 3 November 2005, that the CIA got its biggest catch up till that time when Hellfire missiles, fired from a drone, hit a compound in a remote village in North Waziristan. The target was Abu Hamza Rabia, a 32-year-old Egyptian, who was believed to be al-Qaeda's senior international operations commander. A close associate of Ayman al-Zawahiri, a fellow Egyptian, Rabia was also responsible for training, recruiting, and planning operations outside Pakistan and Afghanistan.[28]

The drone strikes produced some significant breakthroughs in the killing of the top al-Qaeda leadership. On 29 January 2008, a Predator strike killed Abu Laith al-Libi, a top-tier al-Qaeda leader who was believed to have been involved in an attempt to assassinate Vice President Dick Cheney when he was on a visit to Bagram Air Force Base in Afghanistan in February 2007. Abu Laith was said to be a key link between al-Qaeda and its affiliates in North Africa, and his killing was the most serious blow to the group's top leadership in several years. Seventeen more known drone attacks in 2008 reportedly killed at least eight other senior al-Qaeda operatives, including Khalid Habib, the group's operations chief in Pakistan and Afghanistan, dealing a serious blow to al-Qaeda's operation in the region.

After President Barack Obama took over the presidency in January 2009, CIA unmanned Predator missile strikes rose a hundredfold. Drone strikes became the weapon of choice for Obama, which was ironic, considering that he had been awarded the 2009 Noble Peace Prize soon after his installation. What is forgotten is that this was one of his first orders given: *within* 72 hours of his inauguration, Barack Hussein Obama, the 44th President of the United States of America, ordered his first drone strike in Pakistan's tribal region that had become al-Qaeda's new base for cross-border insurgent attacks on US forces in Afghanistan. Soon the drone strikes began occurring weekly, then almost daily.

It was part of the Obama administration's strategy to win the US war in South Asia. He had also hinted that US Special Forces could carry out ground operations inside Pakistan against the insurgents who, US intelligence agencies believed, were being protected by the ISI. President Obama felt the US needed a 'stronger, smarter, and comprehensive strategy.'[29]

The move had followed his decision to send 18,000 more troops to Afghanistan, to combat the rising Taliban insurgency against the US-led occupation forces. The drones flew several times a day—observing and tracking targets—and unleashing missiles on suspected al-Qaeda hideouts in North and South Waziristan.

The main objective of this new and more aggressive approach was to take out al-Qaeda's top leadership and deny sanctuary in the tribal regions to the Taliban and those fighters who routinely slipped across the border to attack US forces in Afghanistan. It also meant attacking militant networks seeking to topple the Pakistan government. The remote-controlled pilotless Predator aircraft became a major weapon in the US campaign.

In 2009, under the Obama administration, 50 more attacks were carried out that eliminated several other senior al-Qaeda and militant commanders. A missile strike in South Waziristan on New Year's Day killed Usama al-Kini, head of al-Qaeda's operations in Pakistan, and his lieutenant, Sheikh Ahmed Salim Swedan. Both were on the FBI's 'most wanted' list and had been indicted for the 1998 bombings of US embassies in Tanzania and Kenya, their respective countries of birth.[30]

With the growing militant insurgency, the US also agreed to target Pakistan Taliban commanders in Pakistan's tribal region. A precision drone strike carried out by the CIA on 5 August 2009, took out Baitullah Mehsud, the chief of the Pakistan Taliban movement and his recently wed young wife. The CIA had been authorised by President Obama to strike Baitullah if they thought they had a clear shot. The Taliban leader was hit after a dramatic escalation of aerial surveillance, with nine unmanned drones assigned to target him.

For years, the US had considered Baitullah a lesser threat to its interests than some other militants because most of his attacks were focused inside Pakistan, and not against US and NATO troops in Afghanistan. Washington had turned down repeated Pakistani requests to target the militant commander who was responsible for a wave of bloody terrorist attacks across the country, particularly targeting the security forces.

The 5 August 2009 strike in Makin was the result of intelligence sharing between the US and Pakistani security agencies. The cooperation had increased after a secret visit to Washington in April 2009 of General Pasha where he met his CIA counterpart, Leon E. Panetta. The two sides agreed, among other things, to focus attention on striking Baitullah and his Taliban supporters.[31]

A change in the US stance also began to appear as Baitullah's power grew and concerns mounted that violence could destabilise Pakistan and threaten the region. In addition, some of Baitullah's fighters were suspected of attacking supply convoys for US and NATO forces travelling through Pakistan. Baitullah's death was seen as a victory for President Obama who relied heavily on the CIA-controlled missile strikes to take out militants based in Pakistan's northwest tribal territory. The strike against Baitullah was another sign that Obama intended to continue and, in some cases, to extend, the policy of using US spy agencies against terrorism suspects in Pakistan.[32]

There was a human cost to this policy; the escalation in the Predator strikes also caused huge collateral damage. According to one estimate, more than 70 strikes between 2006 and 2009 killed more than 700 civilians and only 14 al-Qaeda leaders. In July 2009, the Brookings Institute in Washington released a report stating that 10 civilians died in the drone attacks for every militant killed. There was never any mention of the collateral damage caused and the political cost of these so-called covert operations.[33]

It was quite amusing that even after half a decade and more than 150 drone strikes, the US administration maintained the farce that such operations remained secret and, were therefore, beyond public debate. The political consensus in Washington in support of the drone programme—its surgical, high-tech appeal, and its secrecy—had obscured just how radical it was.

Some US officials maintained that one of the major reasons for not talking openly about drone operations was to protect the foreign governments which had granted permission for strikes under secret deals. It was particularly true in Pakistan's case. It was only when the attacks became more frequent and indiscriminate, fuelling public anger, that Pakistan took a harder position against the drone operations.

The secret campaign provoked condemnation from many international rights groups. On 3 June 2009, the UN Human Rights Council (UNHRC) delivered a report which was sharply critical of US tactics and asserted that the US government had failed to keep track of the civilian casualties or to provide means for citizens of affected nations to obtain information about the casualties and any legal inquests regarding them. On 27 October 2009, a UNHRC investigator, Philip Alston, called on the US to demonstrate that it was not randomly killing people in violation of international law through its use of drones on the Afghan border.

There was mounting international concern over a tactic that had become the Obama administration's weapon of choice against terrorist suspects. The use of armed drones to kill individuals in regions outside active battlefields also raised legal, ethical, and political questions. For the first time in history, an intelligence agency of one country was involved in such an operation in a country with which it was not officially at war.

More worrying, the drone campaign had also contributed to a great swelling of anti-US sentiment in Pakistan. A poll by Gallup Pakistan in 2009 found only 9 per cent of Pakistanis in favour of the attacks and 67 per cent against, with a majority ranking the US as a greater threat to Pakistan than its arch-rival, India, or the Pakistan Taliban. The growing public resentment led many Pakistani political figures to publicly condemn the operations.[34]

But many tribal leaders tacitly supported Predator strikes in their area saying they could accept them as they were clearly hitting high-value targets. The other reason for their support was the fear that the militants could take over Khyber Pakhtunkhwa province if the Pakistan government failed to stop them.

The Obama administration chose the first anniversary of the killing of Osama bin Laden in 2012 to break its doctrine of silence over the CIA's drone warfare. This was one of the most aggressive operations that the CIA had been carrying out in Pakistan and half a dozen other countries.

It remained one of Washington's worst-kept secrets. The drone warfare programme's existence had neither been accepted nor denied by US officials, so far, despite the growing controversy surrounding the campaign which many critics described as extrajudicial executions by remote-controlled unmanned Predators.

A UN report warned that the growing use of armed drones by the US to kill terrorism suspects was undermining global constraints on the use of military force. A major concern was that the US example could be emulated by other countries to carry out attacks outside their borders against groups or individuals, branding them as terrorists.[35]

In the first-ever official public explanation of the CIA drone operations, White House adviser on counterterrorism, John Brennan, offered a vain defense of the controversial strikes against suspected militants declaring them 'legal, ethical, and wise. There is nothing in international law that bans the use of remotely piloted aircraft for this purpose or that prohibits us from using lethal force against our enemies outside of an active battlefield, at least when the country involved consents or is unable or unwilling to take action against the threat,' Brennan declared while speaking at the Woodrow Wilson International Center for Scholars, a Washington-based think tank.[36]

Ironically, the remarks came as Pakistan delivered its strongest public condemnation yet, of the latest drone strike in North Waziristan calling the campaign 'a total contravention of international law and established norms of interstate relations.' The cooperation between the two countries had completely collapsed in 2011, the year when the alignment between the countries had turned hostile.

Once derided by his opponents as a dove, Obama was described by the US media as one of the most militarily hawkish US presidents in recent times. His approach marked a radical shift from Bush's war on terror. Instead of direct military interventions, Obama relied on covert operations. As Roger Cohen, a columnist for *The New York Times*, put it:

'Drone attacks have become the coin of Obama's realm. This new way of fighting is aimed at physically eliminating terrorism suspects and all others perceived to be threatening American national security.'[37]

Inevitably, the latest drone weapon technology has expanded the use of force beyond active battlefields and is completely dehumanising war itself. Strikes carried out by operators sitting in front of a monitoring screen, thousands of miles away from the targets, raise the risk of developing, as a UN commission report said, a 'playstation' mentality to killing.[38]

Justifying the strikes, Brennan argued that the precision strikes had dramatically reduced the danger to US personnel and weakened al-Qaeda and the Taliban insurgents operating from Pakistan's lawless tribal regions. Indubitably, the targeted strikes in the remote tribal regions had eliminated many key al-Qaeda and militant commanders and thrown the terror network into disarray. But the success of this decapitation strategy remains questionable.

6 | Taming Pakistan: Shifting Sands in Washington

President Barack Obama unveiled a new regional strategy to win the war in South Asia. Addressing senior US officials, he declared, 'It has been more than seven years since the Taliban was removed from power, yet the war rages on, and insurgents control parts of Afghanistan and Pakistan.'[1]

While on the campaign trail, Obama had declared that Afghanistan was the 'good war' and a war of necessity that the US had to wage in order to defeat the al-Qaeda and to ensure that Afghanistan never harboured terrorists again. Branding Afghanistan a 'war of necessity' also provided him a cover to denounce the Iraq war as a 'war of choice' that must be brought to an end.

Soon after taking office in January 2009, he ordered a quick policy review on Afghanistan by a former intelligence analyst, Bruce Riedel. But even before it was completed, he accepted a Pentagon recommendation to send 21,000 additional troops, including 4000 'training and advisory' to Afghanistan, bringing the total to nearly 70,000 US troops on the ground.[2]

By this time the fighting in Afghanistan had morphed into a full-blown insurgency with the Taliban extending its control over large parts of the country. Afghanistan was on the brink seven years after the US invasion and there was widespread fear that the Taliban could be in the capital if not stopped. Afghanistan had slipped into chaos.

For the US, the increase in troop numbers was necessary to stave off growing chaos in the south and to provide security for the Afghan presidential election to be held in August 2009. With the escalation in insurgency, there was strong apprehension in Washington that elections would not end well. Karzai, beset with charges of ineffectiveness and corruption, had lost political credibility. Also, political cleavages in Kabul made it extremely difficult to find any consensus solution to the crisis.[3]

The Karzai administration was almost absent in some parts of the country, and the police force, though nearly 65,000 strong, were poorly trained and ineffective. Drug trafficking also contributed to undermining the system. While Karzai had lost the confidence of the Obama administration, there seemed to be no plausible alternative to him. A major concern for the new US administration was that if the Afghan government fell to the Taliban or to al-Qaeda, operating from its safe haven in Pakistan, Afghanistan would once again turn into a base for terrorists.[4]

After years of confusion over the exact US aims in Afghanistan, Obama sought to set a narrow—and what his military chiefs regarded as achievable—objective of denying safe havens to the al-Qaeda and Taliban. The new US strategy, however, didn't present any grand vision of a democratic Afghanistan, or a timeline for withdrawal from a war that had gone wrong.

Instead, in a radical downgrade of the loftier objectives set by President Bush, the aim of the new strategy was 'to disrupt, dismantle, and defeat' the al-Qaeda in Pakistan and Afghanistan. A critical element of Obama's new doctrine was to recast the war as a regional conflict straddling both sides of the Durand Line. That policy decision represented a shift from previous ways of thinking about Afghanistan as an independent problem; now the war front had been extended to include Pakistan.[5]

President Obama also announced a trebling of civilian aid to Pakistan to help prop up the new democratically elected government of Asif Ali Zardari and the PPP. He wanted the US to take full ownership of the deepening conflict.

The main objective of what was initially described as AfPak policy was to look at the problems in the two countries as intertwined. The term denoted the incoming administration's strategy to take a unified approach for these two countries. Obama considered both Afghanistan and Pakistan as the central front of the war against terrorism and that many aspects of the strategic problem of the Afghan war were playing out in both countries.[6]

He asked Congress for $7.5 billion in civilian aid over five years for Pakistan, to help prop up its democracy and infrastructure. 'Now a campaign against extremism will not succeed with bullets or bombs alone,' declared Obama.[7]

Richard Holbrooke, a veteran US diplomat, was appointed special representative for Afghanistan and Pakistan. He was to report through the secretary of state to the president. Holbrooke had coined the AfPak term even before he was offered the new job. He believed that there was a single theatre of war 'straddling an ill-defined border.' Holbrooke had worked for every Democratic president since John F. Kennedy. During the 2008 presidential race, Holbrooke had backed Hillary Clinton in the hope of getting the coveted post of secretary of state in her administration. But that was not destined to be. He owed his new AfPak job to his old friend, Hillary, but he could never win the confidence of the White House. His views on the Afghan war and strategy often fell foul of Obama and his advisors.

Holbrooke would tell his aides that the US was fighting a wrong war. 'You should talk to the Taliban and not fight them.' His views were in sharp contrast with that of the White House and the Pentagon who thought that a military solution to the Afghan war was possible. His views, however, won the confidence and respect of Pakistan's political leadership. His personal relationship with President Zardari and other politicians allowed him to wield influence in Pakistan's domestic sphere.

Obama's AfPak policy, lumping Pakistan with Afghanistan, however, was received with huge scepticism in Islamabad, particularly by the security establishment. A major criticism was India's inclusion in the new US regional strategy. Looking at Pakistan through the Afghan prism was also a cause of resentment. The AfPak strategy also posed a paradox for the Obama administration as it didn't offer any sure way forward or an exit plan. The term was soon dropped.[8] There was, however, a very valid reason for the US to worry about the situation in Pakistan.

The country's northern lawless tribal region along the Afghan border had fallen to al-Qaeda-backed militants, threatening the nation's survival. Thousands of Pakistani troops were engaged in fighting the insurgents who had even advanced to the region close to the capital, Islamabad. The war in Afghanistan had now fully spilled over into Pakistan.

Hours before President Barack Obama announced a new strategy for the Afghan war in March 2009 (an approach US official said would also recognise Pakistan as a key part of the conflict), a suicide bomber demolished a mosque packed with hundreds of worshippers attending Friday prayers in the tribal region near the Afghan border, killing at least 50 people. It was the bloodiest attack in Pakistan that year. The Khyber tribal region, where the bombing took place, was the main supply route for NATO forces in Afghanistan and had become a prime target for the Taliban.

The militants had been regularly attacking convoys. Obama declared the Afghanistan–Pakistan border to be the most dangerous place in the world, 'Multiple intelligence estimates have warned that al-Qaeda is actively planning attacks on the US homeland from its safe haven in Pakistan.' In nearly eight years since the 9/11 attacks, al-Qaeda and its allies had established safe havens in the mountainous Pakistani side of the Afghan border.

Over the years, Pakistan had turned into the main battleground for al-Qaeda and its allies among Pakistani militant groups. In the first several years after the start of the Afghan war, militants based in Pakistan conducted attacks almost exclusively within Afghanistan, seeking to drive out US-led coalition forces from the country and overthrow the Karzai government.

However, by 2007, the militants had changed their modus operandi and started directing their wrath against the Pakistani military and security agencies, launching attacks of increasing sophistication and intensity, as well as escalating a wave of suicide bombings against civilians in the major urban centres across Pakistan.

A distinctive Pakistani Taliban movement under the banner of Tehreek-e-Taliban Pakistan (TTP) had evolved, enforcing their version of a draconian Islamic rule, not only in the tribal areas but also in the neighbouring North-West Frontier Province (now Khyber Pakhtunkhwa). In April 2009, the Taliban forces extended their control still further, taking over the Swat Valley, a popular tourist destination of green alpine meadows and snow-capped mountains, dubbed the Switzerland of Pakistan. The militants blew up scores of girls' schools, declaring female education un-Islamic, and executed hundreds of security and government officials.[9]

Despite these provocations, Pakistan was still reluctant to use military force to stop the militant advance. Instead, the government pursued a policy of appeasement. In yet another humiliating concession, the government had signed a peace agreement in February 2009 with Mullah Fazlullah, the head of the Swat insurgency. The agreement was brokered on his behalf by his 78-year-old father-in-law, Sufi Mohammed, allowing Fazlullah to establish Sharia rule in Swat. The government had acceded to all of TTP's demands, including the establishment of Islamic courts, to be headed by clerics, effectively conceding the area as a Taliban sanctuary and suspending the military effort to crush the insurgents, despite over a year of fighting.

Pakistani officials touted the deal as a way to restore order in the bloodied region—just a few hours' drive from the capital—and to halt the Taliban's advance, but the truth was that a highly demoralised army had no appetite to continue the fight. This much was totally apparent. The newly elected Zardari government, as well as public opinion, also favoured an end to violence, even at the cost of accepting Taliban rule in the Valley.[10]

A major reason for the population losing faith in the security forces was that some top militant leaders arrested during the previous military operation a year ago were all released as part of the deal. They returned to the area and killed scores of people who had cooperated with the military.

Pakistan seemed to be in complete denial of the larger threat the appeasement policy posed to Pakistan's national security. Government officials defended the deal by arguing that it reflected the will of the people. The accord, which had been pushed especially hard by the military, was even described as an arrangement that could be emulated in other areas.[11]

Buying peace was perceived to be the need of the hour, and it was true that many of the locals, who had suffered so much during the past two years of violence, supported the peace accord in the hope that it might bring an end to their misery. Many of them found Taliban's promises of speedy justice and equality attractive. But appeasement came at a huge cost as the following weeks would show.

It was quite evident from the outset that the Taliban were not going to be content with control over the Swat Valley alone, and as feared by many, they used the deal not only to strengthen their hold in the Valley but also to expand their influence. Shortly thereafter, militants in thousands poured into the Valley and set up training camps, quickly re-establishing it as one of the main bases for Taliban fighters. By March 2009, the number of militant fighters in the Valley was believed to be between 6000–8000, nearly double the number at the end of 2008. By late April, they had advanced to within 60 miles of the capital, Islamabad.

The Taliban had turned the country's largest province, Punjab, into their new battlefield, launching a series of bloody suicide bombings and attacks on the urban centres of Lahore, Islamabad, and Rawalpindi, the headquarters of the army. Infiltrating deep into the major cities, the groups had divided into small terrorist cells, making them more difficult to track down.

As the insurgency in Pakistan escalated, it grew not only in numbers but in sophistication. The host of local tribal militant groups, which were earlier only loosely associated or even feuding, had formed an increasingly interconnected and coordinated web, with close collaboration between al-Qaeda and Taliban foreign militants as well as the local militant leaders and Pakistani Taliban. The inexorable advance of the militants towards Islamabad was a devastating blow to Pakistan's claim that the peace deal would contain the Taliban.[12]

The peace accord with Fazlullah had clearly been an abject failure, and the US and other members of the international community called on the Pakistan government to reverse course. Describing the Taliban as an 'existentialist threat,' US Secretary of State, Hillary Clinton, urged Pakistanis worldwide to oppose the government's policy of yielding to them. Pakistanis 'need to speak out forcefully against a policy that is ceding more and more territory to the insurgents,' Clinton testified before a House committee.[13] A major US concern was that Pakistan's nuclear weapons could fall into the hands of the militants who had gotten stronger.

Despite evidence to the contrary, and even in the face of a storm of criticism, the government and the military continued to defend the deal for some time, arguing that it might yet work while also being their only viable option. They also compared the deal to local alliances forged by the US in Afghanistan and Iraq. In Washington, more attention was now being focused on Pakistan than on the war in Afghanistan.

The Taliban advance raised huge concerns just as President Obama unveiled his new regional strategy. The new strategy set Pakistan a benchmark for progress in fighting al-Qaeda and Pakistan Taliban. 'The era of the blank check is over,' declared Obama. The message was clear: US assistance would now be linked to Pakistan's efforts to counter militancy. But many worried that the militants' insurgency had already raged out of control.

Militants loyal to Baitullah Mehsud, the TTP chief, had also stepped up their attacks on Pakistani security forces in South Waziristan and in the Orakzai and Khyber tribal regions, and established their rule along the Afghan border. Some senior US officials described Pakistan as a 'volcano that, should it blow, would send an inconceivable amount of poisonous ash raining down on the world around it.'

David Kilcullen, an expert on counterinsurgency and a key adviser to General David Petraeus at CENTCOM, asserted that 'within one to six months we could see the collapse of the Pakistani state,' a calamity that, given the country's size, strategic location, and nuclear stockpile, would 'dwarf' all other current crises. Such fears may have been highly exaggerated, but it did demonstrate growing concerns about the existentialist threat to the Pakistani state.[14]

In the midst of the crisis, President Obama held a two-day summit in the first week of May 2009 to focus on the security situation in Afghanistan and Pakistan. The trilateral meeting had been raised to a presidential level with President Asif Ali Zardari and President Hamid Karzai in Washington. The focus of the discussion was on ways that Afghanistan and Pakistan, both unstable and strategically vital, could work with each other and with the US to fight militants who presented an existential threat to both countries.[15]

'The security of Pakistan, Afghanistan, and the United States are linked,' stated Obama categorically. He pressed both leaders to take more effective action and work in closer cooperation to counter a rising threat from the Taliban and al-Qaeda in both countries, stating, 'We [are] joined by a common goal: to disrupt, dismantle and defeat Al Qaeda and its extremist allies in Pakistan and Afghanistan....'[16]

Hillary Clinton made much the same point at an earlier briefing, suggesting that it would not be incorrect to think of Pakistan and Afghanistan as 'conjoined twins,' as the US tried to help each tame the forces that spawned terrorism and violence. 'The confidence-building that is necessary for this relationship to turn into tangible cooperation is moving forward,' added Clinton.[17]

Zardari and Karzai, meanwhile, had developed a good personal relationship. Karzai was the chief guest at Zardari's swearing-in ceremony in September 2008. The atmosphere was more congenial in the meeting held on 5 May 2009 than the hostility between General Musharraf and Karzai that had marred the earlier trilateral summit arranged by President Bush in 2006.

But with the Generals being the determinant of Pakistan's Afghan policy, good relations between the two presidents could not bridge the trust deficit between the two countries. Kabul's close relations with

India and the Taliban sanctuary in Pakistan's border region remained a major cause of tension. Besides, both Karzai and Zardari stood on very weak political ground.

Zardari also got a separate 30-minute meeting with President Obama. It was the first direct meeting between them. The talks largely revolved around Pakistan's worsening internal security situation. Zardari also met with other senior US officials, including Hillary Clinton and General James L. Jones, the national security adviser.

Zardari assured US officials that a large number of Pakistani troops were being deployed to fight the insurgents in northern Pakistan. But the US wanted the Pakistan Army to move troops, including country's 11 Infantry Division, from Lahore and the eastern borders with India towards the western border. There was a lot of doubt about the Pakistan Army's capability to carry out the kind of counterinsurgency operation needed to end the Taliban insurgents' control of Swat, and to keep them from infiltrating again or shifting to another region.[18]

Before Zardari departed for Washington in the last week of April, the militants kidnapped four officers of the Pakistan Army special forces from a market in Mingora, the main town of Swat, and paraded them before the media. Days later, their decapitated bodies were found; it was to be the last straw.

Confronting the harrowing prospect of the Taliban moving on Islamabad, the Pakistani military finally took a decision in May 2009, to strike back. As the military prepared to launch a new offensive, there was increasing political support for the move. While the mainstream political parties had earlier favoured soft-pedalling with the Taliban, they had now revised their opinion. Obama administration also played an important role in getting the political parties on board.

The support of Nawaz Sharif, the main opposition leader, was deemed especially important, given his long ties to Islamist political parties; if he spoke out in favour of strong action against them, that, it was felt, would resonate well with the Pakistani public. Richard Holbrooke was in constant contact with him. Holbrooke's intensity had sometimes annoyed Pakistanis, but he had developed excellent relations with Zardari as well as with Nawaz Sharif. 'I very much like him. He constantly keeps in touch with me,' Nawaz Sharif once told me.[19] As expected, Sharif's decision to support a new military offensive in the Swat Valley helped sway the rest of the key parties, as well as the public.

In the first week of May 2009, the army launched a three-pronged offensive involving approximately 30,000 troops, backed by air force jets and helicopter gunships, turning a large area of the Swat Valley into a battle zone. Most of these troops were moved from the eastern border after the US assured Pakistan that India would not make a move after the troops left.[20] Thousands of counterinsurgency commandos were dropped by helicopter into a mountainous Taliban stronghold in the Piochar region.

The commandos had been trained under a new programme for fighting in the region's tough mountainous terrain funded by the US and had proven highly effective in recent assaults in the Bajaur tribal region. It was the bloodiest battle yet in what has been called a 'war for the survival of Pakistan.'[21] There were an estimated 5000 Taliban militants in the mountainous terrain, 10,000 feet (3050 meters) above sea level, which was regarded as the main militant command and control centre. Some top insurgent leaders, including Mullah Fazlullah, were believed to have been hiding there.

A fierce battle ensued, in which Pakistani forces used heavy artillery and helicopter gunships, forcing the residents to flee their homes. Almost one million people from Swat, Buner, and Dir took refuge in neighbouring districts. But hundreds of thousands of others were trapped, and the militants, who had taken positions in some residential areas, used them as human shields. The insurgents had also mined the main roads, making it extremely difficult for the people to flee. The exodus was an unprecedented humanitarian crisis that threatened to undermine public support for the military campaign. The government struggled to cope with the worst catastrophe in Pakistan's 62 years. International humanitarian aid was slow to come. Finally, in July 2009 the government declared the Swat Valley secured and cleared of militants. Although the military may have succeeded in seizing control of the Valley, the region still continued to bleed.[22]

In the midst of fighting in Swat, the TTP received a serious setback when a CIA drone strike killed Baitullah Mehsud and his wife on 5 August 2009. The TTP chief was being treated that night for a kidney ailment at his home in the Makin district of South Waziristan. Baitullah was one of the most powerful of the radical Islamic militant commanders operating out of the remote tribal regions of Pakistan.[23]

They had been launching a steady stream of attacks on the US forces fighting in Afghanistan and had unleashed a wave of terror within Pakistan as well. Baitullah was blamed for the assassination of Benazir Bhutto in December 2007 and had claimed responsibility for a series of suicide attacks in Pakistan. His death, however, brought little relief. His successor, Hakimullah Mehsud, a much younger commander, retaliated by escalating attacks on Pakistani security forces.[24]

Pakistan military's success in Swat dealt a serious blow to the TTP, and it won the praise of the US and other Western allies, but it also prompted the militant group to expand the guerrilla war into the country's heartland. There was a marked increase in suicide attacks on the security forces and installations around the country in the months that followed.

On 10 October 2009, militants launched the most audacious attack on the GHQ. More than one dozen gunmen stormed the large compound in the heart of a bustling commercial district of Rawalpindi, adjacent to Islamabad. Several security checkpoints had been strengthened in and around the GHQ after the surge in attacks targeting military personnel and installations and the access roads were closed to civilian traffic. Despite this, the militants, disguised in army uniform, managed to break through the extensive security cordon and take dozens of army officers and soldiers hostage.[25] They accused the Pakistani military of fighting America's war and killing its own people.

General Kayani was in his office at the time of the attack, less than a hundred meters from the building under siege. The assailants were just a gunshot away from him. That morning the COAS was scheduled for a meeting with the president and the prime minister in Islamabad. When the assault occurred, he was driven out of the GHQ complex by a back gate, returning a few hours later to monitor the situation.[26]

The assailants presented a list of demands, including a demand that nearly 100 Pakistani and Afghan Taliban commanders being held by the security forces be freed. Among the names on the list was that of a woman named Aafia Siddiqui, who was facing trial in a New York court on a charge of assault with a deadly weapon and attempting to kill US soldiers in Afghanistan. An MIT trained Pakistani neuro-scientist, Aafia was named as one of the seven Most Wanted al-Qaeda figures by the FBI.

Aafia had married a nephew of KSM, who was later arrested and sent to the Guantánamo Bay detention camp. She was arrested outside the compound of the governor of Ghazni (province in Afghanistan) on 17 July 2008 and was badly wounded in a shooting incident at a US military detention centre following her arrest. Afifa was flown to the US, where she was charged with two counts of attempted murder and armed assault on US officers and employees, and her arrest and trial had become a rallying point for Islamists in Pakistan.[27]

Pakistani special forces finally ended the 19-hour standoff with the gunmen that left several people dead, including some senior army personnel. The Army's prestige was badly tarnished by the assault on the GHQ. This was neither the first attack on an army installation in the country nor the most deadly, but it was undoubtedly the most serious. The attackers had breached the security at one of the most sensitive national defense establishments in the country and had threatened the safety of the army chief and his top commanders.

It was apparent that despite the setback in the Swat Valley, the militants still had the capacity to hit even the most secure government installations. The raid came only weeks after the killing of Baitullah Mehsud. 'This was our first small effort and a present to the Pakistani and American governments,' said a TTP spokesman.

The GHQ attack indicated the evolution of an ever more intertwined and sinister nexus between former Pakistani military personnel, and the Taliban and the al-Qaeda operating in the tribal regions. They were involved in many terrorist attacks, particularly on sensitive security installations and public places.

One of the most shocking attacks was the bombing of the Marriott Hotel in Islamabad, carried out a year earlier, on the night of 20 September 2008. The incident occurred when a dump truck filled with explosives was detonated in front of the Marriott, located in Islamabad's high security zone. The massive suicide truck bombing killed at least 54 people, including several foreign nationals, injuring at least 266 and leaving a 60 ft (20 m) wide, 20 ft (6 m) deep crater outside. It was one of the worst terrorist attacks in Pakistan's history. The apparent targets were US military personnel who were reportedly staying there.

The storming of the GHQ a year later added to the urgency to carry out the long-delayed military operation in South Waziristan that had become the main headquarters of the TTP. The gains achieved in the Swat Valley were vital, but not sufficient to rein in the insurgency. If South Waziristan remained under the control of the Taliban and al-Qaeda, it was feared that the fighting would continue to escalate. Many leaders of the Swat insurgency, including Mullah Fazlullah, were believed to have taken refuge in the area.

For the US, military action in South Waziristan was crucial in the effort to gain control over the larger Afghanistan–Pakistan border region and turn the tide in the war in Afghanistan. There had been a very close relationship between the Afghan and Pakistani Taliban. The Afghan Taliban did not engage in attacks in Pakistan and focused its efforts entirely on fighting the Afghan and foreign forces in Afghanistan. Although the two differed on the objectives and tactics to be used, Pakistani Taliban and Afghan Taliban were bound by the same ideology.

Pakistani Taliban leaders, including the TTP chief, Baitullah Mehsud, had pledged their allegiance to Mullah Omar. Although in 2008 Afghan Taliban distanced itself from Baitullah Mehsud's activities, it never publicly condemned the TTP attacks on Pakistani forces.

One of the reasons for this was that both Taliban groups had their support base among the Pashtun tribesmen. The Afghan Taliban were also dependent on Pakistani militants to maintain their safe havens and sanctuaries, as well as to recruit Pashtun tribesmen to fight in Afghanistan.

A closer alliance between the TTP and al-Qaeda had reportedly followed a meeting between Baitullah and Ayman al-Zawahiri in South Waziristan in 2008. The TTP had begun to embrace al-Qaeda's message of an expanded, global jihad. The first evidence that the TTP was committed to operations outside of Pakistan and Afghanistan had emerged in January 2008, when Spanish authorities arrested 12 Pakistanis in connection with a terrorist plot in Barcelona. The plotters were discovered to have been in contact with Baitullah, and a spokesman for the TTP claimed the group's responsibility for the plot, saying that it was in response to Spain's military presence in Afghanistan.

With the increase in US financial aid, also came increased pressure on Pakistan to take action against the Afghan insurgents and the Taliban leadership operating from Pakistan's long and porous border region with Afghanistan. Despite the surge in US troop numbers, the fighting in Afghanistan had escalated. For the US, Britain, and their allies, the looming spectre was not one failed state, but two.

Since 2003, the Pakistan military had carried out two operations in South Waziristan, but both ended in peace deals with the militants. It was a flawed strategy that allowed the insurgents to operate across the border with impunity. Peace deals did not stop the militants from continuing to attack Pakistani troops. A UN report released in September 2007 blamed the militants based in Pakistan for almost 80 per cent of the suicide bombings carried out in Afghanistan at that time.

This time the military could not afford to walk away from the job halfway through. Dithering would only allow the Taliban to further expand their operations, and General Kayani had publicly vowed that he would not stop until the region was secured. The long-awaited offensive began on 17 October 2009, with the deployment of more than 45,000 troops, backed by air force jets and helicopter gunships.

The massive use of force was considered critical for winding up the operation before the arrival of the harsh winter, and with these troops added to those still deployed in the Swat Valley, the size of the total force engaged in the fight reached 100,000, almost the same as the total number of NATO forces deployed across the border in Afghanistan.

South Waziristan was a much tougher challenge than Swat in terms of terrain. Its remote mountains and treacherous ravines were perfect guerrilla territory. And unlike Swat, where the Taliban had alienated the local population, the soldiers sent to South Waziristan had to contend with a hostile population that had resisted outside rule for centuries.

As the confidence level between the US and Pakistani militaries grew, General Kayani allowed small teams of US Special Forces soldiers to be secretly embedded with Pakistani forces in tribal areas. US officials had long been pushing Pakistan to allow such deployment, but to no avail. US military personnel had been deployed in Pakistan since 2008, but they were limited to a training role.[28]

The embedding development thus appeared to represent a sea change in the thinking of the Pakistani military leadership. For the US, it was a sign of growing trust in a troubled relationship. Permission for active combat deployment that came with the personal consent of General Kayani marked a departure from Pakistan's earlier policy of limiting US forces to a training role. The embedded US Special Forces personnel helped hunt down Pakistani Taliban and al-Qaeda fighters and coordinate drone strikes. The numbers involved were small—just 16 soldiers in October 2009—but the covert US military operations in some of the most violent Pakistani territories were politically highly sensitive.[29]

The first Special Forces team of four soldiers was deployed to an old British colonial fort in the northern half of the tribal belt in

September 2009, helping the Frontier Corps paramilitaries to carry out artillery strikes on a militant base. A month later, two more teams of six soldiers each were deployed to Pakistani army bases in North and South Waziristan, a lawless warren of mountains considered the centre of gravity of the al-Qaeda-backed insurgency on both sides of the Durand Line.

Their job was to provide 'intelligence, surveillance, and reconnaissance' support, 'general operational advice,' and to help set up a live satellite feed from US drones flying overhead, presumably CIA-operated Predator and Reaper aircraft. The deployment of US Special Forces soldiers to the tribal belt in 2009 coincided with a dramatic surge in drone strikes in the same areas.[30]

A US embassy cable from Islamabad noted: 'Patient relationship-building with the military is the key factor that has brought us to this point. The Pakistanis are increasingly confident that we do not have ulterior motives in assisting their operations.' The participation of US soldiers in combat operations in the tribal campaign has never been publicly acknowledged due to its extreme political sensitivity in a country seething with anti-US sentiment.[31]

Increased cooperation between the US and Pakistani forces helped in the operation achieving its objective, with drones providing high quality intelligence about the locations and movements of the militant forces. The sharing of real-time video feeds, communication intercepts, and other information greatly facilitated the campaign and marked a substantial improvement in relations between the Pakistani and US military.[32]

Video feeds from drones were relayed to a joint coordination centre at a border crossing at the Khyber Pass, where a Pakistani military team monitored the videos and sent them to command centres in Pakistan.[33] The operation was also facilitated by the fact that South Waziristan has a much smaller population than Swat, about 500,000 compared to two million, which allowed the army much more freedom to attack in force.

The military had succeeded in clearing most of South Waziristan within eight weeks of the operation. 'The myth has been broken that this was a graveyard for empires and that it would be a graveyard for the army,' boasted one senior Pakistani military official.[34] President Zardari described the success of the military operation in South Waziristan as proof of his government's resolve to fight militancy, and public support for the offensive swelled.

There was, however, a great deal of doubt about whether militancy could be defeated by military means alone. The toughened resolve of the Pakistani military had certainly resulted in huge gains, but the war was not over yet. Thousands of militants, including top leaders like Fazlullah, Hakimullah, and Waliur Rehman, had escaped the offensive, fleeing to neighbouring North Waziristan and the Orakzai tribal region, where they immediately began regrouping with the help of their allies among Pakistani militant groups there.

Militant forces would regroup and return to once-cleared territory repeatedly and the Pakistani military would not be able to maintain a deployment of 100,000 troops in the regions indefinitely. There were still ongoing attacks on urban centres. In bold defiance of any claim to victory by the Pakistan Army, the TTP immediately unleashed a new string of bombings.

On 13 November, a devastating suicide car bomb attack was perpetrated on the regional office of the ISI, in Lahore, leaving dozens of operatives dead and wounded. Peshawar, a gateway to the tribal region, was hit particularly hard, with bombings on an almost daily basis. Schools were closed many days because of the fear of suicide bombings, and hundreds of civilians were killed in these attacks.

On 4 December 2009, four gunmen stormed a packed mosque on Parade Lane, a five-minute drive from the GHQ in Rawalpindi, spraying gunfire and throwing hand grenades. Most of the 200 worshippers gathered for Friday prayers were serving or retired army officers and their children. As the worshippers ran for cover, the gunmen singled out some for execution;[35] 36 people, including 17 children, an army major general, and a brigadier general, were killed. The strain showed among the Pakistan Army personnel as they buried their fellow officers and their children. The attack was a devastating blow.

Even as the military cleared a large part of the militant-controlled territories, there were still questions about Pakistan's failure to formulate a comprehensive counterterrorism strategy and develop a strong intelligence network. The military's success in Swat and South Waziristan did not allay mounting pressure from the Obama administration to step up operations against the Afghan Taliban and their allies fighting coalition forces across the border. Pakistan was required to 'do more!'

7 | Democracy versus National Security

General Parvez Kayani was visibly irritated when the US Ambassador, Anne Patterson, told him that rejection of the Kerry–Lugar Bill (tabled by Senators John Kerry and Richard Lugar) would be taken as an insult and smack of arrogance. 'Some clauses of the bill could also be termed as an insult to the entire Pakistani nation,' the General retorted.

Patterson was meeting Kayani at the GHQ in Rawalpindi on 6 October 2009, hours after General Kayani had met General McChrystal, Commander of the International Security Assistance Force (ISAF) in Afghanistan.[1] The Kerry–Lugar Bill, aka the aid package, would provide $7.5 billion in civilian aid to Pakistan, spread over five years. It was signed into law by President Barack Obama on 15 October.

General Kayani was offended by some of the conditionalities attached to the Kerry–Lugar Bill, particularly the one that sought to strengthen civilian oversight and control over the military. Kayani told the US officials, in no uncertain terms, that conditionalities like this would not only affect the US–Pakistan bilateral relationship but would also create a division between the military and civilian authorities. He also asserted strongly that the military had absolutely no intention of taking over and pointed out that 'Had I wanted to do this, I would have done it during the long march [of March 2009].'[2]

The Long March of 2009, from Karachi to Islamabad, was a protest march started on a call given by the Lawyers Movement, backed by the major opposition political parties. It was undertaken to force the democratic government, headed by the PPP, to reinstate the Supreme Court Chief Justice Iftikhar Chaudhry and other judges ousted from office by Musharraf. The new President Asif Ali Zardari had been reluctant to do so, fearing that the Supreme Court would take up the issue of the legality of the National Reconciliation

Ordinance (NRO) passed by Musharraf in October 2007 that granted amnesty to politicians, bureaucrats, and others accused of corruption, embezzlement etc. The protest escalated and there was a political crisis, threatening the newly elected government. Kayani's intervention forced Zardari to accede to their demands and Chaudhry was reinstated as the Chief Justice.[3]

Ms Patterson had developed a good rapport with both the civilian and military leadership, but the controversy over the strings attached to the $7.5 billion aid package made things extremely difficult for her. She had struggled very hard to try and make things work between Washington and Islamabad, despite all kinds of complications.

The political storm generated by some additional clauses being inserted in the Kerry–Lugar Bill introduced in Congress on 24 September 2009, and which was unanimously passed by the Senate the same day and by the House of Representatives on 30 September, had reinforced the suspicion that the US was trying to undermine the Pakistani military and the ISI. The critical provisions were almost entirely directed against the Army or at least that was the perception.

It was not that the previous US aid packages to Pakistan had been free of conditionalities, yet the provision in the Kerry–Lugar Bill manifested a clear departure in US approach. It marked a shift from being a solely military-based cooperation, that had historically marked Pakistan–US relations. The Obama administration, in a departure from tradition, sought to build a different relationship with Pakistan's civilian government. The Enhanced Partnership with Pakistan Act of 2009, otherwise known as the Kerry–Lugar Bill, was a major shift in focus.

A day after the meeting with the US officials at the GHQ, the military commanders sent an unambiguous message that the terms set in the Kerry–Lugar Bill were insulting and unacceptable. In an unprecedented statement, the corps commanders expressed 'serious concern' over, what it said, were the 'national security' implications of the aid package. The military contended that the draft of the bill they had received on 15 September did not contain the additional

12 clauses, which had been added subsequently in the final version. They said these clauses were highly objectionable and derogatory. The corps commanders urged the government to build a national response to it in parliament. The military's statement was also a rebuff to the civilian government.[4] The military was particularly furious over the bill's provision that the US secretary of state certify, at six-month intervals, that the military remained under civilian oversight, even specifying such details as the need for the government to control senior command promotions. There was no way the Generals would allow civilian governments to intervene in the matter of the promotion of its officers.[5] It was like waving a red rag in front of a bull!

Another clause required the Pakistani security forces to act against militant networks on its soil, specifying the Afghan Taliban leadership and Lashkar-e-Taiba (LeT), the militant group held responsible for the 2008 Mumbai terror attacks that killed more than 150 people. Although outlawed, the group continued to operate under different banners. The US had long suspected that Pakistani intelligence agencies had never severed their ties with the group that they once patronised. This cynical view of Pakistan's security establishment not acting against militant organisations involved in cross-border terrorist activities angered the generals.[6]

Even more upsetting for the security establishment was the clause that Pakistan grant US investigators 'direct access to Pakistani nationals' associated with nuclear-proliferation networks. That was a reference to Dr Abdul Qadeer Khan, the Pakistani nuclear scientist who had confessed to selling nuclear technology to several countries, including Iran. Although Khan, revered as the father of Pakistan's nuclear bomb, had been removed from his position and placed under house detention, Pakistani authorities had resisted Washington's demand to allow him to be questioned by its investigators.

A haunting US worry was that Pakistan's nuclear arsenal could be taken over by the militants who, by then, had established control in the Pakistani tribal region. To keep military aid flowing, Pakistan was required to cooperate to dismantle nuclear supplier networks by offering relevant information from, or direct access to, Pakistani nationals associated with such networks. But direct access to the scientist remained a thorny issue between Washington and Islamabad.[7]

The Kerry–Lugar Bill had the completely opposite effect to the one that the aid package was supposed to produce for the US. The humiliating conditions were deemed to be a blatant interference in Pakistan's internal affairs. It further fuelled anti-American sentiments and generated a political maelstrom in the country, uniting the opposition parties against the Zardari government.

The controversy over the Bill further widened the civil and military divide. It deepened the suspicion of Washington trying to undermine the military. The confrontation had shaken the Zardari government; it wanted the aid package to go through. For a civilian government in the midst of a serious financial crunch, the US aid came as a boon. It conveniently ignored the conditionalities that came with it.

Zardari thought this was a good opportunity to deal directly with the Obama administration, bypassing the military. An accidental leader who was catapulted to the country's top position, maintaining good relations with the US was critical for his survival. He feared for his life when the tension with the Generals intensified.

Zardari told US Vice President, Joe Biden, in March 2009 that Kayani and the ISI wanted to 'take him out'.[8] In mortal fear for his life, he had extensive security preparations carried out; he even blocked the windows of his bedroom at the President's House in Islamabad with concrete. He informed some US officials that his sister would take over the party leadership if anything happened to him.[9]

His fear was not without reason. Just a few months into the office of president, Asif Ali Zardari found himself in conflict with the COAS who had never trusted him. The military establishment had grudgingly accepted him as president but never totally accepted his authority. It was a rocky relationship from the outset. The first clash came when Zardari's PPP government, only months in power, tried to wrest control of the ISI from the Army and transfer it to the Interior Ministry. General Kayani was at a wedding reception in Rawalpindi's Intercontinental Hotel when he heard the news.

He left the party and rushed to the Army House. He called Prime Minister Yousaf Raza Gillani and warned him of dire consequences if the notification was not withdrawn. Within hours the government made a hasty retreat.[10]

The military had demonstrated who was in charge. The military suspected that Washington was behind the move to undermine the country's premier spy agency.

The suspicion was reinforced as the US officials had accused the ISI of being riddled with Islamist sympathisers who supported terrorists in Pakistan's tribal regions.[11] Washington had alleged that the ISI was involved in the fatal bombing of the Indian embassy in Kabul on 7 July 2008.[12] The ISI was also accused of having warned the militants who carried out the blast to move their headquarters from Miranshah in the North Waziristan tribal region to avoid detection by the US.[13]

Fed up with working with the ISI, the Americans may have planned to circumvent the spy agency and reach out to the Interior Ministry directly. Although Zardari was not yet elected as president, the military was convinced that the notification was his decision as he was virtually running the show and that it was taken with the blessing of Washington.

Zardari's statement on no-first-use of nuclear weapons was deemed an attempt to change the country's nuclear doctrine and his decision to dispatch the ISI chief to India soon after the Mumbai terrorist attack carried out by LeT brought him into direct conflict with the security establishment. Although he was compelled to backtrack on both issues, the tension never dissipated. There was a huge trust gap that could never be bridged.[14]

The army had prepared a contingency plan for his removal. General Kayani told the US ambassador that he might reluctantly persuade Zardari to 'resign'. He even named his choice for the new leader— Asfandyar Wali Khan, leader of the Awami National Party (ANP), a regional party that ruled the country's troubled northwestern province.[15]

Interestingly, both the civil and the military leadership would confide highly sensitive information to Anne Patterson and use her to carry messages to the other side, underlining the growing civil-military divide. The dispatches, released by the WikiLeaks website, showed military and civilian leaders agreeing to policies in private meetings with US diplomats that they would passionately disavow in public. Although the Obama administration did not have a high opinion of Zardari, it was deeply concerned by the situation in Pakistan. 'Pakistan's civilian government remains weak, ineffectual, and corrupt,' Patterson wrote on 22 February 2010: 'Domestic politics is dominated by uncertainty about the fate of President Zardari.'

Even though Washington had serious doubts about Zardari's ability to govern, he was still considered a reliable ally. 'While far from perfect, you will find Zardari is pro-American and anti-extremist,' a February 2009 US embassy cable read. 'We believe he is our best ally in the government.' Zardari was beholden to Ambassador Anne Patterson for her help in getting to power.[16] She addressed President Zardari by his first name.

However, it was the Pakistani military that still mattered when it came to battling militancy and settling the fate of Afghanistan. As one February 2009 cable read: '[We] need to lay down a clear marker that Pakistan's Army/ISI must stop overt or tacit support for militant proxies (Haqqani network, Commander Nazir, Lashkar-e-Taiba).'

The Obama administration thought that by including the conditionalities in the aid package, it could strengthen the civilian government. The resolution of the crisis over the Kerry–Lugar Bill gave the embattled president a critical lease of life. He was grateful and willing to pay back Washington for its support.

On the face of it, the bill in the shape of an aid package should have been welcomed in Pakistan. It promised to provide $7.5 billion in economic aid over the next five years, in order to assist with the development of the country's schools, hospitals, roads, and other infrastructure. The substantial assistance offered was intended to help Islamabad meet its long-term development needs as well as its counterinsurgency requirements and recognised the crucial importance of a stable Pakistan in such a geopolitically sensitive region of the world. But highly intrusive conditions made it impossible for the Pakistanis to accept it.

The backlash to the Kerry–Lugar Bill was fuelled by a widely held perception that Zardari had bowed too easily to US demands. His very strong public support for the bill had reinforced the perception among Pakistanis that their president simply did what the Americans told him to do, and that he was willing to concede part of Pakistan's sovereignty in exchange for the badly needed funds.

The military blamed Pakistan's ambassador to the US, Hussain Haqqani, for getting those tough conditionalities included in the bill with the knowledge of the president. The intelligence agencies claimed to have gathered information, supported by telephone intercepts and other secret recordings showing 'the holder of an important office' insisting that the Pakistan military-related clauses should remain an integral part of the bill. Some top officers in a corps commanders meeting demanded the ambassador's removal.[17] In a country where anti-Americanism was rampant and at an all-time high, the controversy over the stringent US conditions further weakened a president who was already running very low on credibility and public support.

Zardari's tacit approval for the Kerry–Lugar Bill with the conditionalities not only brought confrontation with the military to a head but also left him isolated in Pakistani politics. It also gave an ideal opportunity to the opposition parties to put the government on the mat. Even his coalition partners, including some cabinet ministers, refused to stand by the government on the issue. The government received a major shock when its closest ally and a staunch pro-American ANP came out with a scathing attack on the conditionalities attached to the bill, slamming it as 'tantamount to interference' in the country's internal affairs.

Active lobbying by the military also contributed to whipping up public sentiments against the elected government. The growing public resentment to what was perceived as a move to destabilise the Pakistani state was reflected in an opinion poll: nearly 80 per cent of Pakistanis disapproved of the government's relationship with the US. While the military leadership discussed the serious implications of the Kerry–Lugar Bill on national security, military strategists and commanders also discussed the options, alternatives, and opportunities that needed to be addressed, should the parliament decide not to accept the bill.

It was an extreme miscalculation by the Obama administration to think that by including stringent conditionalities in the bill, it could change the power dynamic in Pakistan and strengthen civilian control over the all-powerful military that wielded greater authority than the elected government. Democracy had just returned to the country after almost a decade of military rule and a confrontation with the security establishment could derail the system. The standoff over the issue further weakened Zardari's political position and widened the distrust between the civilian and military leadership, that threatened to derail the fledgling democratic process in the country.

The growing political pressure put the government in a defensive position. Farhatullah Babar, a presidential spokesman, took pains to explain that most of the criticism of the government was unfounded as it was a piece of US legislation, and not something signed by the Pakistani president or prime minister. 'There is no commitment by the Pakistan government,' he said.

It was apparent that the Zardari government, which had earlier described the passage of the bill as a major foreign policy success, succumbed to pressure. Conceding to the military's demand, the government agreed to have a debate on the Kerry–Lugar Bill in parliament. Zardari, however, insisted that the bill was a 'pro-democracy aid package,' which needed to be defended in parliament and at other public forums.

But the resistance was already waning. Zardari finally agreed to send his foreign minister, Shah Mahmood Qureshi, to Washington to get clarification on the conditions. 'We must address the concerns and fears expressed in Pakistan; we will not allow Pakistan's sovereignty to be compromised and will not allow anybody to micro-manage our affairs,' Qureshi told US officials. It was evident that Zardari's foreign minister was more inclined towards the military's position. And it was just a matter of time before he would jump ship on some other issue a few months later. On 12 October, the Congress agreed to issue a statement addressing all the contentious issues linked to the Kerry–Lugar Bill. Although the conditionalities were not removed, the Congress statement provided some face-saving for the military establishment. Though very angry, the military too were reluctant to block the aid package so critical for salvaging the dwindling economy. Assurances from Senator Kerry, one of the movers of the bill, also helped resolve the crisis. But the whole episode left a bitter aftertaste.

Yet, despite this hiccup, close cooperation between the US and Pakistan Army continued uninterrupted. It did not affect more than one dozen US Special Forces troops deployed in the tribal areas since 2009 to help hunt down militants and coordinate drone strikes. The intensified drone programme killed half of al-Qaeda's top leadership. Ambassador Patterson however admitted in a September 2009 cable to the State Department that the airstrike campaign was risky, with the potential of 'destabilising the Pakistani state, alienating both the civilian government and military leadership, and provoking a broader governance crisis without finally achieving the goal.'[18]

At the heart of Pakistan's military relationship with Washington was the US financial military aid. Yet Kayani did not want his troops to be seen as a 'force for hire,' though the foreign funds were crucial to Pakistan's military operations against militant insurgents in the tribal areas. In a cable in February 2009, the US ambassador noted that the Pakistani economy 'remains too weak to support the Pakistani military's appetite for expensive weapons systems.'[19]

Pakistan, by then, had received $7.5 billion in Coalition Support Funds, a large part of which had gone to the security forces. But hundreds of millions of dollars earmarked for battling militancy had been diverted into the government's accounts. Often Pakistani military claims that it regularly submitted were alleged to have been inflated.

According to a US embassy cable, one such claim was $70 million for radar maintenance, despite the militants having no air attack capability, and another $26 million claim for barbed wire. Still, the

US financial support was never disrupted. 'The relationship is one of co-dependency we grudgingly admit,' a February 2009 US embassy cable said. 'Pakistan knows the US cannot afford to walk away; the US knows Pakistan cannot survive without our support.'[20]

After the Kerry–Lugar Bill controversy, the Obama administration seemed to accept that the balance of power in the country had shifted considerably to the military, which had not only been effectively running national security and foreign policy, but had also cast its shadow over other areas of the government. President Obama, in a tacit acceptance of this reality, dispatched Secretary of State, Hillary Clinton, to Islamabad end-October 2009 to smooth over relations with Pakistan.[21]

In a meeting with her that lasted more than three hours, General Kayani left no doubt that the army was calling the shots. Clinton tried to convince him that the US was not seeking to undermine the army's authority. For the American officials visiting, the meeting with the serving army chief had always been more important, and Clinton maintained that tradition. Meetings with civilian leaders were just a formality; the power laid somewhere else.[22]

Notwithstanding its scepticism of the Generals' stranglehold, the Obama administration understood that it was only the military that could safeguard Pakistan's nuclear arsenal, deal with the problem of militancy, and help the West against the jihadi threat. 'The Pakistani military created (the) problem and seemed to be the only solution to them at the same time,' declared Vali Nasr, an advisor to the State Department, who worked with Richard Holbrooke.

Zardari desperately needed a deal with the US to strengthen his political position in order to show the people of Pakistan that he had something to offer them. He told Senator John Kerry in February 2010 that he was facing casualty at the behest of the world recession and needed something to give his people, as all they had since he came to power were increase in prices! Pakistan had already gone to the IMF for a bailout. But the stringent conditions attached to the loan had fuelled political discontent.[23]

Zardari sought US support to get a reprieve from some of the harsh IMF conditions placed on the Pakistani economy. He wanted the Obama administration to persuade the IMF against further electricity tariff increases. Another increase, he warned, would result in riots in the streets. He said he needed 'a deal' with the US to strengthen his political position. Kerry promised to help build consensus in Washington for liberalising US trade with Pakistan.[24]

The tension over the controversial bill was further diffused when the Obama administration offered hope of a more robust and nuanced approach to strengthening the bilateral relationship. In March 2010, high-level Pakistani officials from both the military and civilian government flew to Washington for the second round of a strategic dialogue.[25]

What set it apart from previous such gatherings was that it was the first which had been raised to the ministerial level, and also included the Pakistan Army Chief, and the head of the ISI? Clinton said the presence of the military leadership 'reflects the importance that we place on this relationship.' The delegation was led by Foreign Minister Shah Mahmood Qureshi, but was dominated by COAS Kayani. The Americans were represented by Secretary of State Hillary Clinton, and National Security Advisor James Jones, as well as additional senior military leaders.[26]

Security, economy, energy, communications, and what was referred to as 'kitchen table issues' by Hillary Clinton, were all up for discussion in the first-ever ministerial level strategic dialogue between the US and Pakistan, which generated important momentum in efforts to create a result-oriented partnership for the future. It was a historic two-day meeting that began on 24 March.

The Obama administration had scheduled the talks as part of a strategy to more vigorously support development initiatives in Pakistan, such as improvements in education, power generation, and trade, and to enhance the country's defence capabilities. 'It's not the kind of commitment that you easily produce overnight or even within a year,' Clinton declared. 'But it is important to get started, to sort it out, and to develop the trust and the confidence between us.'[27]

In a hearing before the Senate Appropriations Subcommittee on 25 March 2010, the secretary of state was emphatic that the US had made it a 'strategic priority' to strengthen its partnership with Pakistan, and that US efforts in Pakistan were vital for America's success in Afghanistan.[28] The hearing set the stage for the debate in the US Congress over the White House requests for $33 billion in new war funding, coupled with $4.5 billion in foreign assistance, chiefly for the Afghanistan–Pakistan (AfPak) policy.

But while the contents of General Kayani's meetings with the US military command remain secret, the dialogue process led by Hillary Clinton and Shah Mahmood Qureshi, resulted in a 56-page comprehensive document that set up the 'architecture' of future cooperation, while outlining Pakistan's interests. This document was made available to the Americans before the dialogue process. Going by the 'architecture' analogy, the two countries had put in place a plan for the future structure of their relationship that would be raised on a more solid foundation.[29]

Pakistani officials touted the meeting as a great success in increasing cooperation. Both countries pledged to reset relations on a more solid footing, moving beyond the Bush administration's almost exclusive focus on military aid to a new emphasis on economic and social sector development in Pakistan.[30] Since 2001, the US had given Pakistan more than $11 billion in aid, which had helped prop up the country's faltering economy. But a large part of that money had gone to financing Pakistan's military campaign against the militants, which hadn't even begun to cover the total cost of those operations. Pakistani and international aid agencies believed that, in total, the war on terror had cost Pakistan's economy more than $35 billion.

In a change of course, the Obama administration agreed to provide help in building power generation capacity, such as dams, as well as other infrastructure.[31] Additional military assistance was pledged as well, including the delivery of the much-delayed F-16 fighter planes. That pledge went a long way to mollify the anger in the military caused by the stringent conditions attached to the Kerry–Lugar Bill. It was evident that despite the pledge for more aid for social sectors, the US approach to relations with Pakistan remained very much embedded in the larger context of its security and military priorities.

Anne Patterson, who left Islamabad in October 2010 after a three-year stint as ambassador, noted that simply giving more money and military assistance would not be persuasion enough. 'There is no chance that Pakistan will view enhanced assistance levels in any field as sufficient compensation for abandoning support for groups which it sees as an important part of its national security apparatus against India.'

8 | What's Your Plan for Afghanistan?

'What's your plan for Afghanistan?' General Parvez Kayani bluntly asked General David Petraeus. 'Integration,' responded the General who had taken command of the CENTCOM after returning from Iraq in 2008. 'We will weave out Taliban foot soldiers from the leadership and integrate them,' General Petraeus tried to explain, at their meeting in Oman.[1]

It was part of the Obama administration's new counterinsurgency strategy that sought to offer some form of amnesty to Afghan and other fighters. 'This bottom-up approach will not work,' General Kayani argued. 'You must go for reconciliation. The top-down approach will work better.' What he meant was that the US should talk directly to Taliban leaders. To him the policy of trying to persuade less committed or less influential insurgents to change sides would not help improve the situation in Afghanistan.[2] Unfortunately, from the outset, even the idea of reconciliation was anathema for the US administration. For the Pentagon, the idea of talking to the Taliban was a form of capitulation.

President Barack Obama later appointed General Petraeus to the new position as commander of the International Security Assistance Force (ISAF) and Commander, US Forces Afghanistan, after General Stanley McChrystal's forced exit following unflattering remarks about Vice President Joe Biden and other administration officials attributed to McChrystal and his aides in a *Rolling Stone* article. McChrystal was recalled to Washington where President Obama accepted his resignation as commander in Afghanistan.[3]

Technically, the new position was a demotion for General Petraeus who had served as CENTCOM chief. It, however, presented a new challenge to the General who was hailed for the success of the counterinsurgency strategy in Iraq. Though there was a huge difference in the situation between these countries, Obama and his military commanders believed that the Iraq experience could be successfully replicated in Afghanistan. General Kayani disagreed.

That meeting in Oman in mid-2010 was the latest in a series of meetings between the two commanders since 2008. Kayani found Petraeus arrogant. There were rumours about General Petraeus being a potential presidential candidate in 2012. General Kayani had observed that the senior US military leadership seemed to be in awe of him; even Admiral Mike Mullen, who was then Chairman Joint Chiefs of Staff Committee, would not speak in his presence. When General Petraeus spoke, others quietly listened. Perhaps that's why he didn't seem very comfortable with General Kayani differing with him during the meeting in Oman that day.[4]

The two had substantial differences of opinion about the appropriate strategy in Afghanistan and how to deal with the wider insurgency. Kayani felt that the US had no effective strategy for winning the war in Afghanistan and that their current strategy posed both significant military and civilian risks. General Kayani had been utterly frank about Pakistan's position on this.

At a NATO conference in Brussels some months earlier, General Kayani asked the top European military officials whether the coalition forces were winning over public opinion in Afghanistan. Describing his notion of success he said the surge in troops alone would not win the war. 'You need to look at the fundamental issues,' he urged the NATO commanders. He was sceptical about the US plan to build and develop the Afghan National Army (ANA) into an effective fighting force in a limited period of time. 'What if the assumption that the ANA could be built rapidly into an effective fighting force turned out to be wrong?' he asked the participants that also included General Petraeus, who was then heading CENTCOM.[5]

General Kayani was certainly not convinced that the new US Afghan war strategy could work. He was not wrong. He would have preferred that the Americans negotiate an exit plan with the Taliban. Kayani expressed the same doubts in almost all his meetings with the US leadership, both military and civil. But there were few in Washington who were interested in his viewpoint or paid attention.[6]

As the initial surge in US troops in March 2009 had failed to contain the Taliban advance in Afghanistan, Obama, after months of deliberations, made a second review of his Afghan policy in November 2009. Under pressure from his military commanders he agreed to send 30,000 additional troops to Afghanistan, though less than what Petraeus and McChrystal had demanded. They wanted 40,000 additional troops for the counterinsurgency strategy to work. The Obama administration was clearly divided over the war in Afghanistan.[7]

Obama was not in favour of sending more troops to Afghanistan. He, however, agreed to the surge after Defence Secretary Robert Gates assured him that it would take 18 months for the US forces to clear the Taliban strongholds and transfer security responsibility to Afghan security forces. With this further increase in the number of troops, Obama also placed a strict timetable on the mission, saying they would have to be withdrawn again, starting July 2011. Obama's tight deadline for pulling out US forces, set at Gates' urging, left very little time for the US commanders in Afghanistan to achieve their objectives and was inexplicable.[8]

The new counterinsurgency strategy known by its acronym, COIN, was aimed at wresting control of the areas under Taliban influence and installing effective administration in those areas. Other objectives included winning over the hearts and minds of the locals by building roads, bridges, schools, and putting in place a well-functioning government. Under the plan, Afghan administration was to be established in 70 districts. The strategy was based on McChrystal's famous theory of delivering 'administration out of the box.'

The US commanders had argued that the strategy (outlined above) had helped turn around the war in Iraq and could be successfully applied in Afghanistan too. The claim of success in Iraq, tipped COIN as the US military's policy of choice. There was a lot of concern, however, about how the massive target set in the new Afghan COIN strategy could be achieved in just 18 months. It was obvious that Obama himself was not convinced that deployment of additional troops alone could win the war. 'There was still the afterglow of the surge in Iraq, and the counterinsurgency narrative that had made the military the saviour of the Iraq war,' said Vali Nasr, a former State Department advisor on Afghanistan and Pakistan. 'I don't believe Obama was in a position to pick a debate with the military on Afghanistan, and to assert what would be his worldview.'[9]

The central premise of the surge was to seize the initiative from the Taliban, particularly in its stronghold in southern Afghanistan, to turn over security responsibilities to the Afghan government, and to begin the withdrawal of US forces by the summer of 2011. But many Pakistani and US counterterrorism experts doubted that the military escalation could be a game changer by that time, or ever.

General Kayani had strong reservations about COIN working in Afghanistan. He was also acutely concerned about the fallout from the proposed 30,000 US troops surge and the resulting intensification of war on the border region in Pakistan, that was already fighting its own war against militancy. The fear was that the surge would inevitably push many Taliban fighters across the border into Pakistan, which would threaten the gains that had been made in the Swat and South Waziristan offensives.[10]

There was also a belief in Pakistan's military and intelligence establishment that America's commitment to the region was waning and that the new US policy failed to offer a viable long-term political solution to the Afghan crisis. Without a stable government in place in Afghanistan before the US troops withdrawal, they feared there would be disastrous consequence.

Under the new strategy the US planned to build up the Afghan army and the police force, doubling their strength, with an aim to gradually transfer power to Afghanistan. It was deemed as a relatively cheap option for the US as the pay of each Afghan soldier was quite small. In a marked departure from previous policy, Obama announced a plan to help rebuild the country's infrastructure.[11]

However, the Pakistani military leadership had a problem with the US plan to expand the strength of the ANA that was supposed to take over the security responsibility, following a drawdown of the US forces from Afghanistan. General Kayani thought the idea of a larger Afghan military was 'foolish. You will fail,' he bluntly told US officials in one of his meetings in Washington. 'Then you will leave and that half-trained army will break into militias that will be a problem for Pakistan.'[12]

'The perception is not correct that we are opposed to the ANA,' stated Kayani when Admiral Mike Mullen asked his opinion about the US plan. But he did express doubts that the US could, and would, continue to pay billions of dollars a year to maintain a 40,000 strong-army. Later, that same question was raised by US Vice President Joe Biden. 'The main issue is the financing [for the ANA] that will cost over six billion dollars annually to maintain it,' said Kayani. 'No, it will cost nine billion dollars per annum,' interrupted a US official. 'How long can the coalition pay that bill?' asked Kayani.[13]

His greatest fear was that, without funding, the ANA would eventually collapse and fragments of the broken army would resort to crime and terrorism to earn their keep. He would give examples of what happened to the Afghan army after the Soviet Union stopped funding the army it had helped build; it melted away within months after the Mujahideen took over Kabul in 1992.[14] General Kayani's concerns may have been exaggerated, but they were definitely not baseless. India's role in training the Afghan forces was also a strong factor in Pakistan's reservation.

The most important plank of COIN was to ultimately transfer all authority to the Afghan government. The assumption behind the July 2011 deadline was that, by then, the Karzai government and Afghan security forces and military would be prepared to take over the primary responsibilities for security. But President Karzai's government, tainted by charges of corruption and ineptitude, had proved too weak to be able to provide effective governance. Karzai himself was accused of protecting his family members and others allegedly involved in drug trafficking and corruption.[15]

President Obama had appointed retired Lt. Gen. Karl Eikenberry, who had earlier served as commander of US forces in Afghanistan, as US ambassador to Afghanistan in April 2009, the post in which he remained till July 2011. His appointment was significant as he too was dubious that the surge of troops could deliver any change in the situation on the ground. His relations with Karzai were extremely tense. Eikenberry, in a classified message to the State Department in November 2009, warned that Karzai was not an adequate strategic partner. 'He continues to shun responsibility for any sovereign burden,' he wrote. His message portrayed a much bleaker accounting of the risks of sending additional US troops to Afghanistan.[16]

The Obama administration had argued that the 18-month deadline was necessary to force President Karzai to improve governance of his country, but that thinking ignored the reality of the political situation in Afghanistan. Karzai's political standing was seriously eroded following the October 2009 elections. Although Karzai emerged victorious in the controversial election, but his legitimacy remained questionable with widespread allegations of poll rigging, involving his close family members. Karzai's relations with the Obama administration had also become severely strained.[17] So bad had the situation become that Holbrooke and Karzai had stopped talking to one another. Karzai's relations with his other Western allies, particularly Britain, had also become quite frosty.

Many, if not most, in the Obama administration already had grave doubts about Karzai's ability to carry through on promises to crack down on corruption or the drug trade or that his government was capable of training enough reliable Afghan troops and police officers for Obama to start planning a credible exit strategy.

In laying out his new strategy on 30 November at West Point, President Obama addressed those concerns. 'In the past, we too often defined our relationship with Pakistan narrowly. Those days are over,' he declared, directly addressing Pakistan. But his words did little to reassure Pakistani officials that the US had a reliable plan for stabilising the hold on power of a legitimate government in Afghanistan.

Disagreements between the US and Pakistan about the situation in Afghanistan and the likely outcome of the US military operations there had become the central point of contention in their complex and tense relationship. Amid concerns about what would follow the proposed US pullout in July 2016, General Kayani warned that Pakistan's strategic interests must be served in any future political arrangement in Afghanistan.[18] 'A friendly Afghanistan can provide Pakistan strategic depth,' he declared.[19]

A looming fear of the establishment of a non-friendly government in Kabul after the US pullout had reinforced the Pakistani establishment's determination not to cut its ties irrevocably with the Afghan Taliban. The deadlines, the drawdown of the US military presence, or even a denial of the additional troops requested by General McChrystal added to Pakistan's concerns. General Kayani had been candidly voicing his reservations on the consequences of the new US–Afghan war strategy for Pakistan.

Even as the US pushed ahead with the surge strategy in Afghanistan, the view became more widespread that the war was unwinnable. The resilience of the insurgency had become crystal clear. Marjah, a farming district in Helmand province, was supposed to be a showpiece of the counterinsurgency plan to clear areas of the Taliban and hand over control to the local government. But many months after the February launch of the operation, involving nearly 15,000 NATO and Afghan national forces, the hold on the area still remained tentative.

The Taliban melted back into the population and assassinated tribal leaders who had collaborated with the coalition forces. In May 2010, General McChrystal called Marjah a 'bleeding ulcer.' The remark was a pointed update of Soviet president Mikhail Gorbachev's characterisation of the Soviet war in Afghanistan as a 'bleeding wound.'[20] A report by the *Afghanistan Rights Monitor* noted that, 'Contrary to President Obama's promise that the deployment would disrupt, dismantle and defeat the Taliban insurgents and their al-Qaeda allies, the insurgency became more resilient, multi-structured and deadly.'

Despite deployment of more than 170,000 US and NATO forces, the Taliban had re-established a strong presence in 75 per cent of the country's districts. The insurgency also continued to spread, expanding even to non-Pashtun areas. In the meantime, US casualties kept rising. The expectation that the Afghan military and police would be able to take over primary control within the given timeframe was highly unlikely.

The difficulties in Marjah were indicative of the enormous challenges of eliminating a deeply rooted insurgency. General McChrystal had predicted that once security was established in Marjah, a 'government in a box' could be swiftly installed. But there was hardly any government in place even months after the operation was declared concluded. A US Senate hearing in May 2010 offered a grim assessment of the state of Marjah, almost three months after the operation was declared over. Senator John Kerry, Chairman Senate Foreign Relations Committee, said that Marjah did not appear to be the turning point it was meant to be in the overall mission in Afghanistan.[21]

Many senior officials in the Obama administration too had serious doubts about the effectiveness of COIN in Afghanistan. The most forceful opposition to the new Afghan war strategy came from Eikenberry, the US ambassador in Kabul. In a cable to Washington, the former military commander-turned-diplomat cautioned that deployment of such a large number of troops would result in 'astronomical costs'—tens of billions of dollars—and would only deepen the dependence of the Afghan government on the US. 'Sending additional forces will delay the day when Afghans will take over, and make it difficult, if not impossible, to bring our people home on a reasonable timetable,' he wrote on 6 November 2009. 'An increased US and foreign role in security and governance will increase Afghan dependence, at least in the short-term.'[22]

A key part of COIN was the training of Afghani military and police forces. But building a professional and competent army and police force had proved to be much harder than US officials had anticipated. The Afghan National Police (ANP) was riddled with corruption. Many officers were implicated in drug trafficking. The public's distrust of the police was evident during the Marjah operation, when the village elders told the Americans that they did not want the ANP to return.[23]

Morale in the ANA too remained low. The rate of defections continued to increase. A report on the ANA by the International Crisis Group, a Brussels-based think tank, described it as a force riven by ethnic and political divisions and plagued by corruption. A major concern among the Pakistani security establishment was that the worsening situation in Afghanistan would have a destabilising effect on Pakistan as well.

With the surge in troops in Afghanistan, the US wanted the Pakistani military to extend its offensive into North Waziristan, the base of the powerful Haqqani network, blamed for carrying out the most lethal attacks against the coalition forces. For the US, breaking the back of the network's operations was vital to achieving success in the Afghan war. A major US worry was that the success of Obama's Afghanistan policy hinged, in turn, on the Pakistani forces eliminating militant havens in the mountainous region near the Afghan border.[24]

The military's success in Swat and South Waziristan also did not allay mounting pressure on Pakistan from the Obama administration to step up operations against the Afghan Taliban and their allies fighting the coalition forces across the border. The launch of operations by Pakistani forces in North Waziristan became central to the new US war strategy and also a major point of contention between the US and Pakistan.

General Kayani was not convinced about the US strategy to concentrate troops in southwest Afghanistan. He would often get into an argument with Petraeus and McChrystal over their plan to focus on Kandahar and Helmand in the southwest which, according to the US commanders, were 'the centre of gravity' of the Taliban insurgency. 'You don't start from the centre of gravity. The reaction of going to Kandahar could be strong,' warned Kayani.[25]

Instead, Kayani wanted Petraeus to send troops to eastern Afghanistan along the border with Pakistan where Pakistani forces were fighting the al-Qaeda-backed insurgency in the lawless tribal region known as FATA (a semi-autonomous tribal region in northwestern Pakistan, which till May 2018, was directly governed by Pakistan's federal government). 'Make it hammer and anvil.'[26]

'Otherwise it will become a revolving door for the militants,' cautioned Kayani, quoting his pet line. Petraeus disagreed, but promised to divert troops to the east once the south was cleared of Taliban control. It would never happen. Petraeus was replaced by General John Allen in 2010 who said it was not possible to divert troops to the east because the deadline for the drawdown was fast approaching. But General Allen said that he was planning to deploy an Afghan brigade which was in the process of formation. It was too late for the operation.[27]

The US decision to pull out troops from Kunar and Nuristan provinces, along the border with Pakistan, added to Pakistan's problems as Kayani had to send additional troops to the border. Military operations in North Waziristan figured constantly in the discussions between US officials and General Kayani. 'I want only (one) condition, that the coalition forces seal the border,' said Kayani. To which the response was silence.[28]

'I had wanted a joint operation. We decided to start from North Waziristan, then Swat happened and we had to divert attention there,' General Kayani told me. 'It was a very difficult operation employing much (resources) and bigger than the entire FATA in (terms of) area.' Apart from other factors, General Kayani argued that it would have been disastrous to open another front without first consolidating the military's hold in the Swat Valley and in South Waziristan. 'It is not the US, but the Pakistani military who should decide when to start a North Waziristan operation,' he stated categorically.[29]

However, the Pakistani military already had a strong presence in North Waziristan. One division was there mainly on the border with Afghanistan, which left Mir Ali and Miranshah unprotected and they became the centre of militant activities. 'We told the Americans that if they deployed troops, sealing their side of the border, we could move against the militants in Miranshah and Mir Ali,' explained Kayani.[30]

President Obama sent his National Security Advisor, General James Jones, to Islamabad for deliberations with the Pakistani leadership as the insurgency in Afghanistan intensified despite the surge in the US troops. The former supreme commander of NATO arrived on 13 November 2009. He had brought a note of warning from President Obama that the US would not view the border dividing Pakistan and Afghanistan as a barrier as this was responding to strikes emanating from Pakistan, which occurred almost daily. The message was clear: US expected the Pakistani military to expand and reorient its fight against the insurgency and target the Afghan Taliban and al-Qaeda more vigorously.

Jones demanded that Pakistan should immediately move against the Haqqani network. It was not the first time that a senior US official stressed the issue, but the message delivered by General Jones was more of a threat. He was not known for his diplomatic skills, and his curt style annoyed the military leadership. The meeting between Jones and Kayani was extremely testy. Jones delivered another tough message to Zardari, exhorting him to intensify action against militant groups and religious extremism. With the threat also came an offer of a range of new incentives, including enhanced intelligence sharing and military cooperation—the carrot and stick approach that had become a hallmark of the Obama administration's policy towards Pakistan.[31]

Two subsequent terrorist incidents—a suicide bombing inside a CIA outpost in Afghanistan on 30 December 2009, and an attempted bomb explosion at New York's Times Square on 1 May 2010—having their roots in North Waziristan, brought Pakistan under renewed pressure to act against the Haqqani network.

It was a huge setback to the US operations in Afghanistan when a suicide bomber blew himself up inside a remote CIA installation known as Forward Chapman Base in the eastern Afghan province of Khost, along the border with North Waziristan. Seven CIA officers were killed in the worst-ever attack against a US intelligence installation. The infiltration of such a high security facility was shocking. The bomber was a 36-year-old Jordanian doctor, Humam Khalil Abu-Mulal al-Balawi, who had apparently been working for

Jordanian intelligence and was assigned to collect information on al-Qaeda operations in Pakistan's tribal regions.[32]

A video later released by the TTP showed the bomber sitting with Hakimullah Mehsud and vowing to take revenge for Baitullah's killing. The bomber was, in fact, planted in the intelligence agency that worked closely with the CIA. The bombing was a joint operation by al-Qaeda, the Haqqani network, and the TTP operating from North Waziristan. The attack underscored that, as effective as the CIA's drone operation had been against the militants, the groups retained the ability to carry out highly sophisticated and ever more audacious attacks.

In the wake of Chapman Base bombing, the CIA intensified drone strikes against suspected al-Qaeda and TTP sanctuaries with Pakistan's support. The raids killed several al-Qaeda commanders, including the mastermind of the Chapman base bombing. CIA director, Leon Panetta, on 17 March 2010, announced that the drone strikes following the Chapman Base incident, had thrown the al-Qaeda into disarray. Pakistan's support with the drone strikes helped ease tension with Washington.

However, the tension between Washington and Islamabad flared up once again when Pakistani-born Faisal Shahzad attempted to detonate a car bomb in Times Square, in the heart of New York City. The son of a retired air vice-marshal in the Pakistan Air Force, he traced the origin of his plot to a 2009 trip he made to Pakistan, just three months after becoming a US citizen. Faisal Shahzad's path to his attempted bombing, was a chilling confirmation that extremists were planning attacks within the US. Shahzad reportedly travelled to North Waziristan where he met with the senior leadership of the TTP.[33] In July a videotape of Shahzad in tribal dress showed him embracing Hakimullah Mehsud. In his video message, recorded after his meeting, he vowed to avenge the death of Muslims in the US drone strikes.

The bombing attempt alarmed the Obama administration and significantly undermined the progress that had been made in the improvement of relations between Pakistan and the US in recent months. General James Jones and Leon Panetta travelled to Islamabad in the second week of May 2010 to (yet again) deliver a stern message to Pakistani leaders. They had brought a dossier with them containing details about Shahzad's contacts with Pakistani militants, and they warned that there would be serious consequences for Pakistan if there was another attack in the US traceable to their country.[34]

They warned that Pakistan had only weeks to show real progress in a crackdown on the group behind the attempt. 'It was almost like reading a riot act to Pakistani leaders,' said a Pakistani official familiar with the talks. General Kayani later wrote to Admiral Mullen complaining about the tenor of the US officials and warned of consequences in case of any US military action. The letter was meant to be delivered to President Obama.[35]

The meeting in May 2010 represented the Obama administration's toughest talk yet to the Pakistani leadership. It reinforced the widespread perception that America's Pakistan problem appeared to have gotten worse, not better, on President Obama's watch. Pakistani officials were also upset that General Jones and Leon Panetta came to Pakistan against the advice of Pakistan's foreign ministry. The military leadership, in particular, didn't want the CIA chief to be part of the US delegation because of the sensitivity of the situation. The ISI chief excused himself from the meeting on the pretext of illness. The military felt particularly uneasy with the aggressive tone of the message that Pakistan was not doing enough to fight militants.

The Obama administration intensified pressure on Pakistan to allow US forces to conduct operations within Pakistan. The Times Square bombing attempt had convinced the Americans that the targeted killing of militants by drone strikes alone was not enough to counter the insurgency and that US military boots on the ground in Pakistan was required. Washington had also demanded improvement in real-time intelligence sharing, including access to flight data for all passengers flying out of Pakistan, and asked to establish an intelligence outpost in Quetta, the alleged headquarters of the Afghan Taliban. The CIA had already been operating such an outpost on the outskirts of Peshawar in northwestern Pakistan. These measures were intended not only to prevent any possible terrorist attack in the US originating from Pakistan, but also to monitor Pakistan's campaign against the militants.

There was a growing concern among the Pakistani civil and military officials that the US might launch a unilateral ground strike on the tribal areas and extend their drone strikes west towards Quetta. That apprehension was fuelled by a television interview with Hillary Clinton after the Times Square bombing attempt in which she declared, 'If, heaven forbid, an attack like this that we can trace back to Pakistan were to have been successful, there would be very severe consequences.'[36] The Obama administration had not ruled out targeting any Taliban sanctuary along Pakistan's western borders. The US believed that most of the top Taliban leaders lived there.

It was extremely difficult for Pakistan to allow US forces to operate inside Pakistan. This could provoke public outrage. There were already dozens of US military personnel present in Pakistan who were involved in programmes to share intelligence with the Pakistan Army and paramilitary troops, and to train them to battle militants in the northwestern region.

Some US troops had also accompanied Pakistani paramilitary forces in the field as observers. But the government had never publicly acknowledged their presence. Additional US troops would create serious problems for the government. However, Islamabad agreed to increase intelligence cooperation. The trust deficit between the two allies had widened further with the Obama administration taking a more aggressive stance. The failure of the US forces in containing the insurgency in Afghanistan had also led to a hardening of Washington's policy towards Pakistan. US officials on several occasions had given a list of the militants that Washington wanted Pakistan to arrest.

In December 2009, the Obama administration authorised further expansion of the CIA's drone campaign with an option to extend the strikes to Pakistan's western province of Balochistan, that had apparently become the headquarters of the Afghan Taliban.[37] The announcement provoked intense anger in the Pakistani military leadership, which declared that it would not allow any such US incursion into the mainland. A major fear was that drone attacks on Quetta would destroy the fragile national consensus in Pakistan for the fight against the militants. The already strained relations between the two countries had reached a new level of tension.

Meanwhile, disgruntled with the Americans, Karzai started showing a degree of autonomy causing great concern in Washington. He sought to build bridges to the Taliban, pursuing his own policy of reconciliation. In early January 2010, the president's brother, Ahmed Wali Karzai, reportedly held two secret meetings with Mullah Abdul Ghani Baradar, a deputy to the Taliban's supreme leader, Mullah Omar in Spin Boldak, a town on the border with Pakistan. The meeting with Mullah Baradar was the first major contact of Karzai government with senior Taliban leadership.[38]

Known as a brilliant and charismatic military commander, Mullah Baradar was credited with rebuilding the Taliban into an effective fighting force and running the group's day-to-day affairs for many years, with Mullah Omar taking a backseat because of his failing health. Besides heading the Taliban's military operations, Baradar reportedly also ran the group's leadership council, known as the Quetta Shura. Karzai's reconciliation efforts had apparently been known to US officials, but did not have their stamp of approval.

Just weeks after the meeting with Karzai's brother, Mullah Baradar was arrested in Karachi, Pakistan, in a joint operation by US and Pakistani intelligence services. He was believed to have travelled often to Karachi, and up to that point he and other Afghan Taliban leaders had moved freely around the country for years. The Pakistani security forces could have arrested him at any time, and his arrest so soon after the meeting with Ahmed Wali Karzai was highly significant.

Mullah Baradar's reported links with Iran has also been a factor for his arrest. A senior Pakistani intelligence officer involved in the operation indicated that Baradar had received funding and weapons from Iran. The Iranian link was a serious cause for concern for the Pakistani security establishment as well, particularly since Tehran had traditionally supported the Afghan Northern Alliance. It also reinforced the suspicion that Iran was seeking to make some inroads into the insurgent movement to maintain its influence in Afghanistan.

Mullah Baradar had conducted the Taliban's financial operations, allocated Taliban funds, appointed military commanders, and designed military tactics. His arrest had dealt a serious blow to the Taliban insurgency. US officials had been quick to declare his arrest a 'significant win.' But his detention did not change the course of the war. He had set the groundwork.

While Washington hailed the capture of one the highest-ranking insurgent commanders, Karzai was furious. He believed the action was a deliberate move to undermine the negotiations he had started with the Taliban leader. He demanded that the Afghan Taliban leader be handed over to the Kabul government. But US officials advised Pakistan otherwise. The gap between the Karzai government and the Obama administration had widened further.

The Obama administration was not yet ready to talk to the Taliban as its entire focus was on a military solution. 'It's our view that until the Taliban leadership sees a change in the momentum and begins to see that they are not going to win, the likelihood of significant reconciliation at senior levels is not terribly great,' Defense Secretary Robert Gates said in January 2010. While ruling out talks with top Taliban leaders, US officials were open to the idea of negotiating with the lower level commanders.[39]

In another dramatic move in June, Karzai fired his interior minister, Hanif Atmar, and the powerful intelligence chief, Amrullah Saleh. Both had worked closely with the US forces since the invasion of Afghanistan in October 2001 and were opposed to any reconciliation with the Taliban. They were also known for their strong anti-Pakistan views. It was primarily for this reason that Pakistan had pressed for their removal in order to facilitate better relations between Kabul and Islamabad. Unsurprisingly, the Obama administration strongly objected to their unceremonious firing. A Pentagon spokesman said both officials were 'people we admire and whose service we appreciate.'[40]

As Karzai became more critical of the US, General Kayani and ISI chief General Shuja Pasha made a number of trips to Kabul in mid-2010, offering to mediate between Kabul and Sirajuddin Haqqani. No direct meeting between Sirajuddin and Afghan officials followed, however, the talks were conducted through emissaries and there was no major breakthrough. The US was well-aware of what was going on. General McChrystal was present at every meeting between General Kayani and President Karzai.

Washington watched this evolving partnership with serious concern and distrust. Despite increasing pressure from the US, Pakistan had refused to take action against the Haqqani network—the most lethal of the Taliban factions. General McChrystal in his assessment on the Afghan war to Washington, reported that there was strong evidence of the network being 'clearly supported from Pakistan,' with aid from some elements of the ISI.

Despite the unceasing pressure from the US, both the Pakistan government and the military had resisted all urging to launch operations against the network, further fuelling US speculation that the ISI had maintained its association with the Haqqanis from the time of the Afghan civil war for the purpose of exerting continued influence in Afghanistan.

Kayani's offer to deliver the Haqqanis in a power-sharing arrangement was, therefore, viewed with suspicion in Washington. Reacting to Pakistan's efforts to broker the talks, Obama said, 'I think we have to view these efforts with scepticism, but also with openness.' But CIA chief, Leon Panetta, was more forceful in expressing doubts about the Haqqani network's intent, 'We have seen no evidence that they are truly interested in reconciliation, where they would surrender their arms, where they would denounce al-Qaeda, where they would really try to become part of society.'

A central issue regarding any brokering of a power-sharing agreement by the Haqqanis was whether they could be reliably separated from al-Qaeda, to which they were closely linked. Some Pakistani intelligence officials believed that the Haqqanis could be persuaded to cut their ties with al-Qaeda if there was a clear indication of a peace deal that would pave the way for the coalition forces to leave Afghanistan. But there were also serious doubts that the Haqqanis could really make a deal with Karzai, given their close ties to the Taliban, and with the Karzai government so heavily reliant on US support.

Pakistan's move to broker a deal with the Haqqani network reinforced tensions with the US over allegations of Pakistan being in bed with some Afghan insurgent factions. Secretary of State Hillary Clinton, during her visit to Islamabad in July 2010, alleged that elements in Pakistan's security agencies knew of the whereabouts of Osama bin Laden, and she again warned of serious consequences if any attack on the US was traced back to Pakistan.

Despite the strains in US–Pakistan relations, General Kayani was still the best bet for the Obama administration looking for an exit from Afghanistan. Therefore, it was not just a coincidence that within 72 hours of Clinton's departure, Prime Minister Yousaf Raza Gillani announced on television his decision to give General Kayani a three-year extension in his term as COAS in view of security challenges faced by the country. It was an unprecedented decision by a civilian government. There were still four months left in his tenure. The US role in his service extension was obvious. Opposition leader Nawaz Sharif, who was publicly critical of the US, thanked Ambassador Patterson for the appointment of Kayani as COAS for a second term.[41]

President Obama was curious to meet Kayani and he had mentioned that to the officials who were engaged with Pakistan. An opportunity emerged when General Kayani arrived in Washington with the Pakistan delegation headed by Foreign Minister Shah Mahmood Qureshi in the third week of October 2010, for the next round of strategic dialogue with the Obama administration.

But there was an issue of protocol. So, it was decided that President Obama would drop by at the office of Vice President Joe Biden at the White House where the Pakistan delegation was due to meet with him. Obama arrived within a few minutes of the start of the meeting. Qureshi spoke for five minutes explaining Pakistan's position and extended an invitation to the president to visit Pakistan.

Obama then turned to Kayani. The discussion mainly revolved around Afghanistan and the role Pakistan could play in ending the war. The President listened to the General attentively. Halfway through the discussion, Kayani gave President Obama a 13-page white paper he had written to explain his views on the outstanding strategic issues between Pakistan and the US. It contained four parts: Afghanistan, Pak–Afghan relations, Pak–US relations, and India. It was the third paper the Pakistanis had given to the White House on the subject in the past.[42]

The summation was this: you are not going to win the war, and you are not going to transform Afghanistan. This place has devoured empires before you; it will defy you as well. Stop your grandiose plans, and let's get practical, sit down, and discuss how you will leave and what end-state we can both live with? It concluded with the sentence: 'Pakistan would not like to find itself standing in a corner in the Afghan endgame.' The message was clear: Pakistan could not be excluded from any negotiations on the future of Afghanistan.[43] Months later, in February 2011, at the Munich Security Conference, Hillary Clinton delivered a comprehensive, point by point, written reply to Kayani. It ended by asserting that both America and Pakistan would stand side by side.

There were already some signs of the White House revising its Afghanistan strategy to embrace the idea of negotiating with senior members of the Taliban through third parties—a policy, which it had previously scorned. Negotiating with the Taliban had long been advocated, not only by Pakistan, but also by President Hamid Karzai and the British government.

There was a slow change of mindset in Washington as it became evident that there was no military solution to the Afghan conflict. While the Obama administration was still officially resistant to the idea of talks with Taliban leaders, behind the scenes a shift was underway despite strong resistance from the US military establishment.

9 | Enemies Now

It seemed like a scene out of a Hollywood thriller: two young men on motorbikes chase a white Honda car in a crowded marketplace in Lahore. From inside the car, a burly foreigner takes out his semi-automatic Glock pistol and shoots through the windshield, shattering the glass and hitting one of the men numerous times. It doesn't end there. Instead of speeding away, the foreigner then gets out of the car and continues to shoot several rounds into the back of the other man trying to flee.[1]

As a crowd starts gathering, the shooter gets back into his car and speeds away from the scene, taking refuge in a nearby police station. Minutes later, a black station wagon appears on the scene, speeding from the opposite direction, breaking the one-way restriction and crushing to death an unfortunate pedestrian, Ibad ur Rahman. It later transpired that apparently these were US consulate officials who rushed to the spot after receiving a call from the shooter. However, after the accident, they managed to escape from the scene and were not heard of again.[2]

The shooting on the cold 27 January 2011 morning in Lahore, brought into the open the cloak and dagger game between the CIA and ISI. It was an incident waiting to happen, with the CIA clandestinely expanding its network in the country. The shooter was Raymond Allen Davis, who had apparently been pursuing Islamic militant groups operating in Pakistan.

It was later revealed he was attached to the CIA's Global Response staff. One of Davis's official responsibilities was to provide security for senior CIA officials tracking militants.[3] But the burly 36-year-old agent seemed to be on a lone mission that fateful day. Among other things, some pictures of sensitive installations in Lahore that he had visited earlier in the day were recovered from him. Raymond Davis had arrived in Islamabad a few months back and had travelled to Peshawar before landing in Lahore. He somehow managed to dodge the ISI.

Davis seemed to know the two men who were following him, but got suspicious when they allegedly pointed a pistol at him. Faizan Haider, 22, and Faheem Shamshad, 26, were not burglars. Nor was there any evidence of either of them being ISI agents, though the American was under surveillance. Davis told the police that he worked for American consulate. Curiously enough, he left his phone switched on during the police questioning, thus recording the conversation.

It was an interesting scene inside the police station where the police officials were not sure how to deal with an American who claimed to be a diplomat but had just killed two men. Davis desperately wanted to contact the US consulate in Lahore. A crowd had started gathering outside the police station. The news of an American having shot dead two men had spread like wildfire.

The incident provided an opportunity to the rightwing Islamic parties to whip up anti-US sentiments. Pakistani intelligence agencies too seemed keen to use the incident to put pressure on the US. The Davis incident exposed CIA's plan of sending a large number of secret agents to Pakistan, as part of the covert US war in the country, thus giving an even more toxic twist to an odd relationship. The uncovering of Davis's role with the CIA brought into sharp focus how the CIA had outsourced its sensitive jobs to contractors.[4]

Of the 274 passengers, who boarded Pakistan's national flag carrier—PIA, flight PK 786—from Heathrow airport on November 2009, 202 passengers were foreigners. They were whisked away from the tarmac at Islamabad through a separate gate, without going through the regular immigration procedures and customs checking.[5]

Some were believed to be diplomats but the identity of others was ambiguous—they were either categorised as 'defence contractors' or shown as associated with the USAID. There had been a marked rise in the influx of US officials into Pakistan.

The prime minister had given Hussain Haqqani, the Pakistani ambassador in Washington, the authority to issue visas at his own discretion without referring each case to Islamabad and thus ignoring any objections from the ISI. It was apparent that the military too had its vested interests for not taking up the issue more strongly; it was not in their interest either to cause a rupture in relations with Washington.

Hussain Haqqani had started out as a journalist and then went on to work for various Pakistani governments—Nawaz Sharif, Benazir Bhutto, and then General Pervez Musharraf's military regime, before leaving for the US in 2004. Once in the US, Haqqani endeared himself to Washington's think tanks by his scathing criticism of Pakistan's military.

His book *Mullah Military Alliance* is considered to be a critical analysis of the unholy alliance of the military and Islamists. Ambassador Haqqani argues that the Pakistan military never severed its ties with the Islamic militant groups, despite the country's alliance with the US after the 9/11 terrorist attacks. He was teaching at Boston University when the February 2008 elections in Pakistan propelled the Pakistan Peoples Party (PPP) into power and ended General Musharraf's nine-year rule.

Hussain Haqqani had served as press secretary to Benazir Bhutto in her second stint in government as prime minister and had remained associated with her and her husband, Asif Ali Zardari, during their self-exile. He had also developed good relations with the US establishment in the interim and organised Bhutto's meeting with US officials whenever she visited Washington.

Zardari thought Hussain Haqqani, with his connections in Washington, could best serve his interests, as he wanted to have his trusted man in Washington to undercut the military that had, historically, been the main determinant of policy with the US. Haqqani replaced General Mahmud Durrani as Pakistan's ambassador to the US. After his return from Washington, Durrani was appointed the national security advisor. But, predictably, he did not last long in the post.

General Kayani and his ISI chief, Lt. Gen. Shuja Pasha, were not happy with Haqqani's nomination as ambassador to the US, but could not prevent the appointment. Ironically, it was General Musharraf—president till August 2008—who gave the approval. The military leadership had never trusted Zardari and the appointment of Haqqani as US ambassador further widened the gap. Haqqani's activities were closely monitored by the ISI and military attaché posted in Washington. There were almost two parallel Pakistani diplomatic channels at work in Washington. The military had established its separate channel of contacts with senior US officials.

The visa liberalisation policy by the new government was hugely resented by the ISI and the issue further aggravated tension between the civilian government and military leadership. The ISI expressed its concern over the large-scale issuance of visas without scrutiny. But President Zardari dismissed their objections.

To get more of its spies into Pakistan, the CIA, while applying for visas for its operators, used the cover of the State Department and Pentagon. They all had separate channels to request visas for their personnel, and all of them led to Haqqani's desk. The ambassador used his discretion liberally. Ostensibly, many of the US citizens coming to Pakistan were—at least officially[6]—going to be administering millions of dollars in foreign-aid money and were shown as working for USAID or for one of the myriad international NGOs based in and around Islamabad.[7]

As far as Zardari and Haqqani were concerned, there was no question of rejecting visa applications, even though ISI officials were convinced that the CIA took advantage of the relaxation in visa rules to insert scores of intelligence 'contractors'. Haqqani was accused of processing more than 400 visa applications on one weekend alone. Nearly 1800 visas were issued to US officials under the new rules.[8] The agency was not wrong: by early 2011, hundreds of US agents were operating inside Pakistan, under both legitimate and false identities.

They rented more than 300 houses in Islamabad alone, many of them suspected of being used as 'safe houses' or what is described in intelligence parlance as 'Omegas.' It was hard even for the ISI to keep a tab on the activities of such a large number of 'operatives.' As one senior ISI official pointed out, 'they' were everywhere. One of the objectives of these 'operatives' was to develop a network among the locals, particularly infiltrating civil society and the military. In this they were successful, recruiting even senior army officers and Pakistani intelligence personnel.[9]

The expansion of the CIA operation in Pakistan was not only linked to the hunt for Osama bin Laden but also to the surge of US troops in Afghanistan by the Obama administration. With a widening trust gap with the ISI, the CIA decided to build its own spy network in Pakistan. 'We knew of all of them but it was hard to keep surveillance on all their activities,' said General Pasha.[10] Since 2009, nearly half the US diplomatic mission personnel in Pakistan were involved in intelligence and counterterrorism activities rather than diplomacy and development. The US consulate in Peshawar, particularly, was almost entirely manned by intelligence personnel, collecting information on various militant groups and on al-Qaeda.[11]

In fact, the CIA agents had outnumbered the ISI. 'We were short of manpower with the ISI doing so many jobs, it was difficult to deal with the workload. We needed at least 3000 personnel to keep watch on all of them,' disclosed General Pasha.[12] Nevertheless, ISI agents would intercept the suspect personnel and stop their vehicles to send a clear message—'we know you.' Vehicles travelling to Peshawar or restricted areas, in particular, would be intercepted by the ISI and the situation would often get very ugly. But the detainees would be let go after a few hours on the orders of the government.

Any action against these suspect agents could jeopardise relations between Islamabad and Washington. The problem was that they were all there on valid visas issued by the Pakistan embassy in Washington. Many visas were also issued by the Pakistan embassy in the UAE. It was a clear violation of the Standard Operating Procedures for visa issuance. Unfortunately, this cloak and dagger game became a daily affair.

Many of the operatives in Pakistan belonged to Blackwater, later renamed as XE, a defence contractor firm often hired by the CIA. Blackwater had been operating in Pakistan for many years and often provoked intense controversy. They were even employed to assemble and load hellfire missiles and 500-pound laser-guided bombs on remotely piloted Predator aircraft—work previously performed only by CIA employees.[13]

The contractors also provided security at other covert bases. The increasing number of CIA drone attacks reinforced the suspicion about Blackwater activities in the country. The presence of thousands of US military and intelligence contractors in Afghanistan and Pakistan pointed to a new and far more dangerous trend: the hitherto unprecedented privatisation of war.

The number of CIA and Blackwater operatives had increased significantly with the surge in the US troops and intensification of the insurgency in Afghanistan. There were also some reports that Blackwater was working with the US Joint Special Operations Command on US forward operating bases in various parts of Pakistan, including Karachi, on 'snatch and grabs' of high-value targets and other sensitive actions inside and outside Pakistan.[14]

It was evident that the stakes for the US in Pakistan were as critical as in Afghanistan or in Iraq. There was strong apprehension in the Pakistani security establishment that the elite commandos of the US Navy SEALs were also part of a US team allegedly training to 'secure' Pakistani nukes. The fear made the ISI even more paranoid.

With the resources and backing of US government agencies, Blackwater had developed a lot of clout using a combination of large bribes and US government pressure. Given the widespread lack of transparency in Pakistan, many in the ISI suspected that Blackwater was using the same combination of money and power to persuade Pakistani politicians and officials to allow it to operate with impunity. But the ISI would not let them off easily. US officials complained about harassment by the security agencies; delayed visas, clogged customs clearance, and sabotaged security contracts as punishment for US support for Pakistan's civilian government and India's nuclear programme.

In a briefing to FBI director, Robert Mueller, ahead of a visit to Pakistan, US embassy officials in Pakistan described a difficult relationship. In a secret 22 February 2010 cable, US diplomats told Mueller 'while we have had major successes in our military and law enforcement cooperation with Pakistan, cooperation has frequently been hampered by suspicion in Pakistan's military and intelligence establishment about US intentions and objectives. Among other things, the Pakistanis believe that we have favoured India over Pakistan—most notably, by approving civil-nuclear cooperation with India—and that we aim to dismantle Pakistan's nuclear weapons programme, which, in light of their conventional military disadvantage vis-à-vis India, they consider critical to their national security,' noted the cable.[15]

Raymond Davis was also among the Americans who arrived in Pakistan in late 2010, benefitting from the liberal visa policy. A native of rural southwest Virginia, Davis enlisted in the military in 1993. He had served in the infantry in Europe—including a short tour as a peacekeeper in Macedonia—before joining the Third Special Forces Group in 1998, where he remained until he left the army in 2003. The army Special Forces—known as the Green Berets—are an elite group trained in weapons, foreign languages, and cultures.[16]

It is unclear when Davis begin working for the CIA, but US officials said that he worked for the spy agency as a Blackwater contractor and later founded his own small company, Hyperion Protective Services. Documents released by Pakistan's Foreign Office showed that Davis was paid $200,000 a year, including travel expenses and insurance. He was described by those who knew him as an unlikely figure to be at the centre of international intrigue.

In the meantime, the US embassy in Islamabad seemed clueless about Davis's status. Cameron Munter, who had taken over as US ambassador in October 2010, replacing Anne Patterson, had gone to Washington for consultation. The deputy chief of mission, an old Pakistan expert, frantically tried to contact the foreign ministry, demanding diplomatic immunity for the detained US citizen.

It was an inauspicious beginning for the new envoy. A career diplomat, with a PhD in history, Cameron Munter had served in Iraq before he was assigned to his new job in Islamabad, considered the most important and most difficult posting.[17] His predecessor had cultivated close ties with the Pakistani civil and military leadership and it was hard for Munter to fit in her big shoes. The communication gap between US diplomats and Pakistani officials made the Davis affair even more complicated. Zardari, who had gotten on well with Patterson, did not like her replacement, so Munter did not have the kind of access his predecessor had enjoyed.

The CIA activities in Pakistan had become more aggressive with the arrival of a new CIA station chief in Islamabad, whose name was later revealed as Mark Kelton. He had replaced Jonathan Banks who was evacuated on 16 December 2010, after his cover was blown in a legal action brought by relatives of a person killed in a drone attack, who accused the CIA station chief of authorising the attack.[18] Neither the CIA nor the US government officially recognise station chiefs, but they are acknowledged to exist by intelligence organisations.

It was apparent that John Bank's identity was deliberately exposed by the ISI in order to send a message to the CIA. It seemed to be in retaliation for a civil lawsuit filed in New York a month earlier accusing the ISI chief, General Shuja Pasha, of being involved in the November 2008 terrorist attacks in Mumbai.[19] The Pakistani military establishment felt that the spy chief of a friendly country should not have been treated like this.

Shortly after the issuance of the summons against the ISI chief, the Islamabad Police moved to register a murder case against Jonathan Banks who was supervising the deadly drone campaign in the tribal areas. It was the first time such a case had been filed against a CIA official in Pakistan. The CIA, in a rare move, recalled John Bank, citing concerns about his safety after his cover was blown.[20] The standoff had pushed the CIA and ISI into an eyeball-to-eyeball confrontation.

It was evident that the replacement CIA chief, Kelton, did not come to Pakistan to be friendly with the ISI. He began preaching 'Moscow Rules' upon arrival, meaning that the ISI should be treated as a foe rather than as a partner.[21] Kelton's main objective was to actively recruit more Pakistani agents to work for the CIA and help expand electronic surveillance of ISI offices. He refused to share any intelligence information with his ISI counterparts. The tension level between the agencies was very high. Despite this, the inevitable clash came sooner than either side expected. Less than 48 hours after Kelton's arrival in Islamabad, the Davis incident occurred.[22]

Davis may have got visa on a diplomatic passport as did many other US intelligence operatives, but he was not a designated diplomat. The embassies are supposed to send a 'note verbal' when a new diplomat arrives in Islamabad. But there was no such exchange of information on Davis. He neither had diplomatic status nor consular immunity.[23] US officials, however, insisted on his immunity.

Davis had landed in Islamabad, but moved around. He stayed in Peshawar for some time before coming to Lahore. The northwestern city, close to the Afghan border, was a hub of CIA activities as the hunt for Osama bin Laden was ramped up. The city was also home to many senior members of the Afghan Taliban. Frequent trips by undercover CIA officials to the city raised concerns in the Pakistani intelligence community. However, the ISI failed to detect Davis's movement and activities in Peshawar.

It was a different mission for Davis in Lahore. Punjab had been the main centre of some of the powerful Islamic militant groups mainly involved in fighting Indian forces in Kashmir. Patronised by the ISI, these groups once operated openly, recruiting holy warriors, before the Pakistani military regime outlawed them under pressure from the US in 2002.

But most of them continued to operate. Among them was Lashkar-e-Taiba (LeT), the most ferocious of the Pakistani militant groups. Davis was tasked with tracking the movements of various Pakistani militant groups, including the LeT.[24]

The broad daylight murders of three Pakistanis in a crowded marketplace heightened anti-US sentiments. Islamic parties came out on the streets calling for Davis's death. Some mainstream political parties too joined the protests, turning the incident into a political issue. The episode exposed Pakistan's predicament; it was not easy to put Davis on trial, nor to free him. It was an extremely tough choice that the civilian government did not want to deal with.

Zardari's government, heavily dependent on US aid, was keen to see Davis released. 'We need them more than they need us,' said a senior Pakistani official. But public sentiment made it hard for the government to be seen as bowing to US pressure. Adding to the government's dilemma was the fact that the foreign ministry would not confirm that Davis enjoyed diplomatic immunity. Foreign Minister Shah Mahmood Qureshi took a hardline position on the issue, against the wishes of President Zardari, which eventually cost him his job.

Frustrated and out of its depth, the civilian government conveniently threw the ball to the military to let them deal with this extremely sensitive matter. Zardari wanted the issue resolved quickly but did not want to take responsibility or ownership of any decision. While not wishing to antagonise his allies in Washington, it was hard for him to let Davis go after his cover was blown. The situation was not comfortable for either General Kayani or General Pasha.[25]

Intelligence chiefs of both countries (Leon Panetta and Shuja Pasha) had developed a good chemistry. Despite strained relations between the two allies on Afghanistan and disagreement over the Afghan Taliban operating from Pakistan that often led to altercation, they had a good working relationship, or at least so Pasha had thought. He, therefore, felt confident that the Davis issue could be sorted out amicably and said as much to the CIA chief in a one-on-one meeting. But Washington's stubbornness deepened the crisis. The situation turned extremely serious when the Pakistan government decided to put Davis on trial.

The US administration and the CIA were still not willing to admit his links with the agency. The US embassy in Islamabad insisted that since Davis entered Pakistan on a diplomatic passport, he must be given diplomatic immunity under the Vienna Convention on Diplomatic Relations. Calling Davis a 'diplomat' was, technically, accurate. But there was a dispute about whether his work in the US Lahore consulate, as opposed to the US embassy in Islamabad, gave him full diplomatic immunity under the Vienna Convention on Diplomatic Relations.[26]

And after shootings in Lahore, Pakistanis were not exactly receptive to debating the finer points of international law. As they saw it, Davis was a US spy who had not been declared to the ISI. General Pasha's telephone conversation with Panetta, and even a direct meeting, did not help resolve the issue.

Panetta and other US officials refused to admit that Davis was a spy and Panetta flatly rejected Pasha's offer to resolve the issue quietly through negotiation. Was Davis working for the CIA, asked Pasha? 'No, he's not one of ours,' Panetta replied. He then went on to say that the matter was out of his hands, and that the issue was being handled inside State Department channels. Pasha was furious, and could not believe that the CIA chief would lie to him. An opportunity to resolve the crisis quietly, was lost.

Panetta thought he could force Pasha to let Davis go, but there was no way that would happen. On the day of Davis's arrest, the new CIA station chief told Ambassador Munter that a decision had been taken to stonewall the Pakistanis. 'Don't cut a deal,' he warned, adding, 'Pakistan is the enemy'. It made the CIA strategy clear.[27]

The Davis episode not only uncovered the clandestine spy network that the CIA was running right under the nose of ISI, but also the extent of America's secret war in a country supposed to be a critical ally. It was an unravelling of the relationship between the two countries built after 9/11. The two agencies had worked closely against the al-Qaeda. But now they were acting as antagonists.

The Davis incident was seen by ISI officials as proof of their suspicions that the CIA operatives were sent to Pakistan as part of the covert US war in the country. The disclosure of Davis's role made it apparent that the CIA had distributed some of the most sensitive jobs to outside contractors. Davis was shifted to an isolation ward of Lahore's high security Kot Lakhpat prison as the row between Islamabad and Washington remained unresolved.

His safety was a major concern for Pakistani authorities. There was a fear of the spy being attacked by his own guards or by other jail inmates, many of them under-trial members of outlawed militant outfits. The concerns had increased after a spokesman of the Pakistan Taliban threatened to kill the American spy if he was released. When in ISI detention, Davis said he was willing to tell all but must not be tortured. He was interrogated for one hour and then it was stopped. Apparently, the ISI chief received a warning from Panetta that Davis must not be touched.

Tension heightened as the court in Lahore charged Davis with murder.[28] Panetta called General Pasha again to convey a message from President Obama that Davis 'must be freed,' Panetta shouted. 'I don't take orders from your president. I take orders from President Zardari,' Pasha retorted, adding, 'We know (the identity of) majority of your agents operating here.'[29] Panetta expressed his disappointment. He had not expected Pasha to take such a tough position. 'Now the matter will be decided by the court,' an infuriated Pasha told the CIA chief.[30]

By then the matter had gone beyond the question of whether Davis was covered by the Vienna Convention on Diplomatic Relations and therefore immune to prosecution by a Pakistani court. The issue got more complicated with the ongoing battle between the ISI and CIA. Partners in the war on militancy, the two spy agencies had never had an easy relationship, but it had recently hit a new low.

The crisis also exposed the divisions within the government and between the civil and military leadership. Zardari was under growing pressure from Washington. Messages were being conveyed directly and through Ambassador Haqqani. They were blunt and often threatening. The case was handed over to the ISI, but there was no clear thinking on how to ultimately resolve the crisis. The US attitude made things more difficult.

On 5 February 2011, US Secretary of State, Hillary Clinton, was due to meet Pakistan Foreign Minister, Shah Mahmood Qureshi, on the sidelines of the Munich Security Conference, to discuss Davis's release. But Qureshi cancelled the visit at the last moment.[31] Unlike President Zardari and Prime Minister Yousaf Raza Gillani, he had taken a much tougher stance on the Davis issue. A few weeks later, Qureshi was removed from the post in a cabinet reshuffle. In apparent retaliation for Davis not being released, Washington postponed trilateral US–Pakistan–Afghan talks, scheduled for 23–24 February, citing 'political changes in Pakistan'.[32]

What further complicated the issue was that the civil and military leadership were not on the same page on critical policy issues. In fact, the 27 January incident had further widened the division between them on issues of national security as well as on relations with the US. The military and ISI publicly blamed the government's decision to relax the visa policy, which according to them, allowed scores of undercover US intelligence officials to enter Pakistan.

Some senior government officials privately blamed the ISI for inciting public opinion on the Davis issue. Such a blame game was unprecedented, even though the friction between the civil and military was inherent in the political setup. The multiple power centres in the country had been a major reason for the Davis affair becoming a politically volatile issue, making it even more difficult to find a diplomatic solution to the problem.

Somewhat surprisingly, two weeks after the shooting, President Obama got directly involved in the fray. On 15 February he called on Pakistan to release Davis under the Vienna Convention on Diplomatic Immunity. It was rare that the US president would intervene in order to protect a spy involved in murder. The matter was simple, Obama said in a news conference: Davis, 'our diplomat in Pakistan,' should be immediately released under the 'very simple principle' of diplomatic immunity.[33] Surely Obama was aware of Davis's spy identity, but there was no mention of that in his message. That further narrowed Pakistan's options.

As threats failed to work, President Obama decided to send Senator John Kerry, an old hand on Pakistan, who enjoyed immense goodwill in Islamabad. But with no indication from Washington of admitting Davis's spy role, General Kayani requested the Senator to postpone the visit. 'We don't want to disappoint you. We cannot hand over Davis to you if you are expecting so,' Kayani told Kerry.[34]

Kerry insisted on coming anyway, saying his travel plans could not be changed. Curiously though, he landed in Lahore on 15 February, instead of Islamabad, as he thought the issue was with the Punjab government. One factor that made the resolution of the crisis more complex was that the PPP's rival, Pakistan Muslim League (N), headed by Nawaz Sharif, led the Punjab provincial government. Nawaz's younger brother, Shahbaz Sharif, headed the provincial government. Although the Sharifs wanted the Davis issue to be resolved, they were not willing to take any responsibility because of public sentiment.

In his meeting with Zardari, Kerry insisted on Davis's release before other issues could be sorted out. But there was still no indication of the US admitting Davis's CIA status. 'The foreign office is doing a favour to Davis by not issuing any statement about his status,' a senior Pakistani official told Kerry. [35] He got the message.

It was evident that Washington too looked towards the Pakistani military leadership to help resolve the Davis affair. There was a feeling in Washington that the civilian government was too weak and unpopular to deliver on the Davis issue. Washington knew that the Generals would be the final arbiter on the issue. They were not wrong. Repeated telephone contact between Panetta and Pasha, however, prevented a complete breakdown in the relationship between the two agencies, which was critical to the US war against the al-Qaeda.

Amidst the standoff on Davis, General Kayani met with the top US military leadership for a daylong secret meeting on 23 February, at a beach resort in Oman, to find a way out of the diplomatic crisis that threatened the US–Pakistan relationship. The US was represented by Admiral Mike Mullen, Chairman of the Joint Chiefs of Staff; General David Petraeus, Commander of ISAF; Admiral Eric Olson,

Commander of US Special Operations Command, and Marine Corps; General James Mattis, Commander of US Central Command. General Kayani, COAS, was accompanied by Maj. Gen. Javed Iqbal, DGMO.[36]

Although the Oman meeting had long been planned to review the war situation in Afghanistan, discussions also focused on the fallout from the detention of the CIA contractor on relations between the two allies. The US officials implored the Pakistani military to step up its involvement in the Davis case, following the government's decision to pass the buck to the judicial system on adjudicating Davis's claim of diplomatic immunity. However, their concerns also went beyond this most recent diplomatic spat.[37]

US did not want the relationship between the two countries to go into a free fall at a time when the US military was at a critical stage in Afghanistan, and Pakistan was the key to control and resolution. General Petraeus exemplified the US determination not to let the Davis affair damage strategic ties between the two countries. A US military official described the meeting as 'very candid, with very productive discussions.' The Pakistani military said the meeting was focused on regional security and would 'explore new ways to better coordinate military operations.'

The Oman meeting did some damage control. Yet there were many other underlying issues which Pakistani security agencies wanted to be sorted before the relations between the two agencies could go back to a pre-Davis situation. 'They have to dismantle those networks if they really want our cooperation,' said an official. 'We have warned them that they cannot do things behind our backs.' The Obama administration, on the other hand, insisted that Davis had to be freed immediately and that a settlement through the court was completely unacceptable.

Pakistan's refusal to accept unreasonable demands finally forced the Obama administration to take a step back and agree on an out-of-court settlement that included a public apology for the incident, a promise to hold a criminal investigation into the killing of the two gunmen by Davis under the US laws, and payment of compensation to the families of the victims. Four weeks into the crisis, the situation was already getting out of everyone's control.

There was also a growing realisation that the stalemate over the Davis incident was not sustainable. The military leadership too did not want the standoff going too far. As the pressure mounted, Zardari called a meeting at the presidency. Kayani and Pasha decided that they would just listen and not give any suggestion. 'Let's do something to get out of this situation,' Zardari asked the Generals. Kayani kept quiet and looked at Pasha. Interior Minister, Rehman Malik, intervened, saying he could help negotiate a deal. Zardari snubbed Malik and told Pasha that only the ISI could deliver.[38]

Pasha insisted that the political leadership must take ownership of any deal. Zardari assured him that he would issue a statement taking responsibility once the crisis was resolved. Pasha was told to find a way out. There was still a problem of getting political parties on board. Pasha met with the leaders of various political parties, including the Punjab chief minister and heads of right wing political parties. There was unanimous agreement by all of them that maintaining good relations with the US was more important than detaining one person.[39] Interestingly, despite agreeing in private, some of them continued with their tough anti-American posturing in public.

Pasha also consulted the Supreme Court Chief Justice, Iftikhar Chaudhry, and some senior lawyers on whether Davis could be released on payment of *diyat* (compensation or blood money for murder). Chief Justice Chaudhry assured Pasha that he would call the Lahore High Court judge and the issue could be settled within days.

Pasha then asked foreign secretary, Salman Bashir, to call US Ambassador Cameron Munter. The three met at the foreign secretary's office. Pasha assured the ambassador that some way out of the crisis could be found if the US administration was willing to cooperate. Davis had become a problem for everyone. A few days later, Pasha called the foreign secretary again and asked him to convey a message to Munter that he should fly to Lahore immediately.[40]

On 16 March after a secret court proceeding, US citizen and CIA contractor, Raymond Davis was released from prison after $2.4 million was paid to the families of the two Pakistani men he shot and killed.

It was all pre-arranged. A senior ISI official sat in a room next to the courtroom monitoring the proceedings. As US laws do not allow payment of ransom money, the payment was reportedly arranged through the Saudi government, though it was never made public.

Davis was taken directly to the Lahore airport where Munter received him. The crisis was finally over, with Davis flying back home. Under the terms of the agreement, the CIA had to pull out scores of its undercover agents from Pakistan and withdraw the summons against the ISI chief. Almost a year later, the US State Department informed New York Court that General Pasha and other Pakistani military officials named in the Mumbai attacks case were immune from the lawsuit.

While it was embarrassing for the Obama administration, the *diyat* deal had put the ISI too in a very awkward situation. Making a spectacle of the entire affair was seen by many senior ISI officers as a great mistake that demonstrated Pakistan's weakness. General Asif Yasin, who served as ISI head of internal security, felt that Pasha should have allowed the interrogation of Davis and then handed him over to the Americans with a clear message that all un-notified operatives must leave the country.[41] Davis finally left, after having shaken up two governments, sans passport. The ISI retained Davis's passport and he boarded the plane without it.

Although fully supportive of the deal, the political leadership was not willing to take any responsibility for its arrangement. Shahbaz Sharif, the chief minister of Punjab, had conveniently left for London a day before the court proceeding. President Zardari too backed out from his earlier promise to Pasha. 'There is now no need for any statement after the issue has been resolved,' he told Pasha when reminded of his responsibility. It was yet another example of the chaos within.

The Davis saga had damaged relations between Washington and Islamabad beyond repair. The fragile alliance had now turned into a hostile relationship. They were now more like enemies than allies. The relations between the two spy agencies would not be the same again.

Less than 24 hours after Davis was freed and flown back home, CIA drones struck a *jirga* (tribal council) in the village of Datta Khel, in North Waziristan, killing dozens of men. The CIA's drone attacks, halted during Davis's captivity, were reactivated the day after his departure. Mark Kelton, the CIA station chief in Islamabad, was venting his anger at the exposure of the spy network that he had built.[42]

Munter was reportedly kept in the dark about the CIA drone strike. The incident further soured the already strained relations between the ambassador and the CIA station chief. From the very outset of the Davis crisis, Munter had argued that lying about Davis would only insult the Pakistanis, who might be persuaded to release him if the agency acknowledged the mistake. But Kelton and his superiors at Langley were adamant not to give in.[43]

Pasha was livid and told Munter that the strike amounted to a 'kick in the teeth' after the Davis deal was arranged.[44] Pasha's relationship with Kelton never recovered, and the two rarely spoke again. Although his tenure lasted only seven months, Kelton signed off on dozens of drone strikes that infuriated the Pakistanis. He also oversaw the final preparations for the assault in Abbottabad that killed Osama bin Laden, a few months later. He was also pulled out, like his predecessor, when his cover was blown in the local media. It was the ISI way of exacting revenge.

In an interview after leaving his post in Islamabad in July 2012, Ambassador Munter described 2011 as 'by far my most difficult year in the Foreign Service.' That it surely was.

10 | Midnight Raid

It was early summer in Islamabad. At the US ambassador's residence, the conversation late evening at the dining table revolved around politics and US–Pak relations. Ambassador Cameron Munter had arrived in Pakistan less than a year ago, in October 2010, to take over, perhaps, the toughest assignment of his diplomatic career. His first few months in the job were spent in dealing with the Davis incident and its fallout.

An official walked into the room interrupting the conversation, handing a note to the ambassador. 'Washington doesn't seem to have any understanding about the time difference,' smiled Cameron. 'I will be back in ten minutes,' he said, as he got up to leave to receive a call in the secure room at the embassy.[1]

Marilyn Wyatt, the ambassador's wife, played host for the rest of the evening. The ambassador returned after almost 90 minutes as the guests were leaving. He looked worried and lost. Whatever he was told by his bosses in Washington, seemed to have troubled Munter. As midnight approached, he returned to the secure room, along with the CIA station chief, to watch live transmissions from a stealth drone circling over Abbottabad as the Osama bin Laden raid began.

Four US helicopters—two stealth Black Hawks and two Chinooks—entered Pakistani airspace at approximately 11:20 p.m. in the vicinity of Ghursal and Shilman in the mountainous northern Khyber tribal area. Flying low and fast, they were able to evade Pakistani low-altitude radar deployments, which were limited in number on the western border since they were on 'peacetime deployment.'

The helicopters dropped US Navy SEALs inside Osama bin Laden's suspected compound at approximately 12:30 a.m. They spent just under 40 minutes carrying out operations. At 1:06 a.m. they blew up a downed stealth helicopter and began their return trip to a US airbase in the Afghan city of Jalalabad, with bin Laden's body on board. The last US helicopter was estimated to have left Pakistani airspace at 2:26 a.m.

General Ashfaq Parvez Kayani was in his study in his official residence in Rawalpindi when at 2:27 a.m. on 2 May, he received a call from the DGMO, Maj. Gen. Ishfaq Nadeem, who informed him that a helicopter had crashed in Abbottabad—the home of the Pakistan Military Academy. He was also told about other helicopters having landed there and then flying away.[2]

General Kayani reached two quick conclusions: the chopper wasn't Pakistani because Pakistani helicopters rarely fly at night; therefore, it must be a foreign incursion that breached the country's air defenses. His major and immediate concern was for the safety of Pakistan's nuclear facility, located a few miles from Abbottabad. He called Air Chief Marshal, Rao Qamar Suleman, and told him that Pakistan's airspace had been violated, and asked him to 'shoot down the intruding helicopters.'[3]

But it was not to be. Intriguingly, F-16 fighter jets and support aircraft were not scrambled for a further 43 minutes—by then it was 24 minutes after US forces had left Pakistani airspace, and more than three and a half hours since the incursion first began. The US helicopters were already well out of Pakistan airspace by the time Pakistani fighter jets took off. The Air Chief didn't have a clear answer for the delay. He blamed 'unpreparedness of the air force on the western borders,' and how the Pakistan Air Force was not meant to engage with the US on the western border.[4]

General Kayani called Prime Minister Yousaf Raza Gillani around 3 a.m. to inform him about the intrusion and asked him to contact the US ambassador to enquire what was happening. He gave the same message to Foreign Secretary Salman Bashir who had returned from Beijing just hours ago. There was a complete panic situation as it was still not clear what had really happened. Munter picked up the phone and said he would get back.[5] General Kayani then waited a further hour and 45 minutes to make his final phone call of the morning at 6:45 a.m. to President Asif Ali Zardari, who was also the supreme commander.

An hour later, General Kayani received a call on a secure line from Admiral Mike Mullen, with the news that a team of US Navy SEALs had killed Osama bin Laden in Abbottabad and returned to Afghanistan. Stunned by the news, General Kayani paused before responding to Mullen, 'Congratulations on the good news,' he said, taking a deep breath.[6]

There was no bitterness or anger in his tone. He didn't even protest over the raid deep inside Pakistan's territory. He didn't tell Admiral Mullen the operation was 'unacceptable.' Instead, he requested Mullen that Pakistan's cooperation must also be acknowledged. Mullen promised that President Barack Obama would handle the issue of the raid in an appropriately measured way. The conversation ended on a pleasant note.[7]

Almost at the same time, President Zardari received a phone call from President Obama who informed him that the US forces had killed bin Laden in a raid inside Pakistani territory. 'Congratulations Mr President,' a stunned and half-awake Zardari responded. He too didn't raise the sovereignty issue. He was genuinely pleased by the news without thinking about the fallout. Shortly after, Lt. Gen. Shuja Pasha received a similar call from Leon Panetta, Director, CIA.

Meanwhile, the residents of Bilal Town, a prosperous middle-class neighbourhood, adjacent to the Military Academy in Abbottabad, were woken up by the sound of helicopters flying low and then a loud explosion. Peeping from their windows, they saw some figures moving in the dark around a double-storey house a couple of hundred meters away. No one came out as they had earlier been warned, presumably by security officials on duty. 'Stay home,' someone shouted in Urdu. Pupils at a madrasa on the edge of the colony witnessed the landing of two helicopters from the roof of their building and just assumed it was Pakistani security forces conducting some operation.[8]

Major Amir Aziz, a serving army officer, lived just a few hundred meters away from the compound known as Waziristan House. Many times the size of other homes in the neighbourhood and separated from the other houses by a corn field, the compound had high barbed-wire fences and two security gates.[9] Major Aziz's family often wondered who lived in the compound, although they had not noticed any unusual activity there; occasionally someone would be seen coming out.

The Major was woken up by the sound of helicopters flying very low. He saw a Chinook landing inside the compound and a Black Hawk landing outside in the field. He witnessed the soldiers in camouflaged uniforms descending at the top of the house from a helicopter still in the air. He also saw one Black Hawk helicopter crashing inside the compound. The explosion he heard was caused by the demolition of that helicopter. He called his unit commander, a Brigadier, to inform him what was happening. But he was apparently told to stay put and not to approach the compound. Later, the entire episode involving the Major and the Brigadier raised many questions. Troops reached the scene an hour after the helicopters had left. No one had any idea what was going on.[10]

Pakistani security officials who were the first to enter the compound found the helicopter wreckage, a house filled with corpses, and several frightened women and children crying hysterically. One of the surviving women, who had been shot in the leg, identified herself as Amal Ahmed Abdul Fatah, a 29-year-old Yemeni and bin Laden's youngest wife. It was then that the officials realised what had happened.[11]

Hours later, on the morning of 2 May, General Kayani and General Pasha arrived at the President House for an emergency meeting of the civil and military leadership to discuss Pakistan's response to the US raid and, more importantly, the embarrassing presence of bin Laden in Pakistan. The atmosphere in the conference room was grim. Besides President Zardari and PM Gillani, the newly appointed foreign minister, Hina Rabbani Khar, and the foreign secretary, Salman Bashir, were also present in the meeting.[12]

There was more of a feeling of embarrassment than that of anger. The discussion mainly revolved around how to explain the episode to the nation. While the president and the prime minister appeared relaxed, Generals Kayani and Pasha looked tense.[13] It was extremely difficult for them to explain how the world's most-hunted man was living right in the heart of an army garrison town.

A major question was whether it was an intelligence failure that made it possible for Osama bin Laden and his entourage to live undetected for more than six years, just a stone's throw from the Military Academy, or was there any complicity? It was a testing time for the military leadership. They were in the eye of the storm.

Only a month earlier, General Kayani had assured the newly commissioned officers at the Military Academy in the town where bin Laden had found sanctuary, that the back of al-Qaeda-supported terrorists had been broken.[14] A major worry for him now was how his officers would react to the US action inside Pakistan's territory. It was an extremely difficult situation for the military leadership. At best, it looked totally incompetent and at worst, completely complicit.

Curiously, there was hardly any discussion at the presidency that day on the breach of Pakistan's territorial sovereignty by the US forces. In fact, there was a complete consensus on downplaying the US raid and to encourage a perception of Pakistan's close cooperation in tracking down bin Laden. President Obama's acknowledgement of Pakistan's cooperation provided some relief to the Pakistani leadership. In his address to the nation the same morning, President Obama commended Pakistan's counterterrorism cooperation that helped 'lead us to bin Laden and his compound where he was hiding. Bin Laden had declared war against Pakistan as well and ordered attacks against the Pakistani people.' He also pointed out that in their conversation, the Pakistani leaders agreed that 'this is a good and historic day for both our nations.'[15]

Still, it was not possible for the Pakistani leadership to publicly condone the US action as they might have done in their private conversations with the American officials. This predicament was illustrated in the cautious phrasing of the statement issued after the 2 May meeting by the foreign ministry.

It was a classic example of playing both sides of the occurrence. While reminding the world of Pakistan's contribution and commitment to fighting al-Qaeda and its history of counterterrorism cooperation with the US, it distanced itself from the US action. The statement did not explicitly praise the sting operation, nor did it condemn it: 'Osama bin Laden's death illustrates the resolve of the international community, including Pakistan, to fight and eliminate terrorism. It constitutes a major setback to terrorist organisations around the world.'[16]

In fact, the statement implicitly validated the unilateral US military action noting that it was in 'accordance with declared US policy that Osama bin Laden will be eliminated in a direct action by the US forces, wherever found in the world.' In order to shield itself from the public outrage over the breach of sovereignty, the statement implied that Zardari and military leaders did not have any prior information about the US raid.[17]

In his op-ed column in *Washington Post* published on the same date, President Zardari went further, expressing satisfaction that 'the source of the greatest evil of the new millennium has been silenced, and his victims given justice.' While conceding that the 2 May raid was not a joint operation, he reiterated that it was 'a decade of cooperation and partnership between the United States and Pakistan that led up to the elimination of Osama bin Laden.' He also endorsed the words of President Obama and appreciated the credit he gave Pakistan for the successful operation. There was no mention of the sovereignty issue.[18]

Marc Grossman, President Obama's special representative for Afghanistan and Pakistan, held talks with PM Gillani just hours after bin Laden's death. In a statement after the meeting, Gillani said he had expressed 'the need for constructive and positive messaging from both sides,' on the operation to kill bin Laden and the avoidance of 'spin.'[19]

However, very soon the tenor started changing and got tougher when US officials and some lawmakers raised questions about whether or not the Pakistani military and ISI had protected bin Laden. The al-

Qaeda leader was found, not in a remote border hideout, but in a mansion in a garrison city, about 40 miles from the country's capital. US officials were not willing to accept that bin Laden lived there without support from within Pakistan.[20]

While the White House tried to play down any suspicion about the role of Pakistani intelligence agencies in protecting the al-Qaeda chief, some other officials were extremely sceptical. President Obama's top counterterrorism advisor, John Brennan, said the US would pursue all leads to find out 'exactly what type of support system and benefactors bin Laden might have had.' In an interview CIA Director, Leon Panetta, stated that US officials did not alert Pakistani counterparts to the raid because they feared the terrorist leader would be warned.[21]

The initial shock and humiliation caused by the US incursion had turned into anger within Pakistan's military ranks. The killing of bin Laden marked an epic victory for US forces. But for Pakistan's military it meant national humiliation. Anti-US sentiments were already high following the Davis incident and now there was widespread scepticism about the official explanation on the Abbottabad raid. There were also questions about how bin Laden could have been staying undetected in a high security zone.

His commanders put General Kayani on the mat. What angered them most was that the US didn't share information about the raid with Pakistani security officials until after it was over. General Kayani almost cried: 'They could have done it jointly with us in the daylight,' he told a retired General.[22]

It was extremely tough for General Kayani and General Pasha to come up with a plausible defense of the failure to find bin Laden and their inability to detect the presence of foreign forces during the course of the raid. In light of the country's defence policy, the US was not considered a threat, and the violation of its airspace and territory on 1 May 2011, was therefore considered a 'betrayal.' There was apparently no 'response capability' on the western border, although one was in place on the eastern borders with India. The generals were certainly not satisfied with Kayani's explanation that the US helicopters could not be intercepted because the radars on the western border were not operative.[23]

In an attempt to rally his troops, General Kayani went from garrison to garrison to explain that he shared their sense of humiliation over the raid but that it was not prudent to sever ties with the US. 'I felt betrayed by the US military action as I have been deeply involved in developing strategic relations with the United States,' he told senior field officers at Islamabad's National Defense University (NDU), a few days later. Officers, one after the other, bombarded him with questions about the US raid and the future of Pakistan's relations with the US for more than three hours and General Kayani sat there answering their questions. After the speech, a colonel in attendance pointedly asked: 'How can we trust the United States?'[24]

The General kept his cool but clearly looked stressed out. 'My feelings would be the same as yours if another such incident happened. We will not hesitate then to curtail all intelligence and military cooperation with the US.' The assurance did not seem to appease the several dozen mid-level officers completing their war course at the NDU. While admitting intelligence failure, General Kayani confirmed that he had ordered an investigation.[25]

Within days, Pakistan's response had changed to reflect the military's outrage. At a meeting at the President House, General Kayani handed over a written statement to Foreign Secretary Salman Bashir. 'It should be released immediately,' the army chief told him. Bashir took out his pen and tried to make some changes. But Zardari interrupted him. 'Let it go as it is,' he told Bashir.[26]

Hours later, the foreign secretary in a news conference warned of 'disastrous consequences' should the US or any other country—such as arch-rival India—attempt a similar raid. 'No self-respecting nation would compromise or allow others to compromise its sovereignty,' stated Bashir, reiterating, 'We want to make it absolutely clear to everyone—do not underestimate Pakistan's capabilities and capacity to do what is necessary for national security.'[27]

It was mainly the ISI chief, General Shuja Pasha, who was in the eye of the storm for his organisation's failure to nab bin Laden or to anticipate the US raid. Pasha was under intense pressure to accept responsibility for the lapse amid calls for his resignation. Under his command, the ISI had expanded its relationship with the CIA, increasing cooperation on drone strikes against militant targets in Pakistan. Yet the ISI chief had also stood up to the US whenever there was a clash or a disagreement over a particular course of action. It was therefore an extremely humiliating experience for the ISI chief to be grilled for several hours by legislators at a joint session of the parliament. General Kayani sat next to him, smoking nervously, as opposition members demanded that someone at the top must resign and some heads must roll. It was indicative of the deep crisis in national confidence brought on by the Abbottabad raid.[28]

In an effort to pacify public outrage, the government announced its intention to launch an investigation into intelligence failures surrounding bin Laden's discovery by the US and killing by foreign forces. There was already an increasing pressure on the government and the military to scale back Pakistan's cooperation with the CIA.

As the Generals needed a scapegoat to blame, both for not knowing about the US incursion, and for not detecting the presence of bin Laden, General Pasha offered to resign. But General Kayani rejected his resignation, as he knew that the buck would not stop there. He had received an extension for another three-year term just a few months ago, evoking resentment among senior officers. His authority had further diminished after the 2 May incident. The opposition politicians joined the protest, spurring public disenchantment with the military.[29]

There was also growing concern that the anger over bin Laden incident could run through the lower-ranking soldiers, making them amenable to the anti-US campaign launched by radical Islamic groups. One group, Hizbut-Tahrir, clandestinely dropped pamphlets in military cantonments after the bin Laden raid calling for officers to revolt against the military leadership and establish an Islamic caliphate. 'It is a slap in the respected officers' faces that on 2 May American helicopters intruded in the dark of night and barged into a house like thieves. It could not have been possible without the acquiescence of your high officials,' read the pamphlet. It was obvious that men within the ranks distributed the pamphlets. The group, though outlawed, had made inroads into the security institutions. A brigadier and a few other officers were later arrested for their affiliation with the group and court martialed.[30]

As domestic political pressure escalated, the military issued a rare defensive response to calm down the critics. In an attempt to pacify the soldiers who openly questioned the rationale for Pakistan's tight military embrace with the US, General Kayani promised to reduce the military's reliance on US military aid and training.

He ordered strict limits on US intelligence operations within the country. A long statement—at various points apologetic, belligerent, and strident—was the clearest indication that Pakistan's military leaders were under immense pressure to assuage their own people, even if that meant scaling back ties to the US.[31]

The statement manifested the crisis that had gripped Pakistan's military. It said the army had 'drastically cut' the number of US troops stationed in Pakistan and ended US training of Pakistani soldiers. General Kayani also told commanders that US military aid for Pakistan should be diverted to help the economy, signalling that he no longer viewed it as essential. Pakistan said it received $8.6 billion in US military assistance in the past decade through the Coalition Support Fund programme meant to reimburse the country for money spent fighting terrorism.

This sent a clear signal that the military was reconsidering its options for expanded cooperation with the US in the fight against militants.[32]

General Kayani told his commanders that Pakistan would not be pressured to agree to a timetable to attack North Waziristan that was seen as the epicentre of militancy, threatening both Pakistan and Afghanistan. The tribal region was home to the Haqqani network— the most lethal of the Taliban factions responsible for attacks on US forces in Afghanistan. He also declared that US drone strikes in the tribal areas 'were not acceptable under any circumstances.'[33] Pakistan had always publicly condemned the programme, while privately acquiescing and, at times, assisting it.

US reaction to the Pakistani statement was muted. American officials said they understood General Kayani needed 'breathing space' to get his own people back on his side. 'The government has been in a difficult spot domestically since the bin Laden raid, and the Pakistani military is probably trying to re-establish some of the credibility it perceived it lost,' said a US official in Washington. In the eyes of the US, General Kayani was still a reliable ally and it was not in the Obama administration's interest to add to his woes.[34]

With a widening trust deficit between Islamabad and Washington, the CIA had built its own clandestine network to track down Osama bin Laden, bypassing the ISI. In fact, the CIA had stopped sharing any information with its Pakistani counterpart about the bin Laden investigation since 2005. During President Obama's tenure, there was a growing suspicion in his administration that elements in the Pakistani security agency might be protecting the al-Qaeda leader. In 2009, on her visit to Islamabad, Secretary of State, Hillary Clinton had declared: 'I'm not saying that they're at the highest levels, but I believe that somewhere in this government are people who know where Osama bin Laden and al-Qaeda is.' Her comments were indicative of difficult relations between the two countries and evoked strong reaction from Pakistani authorities.[35]

The question of how or whether bin Laden eluded the view of Pakistan's military intelligence remained unanswered. It was just too much of a coincidence that bin Laden would be hiding in a neighbourhood close to the military academy, inhabited by retired and serving military officers. Either the ISI knew about his presence there, or it was a complete intelligence failure.

General Pasha claimed that the initial courier tip-off was provided by the ISI. According to him, the agency had conveyed information about an intercepted phone call made to Kuwait to the CIA and to some intelligence agencies of the Gulf countries. But, he added, the

ISI never received any information about the follow-up investigations. While the ISI provided the CIA the relevant information on the courier, they may not have realised its significance.[36]

Intriguingly enough, the ISI had been actively pursuing al-Qaeda operatives in the vicinity around Abbottabad for some time. Just weeks before the US raid, the ISI had captured Umar Patek, one of the masterminds of the 2002 Bali bombing in which more than 200 people were killed, from an area not far from bin Laden's compound. He had come to Pakistan, along with his Filipino wife, to meet the al-Qaeda leader. But he was nabbed before he could reach his leader.[37]

A few years earlier, Pakistani security agencies raided a compound in Abbottabad for Faraj al-Libbi, considered number three in the al-Qaeda leadership hierarchy. He was also believed to have been in contact with bin Laden. He escaped, but was later captured in Mardan, less than 100 miles from Abbottabad.[38]

CIA, meanwhile, had been operating a network in the area after receiving initial intelligence of bin Laden's possible presence in the garrison town. Some Pakistanis, including serving and retired army officers, were recruited for the hunt of the al-Qaeda leader. A USAID office in the city was also used as a cover for the operatives.[39] The Abbottabad Commission report has shed light on some retired security officials who could have helped the CIA in tracking down bin Laden.

Lt. Col. Iqbal, a former ISI officer, was a critical cog in the CIA's hunt for bin Laden. Thrown out from the army on 'disciplinary grounds,' he ran a private security firm that was mainly staffed by former ISI officers. He would often visit Major Amir and take photographs of the bin Laden compound. His wealth had grown astronomically over the years. He drove a million dollar bulletproof, noise-controlled vehicle.[40]

For a retired, mid-level army officer, this kind of wealth was inconceivable. His son, who was also in the army, had served as ADC to former military ruler General Musharraf. Colonel Iqbal was believed to be the person who tipped off the CIA about bin Laden's presence in Abbottabad. He disappeared the day after the US raid.

His profile, according to General Pasha, 'matched that of a likely CIA recruit.' Colonel Iqbal is now residing in California.

Equally curious was the role of Major Amir, who was bin Laden's closest neighbour and hosted Colonel Iqbal. It was not a coincidence that the former ISI officer landed at his house. The Major had been living there for many years. It was strange, because it's rare for a serving officer to be posted at one place for that long. He was the main witness of the US operation, although his initial statement that he was told by his commanding officer not to go out, made him seem somewhat dubious. He was reluctant to appear before the Abbottabad Commission investigating the raid. The ISI chief denied the two had played any role in bin Laden's case.[41]

Another key member of the CIA network was Dr Shakeel Afridi. He was the only one whose service in the hunt for bin Laden was recognised publicly by US officials. A doctor and health official in Pakistan's Khyber tribal region, he headed a polio vaccination campaign in the suburb where bin Laden's suspected compound was located. It turns out that the programme was no ordinary public health initiative. It was a CIA operation designed to confirm bin Laden's presence in Abbottabad by collecting DNA from one of his family members.[42] Afridi was arrested almost a week after the killing of bin Laden.

A judicial commission recommended trying him for treason. He was sentenced to 33 years in prison in 2012—not for his CIA link—but rather for a ransom payment made on his behalf to the Lashkar-e-Islam militant group, which had abducted Afridi in 2008. Pakistan said it constituted financial support for a terrorist group.

Regardless of what Afridi did or didn't know, US officials have talked about him as though he were a key asset in the hunt for bin Laden. Former US Defense Secretary, Leon Panetta (who was Director CIA when the bin Laden raid took place), confirmed during a *60 Minutes* interview in January 2012 that Afridi had worked for the CIA.[43]

While CIA recruits were looking into bin Laden's whereabouts, the ISI had 'closed the file' on Osama bin Laden after the CIA reportedly stopped sharing information on the hunt for the al-Qaeda chief in 2005. This was despite the fact that bin Laden had released an audio recording as late as January 2011, whose authenticity was verified through voice analysis. According to ISI assessments, bin Laden was either dead or inactive, and the lack of intelligence sharing from CIA was seen as indicative that this was the US view as well.

Interestingly, General Kayani had a series of meetings with the top US military commanders weeks and days before the Abbottabad raid. He met with CENTCOM chief, General James Mattis, on 8 April; followed by the visit of the Chairman JCOSC, Admiral Mike Mullen, on 20 April; and US commander for Afghanistan, General David Petraeus, on 26 April. That shows very close coordination between the two militaries at the top level, despite a widening trust deficit between them.

The government tried to bring closure to the issue by ordering an internal (military) enquiry into how bin Laden managed to hide in Pakistan so long. The one-man Pakistan Army Board of Inquiry was headed by Lt. Gen. Javed Iqbal, a close aide to General Kayani. The report concluded that bin Laden was able to escape detection in Abbottabad 'due to the phased construction and occupation of the compound, the extremely low profile that was maintained.'

Curiously enough, a few years later General Javed Iqbal was court martialed for spying for the US and sentenced to 14-years imprisonment. The General was responsible for military operations, one of the most critical position's in the country's defense system until a few months before the Abbottabad raid, lending a new and interesting twist to the bin Laden enquiry.[44]

Meanwhile another judicial commission, known as the Abbottabad Commission, was set up to 'ascertain full facts regarding the presence of Osama bin Laden in Pakistan.' The report was submitted to the government in 2013 but it was never made public. A leaked copy of the report showed a scathing indictment of the security agencies for their failure to detect bin Laden. The report observed that 2 May was the blackest day for Pakistan. This applies to not only the US military raid, but also to the humiliation of being caught hosting the world's most wanted militant. Yet, the latter fact seemed to have been buried under strong rhetoric and clichés about national sovereignty.

The report ruled out complicity of any state institution in harbouring bin Laden. Certainly there is no evidence of that. But, in that scenario, who provided bin Laden protection and logistic support? It is inconceivable that a fugitive, with $25 million bounty on his head, could cross into Pakistan and safely live there without a strong support base within the country.

During the time he hid in Pakistan, bin Laden and his family travelled to many places. He is said to have stayed in Waziristan, Bajaur, Swat, and Haripur before settling in Abbottabad. His wives and children also lived in Quetta, Karachi, and Peshawar. For all that, they must have had the support of a dedicated and ideologically committed group looking after the logistics as well as their security. It is also clear that bin Laden continued to guide al-Qaeda activities while cloistered in his house inside the high security garrison area.

The report summed up the question about the network in just one paragraph and that too in terms of probability: 'It was probably quite small and largely, if not exclusively, al-Qaeda and its associates. It probably had a wider group of less dedicated and less regular support from sympathetic Pakistani jihadi groups and individuals.'

In its Findings section, the Commission notes: 'The implicit assumption that only the CIA had the ability to find bin Laden in Pakistan indicated a complete lack of confidence by the ISI and the intelligence establishment in their own ability to do so. Either OBL was extremely fortunate to not run into anyone committed to doing his job honestly, or there was a complete collapse of local governance,' concluded the Abbottabad Commission report.

11 | Relations on a Slippery Slope

'Now is not the time for retreat or for recrimination,' Admiral Mike Mullen, Chairman Joint Chiefs of Staff Committee remarked during a visit to Islamabad accompanied by Secretary of State Hillary Clinton, on 26 May 2011, to what was described as a tense post-Osama visit of the highest-ranking Obama administration officials. 'Now is the time for action and close coordination, for more cooperation, not less.'[1]

The visit was meant to gauge Pakistan's reaction to the Abbottabad raid. The carefully orchestrated diplomatic encounter was intended both to calm down the Pakistani leadership and to reassure them of political support at a time when the US Congress had threatened to cut economic and security aid. But the vibes in Islamabad, still haunted by the raid, were extremely tense.

Clinton and Mullen looked sombre when they arrived at the presidential palace for a meeting with the Pakistani civil and military leadership. In brief remarks directed to President Asif Ali Zardari, Hillary Clinton said that the Obama administration recognised 'the sacrifice that is made every single day by the men and women of your military and the citizens of your country.'[2]

She said she had 'absolutely no evidence' to suggest that senior Pakistani civilian or military leaders knew that bin Laden was hiding in Abbottabad.[3] But she also warned that relations between the US and Pakistan had reached 'a turning point,' and called on Pakistan's leaders to take urgent measures against Islamic extremists. It was a mixed message.

There was no press conference after the meeting. A short statement issued by the president's office said the two countries agreed to 'work together in any future actions against high-value targets in Pakistan.' That appeared to reflect Pakistan's demand that the US stop carrying out unilateral missions like the 2 May raid. That less than seven-hour stay of the two US officials in Islamabad failed to break the ice, though there was still no desire on either side to break away completely.

A series of spectacular insurgent attacks in Afghanistan blamed on the Haqqani network further heightened tension between Islamabad and Washington. An all-day rocket attack on the US embassy in Kabul on the 10th anniversary of the 9/11 terrorist attacks forced the US's ambassador, Ryan Crocker, to seek refuge in the basement safe room.[4] This was followed by a car bomb attack on an American military base in Wardak province, wounding 70 American soldiers. The audacious attacks had prompted the outgoing Chairman JCOSC, Admiral Mike Mullen, to directly accuse Pakistan of collusion.[5]

In a statement at the Congressional Committee on the eve of his retirement on 30 September 2011, Mullen described the Haqqani network as a 'veritable arm of the ISI'. He went on to tell the Committee that 'the Haqqani Network—which has long enjoyed the support and protection of the Pakistani government and is, in many ways, a strategic arm of Pakistan's Inter-Services Intelligence Agency [ISI]—is responsible for the 13 September attacks against the US Embassy in Kabul.'[6]

Although US officials had long been warning Pakistan against providing protection to the Haqqani network and allowing the insurgents to operate from its territory with impunity, it was the first time a top US official had publicly linked the group with the ISI.

President Barack Obama was reportedly outraged by the public remarks directly implicating Pakistan for the attack on Americans by his top military man. His major worry was that the accusation could trigger another round of the blame game between Washington and Islamabad. Obama, however, didn't need to take action against the Admiral as he was already retiring. 'That's not language I would use,' White House press secretary Jay Carney told reporters in response to Mullen's comments. Other members of the Obama administration sought to play down his remarks.[7]

Admiral Mullen was Obama's main interlocutor with the Pakistani military leadership and his scathing remarks came as a shock to General Parvez Kayani. The two military leaders had developed a good working relationship that had helped diffuse many crises. Over the period from 2007–2011 they had met 27 times. Mullen came to Pakistan 23 times from 2008 to 2011. Over the four years, from Kayani's promotion as COAS in November 2007, until Mullen's retirement on 30 September 2011, hardly a month went by when the two didn't meet.

Mullen would often drop by Kayani's official residence in Rawalpindi for dinner. They would often stay there talking till early morning. One time, Kayani took Mullen to the Himalayas for a flyby of the world's second-highest peak, K2. On another occasion, Mullen hosted Kayani on the golf course at the Naval Academy.

The two men seemed to have developed a genuine trust and respect for each other. Mullen's testimony, therefore, came as a particular shock because it was the rapport between the two that provided some semblance of stability in the turbulent relations between Washington and Islamabad.

Mullen had complained to General Kayani about Pakistan's support for the Haqqani group several times. While Kayani did not deny contact with the insurgent network, he insisted that the group never received any support from Pakistani intelligence agencies. 'If we don't have that contact, it will leave space for other intelligence agencies like CIA and RAW,' Kayani would tell Mullen.[8] He also pointed out that no evidence whatsoever had been provided substantiating the allegation, but the oft-repeated argument from Pakistani military officials did not convince the Pentagon.

The last time the two military leaders had met was on the sidelines of a security conference in Seville, Spain on 16 September 2011 for 90 minutes. After dinner Mullen invited Kayani to his room. They chatted till late. Both knew it was their last meeting before Mullen stepped down at the end of September. It was a pleasant goodbye.[9] Mullen later sent a message to Kayani, after his accusatory remarks to the Congressional Committee, saying that his statement should be read in totality. That was the last communication between the two erstwhile friends.[10] The fateful truck bombing in Kabul and the embassy attack seemed to have rattled Mullen's faith in an underlying common purpose.

As part of a damage control effort, Hillary Clinton led a high-powered delegation to Islamabad on 20 October that included newly appointed CIA Director, David Petraeus; newly appointed Chairman of the JCOSC, General Martin Dempsey; Lt. Gen. Douglas E. Lute, a top White House advisor on the war in Afghanistan; and Marc Grossman, the State Department's Special Representative for Afghanistan and Pakistan.

It was the first such visit since the seven-hour lightning low-key visit on 26 May by Mullen and Clinton to assess the situation post 2 May. The size of the US delegation in October, representing all the agencies, was intended as a signal of unity following conflicting messages in the wake of Admiral Mullen's remarks. Another purpose was to convey the urgency of the situation in Afghanistan and the continued importance of Pakistan as a critical partner in the war against extremist groups.

Unfortunately, Hillary Clinton's scathing remarks during a short stopover in Kabul en route to Islamabad, alleging that the Pakistani security agencies were protecting militant groups, vitiated the atmosphere. In her remarks, she warned Pakistani officials that there would be a 'very big price' if they did not take action against militant groups staging attacks in Afghanistan. 'We will be delivering a very clear message to the Government of Pakistan and to the people of Pakistan,' Clinton told reporters.[11]

Her comments angered the Pakistani military leadership who saw it as 'pressure by verbal assaults and demonization.' There was even some suggestion that the talks should be cancelled. But Prime Minister Yousaf Raza Gillani intervened, saying that such a drastic reaction would not be in the country's interest.[12]

It was already late evening when the high-level US delegation arrived in Islamabad. They were driven directly to the Prime Minister House for the meeting. The talks with Pakistani officials that included General Kayani, General Pasha, and Foreign Minister Hina Rabbani Khar lasted four hours before they adjourned for the night. A senior State Department official described the talks as 'extremely frank' and 'very detailed.' But a member of the Pakistani delegation described it as a highly 'testy' interaction: 'The relationship had descended into a coercive one from a transactional one.'[13]

Hillary Clinton's tenor at a joint press conference with the Pakistani foreign minister remained threatening. While insisting that there is a shared responsibility for fighting terrorism, Clinton hinted of consequences for Pakistan if the government did not 'do more' to stop attacks emanating from the Pakistani side of the border. 'No one should be in any way mistaken about allowing this to continue without paying a very big price,' Clinton warned. She said Pakistan's leaders 'must be part of the solution, which means ridding their own country of terrorists who kill their own people and cross the border to kill people in Afghanistan.'[14]

The Obama administration had dropped its long-standing demand that Pakistan begin an all-out military offensive in the North Waziristan tribal area. Now it demanded that the Pakistanis target the Haqqani leadership, work with the US to do it, or get out of the way. The CIA had intensified drone strikes targeting the alleged militant sanctuaries in Miranshah in North Waziristan. The pressure on Pakistan had increased after the escalation in militant attacks in Afghanistan.

Despite the tension, there had also been a realisation in Washington that both countries shared an interest in resolving the conflict. Hillary Clinton called for the adoption of a common strategy she dubbed 'fight, talk, build.' She wanted Pakistan and Afghanistan to cooperate and do all three things at once.[15]

But there was no possibility of Islamabad and Kabul cooperating. Relations between the two countries had been badly strained after a series of high profile attacks and assassinations, including the assassination on 20 September 2011, of Burhanuddin Rabbani, a former Afghan president and the point-man for reconciliation talks between the Afghan government and the Taliban. The incident happened when a Taliban 'emissary' detonated a bomb in his turban as Rabbani embraced him.[16]

Rabbani's death also killed the prospect of talks between the Kabul government and the Taliban. President Hamid Karzai accused Pakistan of masterminding the grotesque killing in order to scuttle peace talks it couldn't control. Karzai said peace efforts were useless unless Pakistan was heavily involved.

While intensifying pressure on Pakistan to act against the Haqqani network, the Obama administration was willing to consider 'reconciliation' through negotiations with the Taliban. It sought to broker a deal with militants before the last of 33,000 American 'surge' troops prepared to pull out of Afghanistan by September, and for the White House to have the outlines of a deal in time for a multinational conference on 5 December 2011 in Bonn, Germany.[17]

The timing of the visit of the high-powered US delegation to Islamabad was also important as the Congress Committee was to start hearings on Afghanistan and Clinton was to give her testimony a week later on 27 October. She wanted to show some progress in US efforts to end the war in Afghanistan by the time of the NATO summit conference in Chicago in May 2012.

Some backchannel contacts had already been working. A few months earlier, Pakistan had facilitated a meeting between a representative of the Haqqani network and some US officials. The meeting took place in UAE in August 2011 between Ibrahim Haqqani and American officials.[18] But there was no consensus on a political solution to the Afghan war among various US agencies. The Pentagon was certainly not in favour of any 'reconciliation.'

There was some speculation that the State Department was eager to take the lead from the National Security Council (NSC) on a reconciliation policy. The ongoing clash among various branches of the US government had made it more difficult to develop a clear strategy for negotiations with the militants.

Meanwhile, the Taliban responded to the escalation in US military action with the deadliest attacks since the start of the Afghan war. More than a dozen American soldiers and defence contractors were killed in a suicide car bombing in Kabul on 27 October that coincided with the Congress Committee hearing.[19]

The Kabul attack and the other high profile assaults marked a shift in Taliban strategy to shake confidence in the Afghan government, which had been taking over security from NATO in Kabul and other areas of the country. The single deadliest assault on Americans in the capital followed some brazen Taliban attacks on the US Embassy and on NATO headquarters in the city a month ago.

Notwithstanding the freeze, a backchannel contact with the White House kept a critical line of communication open. Former Pakistan ambassador to the US, Maleeha Lodhi worked as a General Kayani's backroom interlocutor to communicate with the White House and the State Department. Having served in Washington as Pakistan's envoy twice she was well connected with the Beltway power circle.[20]

A former newspaper editor, Lodhi was the youngest Pakistani envoy to the US when she was appointed there for the first time in 1993 by Benazir Bhutto's second government. Lodhi returned to Washington following General Musharraf's military coup in 1999. She played an important role in Pakistan's realignment with the US post-9/11.

Lodhi had later served as Pakistan's High Commissioner in London. Her experience and vast contact list had made her a valuable asset for the Pakistani military leadership. Lodhi's main liaison at the White House was General Douglas Lute, Special Assistant to the President on Afghanistan and Pakistan.

General Lute, who had earlier served in the Bush administration, was among the few in the Obama administration who had some institutional memory on the South Asian regional policy. He had developed a good rapport with the Pakistani military leadership that kept the critical backchannel working during the worst crisis in the alliance since 2001. Lodhi mostly communicated to Lute through e-mails.[21]

Historically, the Pakistan–US relationship had largely been military to military. But that connection had turned antagonistic with the US military failure in Afghanistan and accusations of Pakistan supporting Taliban insurgents. Interestingly, the White House had taken a more rational approach than the military and, to some extent, the State Department.

The backchannel communication between Lodhi and Lute helped resolve many crises. Even during the Davis episode, General Kayani used Lodhi to exchange messages with the Obama administration. These communications also helped in arranging some secret meetings. One such meeting was held in November 2011 in the Gulf.[22]

General Kayani quietly flew to Abu Dhabi for a secret meeting with President Obama's NSC Advisor, Tom Donilon who had replaced General James Jones. It was Kayani's first interaction with him since the Abbottabad raid on 2 May. Donilon was accompanied by Douglas Lute, Special Assistant to the President on Afghanistan and Pakistan, and Marc Grossman, recently appointed US Special Representative for Afghanistan and Pakistan (SRAP)—after the sudden death of Ambassador Richard Holbrooke on 13 December 2010, from complications of a torn aorta.

A career diplomat, Grossman was assigned to manage one of the most challenging tasks facing the US. He had served at the US embassy in Islamabad, Pakistan, from 1976 to 1983. Before his new assignment, he had served as Under Secretary of State. Grossman kept a much lower profile than Holbrooke. The SRAP team brought together experts from across the US government (and included several diplomats from NATO countries) to develop and implement integrated strategies to address the complex challenges in Afghanistan, Pakistan, and the region.[23]

After taking over charge of his new posting in February 2011, one of Grossman's main tasks was to interact with a Taliban representative introduced by German officials. The contact was preliminary, but many in the White House and on the SRAP team hoped that this connection might open the door for talks that would be required for a political solution in Afghanistan. Both Lute and Grossman had a central role in framing the Obama administration's regional policy.

The Abu Dhabi meeting was arranged on Donilon's initiative to put the fractured relationship with Pakistan back on track. The Davis affair, followed by the unilateral US Navy SEAL operation, had threatened the cooperation that the Obama administration still required from Pakistan for its exit plan in Afghanistan. There were also serious worries over the escalation in insurgent attacks over the past weeks targeting American forces and installations.

General Kayani was already present at the town house in Abu Dhabi that served as a safe house for a local intelligence agency, friendly to the Pakistan government, when the three US officials arrived. They drove there directly from the airport in unmarked vehicles.[24] The fact that President Obama sent the high-level delegation to meet the Pakistani military chief, and not the civilian leadership in Islamabad, reaffirmed the administration's view about the primacy of Pakistan's military.

The tension was palpable when the delegation took their seats around the conference table. Donilon had come with a firm message: either Pakistan was going to deal with the Haqqani network or the Americans would. Citing intelligence reports, Donilon listed the militant bases in Miranshah, the headquarters of Pakistan's North Waziristan tribal region, from where cross-border attacks on the US and Afghan forces were plotted. He warned that the US would undertake whatever steps were needed to protect its forces if Pakistan refused to act jointly. It was a not-so-veiled threat. The Abbottabad action was a successful model for the US to follow. General Kayani listened to him quietly.[25]

When Donilon finished speaking, Kayani responded in a measured but firm tone making it clear that any more violation of Pakistan's sovereignty by US forces would not be acceptable. He demanded an assurance from the US administration that no Abbottabad kind of raid would ever happen again. Kayani told the US officials that he felt personally humiliated by the Navy SEAL raid. However, Donilon was not prepared to make any such commitment. Almost as a quid pro quo, there was no assurance from the Pakistan Army chief either about acting against the Haqqani network. The divide between the two sides on the Haqqani question seemed unbridgeable.[26]

The discussion moved on to the other critical issue related to Afghanistan's future as the Obama administration's deadline for drawing down of US troops from the country came closer. General Kayani reiterated his concerns about security implications for the region in case Afghanistan fell apart. He once again expressed his fears about the potential disintegration of a well-armed and well-trained Afghan national army along ethnic lines in the event of a withdrawal of US forces without a political settlement in Afghanistan.

Kayani's major worry was the growing Indian influence in Afghanistan. The meeting lasted for almost six hours. Although there was some convergence of views on the need to find a political solution to the Afghan crisis, the chasm over the approach remained wide. Kayani was most upset when the details of the classified discussions at Abu Dhabi were leaked to an American author. 'It was quite shocking,' General Kayani later told me.[27]

The situation between the two allies was very strained but no one at the Abu Dhabi rendezvous could ever have imagined that in just a few weeks, things were going to get much worse. In a pre-dawn 2 a.m. strike on two Pakistani security posts along the Afghan border on Saturday, 26 November 2011, US-led NATO forces killed 26 Pakistan Army soldiers and wounded 12 others.[28]

Backed by two NATO Apache Longbow helicopters, an AC-130 gunship and two F-15E Eagle fighter jets, they targeted the posts at a hilltop at Salala in Mohmand tribal agency in FATA. There were nearly 40 soldiers, most of whom were sleeping or resting at the posts known as 'Volcano' and 'Boulder.' The raid continued for almost two hours, cutting off all communications to and from the posts. Troops at one of the posts engaged the helicopter gunship with anti-aircraft guns. But the resistance did not last long.

Shelling by US gunships at Pakistani border posts had become more frequent in the last few years with the rise in cross-border attacks on the coalition forces by Taliban insurgents. In one such incident two Pakistani soldiers were killed. But the Salala attack, with so many casualties, was extremely serious. Afghan and US officials blamed Pakistani security forces for first firing at the coalition forces conducting an operation against the Taliban insurgents across the border in Kunar province. The US air force, apparently, went into action at the request of the Afghan security forces. The Americans initially refused to even regret the deaths, saying it was defensive action.

While admitting to firing a few flares and a couple of mortar rounds, Pakistani officials insisted that it was meant to stop insurgent infiltration. However, the Salala incident was an accident just waiting to happen with the Afghan and NATO forces intensifying operations against the Taliban in the region close to Pakistan's border. Kunar, in eastern Afghanistan, had become one of the main centres of Taliban and al-Qaeda activities.

Many senior al-Qaeda leaders, including Al-Zawahiri, had once made Kunar their sanctuary.[29] The poorly defined border made it much easier for the insurgents to cross over to the Pakistani side after attacking the coalition forces. US officials had often complained that insurgents were provided cover by the Pakistani security forces and that, in some cases, the Taliban used Pakistani border posts to carry out cross-border attacks.

The Salala issue became more complicated when US officials said NATO forces had informed the Pakistan Army's 11 Corps command near the western border that operations against Taliban insurgents would take place that day. The incident occurred a day after General John Allen, Commander ISAF, Afghanistan, met General Kayani, to discuss border control and enhanced cooperation. The attack was the deadliest US-led NATO strike on Pakistani soil since the start of the war in Afghanistan.[30]

The shock and the anger was palpable at Army House in Rawalpindi that morning. Just hours after the incident, General Kayani called Foreign Secretary Salman Bashir for an urgent meeting. Bashir had heard the news and understood what the meeting was about. On arrival at Army House, he was taken to the sunroom, where General Kayani and Maj. Gen. Ishfaq Nadeem, the DGMO, were waiting for him. The two looked sombre.[31]

The attack on Salala was deliberate and well-coordinated, said Maj. Gen. Nadeem. A short man in his late 40s, the general was appointed to one of the most critical positions less than a year ago. He had earlier commanded an army division in Swat and was highly regarded in the army. He gave a short briefing about what had happened in Salala that fateful morning. According to him, there was no question of a mistake as the coalition forces had been notified about the post.[32] General Kayani was deep in thought. The latest US action, causing deaths of so many soldiers, was not acceptable. Kayani was very concerned about the reaction within the military ranks. And there was still no clear answer from the US military as to why such massive airpower was needed.

The next day, PM Gillani called an emergency meeting of the Defence Committee of Cabinet (DCC). Besides the PM, the foreign minister and the foreign secretary were also present. General Nadeem briefed them about the attack with the help of a map. Despite ongoing tension with the military on another issue—Memogate (*see* Chapter 12)—the Salala incident brought the civil and the military leadership together. What really irked the Pakistanis was that there was not a word of regret offered by the US military officials on the killing of so many soldiers of an allied country. There was also the question of national sovereignty; Pakistan's air space had been violated.

Hina Rabbani Khar, the first Pakistani woman foreign minister and the youngest, sounded more hawkish and wanted all cooperation with the US to be suspended. Coming from a feudal background, she got elected as a member of the national assembly for the first time in 2002 from one of the most backward rural areas in southern Punjab.

Previously, this seat had been occupied by her father. But in 2002, a new rule, instituted by General Musharraf, required candidates to have a university degree, which her father didn't, therefore, he was ineligible to stand in the elections. Since Hina was the only one in the family to hold a university degree, she was chosen to contest on the family constituency and, when elected, was the youngest member in the national assembly.

Hina Khar was appointed the country's foreign minister in March 2011 after the removal of Shah Mahmood Qureshi in the aftermath of the Davis episode. She soon proved her mettle as a tough negotiator. At the DCC meeting, she did not mince her words: 'It is an attack on our sovereignty,' she said. What angered her most was the American hubris. 'They are not even willing to admit that it was not a mistake and apologise for the action.'[33]

The Salala incident, the DCC meeting concluded, was an 'unprovoked and intentional action.' But General Kayani cautioned against closing all doors while dealing with the US: 'One basic lesson of diplomacy is to always keep a window open,' he said with some calming effect. However, he was also under tremendous pressure to prove that he could stand up to the US.[34]

The humiliation of the Abbottabad raid continued to haunt him. He had already decided to break all cooperation with the US. One of the first steps taken, that could hurt the US the most was the decision to close the Ground Line of Communication (GLoC) to NATO forces in Afghanistan. This was going for the jugular. At the DCC meeting, General Nadeem showed the impact of the closure of the GLoC on NATO supply lines.

There are two routes from Pakistan to Afghanistan. Both routes start in Karachi, Pakistan's principal port, on the Arabian Sea. From there, one route crosses the Khyber Pass, enters Afghanistan at Torkham, and terminates at Kabul, supplying northern Afghanistan. The other route passes through Balochistan province, crosses the border at Chaman, and ends at Kandahar in southern Afghanistan. NATO used these routes to transport fuel and other supplies, but it was not meant for transporting weapons.

More than 80 per cent of all supplies to the NATO forces went from Karachi to Afghanistan through the land route, while 80 per cent of the supplied fuel came from Pakistani refineries; this made NATO operations highly dependent on the Pakistani supply lines and its suspension was a major blow to the NATO forces in Afghanistan.

Pakistan tried to use this to leverage the US. There are several alternative routes included in the Northern Distribution Network, but they were all much longer and far costlier. It was not the first time that Pakistan had shut down the NATO supply line. In 2010, Pakistan suspended the supplies to Afghanistan for one week when a NATO helicopter killed two Pakistani soldiers within Pakistan's borders. It was going to be a much longer suspension this time.

In addition to blocking NATO logistical supplies from crossing into Afghanistan, Pakistan also ordered the CIA to vacate the Shamsi airbase in the western Balochistan province from where drone strikes were launched.[35] It was also decided to boycott an international conference on Afghanistan to be held in December in Bonn, Germany. Scheduled meetings with US officials were also cancelled.

Pakistan even refused the Pentagon offer to participate in the investigation into the Salala strikes. Previous cross border incidents like the 2010 American helicopter attacks on Pakistani forces were investigated jointly and the fallout quickly contained. But a year of crises that began with a CIA contractor shooting two Pakistanis to death on a street in Lahore and then the Navy SEAL raid on an Abbottabad compound that killed Osama bin Laden, now risked ending with the breach of an alliance that had been the cornerstone of US national security policy for the past decade.

Pakistan's stance had also hardened this time because of the public outrage on the killing of so many soldiers. On Pakistan's refusal to cooperate in the investigation, the Pentagon decided to rely on phone conversations, e-mail exchanges, and images collected by Predator drones and by other reconnaissance and surveillance aircraft that were operating in or near the region before, during, and after the air strikes.

What angered Pakistani leaders the most about the Salala incident was the statement issued by the White House a day after the Salala attack, in which it said that senior US officials had expressed their condolences to Pakistan and their 'desire to work together to determine what took place, and our commitment to the US–Pakistan partnership which advances our shared interests, including fighting terrorism in the region.'[36] But there was no apology.

Meanwhile, Secretary of State Hillary Clinton called Foreign Minister Hina Khar to extend her 'deepest condolences.' She told her that the Obama administration would support NATO's investigation into the incident. She sounded sympathetic, but the administration was not willing to go beyond a promise for an investigation. Khar had developed a good rapport with her US counterpart but the phone conversation was not calming.

General Martin Dempsey, US Chief of Army Staff, and appointed the Chairman of the Joint Chiefs of Staff on 1 October 2011, following Admiral Mullen's retirement, conceded that Pakistan's anger was justified, given the loss of life. However, Dempsey would not apologise, saying he did not know enough about the incident and an inquiry was still being conducted. These condolences by the US officials, without an apology, added to the humiliation and toughened Pakistan's stance. President Hamid Karzai feared that the Salala incident could push things to a wider conflagration.

The situation took a more serious turn when General Kayani issued a new 'command communiqué,' that allowed his troops to 'respond on their own when attacked, without waiting for orders from the command.' He also warned that any act of aggression would be responded to, with 'full force, regardless of its consequences.'[37]

That indicated a dramatic change in the Pakistan military's rules of engagement. Until then the troops deployed along the Afghan border were only meant to try and prevent cross-border attacks by Taliban insurgents and combat local militants. The new order seemed intended to improve morale and ease anger among the rank and file and elements of the officer corps.

The issue could have been easily defused with just an apology. But the Obama administration was not willing to do so even at the risk of a complete breakdown of relationship with a key regional ally. The Salala incident was a defining point in the post-9/11 relationship between Washington and Islamabad and it seemed to close the narrative of being a strategic partner.

12 | Sorry, But 'No' Sorry

Days after the Salala incident, President Barack Obama phoned President Asif Ali Zardari to express his sorrow over the deaths of the soldiers and made it clear that 'this regrettable incident was not a deliberate attack on Pakistan' and reiterated the US's 'strong commitment to a full investigation,' while stopping short of offering a formal apology.[1]

Zardari was totally incoherent in his conversation with Obama and his ramble was completely off context. There was a precedent for this behaviour: Zardari had an existing bipolar problem. In addition, for the past few days, Zardari had been seriously ill and had collapsed with loss of consciousness. His bipolar problem had got aggravated with the ongoing clash with the military leadership over what was described as the 'Memogate issue.'[2]

Tension had risen between the civilian government and the military when Mansoor Ijaz, a Pakistani-born businessman, claimed in a column on 10 October 2011, in the *Financial Times* (FT) that a Pakistani diplomat had asked him to deliver a memorandum, allegedly from President Zardari, to a top US military official seeking support of the Obama administration to prevent a possible coup and to assist the civilian government to control the military apparatus.

In his *FT* column, Ijaz claimed that he had the memo delivered in May to the top US military official, later identified as Admiral Mike Mullen, on the diplomat's instructions, a week after the Navy SEAL raid on bin Laden's compound. The memo allegedly referred to 'a dangerous devolution of the ground situation in Islamabad where no control appeared to be in place.' It added that if the military did take over, Pakistan may 'become a sanctuary for Osama bin Laden's legacy and potentially the platform for a far more rapid spread of al-Qaeda's brand of fanaticism and terror.'[3] Ijaz later identified the diplomat as

Hussain Haqqani, a Zardari ally, who had been appointed by him as Pakistan's ambassador to the US.

Mansoor Ijaz, who ran the firm Crescent Investment Management LLC in New York, was well known in Washington for his dubious activities. He was a man of doubtful credentials and his motive behind the disclosure raised many questions. In the past he had been very critical of Pakistan's military establishment, though he had close connections with some Pakistani civil and military leaders.[4]

In 1996, he was accused of trying to extort money from Pakistan's government in exchange for delivering votes in the US House of Representatives on a Pakistan-related trade provision. He had also claimed in the past to have had arranged meetings between US officials and former Pakistani prime ministers Benazir Bhutto and Nawaz Sharif.

On the day bin Laden was killed in May, Ijaz wrote that elements in the ISI had almost certainly acted as his 'knowing babysitter.' Yet despite this, in October—after the publication of the article in the *FT*—Ijaz secretly agreed to meet the ISI chief, General Shuja Pasha, at a hotel on Park Lane, London, where he shared the record of his alleged communications with ambassador Haqqani over the memo.[5]

Ijaz said that he saw Pasha because he became concerned that he had been tricked into breaking Pakistani or American law.[6] The enigma of the hard-talking Ijaz, a frequent media commentator, was that he was a ferocious critic of Pakistan's military who had now turned him into its greatest weapon against the government.

Ambassador Haqqani denied that he had any role in crafting the message. But the military took the purported memo, inviting US intervention, very seriously declaring it an act of 'treason.' The Generals had never trusted Haqqani as being too close to the Americans and the scandal, in which he was accused of seeking US help to contain the Pakistani military and stave off a possible military coup, provided them an opportunity to get him out. What worried Zardari and his government was that the buck would not stop at Haqqani.

There was a fear that the treason accusations could reach all the way up to the president. Admiral Mullen had already stated that he neither knew Mansoor Ijaz, nor had he communicated with him. But a Pentagon spokesman confirmed that the former US Joint Chiefs of Staff had received the 'secret memo' through a known intermediary though Mullen doubted its authenticity and didn't take it seriously. 'There was nothing in the memo which indicated that it was from President Zardari,' said a Pentagon spokesman.[7]

Haqqani was called back to Islamabad on the instructions of General Kayani. On 22 November, just days before the Salala incident, he appeared before the top civil and military leadership in a meeting that took place at the Prime Minister House in Islamabad between President Zardari, Prime Minister Gillani, General Kayani, and General Pasha. Haqqani was asked to resign. The ouster of the controversial ambassador, however, did not resolve the crisis or bring down the civil-military standoff on the issue.[8]

In a statement to *Reuters*, Haqqani said that, 'This is not about the memo, this is about bigger things.' A statement issued by the prime minister's office said that Haqqani had been asked to resign to make the inquiry process transparent. 'If he is cleared in the inquiry, the ambassador may be reinstated. The resignation did not mean that Haqqani was guilty,' it said.[9]

The matter turned into an explosive political issue with the Supreme Court taking up the case. The petition was filed by the opposition PML (N) with Nawaz Sharif himself appearing before the court as one of the petitioner's in the case, accusing Haqqani of being behind the 'treacherous' act against the country. The apex court later set up a 'Commission of Enquiry' to probe the allegation. Although Haqqani was sacked, he was not allowed to leave the country on the orders of the Supreme Court as he was required to appear before the Commission.

So scared was the government about the former ambassador's safety that he was kept at the Prime Minister House for his protection. The PM feared that Haqqani could be kidnapped by military intelligence and forced to implicate Zardari in the case. The government's fate, in their eyes, was linked to Haqqani's security.[10]

In the midst of the crisis, in the first week of December—in the immediate aftermath of the Salala incident following on the Memogate issue—Zardari had a breakdown and collapsed in the presidency. The doctors advised that he be taken abroad for medical treatment. It was decided to fly him to Dubai.[11]

As he was boarding a helicopter at the presidency, a spectacle unfolded at the helipad. Zardari insisted on taking Haqqani with him; he didn't want to leave the former ambassador behind. But before Haqqani could board the helicopter, the president's military secretary pulled him back. He made it clear that the helicopter could not fly with Haqqani on board as he was not supposed to leave the country, as per the Supreme Court decision.

The PM, who was also at the helipad and knew the consequence of any attempt to take Haqqani out of the country, finally convinced Zardari that Haqqani could not leave. Zardari agreed but on the condition that Haqqani's wife, Farah Ispahani, a member of parliament who also worked as a presidential aide, would accompany him.[12]

Zardari's sudden departure from the country and rumours that he had suffered a breakdown deepened the country's political crisis. The military's suspicion about Zardari's involvement in the plot to replace senior military officials with the support of the US, gave the generals a reason to act against him. There was apprehension that his ill health could be used as an excuse to get him to stand aside in favour of a new man close to the military.[13] Political uncertainty gripped the country.

In an attempt to end the speculation, the government made public the medical report from the doctors at the American Hospital in Dubai that said Zardari's condition was improving. But it failed to end the speculation. There was scepticism about the government's assurance that the president would be back soon.

The civil and military confrontation came to a head when General Kayani and the ISI chief, General Pasha, appeared before the Supreme Court Commission of Enquiry to record their rejoinder, without getting government clearance, and confirmed the existence of the memo. The civilian and military leadership were now publicly standing against each other on the scandal and relations between them had reached their lowest point since the 1999 coup. Both sides appeared to be digging in their heels.[14]

Prime Minister Gillani launched a scathing attack on the military establishment, accusing the Generals of 'conspiring against the elected government.' In a speech in the national assembly, Gillani warned the military against establishing 'itself as a state within a state. It is unacceptable,' he declared. He also questioned the credibility of the armed forces over the bin Laden debacle that 'resulted in questions being asked on the global stage about Pakistan's sincerity in battling terrorism.'[15]

It was the strongest public criticism of the military establishment by an elected leader in Pakistan's recent history. It was a very sensitive issue for the military leadership who had faced public outrage over the presence of the world's most wanted terrorist in the country and the US special forces raid on Pakistan's soil, an act seen by many Pakistanis as a violation of sovereignty.

Furthermore, the prime minister accused the military of acting unconstitutionally over the Memogate scandal. 'We will have to come out of this slavery. If somebody thinks they are not under the government, they are mistaken. They are under the government and they shall remain under the government, because we are the elected representatives of the people of Pakistan,' Gillani told the lawmakers.[16]

As the crisis escalated, Gillani sacked the defence secretary, a retired General, for unspecified 'gross misconduct and illegal action.'[17] The action was clearly intended to get back at the military. Retired Lt. Gen. Naeem Khalid Lodhi was the most senior civil servant responsible for military affairs, a post usually seen as the military's main advocate in the civilian bureaucracy. Historically, the defence secretary's post has been filled on the recommendation of military chiefs, who often chose retired generals.

Gillani's blitz against the military and his action against the defence secretary drew a strong response from the military leadership. In a rare public statement, the military denounced the PM for accusing it of violating the law by responding to the investigation. 'There can be no allegation more serious than what the honourable prime minister has levelled,' a statement issued by a military spokesman said. 'This has very serious ramifications with potentially grievous consequences for the country.'[18]

For the military, the sacking of General Lodhi had deeper implications: in the event, a PM decided to dismiss the army or intelligence chiefs he needed to have the defence secretary on his side. Gillani appointed Nargis Sethi, a senior civil servant and his close associate, as defence secretary.

It was now an all-out war between the civilian government and the powerful military, worsening political instability in the country. The tough stance by civilian leadership put the military in a box and it seemed as though a coup was imminent. Meanwhile, General Kayani changed the command of Triple One Brigade, which is responsible for the security of Islamabad, and in case of a military takeover, it has a critical role. The military said the change of command was a routine matter. General Kayani dismissed coup rumours as speculation and declared his support for democracy. But the assurance didn't lower the tension. Given the timing, it was perceived to be a signal.

In the midst of coup fears, General Dempsey called General Kayani. There was concern in Washington over growing instability in Pakistan despite their standoff on the Salala incident. Some reports suggested that the US General sought an assurance from General Kayani that there was no coup plan by the Pakistani military. But a Pentagon spokesman was more cautious in his comments saying that it was a matter for the Pakistani military and civilian leaders to work out.[19]

The military was infuriated by what it believed to be Zardari's attempts to ally with Washington against it. While it was apparent that the army didn't want to stage another coup just four years after democracy was restored, it did want a civilian regime that was more responsive to its wishes. So, it relied on the seemingly partisan courts to throw out the government instead.

The controversial memo contained promises of action against the military that the government clearly couldn't have met. There was indeed some credence to the allegation that the entire 'Memo' saga was farcical and the crisis had been engineered on the basis of an unsigned memo, the contents of which were exceedingly unrealistic.

The Memogate saga's standoff finally came to an end after the Supreme Court allowed Hussain Haqqani to travel to the US in late January 2012, on the understanding that he would return when summoned by the inquiry commission. Apparently, the military had sensed that the crisis could have far-reaching implications for the country and for its institution. General Kayani later confided that he didn't want to stretch out the matter. For him, the purpose was served after Haqqani was sacked. The former ambassador was never to return.

Pakistan's domestic political crisis also had an impact on its relations with the US. There was still no resolution of the suspension by Pakistan of the supply line to NATO forces in Afghanistan. The US tried to use alternative routes through Russia, Kazakhstan, Uzbekistan, and Tajikistan, known as the 'Northern Distribution Network.' But the distance was much longer and transportation cost more.

The US was paying six times more to send supplies to troops in Afghanistan via these alternative supply routes. The figures placed the new US costs at $104 million per month, roughly $87 million costlier per month than when the cargo was transported via Pakistan. The higher costs incurred on the alternative supply routes also exerted pressure on the Obama administration to negotiate with Pakistan.

In the midst of all this uncertainty, Sherry Rehman was appointed as Pakistan's new ambassador to the US replacing Hussain Haqqani. She arrived in Washington in the first week of January 2012. A former journalist, Sherry Rehman had earlier held a federal cabinet post in the PPP government. A consummate politician, she had been reluctant to accept one of the most critical and coveted diplomatic jobs. The Haqqani episode had added to the tension with Washington and it was important for the government to get military approval for the new appointment.

US-educated and a suave communicator, Sherry was not unfamiliar to US officials and Washington's think tanks. But it was not an easy time for the new Pakistani envoy with the relations between the two erstwhile allies at breaking point. There had not been any high-level official contact between Washington and Islamabad since the Salala incident. Initially, Sherry's main contact in Washington was Marc Grossman, the special envoy for Pakistan and Afghanistan at the State Department. But she had to learn to navigate different power centres in Washington.

At the White House, Sherry found a more receptive interlocutor, Douglas Lute, who was the NSC advisor dealing with Pakistan and Afghanistan. He was a very pleasant person to deal with. However, the discussion between the two would get stuck on the demands for an 'apology' from her and the 'opening of the GLoC' from the American side. 'There is no question of apology,' Lute told her in their first meeting at the White House.[20]

Not intimidated, Sherry shot back, 'We are allies and you can't even apologise for an incident that has killed our soldiers?' She reminded him of American fair play. It resonated with Lute. 'Let's work together to find some way out,' he said.

The two developed a good rapport and would meet regularly. Lute was fond of Pakistani food, particularly barbecue and *gulab jamun*, and Sherry would often invite him for dinner. But there was still no sign of the US officials budging from their position of 'no sorry.'[21]

Nonetheless, Sherry felt that the US administration was keen to restore relations with Pakistan. The closure of the GLoC had exponentially increased the cost to the US of sending supplies to the troops in Afghanistan. And Pakistan's cooperation was still critical for the US and NATO forces fighting the Taliban insurgency that was getting stronger.

Hillary Clinton too, had a more sympathetic position on the apology issue. From the very outset, she had suggested that the US should say 'sorry' and move on. But the White House ignored her. For his part, Obama was worried that offering an apology would give his

Republican opponent an excuse to accuse him of 'apologising for America.' Meanwhile, a series of attacks by the Taliban in Kabul and other Afghan cities had hardened the US stance. The attitude of the Pentagon was that Pakistanis had got what they deserved for supporting the Taliban.

Another contentious issue that would often come under discussion with the US officials was the increasing drone strikes by the CIA in Pakistan's tribal region, causing civilian casualties. The US Navy SEAL raid in Abbottabad and the air strike on the Salala border post killing Pakistani soldiers had also raised the sovereignty question. One of Sherry's main talking points in Washington was: shut down drone strikes, they are creating problems for Pakistan. 'It is an exhibition of America's reckless use of extrajudicial killings,' she burst out during a meeting at the State Department. 'But your leaders approve,' retorted Grossman.[22] He was not wrong.

But Pakistan's position on drone strikes had changed with the breakdown of the bilateral relationship from the beginning of 2011. Some US officials acknowledged the problem, but nothing changed; drone strikes had become a weapon of choice for the Obama administration.

Sherry had also developed a good rapport with General Dempsey. 'We are very keen to restore relations with Pakistan,' the General told the ambassador at a dinner at his house. 'Then stop drone strikes,' demanded Sherry. 'That may not be possible,' said the General, parroting what Sherry had already heard in her previous meetings with US officials. An ongoing US concern was Pakistan's support for the Haqqani network, the most lethal of the Afghan Taliban factions. General Dempsey too had raised the issue with Sherry. A series of militant attacks in Kabul was blamed on the network.

'First make up your mind whether you want us to eliminate them or bring them to the negotiating table,' Sherry told the General. 'You can't have both.' General Dempsey went red-faced. He was not expecting such blunt talk from the young envoy. There was silence for a few seconds as the General tried to calm himself down. 'Please stop using the H word for one year and I assure you we can find some solution,' Sherry argued.

That hit the right cord. 'I think ambassador, you are right,' said the General after a long pause. And for the next few months the Pentagon didn't raise the issue, at least publicly. But the rising Taliban insurgency and alleged support from elements in the ISI remained a point of conflict.

The growing use of Improvised Explosive Devices (IED) by insurgents against the coalition forces, with devastating effect, was yet another issue added to the already explosive mix. US officials confronted the ambassador with reports that potassium nitrate, used for making these explosive devices, were supplied from Pakistan. The chemical was used as a precursor in some of the products in Pakistani fertiliser factories. It was certainly a serious situation. With a huge porous border and the support network for the Taliban among Pakistani religious groups, it was not possible for Pakistani security agencies to stop the transportation of the chemical to Afghanistan.

Sherry was invited for a briefing at the CIA headquarters at Langley where she was given a slide presentation by Mike Morell, acting director CIA, on the devastation caused by IED attacks carried out by the Taliban and the connection that led to Pakistan. But the evidence presented at the briefing didn't impress her. Sherry later sent a report to Islamabad about the briefing titled 'A movie and a dinner.'[23]

After prolonged deliberation, the US agreed to help Pakistani fertiliser factories find an alternative precursor for their product. The problem seemed to have been resolved. Then retired General David Barno, who was head of the Combined Forces Command-Afghanistan from 2003–2005, gave a testimony to the Congressional Committee accusing Pakistan of helping make the IEDs. Sherry was furious and called the State Department to complain. There was no further mention of the issue by the Pentagon or the State Department for a long time.

Meanwhile, the issue of apology over the Salala incident also got complicated because of internal discord between the Pakistani civil and military leadership as well as differences within the Obama administration. An opportunity to end the conflict emerged when Hillary Clinton met with Hina Khar in London on 23 February 2012, at a conference on Somalia.

At a sideline meeting that lasted more than one hour, Hillary Clinton told Hina Khar that she was willing to tender a public apology on the tragedy to end the crisis. But Khar told her to wait till the joint session of parliament had decided on the terms for resetting relations with the US. Ms Khar had received instructions from the PM on the phone as she was walking with Hillary Clinton to the meeting room. Clinfton responded by saying that while she fully respected the Pakistani parliament's need to review relations carefully, she also stressed the need to resume joint work. The opportunity for an early resolution of the standoff was lost.[24] Meanwhile, President Obama was held back by the military from making an apology in a televised message.

However, prolonging the closure of the GLoC was also not in Pakistan's interest. Recognising the need to repair relations with the US, the parliament authorised the government to take the decision on the reopening of the GLoC supply line and resetting relations between the two countries on new terms. But it was not going to be an easy decision for the government to take, given the growing anti-American sentiment in the country. The upcoming parliamentary elections were another reason for the government's reluctance to reopen the supply line without the US administration responding positively to Pakistan's demand for an apology for the Salala incident.

Talks between Pakistan and the US in April 2012 failed to resolve the standoff. The Obama administration's stubbornness in refusing to tender an apology for the Salala incident remained the main sticking point. The situation became more complex with Pakistan placing an additional condition for reopening of the supply line that required the US to pay $5,000 per truck. US Secretary of Defence, Leon Panetta, rejected Pakistan's new conditionality saying, 'Considering the financial challenges that we're facing, that's not likely.'[25]

In an apparent move to break the ice, NATO invited Zardari to the Chicago Summit conference (21 May 2012) of some 60 nations to discuss Afghanistan's future. The Obama administration thought that the summit invitation could provide an incentive for a deal on resuming supply shipments through Pakistan.[26] But if there was any hope of Pakistan's fractured relations with the US getting back on track soon, it came crashing down in Chicago.

On the eve of Zardari's departure to Chicago came the conviction, on treason charges, of Dr Shakeel Afridi, a CIA operative who helped in the US mission to kill Osama bin Laden.[27] Afridi's trial, under Pakistani tribal laws, and a sentence for 33 years in jail, got the angry US lawmakers to propose a cut in aid to Pakistan. The timing of the controversial verdict, by an assistant political agent in FATA, could not have come at a worse time.

While there were many sources of tension building up for a long time, the situation also owed a lot to the way the leadership of both countries had handled these critical bilateral relations—superpower arrogance on the one side, and complete disarray and absence of any policy direction on the other. This was glaringly demonstrated during the Chicago NATO summit meeting. Obama's impertinent dealings with President Zardari and deliberate omission of Pakistan from the list of countries that he thanked for support in Afghanistan, was a reflection of superpower hubris.

A last-minute invitation may have won Pakistan a seat at the NATO summit to discuss the Afghan endgame, but its participation in the forum of some 61 nations and organisations, was clouded by the stalemate over reopening of the NATO supply line and other unresolved issues with the US. A handshake and a brief exchange of words at the start of the session on Afghanistan was the only direct interaction between Obama and Zardari.

'We just talked very briefly while walking into the summit,' Obama said later, indicating an unmistakable snub. This public show of annoyance and embarrassment piled on the Pakistani leader during a crucial summit meeting was unprecedented. It seemed a deliberate move to mount pressure on Islamabad as it negotiated new terms of engagement with Washington. That attitude turned a fragile process of resetting a relationship between the two countries into a debacle.[28]

An increasingly aggressive position taken by Washington had made it much harder to revive already dysfunctional relations. The Obama administration had made public humiliation a policy, especially while dealing with Pakistan, forgetting that there could be a strong reaction to it. That approach was one of the reasons for the rise of anti-American sentiments in Pakistan.

The Pakistan government was equally responsible for getting itself into this humiliating situation. A major question was whether Zardari should have gone to Chicago on just three days' notice, with some key issues like reopening of the NATO supply route remaining unresolved. Although Pakistani officials gloated over an 'unconditional invitation' to the meeting, it was not to be.

There was an expectation by the US that Pakistan would at least allow the goods stuck at the Karachi port to go through while the new transit terms were being negotiated. Either the Pakistani officials were completely oblivious of the hostile mood in Washington because of the stalemate in reopening of the GLoC or they had simply ignored it in the desperation to be invited.

It was a huge miscalculation. President Zardari got a rude shock when he was cold-shouldered by Obama. He had certainly not expected this treatment when he left for Chicago. It was apparent that the Pakistani government officials came to Chicago without any clear policy strategy. In a repeat of his conversation with President Obama, while meeting with Hillary Clinton, President Zardari was completely incoherent and talked only rhetoric without any substance.[29]

Pakistani officials were not able to place any consolidated proposal on the table and there was no clarity on how they wanted to shape the new relationship with Washington. It had been almost six weeks since parliament approved guidelines for the resetting of ties with the US, but there was no substantive policy framework in place as yet.

The negotiations with the US seemed to be stuck on the haggling on transit fees for NATO supply trucks. Instead of taking a wider strategic view of the relationship, Pakistani officials were only talking about money, earning the reputation of a rent-a-service country. There was no obvious reason why the government could not reopen the GLoC after approval by the parliament.

Despite the tension, the two countries had shared interests, particularly in bringing an end to the 11-year-old war in Afghanistan. Pakistan had a critical role to play in the Afghan endgame and a complete rupture between the two countries could be disastrous for regional stability and Pakistan's own security.

The Chicago conference endorsed an Afghan war exit strategy and a plan to transfer security responsibility to Afghanistan's own security forces by 2014. But it left many questions unanswered about a negotiated political settlement with the Taliban, crucial for a peaceful transition.[30] There was not even a mention of a regional approach, guaranteeing the neutral sovereignty of Afghanistan.

The restoration of ties between the US and Pakistan was critical for a negotiated political settlement, as well as a regional solution to the Afghan conflict. Ominously, hostility between the two countries was encouraging radicalisation. Rightwing Islamic parties, and even outlawed militant groups, were out on the streets in Pakistan opposing the reopening of NATO supply lines. There was credible evidence that rallies under the banner of 'Defence of Pakistan' were backed by elements within the security agencies to exert pressure on Washington to accept Pakistan's demands.

In the meantime, Pakistan and the US were engaged in negotiations to end the bitter impasse over the supply route with a high-level Pentagon negotiating team. The talks broke down in June when Defence Secretary, Leon E. Panetta, said US was 'reaching the limits of our patience' over Islamabad's failure to root out Afghan insurgents in its tribal areas.[31]

In the wake of Panetta's comments, Deputy Assistant Secretary of Defence, Peter Lavoy, was not allowed to meet with General Kayani.

In protest, the Pentagon called back its negotiating team. Panetta's criticism of Pakistan was indeed a setback in the talks. But the major sticking point was still the apology issue.

With the impasse getting even more entrenched, Hillary Clinton took charge, telling the White House that 'enough was enough.' Her position was clear; the US should say 'sorry' without further delay, to end the standoff that had been hurting US interests. She asked her deputy at the State Department to fly to Islamabad to negotiate with General Kayani. The White House acquiesced to Clinton's demand to salvage the situation.[32]

Hillary Clinton's cordial relations with Hina Khar helped her to move forward. The response from Pakistan was encouraging. A week of marathon negotiations followed, that included two trips to Islamabad by General John R. Allen, the US commander in Afghanistan, and a weekend trip by Thomas R. Nides, the deputy secretary of state. Nides and Pakistan Finance Minister, Abdul Hafeez Shaikh, were principle negotiators from their respective countries. After weeks of behind-the-scene phone calls, e-mails, and meetings between Nides and Shaikh, an agreement was reached on the term that NATO supply lines will be reopened.[33]

A final agreement on the wording of Clinton's statement of her conversation with Khar came after intense behind-the-scene talks. A statement from Clinton on 2 July 2012, said: 'Foreign Minister Khar and I acknowledged the mistakes that resulted in the loss of Pakistani military lives. We are *sorry* for the losses suffered by the Pakistani military. We are committed to working closely with Pakistan and Afghanistan to prevent this from ever happening again.'[34]

The single word—*sorry*—finally resolved the seven month-long crisis that had held both countries hostage and led to the reopening of the GLoC. The wording of Clinton's statement was a much watered-down version of what she had been willing to do in February.

During their telephone call, Khar made it clear to Clinton that no lethal equipment could transit into Afghanistan through the GLoC except those meant for equipping Afghan national security forces.

Pakistan's Defence Committee of the Cabinet released a statement declaring that the agreement was in the country's best interest and a boon to the Afghanistan peace process: 'Allowing NATO convoys to enter and exit Pakistani territory would speed the withdrawal of Western forces and enable a smooth transition in Afghanistan.'[35]

Besides the apology, US also agreed to reimburse Pakistan around $1.2 billion under the CSF programme for costs incurred by 150,000 Pakistani troops carrying out counterinsurgency operations along the border with Afghanistan. Those payments had been suspended since Pakistan had shut down the GLoC routes. Pakistan, too, dropped its demand for payment of $5,000 for each truck carrying NATO's non-lethal supplies from Pakistan into Afghanistan, and agreed to keep the fee at the existing rate of $250.[36]

Both Washington and Islamabad took a step back, realising that the impasse risked transforming an extremely complicated relationship into a hostile one at a time when they still needed each other. A 'sorry' may have finally defused the situation arising from the Salala incident. But there were other sources of conflict that continued to cloud relations between the two countries. Pakistan's opposition to unilateral CIA drone strikes and Washington's allegations of Pakistan's links with the Afghan Taliban continued to remain a source of friction.

In the first week of December 2012, General Kayani and Hina Rabbani Khar met Hillary Clinton in Brussels on the sidelines of a NATO and EU conference on Afghanistan. In what was described as the 'Rabbani-Kayani charm offensive,' the Pakistani leaders stressed the need for seriously pursuing reconciliation in order to end the war in Afghanistan.[37]

This message was timely as a tangible shift in the US administration's policy towards reconciliation was discernible. This was to be Hillary Clinton's last meeting with Pakistani leaders as Secretary of State. Paying a rare tribute, General Kayani recalled that Hillary Clinton 'was a highly intelligent person.'

13 | Talking to the Taliban

It was John Kerry's first visit to Islamabad after his appointment as Secretary of State in February 2013, taking over the mantle from Hillary Clinton, as President Barack Obama was sworn in for a second term in January 2013. Kerry, as Chairman of the Foreign Relations Committee for the past four years, had been used as a troubleshooter for Pakistan by the Obama administration several times, and he was familiar with the country and its leaders.[1]

There had been a change of leadership in Pakistan as well after the general elections held on 11 May 2013, that swept Nawaz Sharif's party—the PML (N)—to power for the third time. And that led to Sharif's third stint as PM. It was a remarkable turn of fortune for a leader who was ousted from power by the military at gunpoint in 1999 and convicted on treason charges.

Sharif's return to power was yet another episode of Pakistan's ongoing political soap opera. It was also the first time in Pakistan's political history that there was an orderly transition from one elected government to another. It may not have been the same 'heavy mandate' that Sharif had enjoyed during his second term (17 February 1997–12 October 1999) in office, but it nevertheless gave him enough space and power to take tough decisions urgently needed to bring about the economic and political stability that the country needed.

The country's political landscape had changed extensively since Sharif's last term in office and it was certainly not going to be smooth sailing for the third-timer. A major challenge for the new government was how to deal with the new geostrategic reality. The decade-long US war in Afghanistan had spilled over deep inside Pakistan's territory. The country itself had become the theatre of a war unleashed by the militants and the local Taliban. More than 100,000 army troops were engaged in a bloody war with the militants in the lawless tribal regions. Pakistan had experienced a spate of attacks by the al-Qaeda-linked militants since Sharif was sworn in, raising concerns about regional stability.

With the approaching 2014 deadline for the withdrawal of US troops from Afghanistan, Pakistan needed to have a coherent national security strategy in place, with the civil and military leadership on the same page. The civilian government needed to take charge of formulating the national security and foreign policies.

But in order to do that, they needed to have proper understanding of the situation, as well as the capability, to come up with a clear national narrative. And that was largely dependent on how civil-military relations evolved under Sharif's stewardship. That had been the biggest problem during his previous two terms.

For the military leadership too, it was time for retrospection and building bridges. General Parvez Kayani's initiative in visiting Sharif and briefing him on national security issues a day after the elections seemed to have helped build confidence between the civil and military leaderships.[2]

General Kayani told Nawaz Sharif that he needed to unite the nation, and that it was imperative to evolve a strong working relationship among all institutions of the state to deal with the grave challenges faced by the country.[3]

However, given the inherent contradictions in the political system in the country, the military remained the most powerful political force in and out of political power. Despite initial overtures by General Kayani, the past baggage of mutual distrust stayed on.

Meanwhile, US Secretary of State, John Kerry, landed in Islamabad late night 31 July 2013, on his way back from Kabul. An old hand in the foreign policy arena, his modus operandi was quite different from Hillary Clinton's in many ways.

The short visit was aimed at exchanging views with the new Pakistani administration and to discuss ways to revive deadlocked talks with the Taliban. Both sides were keen to start a new chapter in their relationship. President Obama had hailed Sharif's victory in May as a 'significant milestone' for Pakistan's democracy.

Sharif, like Zardari, was keen to have good relations with Washington that every government in Pakistan saw critical to stay on in power. While publicly criticising Washington, Sharif would assure US officials of his support.[4] He owed his release from prison in 2000, and being sent to Saudi Arabia, to the Clinton administration.

The Kerry visit was, therefore, a good opportunity for him to revive contacts with Washington. The Obama administration had its own agenda; it wanted the new government to come up with a clear plan to step up its campaign against groups such as the Haqqani network, which regularly attacked US forces in Afghanistan from its hideouts in Pakistan.

Sharif was conscious of the military's predominance in framing the country's foreign policy, particularly its relations with Washington. He wanted to demonstrate to the US that he was the boss. But it would not be easy.

He was upset when Kerry's itinerary showed a separate meeting with General Kayani at the GHQ in Rawalpindi. Sharif insisted that Kayani should only meet Kerry as a part of the Pakistani delegation at the Prime Minister House. But he reluctantly agreed to let the matter rest, when told by his aides that a change in the programme may not be acceptable to US officials.[5]

Kerry had previously met Sharif when he was chairing the Senate Foreign Relations Committee and the two had developed a good rapport. Kerry had visited Sharif's home in Lahore several times. Sharif described him as 'a wonderful friend.' Before heading into a closed-door meeting, Sharif asked Kerry about his wife, Teresa Heinz Kerry, who was hospitalised after a seizure a month earlier. 'She's doing better,' responded Kerry.[6]

It was, however, a stormy session at the Prime Minister House when the two delegations met after a 30-minutes one-on-one meeting between Sharif and Kerry. As they settled down in their seats, Sharif repeated the allegation that Kerry had made in their exclusive meeting about the connection between the Haqqani network and Pakistani security agencies. Sharif looked towards General Kayani for an explanation.[7]

The army chief lost his cool and questioned the purpose of bringing up an issue that had already been discussed several times in the past. 'The US officials have never provided any evidence despite our repeated insistence,' Kayani said, raising his voice. 'I have told US officials that 'give us evidence and we will strike.' Turning towards General Martin Dempsey, Chairman of the Joint Chiefs of Staff, who was accompanying him, Kerry said that he had been informed otherwise. Dempsey kept quiet.[8]

After the meeting, Kerry took General Kayani aside and told him that he would discuss the issue again with US officials. They were to meet again in the evening at the Army House for dinner. Kayani had met Kerry several times before, and both had developed a liking for each other. Also present at the evening meeting was Lt. Gen. Zaheerul Islam, the newly appointed ISI chief who had replaced Lt. Gen. Shuja Pasha.

He came from a military family background and had headed a corps before his new assignment. He was earlier head of internal intelligence in the ISI. Islam was considered to be close to Kayani and also had a reputation of being a hardliner, particularly on India.

General Islam had visited Washington in July 2012, a few months after his appointment, where he had met his counterpart—the CIA Director, General David Petraeus. That was the time when the conflict over the Salala incident had finally been resolved after US had apologised for the killing of 24 Pakistani soldiers.

Subsequently, the NATO supply line was reopened, easing the tension between Washington and Islamabad. General Islam's three-day visit to Washington was, thus, an indication of a thaw in relations.[9]

That evening the meeting between Kayani and Kerry at the Army House continued for five hours. At the end, Kerry asked to see Kayani alone. But Kayani asked Zaheerul Islam to stay in the room. Kerry started with an apology for his morning's behaviour.[10]

He said he had checked with US officials and that Kayani was right: no substantive evidence about ISI's connection with the Haqqani network had been handed over to Kayani. With the 2014 deadline for withdrawal of US forces from Afghanistan coming closer, a major US demand from Pakistan was to bring the Taliban back to the negotiating table.

US had designated the Haqqani network as a foreign terrorist organisation in September 2012.[11] But the Obama administration deliberately refrained from designating the Taliban movement as a terrorist group because it intended to negotiate with it for reaching a political settlement in Afghanistan. There was more seriousness in the administration in Obama's second term to hold direct talks with the Taliban as the 2014 US troop withdrawal deadline edged closer. Obama, however, still faced resistance from his military establishment on conducting negotiations with the Taliban.

It was in March 2011 that US officials had, for the first time, engaged in direct talks with an emissary of the Taliban leadership. A former personal secretary of Mullah Omar, Tayyab Agha (who had been in touch with the German foreign intelligence service, BND, since the end of 2009) was brought to Munich for a meeting with a delegation from the US State Department and the CIA.[12]

Over the next few months, US officials held several secret meetings with Taliban representatives in Germany and in Qatar. Michael Steiner, Germany's special representative for Afghanistan and Pakistan, chaired those meetings. The talks were described as a preliminary exercise aimed at assuring the Taliban that the US and its allies were serious about a negotiated settlement.[13]

But after only three sessions, details of the meetings were leaked to the *Washington Post* and the *Der Spiegel* news magazine. The leaked reports made the Taliban leadership extremely nervous because of the fear that such secret parleys with the 'enemy' would not go down well with the commanders on ground.[14]

The development represented a clear shift in the attitude of the Obama administration towards peace talks with Taliban. This was first signaled in a speech by Secretary of State, Hillary Clinton, at the Asia Society in New York in February 2011, in which she said that previous requirements for talks could be considered as 'desired outcomes.' In the past, the US had set three preconditions for talks: the Taliban should break all ties to al-Qaeda, renounce violence, and accept the Afghan constitution.[15] The removal of preconditions cleared the way for the start of what was known as the 'Doha process.'

The Taliban too showed flexibility. The militia, for the first time, publicly expressed interest in negotiating with Washington, outlining a vision for talks with US officials that conspicuously excluded a role for the Afghan government. The announcement marked a major departure for the militant group that had long said it would not negotiate while foreign troops remained in Afghanistan.

The Taliban had one goal in mind—to get the release of senior Taliban leaders being held at Guantánamo. In agreeing to these mediated discussions, the Afghan government had hopes that they could turn the Taliban from a militant organisation into a political one, in order to curb violence and maintain peace. They also wanted to break the Taliban away from their support base in Pakistan.

Those preliminary interactions led to some confidence building measures, including an agreement on the opening of a Taliban liaison office in Doha in order to give Afghan and Western peace negotiators an 'address' where they could openly contact Taliban intermediaries. The opening of the Doha mission was seen as a de facto legitimisation of the insurgent group. Tayyab Agha was appointed as the head of the Taliban liaison office in Doha and authorised to meet foreign delegates as a representative of Mullah Omar.[16]

US officials had described the opening of a Taliban mission as the single biggest step forward for peace efforts. The aim was to offer protection to a few Taliban leaders in a foreign country so that the Afghan government and Taliban could begin the reconciliation process by engaging in peace talks.[17]

President Hamid Karzai had initially wanted the Taliban office to be located in Saudi Arabia or in Turkey due to their good ties with Kabul. But the Taliban saw Saudi Arabia and Turkey as being too aligned with the Afghan government to be impartial. They opted for Qatar because they thought it was more neutral and balanced. While Qatar did not recognise the Taliban regime from 1996 to 2001, they had maintained 'cordial' relations with the militant group.[18]

The US, too, was amenable to the decision to make Qatar the home for peace negotiations. Karzai eventually approved of the decision to open an office for the Taliban in Qatar. However, Karzai urged his Western allies not to negotiate with the Taliban in Qatar except in the presence of Afghan leaders. He was not happy with the situation.

There were several missed opportunities delaying the opening of the office. For example, in December 2011, an agreement seemed to be at hand for stakeholders to consider announcing the opening of the Doha office at the Bonn Conference held the same month. But Karzai's fierce opposition torpedoed this. The impossible conditions he set, also became stumbling blocks subsequently. For example, he insisted on assurances from Qatar, specifying terms for the office as determined by him. Neither the Qataris nor the Americans obliged.[19]

Initially, the US sought to keep the dialogue with Taliban independent of the ISI. That decision upset Pakistan, which wanted to be a part of the negotiations.[20] Washington was suspicious of the ISI playing a spoiler's role. However, it was not possible to keep Pakistan out of the loop as most of the Taliban leaders and their families were living in Pakistan and the insurgents were also dependent on logistical support from their allies in Pakistan. The Taliban may have also been apprehensive of the ISI, but the militia could not afford to alienate Pakistan.

Meanwhile, the opening of the Taliban mission raised the prospect of exchange of prisoners. The Obama administration had indicated that it could consider transferring five high-ranking Taliban leaders from Guantánamo to Doha, where they would be reunited with their families and placed under house arrest. In return, the Taliban was willing to release three US citizens, including Sergeant Bowe Bergdahl who they had held since June 2009.

The two sides came very close to a deal on prisoner exchange and a Taliban emissary even visited Guantánamo to meet the detainees.[21] The exchange of these detainees for the only US prisoner of war in Taliban custody, was supposed to be part of a package of confidence building measures that was supposed to include a Taliban statement disassociating itself from al-Qaeda. But the talks broke down over how these steps should be sequenced, with the Taliban insisting on the prisoner swap first.

Differences within the US administration and fear of a congressional backlash were also factoring in the impasse in the proposed agreement. In March 2012, the Taliban abandoned preliminary talks with US interlocutors, after US Army Staff Sergeant Robert Bales killed 16 people in their beds, including 9 children, in the Panjwai District of Kandahar province, home to many in the Taliban leadership.[22] The group also accused Washington of reneging on promises.

Once the Taliban suspended talks, their leaders too came under pressure from the rank-and-file to 'wait it out' and to not make concessions. But they indicated, via various channels, that this did not mean the end of the Doha process. The deadlock contributed to the 18-month hiatus in direct US–Taliban contacts.

Notwithstanding the faltering start, the agreement on the opening of a Taliban liaison office was a very significant development and a step towards the start of formal and direct negotiations between the Taliban and Obama administration. It marked a significant milestone in diplomatic efforts aimed at a negotiated settlement of the 12-year-old war.

Not being involved in the talks, the Afghan government was critical of the US initiative. Afghan opposition parties, too, had voiced their reservation over the Doha process and demanded involvement of all Afghan groups, particularly those who had fought with the militia before 2001, in any talks with the insurgents.

In order to break the logjam in the Doha talks and ease rising tension between Kabul and Islamabad, Secretary of State, John Kerry, hosted a trilateral meeting with Pakistan and Afghanistan in Brussels on 24 April 2013. The meeting was held amid a new round of recriminations between the two governments and rising nervousness on both sides of their shared border over the fast-approaching departure of US combat troops from Afghanistan.

The meeting that followed the NATO foreign minister's conference a day earlier on 23 April 2013, was attended by President Hamid Karzai and General Kayani representing Pakistan. At the time, Pakistan had a transitional government, with parliamentary elections scheduled for May. As there was no foreign minister in place, Kayani was accompanied by Foreign Secretary, Jalil Abbas Jilani.

The three leaders—Kerry, Kayani, and Karzai—met for three hours in the suburbs of Brussels at the residence of Douglas Lute, the US envoy to NATO. The tension was tangible between the Pakistani and Afghan leaders as they appeared before the media at the start of the meeting.[23]

Afghanistan had accused Pakistan of playing a double game, saying publicly that it favours talks between the Taliban and Karzai's government while privately keeping the Taliban leadership on a tight leash to prevent the negotiations from getting off the ground. Karzai was upset because of his government being kept out of the US–Taliban negotiations. He suspected that Pakistan had purposely stopped the Taliban from talking to the Kabul government.

The Obama administration had tried for several years to bring the Pakistan and Afghanistan governments together with the US in tripartite talks. Although there had been some progress, with an increase in cross-border trade and pledges of further cooperation, both sides remained mutually suspicious of each other and occasionally even hostile.

Kerry began by saying that his government was keen to resume negotiations with the Taliban and wanted a statement from them declaring their willingness to return to the negotiating table. Lute, who was also present in the meeting, said that one line would be enough.[24]

The trio looked more relaxed after a grueling session. They ate lunch together and walked the grounds of the estate as part of their meeting. Kayani and Karzai shook hands warmly at the end. Kerry promised that they would continue the dialogue in hopes of finding a way to work together on peace negotiations with the Taliban.[25] But there was still no sign of Kabul and Islamabad bridging the divide.

On his return from Brussels, General Kayani asked the ISI chief to contact Taliban leadership and persuade them to return to the negotiating table.[26] With the year's fighting season well underway, there was a division between Pakistan-based leaders and its ground commanders inside Afghanistan over whether to wait out the departure of the US forces or to join the Afghan political process; but those in favour of talks, prevailed.

The Taliban were persuaded to accept a sequence in which they would first issue the statement of restarting the dialogue process, rather than insist on the prisoner release as a prerequisite. The statement would also convey the Taliban's willingness to enter into an intra-Afghan dialogue. This was expected to include members of Kabul's High Peace Council, once this body was broadened. The Taliban agreed to this. Instead of a one-line statement, the Taliban issued a one-page long statement, thus clearing the way for the resumption of the stalled talks.[27]

The talks were revived only after Obama's re-election, changes in his national security team, and Pakistan's vigorous intercession with Washington to give the Doha track a decisive push. What injected urgency into the effort was the looming deadline of 2014 when NATO combat troops were scheduled to depart Afghanistan.

In June 2013, the Taliban finally—and officially—opened their office in Doha. The opening of the Doha office represented the first concrete sign of willingness to negotiate on the part of the two parties to the Afghan conflict: the US and the Taliban. It was the strongest signal yet of their interest in seeking a political end to the war. It also marked international recognition of the Taliban as a legitimate negotiating partner.

In acknowledgement of this recognition, Taliban representatives read out a statement at the Doha office's opening that contained two key messages which Washington had long called for and which were prerequisites for the office to open. The first was the undertaking that Afghanistan's soil would not be used to 'harm' and threaten other countries; the second was Taliban's willingness to 'meet (other) Afghans.'[28]

Both sides had stepped back from their previously held positions to reach an agreement on the office. Taliban's statement did not quite contain the language US officials may have wanted to affirm the Taliban's public 'break with al-Qaeda.' But it was accepted by Washington as 'the first step in distancing them from international terrorism.'[29]

The opening of the Taliban office was to be followed by a meeting between the US delegation led by James Dobbins, the new special representative for Afghanistan and Pakistan, and representatives of Taliban's political commission, led by Tayyab Agha. The Taliban delegation also included a member of the Haqqani network, the deadliest foe to the US in Afghanistan, that was recently declared a terrorist group.

The first issue that triggered a strong reaction was the office's sign and flag. Taliban offices flew the Taliban flag and bore signage that named the office as the 'Islamic Emirate of Afghanistan' (the Taliban-era name for the country). No sooner had President Obama described the opening of the Taliban's Doha office as an 'important first step' towards reconciliation at a G-8 summit, President Karzai announced a boycott of the Qatar process. He also suspended talks on a security deal aimed at a post-2014 US military presence in Afghanistan.

Karzai's fury over a development that was long in the making, manifested his mercurial stance of the past two years—ever since efforts to establish a negotiating channel in Qatar got underway. This time, however, Karzai's anger was prompted by Taliban's use of the 'Islamic Emirates' sign and flag at the Doha office.[30]

Kabul accused Qatar and the US of violating an understanding that the office would only be a venue for peace talks and not have the appearance of a rival Afghan embassy. However, instead of seeking to quietly resolve the issue, Karzai went public in display of rage and retributive actions. The banner became the source of immediate contention. But Karzai's fundamental problem was in joining a process that, if successful, would make him politically irrelevant.

The issue itself was swiftly resolved. Within a day, the plaque was removed, and the flag lowered. Washington acted quickly through the Qataris and also moved to placate Kabul to prevent the process from unravelling. Qatar removed both symbols after the Afghan president halted peace talks, claiming that the Taliban were being allowed to call their office an embassy and were being presented as a government in exile.

A US statement in support of the Doha office was put on hold, to wait until tempers cooled in Kabul. The talks could not take off because of Karzai's tantrum. The Taliban complained that they had been misled by the Qatari government about the flag not being an issue. Whatever the reason, a great opportunity for negotiating peace was lost.

It did not, however, obscure the significance of the Doha development or minimise the intense diplomatic effort that went into it, in which Pakistan played a vital behind-the-scene role. The members of Taliban delegation in Doha kept a low profile though they were seen at mosques, shopping malls, and registering the birth of family members at the Afghanistan embassy in Doha. Their homes were stated to be quite lavish and were paid for by Qataris.

Short of declaring victory, the Obama administration announced in the first week of June 2014 that it was ready to 'turn the page' on America's longest war. Under yet another new timetable announced by President Obama, the last US troops were scheduled to leave Afghanistan before the end of 2016, at the end of his second term in office. Although security and combat responsibilities had been transferred completely to the Kabul administration, the presence of a sizeable residual force would keep US involved in the Afghan conflict beyond 2014.[31]

With the special forces continuing to operate in Afghanistan, presumably to disrupt the al-Qaeda threat and train Afghan security forces (the very pursuits the US forces were engaged in, throughout the 13-year-long war), it effectively meant that there would be no end to the US war by the earlier 2014 deadline.

The US exit strategy seemed as confused as it was during the course of the war. With no political reconciliation with the insurgents in place, long-term stability in Afghanistan remained questionable. Apart from other factors, the US refusal to release five high-ranking members of the previous Taliban government in Afghanistan—who were being held indefinitely without charges—in exchange for the lone US soldier, Bergdahl, was a major reason for the Doha process not taking off. The trade-off question had been on the negotiating table for more than two years. The issue was directly linked with the start of a formal negotiation process between Afghan Taliban and US on the future of Afghanistan.

All five Guantánamo detainees were to be part of the Taliban negotiating team. After considerable dithering, the Obama administration finally released the five senior Taliban prisoners held at Guantánamo Bay in May 2014, in exchange for the US soldier, but the deal may have come too late for the revival of a dead negotiation process. Some US officials still remained optimistic about the resumption of engagement between the US and Taliban. 'Maybe this will be a new opening that can produce an agreement,' US Defence Secretary, Chuck Hagel, told NBC network after the exchange of prisoners.[32]

For the Afghan insurgents, the prisoners swap deal came as a great victory. The five released Guantánamo detainees, identified as Mohammad Fazl, Mullah Norullah Noori, Mohammed Nabi, Khairullah Khairkhwa, and Abdul Haq Wasiq were very important members of the ousted Taliban regime in Afghanistan. They reportedly remained influential in the insurgency movement despite having been in detention for so long. They were transferred to Qatar from Guantánamo where they stayed under travel restrictions for one year.

Taliban's supreme leader, Mullah Omar, was buoyed by the release of the five senior Taliban leaders. He described the deal as a success for the Taliban's political negotiations and a recognition at the international level of the 'Islamic Emirate as a political reality. In a rare statement, he extended his 'heartfelt congratulations to the entire Afghan Muslim nation and families of the prisoners for this big victory.' But perhaps the Bowe Bergdahl deal came too late.

There was no indication in Mullah Omar's traditional Eid message about any prospects for a resumption of direct talks with the US authorities after the deal. However, the message that year blended tones of triumph with an offer of reconciliation. While claiming victories on the battlefield, Mullah Omar called for the establishment of an inclusive government protecting the interests of all ethnic factions after the withdrawal of Western forces from Afghanistan. Indeed, for the Taliban, the prospective withdrawal of US-led combat troops was a victory for their resistance.[33]

Even if the prisoner exchange didn't lead to resumption of the dormant Doha process, it had certainly improved the prospects for some kind of engagement between the US and the Taliban. Most intriguing was the timing of the prisoner swap deal. After holding back on the decision for two years, the Obama administration moved ahead on the issue, putting aside all caution.

The secret deal came at a critical stage of the political transition in Afghanistan with the final round of the presidential elections less than two weeks away, on 14 June (the first round was held on 5 April 2014), further fuelling uncertainty about the US endgame. Without doubt the secret negotiations, that ultimately led to the prisoner exchange deal, were carried out at a very senior level from both sides. Even President Karzai was kept in the dark about the impending agreement.[34] That showed the widening distrust between the Obama administration and the outgoing Afghan leader. Their relations hit a new low after Karzai refused to sign the bilateral security agreement and blocked the Doha process. Still, one could not blame Karzai for his outrage over the deal negotiated by the US with the insurgents behind his back. The Obama administration could afford to ignore the lame duck Afghan president. But any such unilateral and secret deal with the Taliban by the Americans would not be acceptable even to the new Afghan leadership.

Having failed to disrupt the 2014 Afghan presidential elections, the Taliban had stepped up attacks on coalition forces during its summer offensive. In August that year, for the first time since the Vietnam war, a US army general was killed in a foreign war when an Afghan soldier, apparently a Taliban infiltrator, shot him at a training facility.

The killing of General Harold Greene—the highest-ranking member of the US-led coalition killed in the Afghanistan war—underscored the challenge facing coalition forces as they tried to wind down their involvement in the 13-year-old conflict. Far from vanquished, the Taliban had widened their operations, particularly in the eastern and southern region of Afghanistan, where the security transition had completely taxed Afghan forces.

Over the years, the Taliban insurgency had grown in intensity, spreading to even non-Pashtun Afghan territories. While the Taliban had consolidated their war gains in Pashtun-dominated southern and eastern Afghanistan, attacks in the northern regions had also intensified in recent years. The Taliban demonstrated their growing strength in the north by launching regular attacks in the provinces of Takhar and Badakhshan, which had been among the country's most peaceful, and in the provinces of Balkh and Samangan.

The Taliban managed to consolidate their war gains by tapping into widespread discontent with the entrenched incompetence and corruption among Afghan government officials. In many areas the Taliban had even effectively supplanted the official authorities, running the local administration and courts, and conscripting recruits.

In the protracted conflict between the Kabul government and Taliban, relatively low, but still significant levels of violence had seriously affected Afghan stability and reconstruction. Another consequence of the continued violence and political instability was a de facto partition of Afghanistan arising from a steady increase in Taliban control in Pashtun-majority areas in the southern and eastern provinces.

Meanwhile, presidential elections went ahead in Afghanistan in April, with a second round held in June. Incumbent President Hamid Karzai was not eligible to run due to term limits. The elections were controversial and failed to stabilise the situation in Afghanistan. It was a very close contest between Abdullah Abdullah, a former foreign minister and a consummate politician, and Ashraf Ghani, a former finance minister as well as a former senior World Bank executive. But there was no clear winner in the elections, marred by allegations of widespread malpractices.

A last-minute power-sharing deal averted a crisis that had threatened Afghanistan's political transition, which was extremely critical to the Obama administration's plan for troop withdrawal. Under the agreement, brokered by Washington, Ashraf Ghani was named the country's new president while Abdullah Abdullah, his rival in the bitter fight over the fraud-riddled run-off election, occupied the newly created position of chief executive. They assumed office finally in September 2014 after months of wrangling.[35]

Although far from democratic, this dubious arrangement had broken the deadlock that had delayed the transfer of power for months. However, ambiguity surrounded the newly created role of the chief executive that did not have any legitimacy in the Afghan constitution. The spectacle of the two leaders—Ghani and Abdullah—apathetically sharing an embrace after signing the agreement did not give out much hope for the durability of the bizarre power-sharing formula.

There was not even an exchange of greetings between the two leaders. The tension was palpable, as they did not even turn up for a planned joint press conference. But neither of them had a choice. Further impasse would have meant a new civil war. However controversial it might have been, the presidential election and subsequent power-sharing agreement completed the first democratic transfer of power in country's history.

For the US, political transition finally cleared the way for a bilateral security agreement to be signed by the new government, allowing its residual forces to stay on in Afghanistan beyond 2014. The presence of even a small number of foreign troops was essential for boosting the morale of the Afghan forces assuming complete combat responsibility.

The transfer of power to the new administration also marked the end of the 13-year rule of President Hamid Karzai. His exit resulted in a sigh of relief in Washington for whom the controversial Afghan leader had become a liability. Their relations had hit a new low over the last few years, especially after the outgoing Afghan president refused to sign the bilateral security agreement.[36]

With the end of Karzai's presidency, it was hoped that a new administration in Kabul could open up a new window of opportunity for Pakistan and Afghanistan to improve their relations. The security of the two countries had never been so intertwined as it was now, with the drawing down of the coalition forces. Growing instability across the border had serious implications for Pakistan's internal security, raising the cost of its counterterrorism efforts. But there was also a high wall of distrust that was going to be hard to dismantle.

14 | Storming the Witches' Brew!

It was around midnight. The study at the Army House was filled with smoke. General Parvez Kayani reflected on the momentous developments in the region—from the roller coaster Pak–US relations to the situation in Afghanistan and the battle against insurgency—under his stewardship. It was a few weeks before he took off his uniform after six years as COAS, arguably the most powerful position in the country.

Lighting another cigarette, he talked to me about his efforts to put the Doha process back on track. There was frustration in his tone as he discussed the problems in relations with Kabul and the US. 'I have told both Kabul and Washington that we don't want Taliban rule in Afghanistan. The majority of the Afghan population is Pashtun and we want them to look towards Kabul,' he said. 'We have even have been in contact with former Northern Alliance groups and had arranged several meetings between them and the Taliban.'[1]

Kayani said he tried to reassure President Hamid Karzai that Pakistan did not want to impose any particular group in power in Afghanistan, and said he even went as far as offering to 'remove the term "a friendly Afghanistan" from our official statements if it bothered the Afghan government. We can just say a stable and peaceful Afghanistan is essential for the stability of Pakistan.' But these assurances failed to breach the wall of distrust, much to his disappointment.

The General had shared his worries with President Barack Obama's administration about the potential nexus between the Pakistani and Afghan Taliban. 'We need a window to break that nexus,' he had repeatedly told US officials. What had perturbed him the most was the chronic fear of conflict on two fronts—on both the eastern and western borders. For Kayani, the concept of strategic depth was that the western border remained peaceful. The discussion became more philosophical as the night progressed.[2]

General Kayani had just made a public statement a few weeks before, on 6 October, confirming his retirement, when I met him. Considered by many analysts as one of the most powerful military generals in Pakistan's history, General Kayani was a reclusive man. He was a night person and would engage in discussions till late at night, even when in active service.

As the COAS, General Kayani had led his forces in one of the most successful counterinsurgency campaigns in a treacherous terrain. He was a thinking soldier and had a strategic mind. Although he was credited with the restoration of democracy, the spectre of military continued to cast shadows over the political spectrum. Despite constant conflicts with the civilian leadership, he didn't let the democratic process get derailed. General Kayani oversaw two democratic political transitions (2008 and 2013) during his six years in office.

It had been a roller coaster relationship with the US under General Kayani, particularly in 2011, that saw the two allies downsizing their relationship—from strategic to mere transactional. In fact, there had never been any real strategic conversion in the alignment that emerged after 9/11. The unilateral US Navy SEAL raid on Osama bin Laden's compound in Abbottabad and the fact that the world's most wanted terrorist had been living in a high security garrison town came as a personal humiliation for him, putting his authority among his soldiers at stake.

Kayani's reluctance to launch a military operation in North Waziristan, the last bastion of the Pakistani Taliban and also the base of the Haqqani network, remained a controversial issue and a major sticking point in Pakistan's relations with the US. He had consistently argued with US officials that there was no military solution to the conflict in Afghanistan and stressed the need for a negotiated political settlement with the Taliban.

General Kayani may be criticised for his inaction during his second term, but one must acknowledge the fact that it was his counterinsurgency strategy that helped re-establish the writ of the state in most of the tribal areas and the territories in Khyber Pakhtunkhwa that were lost to the Taliban. After clearing Swat, General Kayani launched simultaneous operations in South Waziristan and other tribal areas. That turned the tide against the Taliban.

On 28 November 2013, General Kayani stepped down as COAS that ended a decade long chapter of him being a focal person—first as head of the ISI and then as army chief. During the latter period, he was often in a contentious relationship with the US and a partner in an often pugnacious strategic dance. His successor certainly had his work cut out for him. In addition to continuing the fight against the Pakistani Taliban, he would have to help the US find a political solution to get out of the Afghan conflict.

Prime Minister Nawaz Sharif, not surprisingly, chose a dark horse as the country's new army chief. It was Sharif's way of playing it safe by picking a relatively low profile officer for the most critical and powerful post in the country. Having been ousted by his handpicked army chief once, and given his history of tumultuous relations with all others holding the post during his past two terms, Sharif had become more cautious.

He ignored General Kayani's recommendation and instead picked an unassuming man with no past baggage and lower down in the seniority list, who was considered a safe bet—General Raheel Sharif. His appointment signified a complete break from the Musharraf-era military hierarchy. A critical issue was how civil-military relations would evolve under the new military leadership.[3]

General Raheel Sharif belonged to a prominent military family. His elder brother, Major Shabbir Sharif, who was killed in the 1971 war with India, received the country's highest gallantry award. General Raheel Sharif himself had served as Corps Commander Gujranwala for two years and then took over as Inspector General for Training and Evaluation (IGTE) before his appointment as COAS.

As the IGTE, he had dealt with the evaluation of military doctrines and war strategies with a view to shaping future training programs.

He had changed the army's focus towards carrying out counterinsurgency operations against militants. It was he who had spearheaded the thinking in the Pakistan military since 2007 that fighting the Taliban inside Pakistan was more important than focusing on India.

General Sharif viewed jihadists, principally in the form of Pakistan's own Taliban, as the country's greatest threat, and sought the help of the US in countering it. He had a reputation of being non-political. But the army chief in Pakistan is also, politically, the most powerful man, and he soon found himself being pushed into the political power game.

With the change of guard in the army and a new Supreme Court chief justice about to take over following the retirement of Iftikhar Chaudhry, who had been known for his imperiousness, the transition of all the power centres of the state had been completed. Indeed, a remarkably smooth changeover that started with the transfer of power from one elected government to another, marked a huge stride forward for the democratic political process in the country. PM Nawaz Sharif felt more confident with the power balance strengthening his civilian rule.[4]

But it was not to last long. The trigger was the government's silence over public accusation of the ISI chief being directly involved in an assassination attempt on a leading TV talk show host that had angered the military and the spy agency. The military, too, lost all rationality by unleashing an anti-government campaign through a section of the media under its influence.[5]

Less than seven years after the return of the democratic order, the military was back in the arena, upping its public political profile. It was a return to the old cloak and dagger game between the civil and military authorities. The Nawaz Sharif government found itself in a tight corner and was forced to issue a public statement condemning the anti-ISI campaign. Things cooled down a bit, but the episode had vitiated the country's political atmosphere.

In fact, it was almost like the chronicle of a story foretold when Nawaz Sharif returned to the helm for the third time. It was partly the case of past baggage that refused to go away, keeping alive the distrust of each other. The generals had accepted Sharif's return to power, though with some reservations. And it did not take much time for the uneasy relationship to flare up.

The spark was provided by Sharif's decision to put former military leader General Pervez Musharraf on trial for treason. Interestingly, the treason case was filed more than five years after Musharraf's exit. It was Nawaz Sharif who put his nemesis in the dock, ignoring the military's warnings. He had not forgiven the former military ruler for taking him out, handcuffed from the Prime Minister House and putting him on trial for sedition.[6]

Most worrisome for the military leadership, was mounting discontent within the ranks, particularly among junior officers. It was this pressure that forced the new army leadership to provide protection to the former army chief and avoid his appearances before the special tribunal for several months. Musharraf finally appeared after a reported deal that he would be allowed to leave the country after the indictment. But that did not happen. Nawaz Sharif would not let his tormentor out. The most sensitive issue, however, that was souring relations, was the government's ambivalence over the military's war against militancy.

After returning to power, PM Nawaz Sharif had decided to open negotiations with the Tehreek-e-Taliban Pakistan (TTP), who had earlier been driven out of almost all the tribal agencies in the FATA except for North Waziristan. Even as the Sharif government continued with the 'peace dialogue' with militants, many more soldiers and officers were killed in the battlefield.

The charade of peace talks continued despite a series of gruesome terrorist attacks across the country. Hardly a single day passed without a terrorist attack causing more deaths and destruction. While the TTP owned most of these attacks, it cleverly maintained a policy of plausible deniability on some others, carried out by its affiliated groups.[7]

What was inexplicable was why the government and its negotiating team deliberately bought into this ploy and continued to play apologist for the militants' actions. While seemingly engaging in talks, the TTP used violence to keep up the pressure on the government. This strategy worked well for the militants; after each attack, the government appeared even more conciliatory. Nothing could be more pleasing for the militants than the fact that both major political forces in Punjab and Khyber Pakhtunkhwa (KP) were playing on the Taliban's turf. Not only the federal government, but also its main opposition group—Pakistan Tehreek-e-Insaf (PTI) led by Imran Khan—seemed to be reading from the same TTP book.

By dragging on the charade of a peace dialogue, the government lost a critical window available to the security forces that summer, to successfully launch an operation to destroy the terrorist bastion in North Waziristan. The consequence of indecision proved extremely costly. The demand by TTP for the withdrawal of forces from a part of South Waziristan, as a confidence building measure, was not acceptable to the military. The widening gap between the civil and military leadership was tangible. The military leadership was losing its patience.

There was a certain degree of inevitability about the military strikes on the militants' hideouts in North Waziristan in FATA after the Pakistani Taliban slaughtered more than two dozen Pakistani paramilitary soldiers in February 2014, who they had held captive since 2010, even as other elements of the group ostensibly carried on peace talks with the government.[8] The Sharif government was left with no choice but to suspend the peace talks following this tragedy. Air force jets retaliated by pounding suspected terrorist camps and taking out several militant commanders.

The failure to build a strong counterterrorism narrative had given a huge advantage to the TTP and their allies among the mainstream political parties. But the barbaric beheading of Frontier Constabulary soldiers and the posting of ghastly internet videos, showing militants playing football with their severed heads, had proved to be a turning point in defeating the narrative of violence.

The military was finally convinced that without clearing North Waziristan, Pakistan could never win the war against militancy and the time had come for decisive action. It was no longer a question of US pressure, but Pakistan's own security concerns that demanded an attack on the nerve centre of terrorism if the gains made by the security forces in earlier counterinsurgency operations were not to be negated.

In the meantime, the terrorist attacks were becoming bolder and more fearless. On 8 June 2014, militants armed with automatic weapons, rocket launchers, and wearing suicide vests, attacked the Jinnah International Airport in Karachi. The ferocious and well-coordinated terrorist attack was a grim reminder of a state under siege: the security forces cleared the airport after a fierce gun battle stretching to several hours that left 36 people dead, including all 10 attackers, and some aircraft damaged.

Most of the attackers were foreigners of Uzbek origin who belonged to the Islamic Movement of Uzbekistan (IMU), an al-Qaeda-linked militant organisation that worked closely with TTP. They had taken sanctuary in North Waziristan. The main objective of the attackers was to inflict maximum damage and high profile targets were selected to get international publicity. They were successful on both counts. The attack on the country's biggest international airport and commercial gateway carried much greater long-term consequences for the country's image and economy.[9]

It was shocking the way the terrorists, carrying huge bags of firearms and explosives, breached the supposedly high security zone and entered the runway. It was apparent that the assailants had all relevant information about the airfield—not possible without internal help. Claiming responsibility for the attack, the Taliban spokesman claimed that one of their aims had been to hijack a passenger aircraft. The attackers nearly achieved their goal.[10]

Despite the brazen attack and the fact that thousands of soldiers had been killed in attacks by militants, the government had not yet given the go-ahead to the military to eliminate militant sanctuaries in North Waziristan. One major reason for avoiding an operation was the fear of backlash in Punjab, the country's biggest province and also a stronghold of the prime minister.

The notion of Punjab's safety, first and foremost, entailed serious consequences for the country's unity and stability. Ironically, this inaction made Punjab much more insecure in the long-term. The province was the biggest incubator of sectarian extremists and jihadists. Many of the Punjabi militant groups had made North Waziristan their operational base and were working closely with the TTP and al-Qaeda.

However, the bloody siege of the international airport in Karachi proved to be the proverbial last straw. The Sharif government was left with no choice but to declare an all-out war against those responsible for the brazen assault on the state. The incident had shaken the country and demand for action became ever louder. Ending its prolonged dithering, the government finally ordered a full-scale military operation in North Waziristan, rightly described as the 'epicentre of gravity' of terrorism. The operation was finally launched on 15 June 2014, along the Pakistan–Afghanistan border.[11]

Thousands of ground troops, backed by air force jets, moved into action in the third week of June after the announcement of the offensive to reclaim control over the strategically placed territory. It was indeed the most critical battle in Pakistan's long war against militant insurgency, and far more complex than any other undertaken by the security forces in its decade-long war in this treacherous mountainous territory. Even though the military was by then much more battle-hardened and experienced in fighting insurgency, the asymmetric war was never easy. It was going to be a long haul.[12]

It was not the first time the Pakistan Army had carried out an operation in North Waziristan. The earlier expedition, launched in 2004, ended in a peace deal with the tribal militants after two years of fierce fighting. The truce turned out to be a boon for the militants; it gave them breathing space to not only regroup, but also to strengthen their positions. They were now going to be much harder to dislodge.

The biggest of the seven tribal agencies in FATA, North Waziristan was a haven for a lethal mix of foreign and local militants presenting an existential threat to the country. Many of the terrorist attacks in other countries also had roots in the region. North Waziristan had aptly been described as a 'witches' brew' with militant groups making the agency their training ground.[13]

The number of foreign fighters in the territory was roughly estimated by the intelligence agencies to be around 8,000. More than half of them—some 4,800—were reportedly Uzbek. They had not only been involved in the Karachi airport attack, but had also participated in other high profile attacks inside Pakistan. Apart from the Uzbeks, there were other foreign militant groups as well, such as networks of isolated Chechens, Libyan Islamic Fighting Group, and Chinese Uighur militants.[14]

One of the largest groups operating from the agency consisted of militants belonging to the East Turkestan Islamic Movement, which had been blamed for carrying out terrorist attacks in China's Xinjiang province. Reportedly, the majority of Arab militants had either been killed by US drone strikes or had left the region. Thousands of home-grown Punjabi militants had also moved to North Waziristan over the years, and established training camps in the restive border region.

The battle for control over this lawless region had assumed much greater significance with the approach of the 2014 deadline for withdrawal of US combat forces from Afghanistan. Al-Qaeda-linked groups presented a worrying, long-term security threat for Pakistan and, in fact, for the entire region.

A major concern for the Pakistani security forces pertained to terrorists' crossing over into Afghanistan, as had happened in the past, and the use of the sanctuaries for cross-border attacks. The Pakistani military had requested Afghan security forces to seal the border on their side to facilitate the elimination of terrorists who attempted to flee across the border.[15] But that did not work out, given the tension between the two neighbours.

The military operation in North Waziristan was only one dimension of the wider battle against militancy and violent extremism in the country. The militant groups had strong networks across the country. For a long-term solution, the government needed to develop a coherent and overarching counterterrorism strategy in order to strengthen the capacity of the civilian law-enforcement and intelligence agencies.

A major objective of the North Waziristan offensive, of course, was to secure control of the lawless territory. But military action alone didn't offer a long-term solution to an extremely complex problem. The government needed to take urgent measures to end alienation and backwardness of the FATA tribal regions as well. The military operation also provided a great opportunity to push for the long-delayed integration of FATA with the rest of the country in order to end its ambiguous semi-autonomous status.[16]

Just before the advent of winter 2014, Pakistani security forces had cleared most of the region under Taliban. Once described as the 'epicentre of terrorism,' Miranshah was reduced to mere rubble when I visited the area a few months later.[17] The long row of hotels that had sprung up over the last few years and had been used by foreign militants as rest and relaxation centres had been blown up by air strikes and heavy artillery fire.

Sitting in the midst of the destruction was a sprawling mosque, which was more than a place of worship. A labyrinth of rooms in the basement served as joint headquarters of various terrorist groups operating from the area. Soldiers stood guard on top of the half-destroyed structures. Although the town and the surrounding villages were by then under full control of the army, small bands of militants were still lurking around in the hills. The scene was not very different in Mirali, another hub of foreign fighters.

Weeks of fierce fighting had left the town completely ravaged. Nothing was left of the shops that supplied IEDs and suicide jackets to the militants, but the town was still not completely cleared of land mines. From the helicopter, the entire region looked deserted with no sign of human life except for soldiers taking position on the hills.[18]

This was what it looked like after five months of the army operation in North Waziristan. But the fighting was far from over as winter set in. Some of the high peaks were already covered with snow. The militants had scattered in small bands, engaging the troops in hit-and-run ambushes. Air force jets frequently bombed suspected militant hideouts. The Haqqani network played a pivotal role in turning North Waziristan into a centre of international militancy. Having been protected for long by the security agencies, the network had effectively been the main patron of almost all militant groups, including the TTP, operating from the agency. The footprints of the Haqqanis were visible all over Miranshah and Dande Darpa Khel.[19]

It was in the basement of the mosque in the main Miranshah bazaar that the Haqqani group held US soldiers captured in Afghanistan. An American Humvee vehicle and a pick-up used by the Afghan police were among the weapons and other stuff seized by the troops during operation. Most of the fighters associated with the Haqqani network were believed to have moved out before the offensive in North Waziristan began. The military claimed that the group would not find Pakistani territory a safe haven anymore. However, there was suspicion that they were still being protected by Pakistan's security agencies and had been moved to some other sanctuary.[20]

North Waziristan operation was unique in many ways. The role of intelligence contributed hugely to the precision targeting of militant sanctuaries. Intelligence-based crackdown on the terrorist network across the country before the start of the army operation in the agency had also helped contain the blowback in other parts of the country. Indeed, it had been the most difficult battle that the Pakistani forces had to fight in the forbidding terrain. The valour of the soldiers was critical to winning that war. The high ratio of officers killed in the operation gives some idea about the way this battle was fought; officers leading from the front had established a new legacy.[21]

In the midst of the North Waziristan operation, opposition leader Imran Khan stormed the capital on 14 August 2014, with thousands of his supporters vowing to topple the Sharif government that he accused of returning to power through rigged elections. The protests,

held more than a year after the elections, was a well-orchestrated move
to destabilise a democratically elected administration.[22] The march
on Islamabad and the demand for the prime minister's resignation
coincided with reports of increasing tension between the civil and
military leadership.

The cricket hero-turned-politician had lost the 2013 elections with his
party, the PTI, winning far fewer seats in parliament than expected.
After languishing on the sidelines of Pakistani politics for more than
16 years, Imran Khan was confident that his moment had arrived.
His biggest support came from the young generation that constituted
more than 60 per cent of the country's population.

He drew support from his slogan for change, for a 'Naya Pakistan'
(New Pakistan). However, while Imran Khan promised to fight
against the status quo parties, he hobnobbed with rightwing groups.
PTI's electoral alliance with Jamaat-e-Islami and some other Islamic
groups had raised questions about his concept of change. In fact, he
was one of the staunchest opponents to the military operation against
Pakistani Taliban.[23]

It was hard for the new PTI party to defeat well-entrenched political
parties. But Imran refused to accept electoral results, although
intriguingly, it took him more than a year to take to the street to
challenge the results. It was evident that there was no way Imran could
have forced early elections with his party's relatively small presence
in parliament. Early elections could only have been possible if Sharif
was forced to dissolve the national assembly. That, in turn, could only
happen if there was enough pressure built up through violent street
protests. All that was certainly in Imran Khan's calculations when
he decided to up the ante, declaring war on the Sharif government.

A perfectly choreographed political show unfolded in Islamabad. The
siege of the Red Zone—the high security area where parliament and
other important government offices are located—and the storming of
the Prime Minister House was supposed to be endgame for the Sharif
government. The nation was gripped by the spectacle of a violent mob
rampaging through Constitution Avenue.[24]

The government had called in the army to protect the capital. Article 245 of the constitution had routinely been used in conflict zones in order to give legal cover to security forces fighting insurgencies. But this provision had rarely been invoked in urban areas in times of peace. One oft-repeated argument offered by the government was that the invocation of Article 245 was linked with the operation in North Waziristan, meant to give legal cover to the troops dealing with any militant backlash.[25]

The Sharif government had miscalculated, in taking for granted, that the army would come to its rescue at this time of crisis. It was, in fact, the other way around. The troops deployed at the Red Zone refused to act against the protesters who had besieged parliament and the Prime Minister House. Instead, the generals called on the political leadership to expeditiously resolve the crisis politically and without the use of force.

It was the second such warning by the army in as many weeks. The military felt empowered to do so as the situation seemed to be slipping out of government's control. The warning showed that the centre of gravity of political power had shifted to the GHQ. However, parliament rallied around the government to save the system, giving the prime minister some breathing space. The joint session of parliament continued for more than two weeks, sending a strong message to the military that no unconstitutional move to remove the elected government would be acceptable.[26]

As hostilities grew, the prime minister reportedly thought of sacking General Zaheerul Islam, the ISI chief, for allegedly trying to destabilise the civilian government.[27] That brought the confrontation to a head. Defence Minister Khawaja Asif, accused the ISI chief of having encouraged Imran Khan's anti-government march. Specifically, the minister said, Islam had a 'personal grievance' against the Sharif government. The PM was forced to back down. Khawaja Asif was subsequently sidelined and snubbed at a dinner with army generals. His position as defence minister became completely irrelevant.

Despite the backing of a group of generals, if not the army chief's, Imran failed to extend the protest to other cities and bring down the government. The siege of Islamabad dragged on for months, affecting governance, but parliament stood firm and refused to succumb to pressure. The intensity of the siege started to recede after General Islam and some other commanders retired in November 2014. The threat of a coup may have dissipated but the entire episode had intensified the civil-military tension. Imran Khan needed a face-saving option to call off his anti-government campaign.[28]

And then the unthinkable happened on 16 December 2014. Taliban took their war to a ruthless new low with an assault on a crowded school in Peshawar that killed 149 people—134 of them uniformed school children and other staff members. It was the deadliest terrorist attack in country's history. During an eight-hour rampage at the Army Public School in Peshawar, KP, six gunmen, all foreigners (one Chechen, three Arabs, two Afghans) wearing suicide jackets, stormed through the school corridors and assembly hall, firing at random, and throwing grenades.[29]

Some of the 1,100 students at the school were lined up and slaughtered with shots to the head. Others were gunned down as they cowered under their desks, or forced to watch as their teachers were riddled with bullets. A rescue operation was launched by the Pakistan Army Special Services Group (SSG), who killed all six terrorists and rescued 960 people.

A TTP spokesman said the attack was in retaliation for the continuing military operation in the North Waziristan tribal region. The attack demonstrated how Pakistani Taliban's war had often been taken out on the country's most vulnerable citizens. It also reflected the failure of the security agencies to counter the ongoing terrorist threat. PTI's 126-day-long siege of Islamabad ended.

The Army Public School (APS) Peshawar massacre was described as the 9/11 of Pakistan, but the government's response was unforgivable. Consultation with other political parties on a critical national security issue was one thing, but abdication of its responsibility was something else. It was shameful that it took the deaths of over 130 school children for the government to wake up to the need for a coherent counterterrorism strategy and even then, the task was assigned to a multiparty committee. Even a tragedy of such unimaginable proportions had failed to shake the political leadership out of its inertia and get Prime Minister Sharif to adopt a more proactive role.[30]

While the government 'outsourced' the task of framing a national counterterrorism policy to a multiparty committee, the military took charge of deciding on a plan of action. The picture of the meeting at the GHQ showed that it was not Sharif, the PM, but Sharif, the COAS, who was at the helm. Perhaps it was just wishful thinking to expect a committee, comprising members of political parties with diverse views on the very meaning of militancy and violent extremism, to come out with any comprehensive plan of action.[31]

Beneath the rare show of unity over the APS tragedy, the divide was even more apparent. While seemingly united in grief over the ghastly massacre, there was still no clear national narrative about how to deal with those responsible for such a horrific crime. It was not just the matter of the six killers who slaughtered innocent children, but also the apologists for militant groups that continued to operate with impunity.[32]

While a counterterrorism policy had long been under discussion, it never took shape despite some major terrorist attacks claiming thousands of lives. In the aftermath of the APS attack, the government declared that it would not make any distinction between the 'good Taliban' and the 'bad Taliban,' but there was still no clarity about extremists and jihadi groups who did not fall in either of these two brackets.

It was this very ambiguity that had harmed the country's national security more than anything else and turned the country into a breeding ground for militancy. It was the same group with whom the government had been engaged with in peace talks just a few months ago, that had claimed responsibility for the slaughtering of the school children, and other major terrorist strikes prior to that.

Although the military had a critical role in the internal security policy, it should have been primarily the responsibility of the elected civilian leadership to take lead and decide on the course of action. This was certainly not the case. The government's inaction and apathy had shifted initiative to GHQ.

Within hours of the APS incident, apparently on the insistence of the military, the government lifted the moratorium on executions, following which, several convicted militants were hanged. For many, all these actions were justified under the prevailing circumstances. Yet they were not a substitute for a coherent counterterrorism policy. Though both the civilian and military leadership had pledged to fight militants of all hues, there was no indication of any action taken against those openly preaching jihad against other countries. Mere condemnation of the Peshawar incident didn't make them acceptable.

The APS massacre could have become a turning point in Pakistan's struggle against militancy and terrorism—but only if the political and military leaders sincerely adhered to their pledges. The tragedy had united the nation as never before; even those who had refused to accept it as Pakistan's own war had a change of heart. But the resolve didn't last long. Pakistan's response to the militant attacks had mostly been reactive with no clear strategy for a decisive war.[33]

Military coups in Pakistan have always had a certain element of predictability and imminence about them. One could almost see them unfolding. There was nothing subtle about them—always a swift and hard power play. This time perhaps, there was a different phenomenon at play: an incremental shifting of power without tanks rolling on the streets. Even the term 'soft coup' may not be an appropriate one. It was more of an assertion of power. It was indeed a dramatic turnaround from a year and half ago when Pakistanis celebrated the first-ever transfer of power from one democratically elected government to the next. Many had then considered military rule as a relic of the past.

It was not just about the 21st amendment, passed by both the national assembly and the senate on 6 January 2015, and which received presidential assent by Mamnoon Hussain a day later, on 7 January. This amendment established speedy military trial courts, for a maximum period of two years, for terrorist offenses, for waging war against Pakistan, and acts threatening the security of Pakistan. The shifting of the power base this time was a far more subtle and significant shift: it was about the acceptability of the return of the military as an arbiter of power by political leaders themselves and the public in general. The generals, sitting among the civilian leaders, virtually dictating a national counterterrorism action plan, were only one of the manifestations of this new reality.[34]

It was not surrender as was being described by some analysts, but more of an abdication of responsibility by the civilian leadership. It was glaringly obvious that Prime Minister Sharif was not willing to lead the nation in this critical war. Shy of even coming on TV when the entire nation had sunk into a state of shock after the carnage of school children in Peshawar, he had let the generals take charge.

Prime Minister Sharif did not even bother to visit the Army Public School when the pupils returned to their classes, haunted by the memory of the massacre of their schoolmates. It was the other Sharif, the general, who was there to greet the returning children. Symbolism did matter, particularly, at a time when a national tragedy had occurred. But it went beyond symbolism. The military commanders were presiding over the provincial action committees as well, set up to implement the national action plan.[35]

It was a further reflection of the civilian administration conceding more and more ground to the military on internal security matters. The impression of the civilian government and military being on the same page in fighting terrorism was deceptive. The gap between them on counterterrorism policy and other issues was as wide as ever.

The high profile visit of General Raheel Sharif to Washington and London had further reinforced the perception that it was not the prime minister but the army chief who was in charge. This was not the first time that a Pakistani army chief had visited Western capitals, but the kind of interest that General Raheel Sharif attracted during the trips was rare, if not unprecedented. There had been a noticeable

public perception that the Western allies considered Pakistani
military as the main decision-maker and were, therefore, seeking its
cooperation in the quest for regional security. Though the military
had always had a strong say on key aspects of foreign policy, it was
now much more overtly defining overall policy direction.[36]

Such a high public profile for a chief of army staff was extraordinary,
even in a country where army rule had been the norm. While this
could be largely attributed to General Raheel Sharif's role as a military
commander leading from the front, it probably also owed a lot to
the massive publicity campaign undertaken by the publicity wing
of the military, known as the Inter-Services Public Relations (ISPR).
The life-size hoardings of portraits of Raheel Sharif springing up
across the country was not a spontaneous show of public love: it was
orchestrated. The military's influence over the electronic media had
become more effective than ever. That had also helped a great deal in
building the image of the general as a saviour.

15 | Death of Mullah Omar: Battle for Leadership

It was almost 10 p.m. on the night of 7 July 2015, when a three-member Taliban delegation, sporting their signature turbans, took their seats, facing the representatives of the Kabul government in the conference hall of the State Guest House in Murree, Pakistan. Pakistani, Chinese, and US officials, in an observer status, were seated on the sides.

It was the month of Ramadan, so that was the reason for the after-dinner overnight sitting. Murree, about 40 miles from the capital Islamabad, was chosen to maintain some confidentiality. It was the first direct interaction between the Taliban and US-backed Kabul administration, though some informal contacts had been made between the two sides in the Chinese city of Urumqi and, later, in Norway.

While the Taliban were represented by mid-level leaders based in Pakistan, the Afghan government, significantly, sent a sizeable delegation to ensure that all major Afghan power groups were represented. Since most of the participants from both sides were ethnic Pashtuns, the discussion was largely in Pashtu or Dari.[1]

Both sides presented their views forcefully, but the Taliban representatives were much more aggressive. They taunted the Afghan delegation that the Kabul government could not provide security even in Kabul. The atmosphere, however, didn't turn acrimonious.[2] It ended with both sides sharing *sehri*, the pre-dawn meal Muslims eat before a new day of fasting begins, consisting of tea, omelettes, yoghurt, fruit, curry, and *paratha* (flatbreads). The meeting ended with a promise of continuing the talks. White House spokesman, Josh Earnest, called the talks 'an important step toward advancing prospects for a credible peace.'[3]

239

The recently elected Afghan President, Ashraf Ghani, had made the opening of a political process with the Taliban his top priority and he had focused on getting Pakistan to deliver the Taliban. After his installation as Afghanistan's president in September 2014, Ghani reached out to Pakistan in a marked departure from former president Hamid Karzai's antagonistic approach towards Islamabad.[4]

President Ashraf Ghani's visit to Pakistan on 14 November 2014, promised a new beginning in the relations between the two countries. The Pakistani civil and military leadership, too, were eager to start a new chapter with the new administration in Kabul. President Ghani was given a guard of honour at the Pakistan Army's headquarters and he joined Prime Minister Nawaz Sharif in watching a cricket match between teams representing the two nations.

President Ghani told General Raheel Sharif that it was time to end 'thirteen years of undeclared hostilities.' He offered to address all the concerns the Pakistan military had about Afghanistan. Ghani said he would withdraw a request his predecessor had made for heavy weapons from India, and he proposed unprecedented transparency and cooperation between the two states' military, and intelligence agencies.[5]

He ordered the Afghan army into battle against elements of the Pakistani Taliban that had taken refuge in Afghanistan, and he agreed to a long-standing Pakistani request for Afghanistan to send officer cadets to be trained at the Pakistan Military Academy. He also proposed establishing jointly-operated border checkpoints, to promote the regulated movement of people and goods.

The two sides also signed a landmark agreement to take action against all militants and their hideouts on either side of the border without discrimination. Ghani had put his political future at stake by charting a friendly course with Pakistan in a desperate hope to bring peace to his war-torn country. In return, he expected Islamabad's cooperation in curtailing the Taliban's military capability and forcing the insurgents to come to the negotiating table.[6]

But all those promises of cooperation remained unfulfilled. The bonhomie was short lived. President Ghani's discontent with Pakistan had increased following the brutal spring and summer fighting seasons in 2015, which witnessed a record number of Afghan national forces and civilian casualties. The Taliban offensive that summer had been the fiercest and much more widespread than ever before. Kabul had seen almost daily, and increasingly audacious, attacks in its high security zones. The most worrisome aspect, however, was the spread of the insurgency even in northern provinces. The fall of Kunduz demonstrated Taliban's growing military prowess.

That gave more ammunition to critics of Ghani's reconciliation policy at home. Besieged from all sides, the Afghan president was losing his patience. His frustration was very evident by his communication to the Pakistani civil and military leaders calling for clamping down on Taliban commanders residing in Pakistan. He warned of reversing his policy of outreach if Pakistan failed to deliver.[7]

President Ashraf Ghani had also been airing his dismay to some of his old Pakistani friends and political leaders who met him over, what he described as, Islamabad's failure to deliver on its promises. There was nothing tangible that Islamabad had to show for its cooperation on any issue, he reportedly told the Pakistani visitors. His tenor got increasingly bitter as the Taliban offensive turned more lethal. He felt that the Pakistani military action in North Waziristan and other tribal areas had pushed the insurgents over to the Afghan side, while not doing enough to curtail their activities in Pakistan. Another serious concern of Kabul was that thousands of Pakistani militants were reportedly involved in the Taliban offensive.[8]

The Afghan president even suspected elements within the ISI of aiding fighting in the western Afghan province of Kunduz that had become the Taliban's main battlefield. However, with the drawing down of the US-led coalition forces, the increase in intensity of the Taliban offensive was almost predictable. Insurgents had also benefited hugely from the internal political divide and uncertainty in Afghanistan. It was also clearly apparent that the Afghan national forces were still not fully equipped and trained to deal with the widespread and organised insurgency without active support of the US and NATO forces.[9]

Pakistan openly, and very strongly, criticised the Taliban offensive calling them acts of terrorism. But for Ghani such statements alone were not enough to assuage sentiments at home. Each fresh terrorist attack on Kabul weakened Ghani's control. The real issue was what Pakistan could do to help him and prevent the situation from reverting to the previously held hostile relationship. In this context, the Murree meeting salvaged the situation somewhat, though temporarily. President Ghani thought the talks would win him some much-needed political space at home. But there was a major question about the sustainability of the talk process.[10]

Although the ISI had managed to bring the Taliban to talk to the Kabul government, that had involved a level of coercion, which sharpened differences within the Taliban ranks. Not all Taliban factions were amenable to the reconciliation process. Divisions within the Taliban ran deep. The strongest objection came from battlefield commander, Abdul Qayyum Zakir, a former Guantánamo Bay detainee. Zakir, who commanded several thousand fighters in eastern Afghanistan, was opposed to direct talks with the Kabul government.[11]

Pakistan had to resort to strong-arm tactics to pressurise senior Taliban officials to attend the Murree talks. The Taliban leaders living in Pakistan had been warned by security agencies that they would face consequences if they didn't come on board. After some resistance, the Pakistan-based Taliban Leadership Council, led by Mullah Akhtar Mansour, succumbed to the pressure and agreed to send a delegation to the Murree talks.[12]

Taliban had struggled to maintain unity and the relationship between various Taliban committees operating from outside Afghanistan and the field commanders inside Afghanistan was complex. The influence of the old guard had waned over the years and the new generation of field commanders was even more radical. Most of the new generation were teenagers during Taliban rule, but they now formed the core of the insurgency.[13]

Alarmed by Pakistan's arm-twisting, many Taliban leaders started to discreetly move out of the country, often with their families.

One favoured destination, surprisingly, was Iran, as well as the Gulf countries and Afghanistan itself. Tayyab Agha, the head of the Taliban Political Commission based in Qatar, visited Tehran on 19 May 2015, and the trip was believed to be part of efforts being made to evacuate as many Taliban seniors as possible from Pakistan.[14] Iran was increasingly worried about the Islamic State (IS) getting a foothold across the border in Afghanistan and was willing to cooperate with its erstwhile foe as a plausible counter-force against the emerging common threat.

The confusion over the Murree meeting was further fuelled by a media report quoting a representative of the Taliban office in Qatar stating categorically that the meeting was 'not authorised.' The statement was a confirmation of division between the Qatar office and Pakistan-based Leadership Council also known as the Quetta Shura. The Qatar office refused to send its delegate, ignoring the Shura's advice and despite Pakistan's persuasion.[15]

A statement issued by the Qatar office a day after the 8 July meeting, without referring to the meeting itself, said that the Political Commission was the only authorised channel for talks. The last two sentences of the English version read: '… from now onwards, all of Islamic Emirate's foreign and internal political affairs are entrusted to the Islamic Emirate's Political Office as their sole responsibility. The Political Office has full capacity and agency powers to conduct or postpone, in light of Islamic principles and national interests, negotiations with internal and foreign parties wherever and whenever it deems suitable.' The Murree talks were not referred to directly and were neither rejected nor approved.[16]

Meanwhile, an article attributed to an individual author briefly appeared on the Taliban's English website on 9 July 2015, which explicitly rejected the authority of the Taliban delegates attending the Murree meeting and condemned Pakistan for presenting those Taliban attending in what it called 'their personal capacity' as official negotiators. However, that article was taken down hours after its publication.

Notwithstanding fractures within the insurgent movement, the participation of senior Taliban leaders in the Murree meeting was seen as a positive development. Those Taliban who participated in the Murree talks indicated that the meeting had been endorsed, at least tacitly, by the movement's leadership. The presence of Akhtar Mansour's (Taliban leader and second-in-command to Mullah Omar) 'chief of staff,' Latif Mansour, and Mullah Muhammad Abbas Akhund, who was also a member of the Quetta Shura, was enough to render the meeting 'official.' The third delegate was Ibrahim Haqqani, a senior member of the Haqqani network that had been declared a terrorist organisation by the US State Department a few years earlier.[17]

One week after the meeting, the Taliban website published the customary Eid message issued, as always, in the name of Mullah Omar. No surprise there, as Akhtar Mansour had effectively been running the Taliban for years and, most likely, he himself had the messages drafted. However, this Eid message was a departure from the norm; it was a clear indication of a paradigm shift in the views of the Taliban on war and peace in Afghanistan.

Its approval of peace talks marked a clear deviation from the Islamic militia's earlier hardline position of shunning any interaction with the Kabul government. The statement had also tried to convey a more moderate outlook on education and relations with the outside world. That indicated a welcome change indeed, but its veracity was yet to be fully tested. But it cleared the confusion about one thing: the statement had removed any doubts over the Murree talks having the blessing of the Taliban leadership. And that certainly lent greater credibility to the process of reconciliation, and negated the confusion fuelled by reported comments by some members of the Qatar political office rejecting the Pakistani-sponsored talks.[18]

There had also been questions about whether Mullah Omar, the elusive supreme Taliban leader, was even alive. Nothing had been heard about him, or from him, for the past several years, except for the annual Eid day messages posted on the Taliban's official website. He had not been in contact even with senior Taliban leaders. Mullah Omar's prolonged absence from the scene had widened the split within the ranks. The Eid message presented a long explanation justifying the softening stance on talks with the Kabul government. 'Concurrently with armed jihad, political endeavours and peaceful pathways for achieving these sacred goals is a legitimate Islamic principle and an integral part of Prophetic politics,' the well-crafted statement declared.[19]

Undoubtedly, the July 2015 Eid message purported to be from Mullah Omar was a remarkable shift from the tenor of the bulletin just a year earlier. That Eid message had been completely silent on the reconciliation issue, which was consistent with the Taliban policy of having no dialogue with the Kabul government until all foreign forces had been pulled out. In sharp contrast, the latest message elaborated that 'the objective behind our political endeavours, as well as contacts and interactions with countries of the world and our own Afghans, is to bring an end to the occupation.'[20]

Another important part of the Eid message was the appeal to maintain unity among the Taliban ranks. That may have been a reflection of concern over the reports of schisms within the organisation on the future course of struggle with only a small US residual force left in the country. There were some Taliban factions, particularly those led by a new generation of field commanders, that were rigidly opposed to any peace negotiations with the Kabul government.[21]

That internal organisational struggle was not new, but it seemed to have intensified with the withdrawal of most of the coalition forces. Mullah Abdul Qayyum Zakir, the hardline chief military commander, was forced to step down in a major leadership overhaul after his opposition to peace talks with the Kabul government. He rose to prominence after being freed from Guantánamo Bay in 2007. His exit allowed more moderate leaders like Mullah Akhtar Mansour to assert their authority.

Although Mullah Zakir remained in the Leadership Council, his powers were drastically curtailed, but he still had the support of some of the field commanders who believed that they could win the war.[22] How deep the divisions within the Taliban really penetrated was not at all clear. There were conflicting views about the state of unity within the insurgency. Lack of clarity made it hard to predict things even if the negotiations made a promising start. The reservations expressed by some members of the Qatar political office did not come as a surprise. Such differences were inevitable as the organisation tried to explore a political solution after fighting for more than 13 years.

Another interesting passage in the message was emphasis on scientific education. 'Some people, without having any sound proof, think that the Islamic Emirate is against all new developments, modern sciences and resources,' the statement declared. That was clearly meant to assuage the fear of Afghans and the international community that the Taliban wanted to reimpose retrogressive system rejecting modern education. Yet there was no mention about female education and the protection of women's rights.[23]

There were several factors behind this remarkable shift in the Taliban's position and their willingness to come to the negotiating table after refusing rapprochement for so long. One major reason for this shift was the concern within the Taliban leadership that the end of foreign occupation would inevitably lead to a sharp drop in recruitment among Afghans who had been fighting a 'defensive jihad' against invaders. A continuation of civil war might not get the Taliban the same level of support. War fatigue was evident.

It was also apparent to the leadership that the Taliban could not win an outright military victory, leading to the conquest of the whole of Afghanistan, or of the approximately 90 per cent of the country that they held in the summer of 2001, prior to the 9/11 attacks. A political settlement could bring them into the mainstream. One other major factor in the Taliban moderating its position was the alarming rise of the self-styled Islamic State (IS) or Daesh in Afghanistan. That was not only challenging the Afghan government, but also the Taliban. Scores of Taliban fighters were reported to have been killed in clashes as the IS tried to displace the Islamic militia. There was a strong concern that the IS could gain more ground if the civil war continued.

The first signs of the IS getting organised in the Afghanistan–Pakistan region emerged as early as 2014. Leaflets urging fighters belonging to the Taliban and other Afghan insurgent groups to join the Middle East-based militant group appeared in various districts. These appeals were posted not only in eastern Afghanistan, along the border with Pakistan, but also in Kabul. Early IS recruits came from the ranks of splinter factions of the Pakistani Taliban who had been driven into Afghanistan after large-scale operations in the tribal region by the Pakistan Army. Spurred by the declaration of a Caliphate by Abu Bakar Al Baghdadi, several smaller militant groups in Pakistan and Afghanistan pledged their allegiance to the group.[24]

In September 2014, Daesh named Abdul Rahim Muslim Dost—a former Afghan Taliban commander from Kunar province—as an organiser for the group's Khorasan chapter. A prominent Salafi jihadist scholar, Muslim Dost enjoyed a significant following among Salafis in eastern provinces like Kunar and Nuristan. Some high profile defections of Afghan Taliban commanders helped the group create a formal organisational structure.

In January 2015, the group released a video proclaiming themselves administrators of an official wilayat (or province) for IS in Afghanistan and Pakistan. The creation of the Shura for Khorasan (the historic name of the region including Afghanistan, Pakistan, and Central Asia) was endorsed by the IS supreme command. It named former TTP commander of Orakzai Agency in Pakistan, Hafiz Saeed Khan, as the Emir for Daesh in the Khorasan region and Mullah Abdul Rauf, a former Afghan Taliban commander who had spent many years in Guantánamo, as his deputy.[25]

Initially the IS focused on Afghanistan's eastern provinces of Kunar and Nangarhar, where many Pakistani Taliban commanders, fleeing the military operation in the tribal areas, had settled. Mullah Abdul Rauf organised the group in southern Afghanistan. Soon after the formation of its Khorasan chapter, IS became active in eleven provinces of Afghanistan, including Ghazni and Logar. In most cases, defections from the Taliban ranks to the IS were motivated by the group's huge financial resources rather than its radical and rigid worldview and ideology.[26]

All was set for the second round of the Murree dialogue at the end of July and some Taliban delegates had already arrived in Islamabad when the news that Mullah Omar had died was leaked by the Afghan secret service, the NDS. The timing of the announcement, just a day before the most critical phase of the peace talks was due to restart, was most curious. The Afghan government said Mullah Omar died in a hospital in the Pakistani city of Karachi two years ago and accused Pakistan of deliberately hiding the news.[27]

The news of Mullah Omar's death doomed the peace negotiations. It also further complicated the peace process as it removed a figurehead for the insurgents, who until now had appeared to act collectively but were split on whether to continue the war or negotiate with Ghani's government. The indefinite postponement of reconciliation talks and the subsequent breakdown of President Ashraf Ghani's outreach to Pakistan dealt a fatal blow to a fledgling peace process that Pakistan and other countries had worked hard to shepherd along.[28]

Enigmatic and reclusive in life, Mullah Omar's death was no less mysterious. Since his famous escape on a motorbike from Kandahar after the US invasion in October 2001, very little was heard of him except for occasional audio messages. Those, too, went silent a few years ago. The well-crafted Eid messages posted on the Afghan Taliban website attributed to him remained the only hypothetical communication with his supporters. The last such message appeared just a week before the breaking of the highly kept secret about his death, which had occurred some two years ago.[29]

The circumstances and place of Mullah Omar's death remained a matter of speculation. Both the American and Afghan officials had claimed that after fleeing from Kandahar in December 2001, Omar had crossed into Pakistan and was guiding the group from Quetta. The allegation brought huge pressure upon Pakistan with some Afghan officials suggesting that the US should use drones to strike Omar's alleged hideout in Quetta.[30]

When I interviewed former Afghan president Hamid Karzai in 2004, he gave me an address in Quetta where he claimed Mullah Omar was residing under the protection of Pakistan's intelligence agencies—a revelation which incited strong reactions from Pakistani authorities. Later on, I found out that that address belonged to the owner of a grocery shop.

Dutch journalist Bette Dam in her book published in 2018—*The Secret Life of Mullah Omar*—made the sensational disclosure that the Taliban's founder had lived and died in a village in Afghanistan's Zabul province, located close to a US military base. This reinforced doubts about the widespread perception that Mullah Omar had operated from a safe haven in Pakistan. The findings of the book confirm Taliban's assertion that their elusive leader never left the country after their conservative regime was ousted by US forces in 2001.[31]

Mullah Omar had reportedly stayed in the house of Jabbar Omari who had worked for the Taliban supreme leader as his driver and bodyguard during Taliban's regime. Omari had brought Omar to his home in the Zabul province after the Taliban's ouster in 2001, and built a secret room where the Taliban leader could live safely. According to Bette Dam's book, the reclusive leader had severed all ties and would not even meet his family members or other Taliban officials, delegating all responsibilities to his deputies. Interestingly, the house where Mullah Omar resided for more than a decade had been part of several search operations by both the US and Afghan forces.[32]

Even Omari's family was unaware of the real identity of their reclusive guest. Despite his deteriorating health condition, Mullah Omar refused to go to Pakistan for treatment. When Mullah Omar finally died in 2013, after a prolonged illness, few people attended his funeral. He was buried in a quiet corner of the village. Mullah Omar's family and other Taliban leaders learnt about his demise much later. They promised to keep the news a secret, knowing very well that if the information was to become public, it could have a very adverse impact on the insurgency.[33]

What gave credence to Bette Dams's disclosure that Mullah Omar never left Afghanistan, was that even during the Afghan resistance war against the former USSR, and unlike other Mujahideen commanders, Omar would not travel to Pakistan. The only time he reportedly visited Quetta was when he needed surgery for his eye after being injured in a battle.

Over past 13 years, the Taliban resistance had been built under Mullah Omar's banner, though little was known about his whereabouts and his role in the battlefield. Most of the field commanders had, perhaps, never even met him. Worryingly, in spite of successes on the ground, thinking within the Afghan Taliban concerning the future of Afghanistan remained obscure.

Although Mullah Omar enjoyed the absolute loyalty of the Leadership Council, his influence seemed to have waned over the years with the growing radicalisation of a new generation of field commanders. Being out of the field for so long had turned Mullah Omar into more of a symbolic figurehead. Nevertheless, that kept the faction-ridden organisation united. One wonders whether, given his stubbornness, Mullah Omar would have agreed to reconciliation.

The death of their supreme commander, albeit a figurehead for so many years, further divided the Taliban. The succession issue was never easily resolved in an organisation so deeply invested in an undisputed authority. It was a battle for leadership between his handpicked deputy, Mullah Akhtar Mansour, and family members. The ensuing power struggle further fractured the militant group. The belated disclosure of the death of a man with a bounty of $10 million on his head did not stir the world. Rather, there was concern over the possible unravelling of the radical Islamic movement.[34]

Within days of the disclosure of Mullah Omar's death, the Taliban Leadership Council named Mullah Akhtar Mansour the group's new emir. A longtime deputy to the Taliban, late leader, Mansour had been effectively in charge and was seen as a logical choice for the leadership particularly since Mullah Abdul Ghani Baradar, co-founder of the Taliban movement in Afghanistan and deputy of Mullah Omar, had been under detention in Pakistan. But Mansour's election intensified the internal power struggle. Several senior figures in the movement, including the eldest son (Mullah Mohammad Yaqoob) and brother (Mullah Abdul Manan Akhund) of Mullah Omar walked out in protest at the conclave held in Pakistan's western city of Quetta, saying that it was not a representative meeting.[35]

Mansour had powerful rivals within Taliban, notably battlefield commander, Abdul Qayyum Zakir, who pushed for Mullah Omar's son, Mohammad Yaqoob, to take over the leadership of the movement. The dissidents challenged Mansour's appointment saying that the Taliban Council meeting was not representative. They said Mullah Mansour was not appointed 'by all Taliban,' as not all members of Afghan Taliban's Supreme Council had been consulted over his election. They alleged that Mansour had invited only members of his group to pave the way for his election.

Such a display of dissent within the group's secretive core was the clearest sign yet of the challenge the new leader had faced in uniting a group already split over whether to pursue peace talks with the Afghan government. The split in the movement on the leadership question further widened with the resignation of the head of Afghan Taliban's political office in Qatar.

In a statement, Tayyab Agha criticised the way in which Mullah Omar's successor had been chosen. He said he was stepping down to avoid 'expected future disputes.' He described it as 'a great historical mistake that the new leader had been appointed outside the country and from the people who are residing outside the country.'[36]

Agha was extremely critical of the way Mansour's election was rushed through and that the decision was made on Pakistani soil. It was a direct inference to Pakistan having influenced the appointment of Mullah Mansour. Tayyab Agha also called on the militant movement to handle all of its affairs from within Afghanistan, and criticised the fact that Mullah Omar's death 'was kept secret for almost two years.'[37]

Tayyab Agha's differences ran much deeper than his opposition to Mansour's appointment as a successor to Mullah Omar. He was upset with Pakistan's influence over the Taliban leadership and its contacts with Iranian and other secret services. In an open letter written months later he exhorted the leadership to remove all Taliban military or non-military figures who kept 'direct or indirect contact with the Pakistani, Iranian, or other foreign intelligence services.' He particularly advised Taliban to break free from 'Pakistan's manipulative influence.'[38]

He felt that the presence of the movement's key decision makers in Pakistan allowed the country to 'impose things against the interests of the movement and Afghanistan.' He wanted the members of the Taliban leadership to leave Pakistan in order to make independent decisions. He also wanted to reform Taliban's unpopular practices in the areas in Afghanistan under their influence. The chasm in the Taliban movement had widened, bringing greater pressure to bear on Mansour.[39]

In his first statement after being acclaimed the supreme leader of the Taliban movement, Mullah Akhtar Mansour, vowed to continue fighting. He dismissed talks about peace as 'enemies' propaganda.' The statement posted on the Taliban website indicated a clear change of tone from someone who had long been seen as one of the most pro-peace and moderate figures in the movement's leadership. While not ruling out peace talks, Mansour emphasised that jihad would continue to be waged to achieve the objective of the establishment of an Islamic order. It was obvious Mansour was pushed to adopt a hardline stance on peace talks in order to consolidate his power and unify the movement in the face of dissent.[40]

Mullah Mansour was clearly under pressure to establish his authority as a strong leader. Any peace overtures, without emphasising jihad, could be interpreted by Taliban fighters as a compromise and a betrayal of their struggle. It was therefore not surprising that there was a marked escalation in the Taliban offensive after Mansour's elevation to the top leadership. Pushing the war option more than peace could help to project him as an uncompromising leader.[41] The peace talks started under the Murree process were in jeopardy—but was that really a sustainable process anyway?

Pakistan's predicament had worsened with the breakdown of its relations with President Ashraf Ghani's government after a brief period of bonhomie. Hostilities had further heightened with the escalation in Taliban attacks, ending any possibility of the resumption of negotiations between Kabul and the Afghan Taliban. Neither the Taliban nor Kabul was willing to move forward, putting Islamabad in a tight corner.

President Ghani wanted Islamabad to take action against the Taliban leaders and the insurgent sanctuaries on its soil. That would have been tantamount to Pakistan declaring a full-scale war on Afghan Taliban leaders and fighters who were by then deeply entrenched in the border regions. The Taliban blitz had, once again, increased the international pressure on Islamabad to act—particularly against the Haqqani network that was still deemed close to the Pakistani security establishment.

Despite military operations in North Waziristan, there was widespread scepticism about Islamabad's promise not to allow Haqqani network to use the region as its base. The reports of Mullah Mansour freely roaming around Quetta, and gaining the allegiance of insurgent commanders in mass gatherings, had further provoked the ire of the Ghani administration.[42]

The Taliban were not willing to re-enter into the dialogue process without some preconditions. They wanted some preliminary steps to be taken prior to the talks that included recognition as an Islamic Emirate, removal of their officials from the black list, lifting of travel restrictions, release of prisoners, and unfreezing of their funds. It was a tall order for both the Kabul government and the US to accept these conditions without a decrease in insurgent hostilities, which was taking a very heavy toll on Afghan security forces and on the civilian population.[43]

The year 2015 was the bloodiest since the 2001 US invasion of Afghanistan. The Taliban had also been able to extend their offensive to the northern Afghan provinces where the militia had not had much of a support base in the past. The residual US forces could hardly be expected to stop the Taliban advance from the militia's traditional stronghold in eastern and southern Afghanistan.

A real problem for the Afghan security forces was the crisis of confidence that had been more than evident in Kunduz, where over 7,000 soldiers failed to defend the city against a far fewer number of insurgents. Reports from Baghlan and other northern districts had not been encouraging either. Desertions from the Afghan National Army had further increased in the face of growing intensity of Taliban attacks.

Parts of Kunduz province had been under siege for more than a year, but the Taliban's inroads into other northern provinces had been quite startling, shifting the battlefront away from the insurgent heartland in the south. A major factor in the latest offensive was the coalescing of various transnational militant groups driven out by the Pakistani military operation in North Waziristan. The fighting close to the Tajik border had alarmed the Central Asian nations facing their own militancy problems.[44]

The Taliban escalation was a clear indication of Mullah Mansour consolidating his control over the group. Any challenge to his leadership seems to have vanished after the son and brother of Mullah Omar finally pledged their allegiance to the new emir. It had also disproved the widespread perception of the insurgent group disintegrating after the death of their 'supreme leader.'

However, the killing of Mullah Akhtar Mansour in a CIA drone strike on 21 May 2016, in Balochistan, near the border with Iran, gave a new twist to the festering Afghan crisis. It signaled a more aggressive US policy stance, as hopes of the Afghan Taliban coming to the negotiating table had faded. That the attack was carried out well inside Pakistan's territory exposed Pakistan's vulnerability in balancing an alliance with the US along with maintaining relations with the Afghan Taliban.[45]

Mullah Mansour was returning from Iran and travelling on a Pakistani passport, which raised some serious questions about the Taliban's Iran connection. He had moved his family to Iran. His stay in Iran was secretly facilitated by the Iranian Revolutionary Guard that shed new light on the movement's complicated relationship with Tehran. Iran had also provided weapons, cash, and sanctuary to the Taliban. Despite the deep ideological antipathy between a hardline Sunni group and a cleric-run Shia state, the two sides were quite willing to cooperate against mutual enemies and in the pursuit of shared interests.[46]

Authorised personally by President Barack Obama, the strike marked the most significant US incursion into Pakistan since the 2011 US forces raid that killed Osama bin Laden. Mullah Mansour was targeted on the main RCD Highway, which connects Pakistan with Iran. Pakistan accused the US of crossing the 'red line' and claimed the attack was a violation of its sovereignty, while failing to offer any plausible explanation to account for the presence of the insurgent leader on its soil.[47]

By striking in Balochistan—hitherto off-limits for remote-controlled Predators—the US signaled its willingness to extend the war against Afghan insurgents to targeting sanctuaries within Pakistan. It was a huge blow to the Taliban—still reeling from news of the death of their founder and supreme leader, Mullah Omar.

While the Obama administration declared the death of Mullah Mansour as a 'game changer' and a 'milestone' for Afghanistan's elusive peace process, there was no indication that the militia would change its hardline position on peace talks after the death of its leader.[48]

The death of Mullah Mansour may have shaken the Taliban movement but it did not lead to its disintegration as anticipated by the US officials when they decided to eliminate him. Within days of the incident, the Taliban leadership chose Mullah Hibatullah Akhundzada, a hardline religious scholar from Kandahar, as their new leader.

Owing to the fact that he came from the Taliban's traditional stronghold, he was largely accepted by the rank-and-file fighters. He had served as a deputy to the slain Taliban supremo, Mullah Mansour. The new leader was not as controversial as his predecessor.

Akhundzada was appointed by senior Taliban figures who met somewhere near Quetta. The Taliban called the new appointment unanimous, although that did not signify much, since they said the same when Mullah Mansour took over in summer a year earlier.[49]

A veteran of the anti-Soviet resistance in Afghanistan in the 1980s, Hibatullah Akhundzada was reputed to be more of a religious leader than a military commander. He had been a senior figure in the Taliban courts for years and was believed to have issued rulings in support of Islamic punishments—such as public executions of convicted murderers and adulterers, and amputations of those found guilty of theft. He had lived most of his life inside Afghanistan, with little evidence of travel. He belonged to the Noorzai tribe that is settled in Panjwai district in Kandahar. He also ran a madrasa near Quetta, which many top Taliban commanders had attended.[50]

The Leadership Council also named Mullah Mohammad Yaqoob, son of Mullah Omar, as a joint deputy head of the movement, alongside current deputy leader Sirajuddin Haqqani, a leader of the Haqqani network, under the Taliban supreme commander, Mullah Hibatullah Akhundzada.

16 | A Maverick in the White House

The gathering in Moscow in January 2017—the third in the series of consultations between Russia, China, and Pakistan—underlined growing concern about the spillover effect of the Afghan crisis in the region. The initiative was the latest example of Russian assertion of its diplomatic power amidst growing frustration over the US's failure to deliver peace in Afghanistan.

An underlying cause of anxiety had been the growing threat of the militant IS group spreading its tentacles in the war-torn country. But it remained questionable whether the new alliance could help reach a negotiated political solution to the Afghan conflict. Although the Kabul government was invited for the next round of talks, its exclusion from the earlier meetings cast a shadow over the process.[1]

With the US not invited to the Moscow-initiated process, the new nexus could not be expected to replace the quadrilateral forum that included the US, along with Pakistan, China, and Afghanistan. The quadrilateral talks had been suspended for almost one year after the collapse of efforts to bring the Taliban to the negotiating table. The killing of Mullah Akhtar Mansour, the leader of the Taliban, in a CIA drone strike on a vehicle which had crossed into Pakistan from Iran on 21 May 2016, had further diminished hopes for the talks to resume.[2]

Things had become more complicated with the political transition in Washington. Like other foreign policy issues, there was complete confusion over the Afghan policy in the soon-to-be installed Donald Trump administration. That had perhaps compelled the three countries to find a regional solution to the Afghan crisis that directly affected their own security.

The Moscow trilateral meeting had called for lifting of the travel ban on the insurgent leaders, one of the major demands that the Taliban had presented as a precondition for talks with the Kabul government.

The Taliban were obviously pleased by the Moscow meeting endorsing its demand. But lifting of the ban required US consent.

China had, for some time, been actively involved in the Afghan peace efforts, being a major investor in mining and infrastructure development projects in that country. Its good relations with both the Kabul government and the Taliban had helped Beijing facilitate a few rounds of informal talks between the two warring sides. Beijing had also been gravely concerned about the increasing instability in Afghanistan and recent reports of growing IS activity in the country.[3]

Although Russia was not a fresh entrant on the Afghan scene, its initiative to build a regional alliance to counter the IS threat pointed to a new alignment of forces in a changing geopolitical landscape. Interestingly, the meeting on Afghanistan followed another set of trilateral talks in Moscow that included Turkey and Iran on the settlement of the Syrian crisis. The US was excluded from that meeting too, indicating that Moscow was taking a lead in settling the Syrian and Afghan crises, thereby considerably altering the balance of power in the international arena.[4]

This Russian assertiveness seemed to be driven by the Obama administration's inaction and in anticipation of expected changes in US foreign policy under the incoming Trump administration. Though Trump had openly castigated the Obama administration's approach on Syria and Afghanistan, there was no clarity on future US policy, especially on Afghanistan. That had also provided Moscow an opportunity to alter the current negotiating format and try to break the persisting deadlock in the diplomatic efforts to find a political solution to the Afghan conflict.

There had also been serious concern among the three countries over the deteriorating situation in the proximity of their borders. 2016 was the bloodiest year in Afghanistan with the Taliban intensifying their attacks considerably. More perturbing, however, was the expanding footprint of the IS, apparent in several terrorist attacks in Afghanistan that took a huge toll on the civilian population.

The increasing activities of IS in northern Afghanistan, close to the borders of the Central Asian countries, were particularly alarming for Russia. There was also a growing fear in Moscow of the IS making inroads in the Muslim population in those countries, especially as the Chechens form one of the largest foreign contingents in the IS war in Iraq and Syria. That had also been the reason for Russia establishing contacts with the Afghan Taliban and providing them weapons and financial support in order to fight the IS.[5]

Both China and Pakistan shared Moscow's concerns. Islamabad, particularly, saw some hope of the new regional format being in a better position to persuade the Afghan Taliban to come to the negotiating table. However, it was not easy to make a breakthrough given the complexities surrounding the issue. Most importantly, it required a great deal of concerted efforts to remove the reservations of the Kabul government over the new format that involved Pakistan.

There had also been a question mark over the Taliban agreeing to formally sit across the table with the Kabul government without any preconditions, particularly at a time when they had achieved significant success in the battlefield. Afghan officials had informally met the representatives of the Taliban's Qatar office. But formal peace talks were a completely different ballgame.

Meantime in Pakistan, following the Panama Papers leak in February 2016, involving Prime Minister Nawaz Sharif's family members, the political crisis had worsened. The tension between the civil and military leadership there, also cast its shadow over Islamabad's dealing with the US and with Afghanistan.

It was not merely an issue of being implicated in a scandal. The charges against the prime minister had come when he already had enough problems on his plate—each one more difficult to resolve than the other. The Panama Papers leaks had stirred up a political hornet's nest. The 'Panamagate' scandal, as it was called, had changed the entire political dynamic in the country.[6]

Although he was not directly named in the Panama Papers, the revelations pertaining to his apparently massive family business abroad, had put the beleaguered prime minister in a tight spot. Sharif was feeling increasing heat from the military. The tension had been mounting since the COAS, General Raheel Sharif, made a rare public statement calling for across-the-board accountability. The government saw it as a warning.

Until the Panama Papers revelation, the balance of power seemed to have tilted more towards the civilian government, though the military continued to maintain an upper hand in internal security matters. But with the credibility and legitimacy of the government now thrown in question, the situation allowed the military greater space. It was déjà vu all over again for Nawaz Sharif who had lost power twice in the past, halfway through both his terms, as a result of confrontation between various centres of power.

It was the biggest challenge Nawaz Sharif had faced in his third term in office. The situation was far more serious than it was during the 2014 siege of the capital by Imran Khan. With his family directly implicated in the scandal, Sharif was on a sticky wicket with his moral authority at its lowest.

Even more worrisome for the PM was the growing assertion of the military as the political crisis worsened. One of the major factors behind the tension was the pressure on Nawaz Sharif to grant General Raheel Sharif, who was due to retire in a few months, an extension as army chief. Although the General had earlier, in a rare public statement, announced that he would not accept an extension, there had clearly been a change of mind.[7]

In the midst of the crisis, a leaked report of the details of a confidential National Security Committee (NSC) meeting, highlighting differences between the civil and military leadership over action against militant groups, brought the conflict to a head. Published in the *Dawn* newspaper on 7 October 2016, the report revealed a testy interaction between the two sides as civilian officials warned against the country's growing international isolation because of the failure of security agencies in eliminating militant groups.[8]

Presided over by the PM, the meeting was attended by the top military leadership, including the ISI chief Lt. Gen. Rizwan Akhtar who had replaced Lt. Gen. Zaheerul Islam. According to the report, the Punjab Chief Minister, Shahbaz Sharif, got into a verbal confrontation with General Rizwan while blaming the military-led intelligence agencies of preventing the civilian law enforcement agencies from taking action against banned militant groups. The PM also reportedly directed that 'fresh attempts be made to conclude the Pathankot investigation and restart the stalled Mumbai attacks-related trials in a Rawalpindi anti-terrorism court.'[9]

The Pathankot air force base terrorist attack took place on 2 January 2016. Part of the Western Air Command of the Indian Air Force, the Pathankot incident had yet again brought the issue of non-state actors to the fore. The attack, weeks after Indian Prime Minster Narendra Modi's visit to Lahore, was allegedly carried out by Jaish-e-Mohammed. The terrorist attack had, once again, put Pakistan in the dock. It was not just cross-border involvement but also the activities of banned outfits at home that had raised questions.[10]

Some senior officials actually conceded that militants had sneaked across the border. By assuring India of full cooperation in the investigation and promising to take action against those found involved, the prime minister had shown a degree of maturity not seen before. But it needed more than mere assurances. Although fully committed to the principle of fighting insurgents in the tribal regions of Pakistan, the military leadership and the ISI were still reluctant about taking action against militant groups. The military leadership didn't want to be seen to be acting under perceived Indian pressure while Sharif was worried over the warning about the country's international isolation, this should not happen. The cleavage between the civilian and the ISI was tangible in the national security meeting as reported by *Dawn*.

There was nothing in the report that would have actually compromised national security. Despite this, the military leadership accused the Sharif government of deliberately leaking the story to the media to undermine the security establishment. Tension mounted as the retirement of General Raheel Sharif came close. The *Dawn* Leaks scandal, as it came to be known, was a handy tool in letting the military leadership beat up the government about it.

It was also meant to pressurise the prime minister to accede to the General's extension demand. But Nawaz Sharif was adamant about not changing his decision, even though General Raheel Sharif had assured him of full cooperation and promised to close the investigation on the media leak.[11]

The tension, thus, further intensified casting a long shadow over General Sharif's final days in office. The military leadership had refused to attend any meeting at the Prime Minister House pending the investigation of the 'leak' to the media of the proceedings of top-level parleys on national security. The sources of civil-military tension would not go away with the change of the army guard in November 2016. It was more about the institution than an individual.

General Raheel Sharif may not have been a great strategist or thinker, but he took tough decisions that turned the tide against militancy, though there were valid questions about some of his actions. He proved wrong the sceptics who warned against going into the treacherous terrain and advocated for a conciliatory approach towards the insurgents there.[12]

However, the distinction between 'good' and 'bad' militants remained a highly contentious issue. That perception had partially changed following the North Waziristan operation and the crackdown on militant networks operating on the mainland. But the continued activities of some banned militant groups and their alleged involvement in cross-border terrorist attacks, raised questions about the resolve to eliminate all kinds of militancy.

There was still the huge and unresolved problem of a lack of a holistic and overarching approach in dealing with the challenge of violent extremism. This threatened to reverse the gains achieved in the counter insurgency campaign. The ISI's reluctance to effectively act against the India-centric militant groups had also been a cause of tension with the civilian administration.[13]

Predictably, Prime Minister Nawaz Sharif once again picked a dark horse for the coveted post of army chief, after the retirement of General Raheel Sharif in November 2016. The choice of General Qamar Bajwa was based more on political considerations than the order of seniority or merit, though there is no question about his professionalism and experience.

Probably the thinking behind the decision was to have someone who was amenable to civilian authority. It was the third time Nawaz Sharif had appointed the army chief. Each time he had chosen an officer who was lower down the list. Yet his relations with the military leadership had never been tension-free. The confrontation with the generals cost him his second government.

An increasing role in internal security had led to greater involvement of the military in political matters. One could hardly dispute the rationale behind picking a low profile officer to head the army, given the perpetual tensions between the two state institutions. It was not just about the imbalance of power that had allowed the military to dominate foreign and national security policies but also the power tussle that often threatened to destabilise the democratic system.[14]

General Bajwa had the reputation of an easygoing officer but a tough professional. However, given the inherent complexities, he was not expected to be pliable. It was quite simplistic to think that the sources of tension would simply go away with the transition in the army leadership. In a country where the position of army chief is considered to be the most powerful, even a smooth transition in the leadership held high political significance.

Nawaz Sharif thought that the change of army command would give his government some breathing space as it confronted several political challenges. But there was not to be any significant shift in the existing civil-military imbalance. Given the gravity of the internal security challenges, the government's reliance on the military had increased. The counterinsurgency campaign in the tribal areas was far from over despite the military successes achieved in North Waziristan. A large number of troops were still involved in combing and holding operations in almost all seven FATA agencies.

While the controversy over the *Dawn* report may have triggered the latest crisis, there were a number of other factors that had contributed to the civil-military standoff. There was an almost complete breakdown of trust between the two branches of state. The latest round of confrontations had also removed any illusions about improving civil-military relations with the change of army guard.

The situation had become even worse with the major opposition political parties putting their weight behind the military. The ruling by the Supreme Court in April 2017 to form a Joint Investigation Team, comprising of personnel from civilian and military agencies to investigate the Panama case, had tightened the noose around the prime minister.[15]

In the midst of all that, the PM's office issued a notification regarding the termination of the services of prime minister's special assistant on foreign affairs, Tariq Fatemi, and a senior information ministry official as per the recommendation of the investigation commission probing the *Dawn* report. The order was instantly rejected by the military for being incomplete. However, no substantial reason was given for the rebuttal. It was evident that the entire issue of the 'leak' had been blown out of proportion.[16]

Nawaz Sharif's fate was sealed when the Supreme Court, not only disqualified him for life but also indicted almost all the Sharifs. Nawaz Sharif resigned as prime minister of Pakistan in July 2017, following a unanimous decision by the country's Supreme Court to disqualify him from office. The inglorious exit of Nawaz Sharif came as a serious blow to the country's most powerful political dynasty. The unprecedented judicial action apparently backed by the security agencies against a sitting prime minister was a watershed moment for the country's political history.[17]

Meanwhile, in June 2017, President Donald Trump announced his decision to bolster the presence of US troops in Afghanistan, raising questions about the US getting into the third phase of its Afghan war. With 8,800 personnel already engaged in the war in Afghanistan, the number of US troops increased to 13,000. There had not been any formal Afghan policy announcement by the US president; instead, he just authorised the Pentagon to take a decision on the surge figure.[18]

The decision to send additional troops underscored a reversal of the Obama administration's policy envisioning the complete withdrawal of US combat forces from Afghanistan; it was also a departure from Trump's own election pledge to not get militarily involved in foreign conflicts. For the new administration, the troop surge was necessitated by spreading Afghan Taliban insurgency, causing an increasing number of military and civilian casualties in the war-torn country.[19]

The series of terrorist attacks in Kabul were the deadliest since the US invasion in 2001. The killing of more than 160 Afghan National Army soldiers in an attack on a military garrison in Herat, believed to be a more secure region, underlined the deteriorating security situation in the country. Thousands of Afghan soldiers had been killed in insurgent attacks since the drawdown of US troops in December 2014. The Taliban had extended their area of influence.

Trump's 'stopgap' arrangement was not going to work. With a deteriorating security situation and a weak and divided government in Kabul, unable to maintain its control over territory, the challenges that confronted the US in Afghanistan were somewhat similar to those faced in the immediate aftermath of 9/11.

Finally, President Trump, on 21 August 2017, laid out his Afghan policy that he declared would bring an end to the US's longest war. In a televised address to troops at Fort Myer in Virginia, the US president declared that the new strategy would focus more on counterterrorism and increase pressure on Pakistan to deny safe haven to terrorists and militant groups. Even as he was speaking, the fresh US deployment to Afghanistan had already begun. Trump did not say how long the new troops would stay, or what their ultimate objective was.[20]

Although Trump declared that US troops would not stay in Afghanistan for long, there was still no clear exit plan. Before standing for the presidency, and privately since entering the Oval Office, Trump had argued for a military withdrawal, but in his speech, he made a rare admission that he had changed his mind. 'My original instinct was to pull out, and historically I like following my instincts, but all of my life I heard that decisions are much different when you sit behind the desk in the Oval Office,' the president said. As in the past, the emphasis was on the military solution. The surge in troops marked a complete turnaround in Trump's election promise to pull out US troops from Afghanistan. He got the US more deeply engaged in what he had earlier described as a 'futile war.'[21]

Trump reserved his strongest criticism for Pakistan. While acknowledging Pakistan's sacrifices and its efforts in fighting terrorism, he declared that it had also been part of the problem. 'We can no longer be silent about Pakistan's safe havens for terrorist organisations, the Taliban and other groups that pose a threat to the region and beyond.' Trump warned that Islamabad would have 'much to lose' if it did not comply. It was perhaps for the first time that a US president had, publicly, warned Pakistan of severe consequences if the country did not take effective action against the alleged terrorist sanctuaries along its borders. Like the previous administrations, the Trump administration too believed in unquestioned cooperation, ignoring Islamabad's interests completely.[22]

It was apparent that President Trump had given in to pressure from the American military establishment, though one tends to agree with him that complete military withdrawal would have disastrous consequences for regional security. The new US strategy came at a time when the Taliban insurgents had expanded their influence to over 40 per cent of the country that was plagued by rising internal political discord.

It was evident though, that there was still no realisation in the Trump administration about the seriousness of the Afghan situation. It was not easy for the US forces to contain the Taliban advance and to maintain the status quo for a longer period. What was extremely alarming, was the spread of the insurgency even to regions in north Afghanistan that were previously considered secure. It was also obvious that the surge in US troops would not significantly shift the balance of war. Deployment of additional troops was more of a patchwork effort than a serious attempt at exploring the possibility of a political solution to the Afghan conflict. Diplomacy and political options were clearly not a priority for the Trump administration, though there had been a fleeting mention of the administration's willingness to begin talks with the Taliban insurgents.[23]

There was no roadmap for peace. Like his predecessor, Barack Obama, Trump had made it clear that the US would not be engaged in nation building in Afghanistan. Unfortunately, there was no clear thinking in Washington on exploring the possibility of a political solution to the Afghan crisis. The use of the 'mother of all bombs' could not bring an end to this bloody war. The much-awaited strategy that linked Afghanistan with the US's South Asia policy deepened regional tensions. Trump repeatedly presented his ideas for South Asia as a radical departure from the Obama administration policies, with a tighter focus on counterterrorism, describing his approach as 'principled realism'.[24]

While assigning India a greater role, there was no plan to engage other neighbouring and surrounding countries in the effort to resolve the Afghan conflict. Trump's policy of getting India more deeply engaged in Afghanistan, had made the situation for Pakistan more complicated. Islamabad's concerns about India's economic and strategic cooperation with Kabul may have been exaggerated, but the previous US administrations were careful not to encourage Delhi to expand its role in Afghanistan.

For Pakistan, the Trump administration had crossed the red line by making India a part of its Afghan strategy. The US policies towards Pakistan had long underestimated the centrality of this regional dynamic. The US Secretary of State, Rex Tillerson, called Prime Minister Shahid Khaqan Abbasi (who took over on 1 August 2017, as PM after Nawaz Sharif's ouster) a few hours before Trump's speech to convey a more nuanced message to alleviate Pakistan's concerns. But there were still lots of questions about the new US policy of lumping South Asia with Afghanistan. There was an implicit US threat of expanding action against the Afghan Taliban insurgents to the Pakistani border regions.[25]

Missing in the policy matrix was the source of tension between Afghanistan and Pakistan that had made prospects for Afghan peace bleaker. Relations between the two countries had never been cordial since 2001, but they had hit a new low with the escalation in terrorist attacks that Kabul blamed on the Haqqani network operating from Pakistan's border areas. There had been a further breakdown of relations between the two countries with measures taken by Pakistan to tighten border management. No matter how intense the US administration's pressure, it failed to force Pakistan to change its position.

Pakistan's own dubious policy contributed to the widening of the gap. There was no serious effort for getting Islamabad's concerns heard in Washington. Pakistan failed to establish meaningful contacts with the Trump administration. It also showed a crisis of leadership in both the civil and military spheres that it could never formulate a clear Afghan policy. Pakistan's Afghan policy had largely been reactive and based on duplicity in Kabul.

Relations had hit a new low following a short period of bonhomie between the two countries in the early period of President Ashraf Ghani's presidency. The biggest opportunity to mend fences was completely lost. Since then, the two countries had been engaged in a bitter war of words accusing one another of providing sanctuaries to each other's insurgents. President Ghani's frequent outbursts and blaming Pakistan for each incident of violence in his country did not help.

Trump began the New Year by launching an attack on Islamabad in his first tweet of 2018: 'The United States has foolishly given Pakistan more than 33 billion dollars in aid over the last 15 years, and they have given us nothing but lies and deceit, thinking of our leaders as fools,' he wrote. 'They give safe haven to the terrorists we hunt in Afghanistan, with little help. No more!'[26]

A few weeks earlier, the US vice president, Mike Pence, said the US administration was putting Pakistan on notice to end its support for the Taliban. Meanwhile, the Trump administration suspended all financial aid to Pakistan over Islamabad's alleged failure to confront militancy in the country.[27] Pakistan's refusal to allow US access to a captured militant from the Haqqani network had added to Washington's ire. The militant was arrested in October 2017 by Pakistani troops as they rescued a Canadian–American couple that had been held captive for five years.

President Trump's tweet was humiliating but what he declared, in the crudest way possible, had been stated in a more nuanced manner by other US officials many times in the past. The aid was now directly linked to Pakistan more actively supplementing the US war in Afghanistan. More precisely, the Trump administration sought to extend the Afghan war well inside Pakistan.[28]

It was not the first time Pakistan's relations with the US had hit a low, yet such an open show of hostility by the US administration was unusual. Pakistan–US ties had hit their lowest ebb in 2011, following the air strike on the Salala border post that killed more than a dozen army soldiers and officers. But Pakistan had then handled the crisis more deftly without compromising its national security interests. The Salala incident had resulted in a recalibration of relations between the two allies—morphing from being a strategic alliance to more of a transactional arrangement. Both civil and military aid from the US had already been drying up during the fag end of the second Obama term. Now the residual transactional relationship, too, had come under strain after Trump's punitive move.

Almost all US military aid had been stopped and only a trickle of civilian aid was now coming to Pakistan. The interaction between the two countries was reduced to a low official level though military-to-military contacts still survived. While the illusion of any strategic convergence had been absent for long, even a transactional relationship was becoming hard to maintain. There was no clarity on how the Pakistani leadership intended to deal with the new challenges arising from toughening of the US stance. The political instability in the country had added to Pakistan's foreign policy and national security problems.[29]

Like previous US presidencies, the Trump administration also saw relations with Pakistan from a purely Afghan prism. Washington's demand for unquestionable compliance was unacceptable to Pakistan and Trump's policy of using pressure tactics to bring Pakistan to its knees, did not seem to be working. The Trump administration's policy towards Pakistan was mainly driven by its own growing frustration over the US failure to defeat the Taliban insurgency in Afghanistan. But there were other geopolitical factors, too, determining the new US hardline approach.

It was not just about the Afghan issue straining relations between Washington and Islamabad. The Trump administration had also expressed its concern over Pakistan's growing strategic and economic ties with China. Washington regularly questioned Beijing's strategic stakes in the China–Pakistan Economic Corridor (CPEC). The CPEC had added a new dimension to the 'all weather' friendship between Pakistan and China. From a purely strategic and security cooperation spanning over more than five decades, the relationship had evolved into a dynamic economic and commercial partnership as well.[30]

The multi-billion dollar investment programme underscored an expanded bilateral cooperation at a time of China's rising geopolitical ambition and growing concerns about Pakistan's security and its fledgling economy. More importantly, the project was eventually to connect China to the Indian Ocean through the Pakistani port of Gwadar, also giving it an access to the Persian Gulf. The CPEC is an important part of a much grander Chinese agenda of regional economic connectivity—the One Belt One Road (OBOR) initiative.[31]

China considered CPEC a 'flagship project' in the whole scheme of OBOR that envisaged a continental Eurasian 'Silk Road Economic Belt' and a Southeast Asian 'Maritime Silk Road.' Given its geostrategic position, Pakistan has the potential to serve as a nexus for the two routes. Pakistani leaders describe CPEC as a game-changer both in terms of the country's economic development and security. CPEC represents an international extension of China's effort to deliver security through economic development. Eventually, an overland link across Pakistan to the Arabian Sea could help ease China's vulnerability to the fact that roughly 85 per cent of its oil imports travel through the single chokepoint of the Strait of Malacca.

CPEC was a practical manifestation of intensified and expanded bilateral cooperation at a time of rising Chinese geopolitical assertiveness and rising concerns about Pakistan's security and development. The changing regional geopolitics and consequent realignment of forces has brought the 'all weather friends' closer. The cooling of its relations with the US, and rising tension with arch-rival India, has given further impetus to Pakistan leaning towards China.[32]

China's growing geopolitical assertiveness and its investments in Pakistan was a major cause of worry to India. One of the Indian concerns was that China could use Gwadar as a naval base for its expanded blue water fleet and operations throughout the Indian Ocean.[33] Now the fear is that CPEC might become another point of contention between the two nuclear South Asian powers. In June 2015, barely two months after Chinese President Xi Jinping announced plans to invest $46bn in CPEC, India's Prime Minister Narendra Modi told China that it was 'unacceptable.'[34]

Washington had its own concerns about CPEC helping China fulfil its ambition to expand its access to, and likely influence, within Eurasia. US administration was also concerned about Pakistan's growing closeness to China. The new geopolitical nexus between Pakistan and China was seen as a threat by Washington which did not want to lose leverage over its long-term South Asian ally.[35] The new realities posed a serious challenge to Pakistani policy makers on how to balance Islamabad's relations with Beijing and Washington.

Notwithstanding these tensions, there was still some convergence of interests between the two estranged allies when it came to ending the war in Afghanistan. But the Trump administration's tactics did not help the two sides work together. Managing these troubled ties also posed a serious challenge to the new administration in Pakistan. The parliamentary elections held in July 2018 swept Imran Khan into power. However tainted they might have been, the 25 July elections had cleared the clouds of political uncertainty—though not entirely.

There was much goodwill among the top brass for the government that had been missing in the past. It was evident that the generals felt much more comfortable working with the new civilian dispensation that did not come with any past baggage. It was important for the military leadership to help stabilise the political and economic situation that also threatened its institutional interests. The fact was that the security establishment had gained greater space and there was no apparent reason for it to rein in the new civilian administration.[36]

17 | Shifting Sands of Afghanistan

The beginning of 2018 had seen a massive escalation in violence, with the Taliban launching an unprecedented number of attacks. Between 20–20 January 2018, there were five high profile attacks in major cities and districts in Afghanistan; the three largest ones took place in the capital, Kabul, claiming dozens of civilian lives. The attacks in high security zones marked the bloodiest phase of the 17-year war with the insurgents getting more audacious.[1]

The escalation in fighting raised questions about the new US–Afghan strategy. Not that the Afghan capital had not witnessed such high profile terrorist attacks before, but the ferocity and the frequency of assaults was alarming. The attacks indicated the increasing capacity and the organisational ability of the insurgents despite a massive escalation in US air strikes.[2]

While the Taliban claimed responsibility for two attacks in Kabul, the militant IS group reportedly carried out the third one. The deadliest one was when Taliban militants drove an explosive-laden ambulance into a secure zone in the capital, housing government offices, and foreign missions, killing and wounding hundreds of people. The insurgents had taken the war into the nation's capital. The rising toll of civilian casualties was disturbing.[3]

It signaled a shift in insurgent strategy—from gaining territorial control to focusing more on the capital to test the mettle of the Afghan security forces. It seemed that the Taliban and the IS were competing on who could create the most terror and carnage in the besieged capital and in other towns and cities in Afghanistan. The chaos resulting from the violence, served the objective of these militant groups—to undermine the confidence of the Kabul administration. While the Afghan National Army had improved its performance greatly over time, it was still not capable of dealing with such organised terrorist attacks on its own. The frequent breach of security by the insurgents had further exposed the inadequacy of the Afghan security agencies.[4]

Even as the Taliban expanded its control over vast swathes of territory, increasing presence of IS in Afghanistan was extremely worrisome. The terrorist group that was fighting both Kabul and the Taliban had been responsible for several high profile attacks in the capital over the last few months and had made inroads in some areas of eastern and northern Afghanistan. The rise of IS had brought greater devastation to an already battered country and caused a spike in the number of civilian casualties.[5]

The latest surge in militant attacks came as the relentless US air strikes had forced the Taliban to retreat from some of their strongholds in western Afghanistan. But the US military offensive had failed to contain the insurgency that had spread to vast areas. There had not been any cessation in the fighting, not even in the winter months. The weakening writ of the Afghan government in the hinterland had given further impetus to the insurgents.

In the midst of this intensification in hostilities, President Ashraf Ghani made an unexpected offer of unconditional peace talks with the Taliban on 27 February 2018. This envisaged giving the Taliban recognition as a legal political party and the release of insurgent prisoners. The offer marked the most significant peace overture by the Kabul government since the war started.[6]

Later, in March 2018, Ghani approved a joint declaration at a conference with major foreign partners held in Uzbekistan's capital, Tashkent, stating that they 'collectively agree that direct talks between the Afghan Government and the Taliban—without any preconditions and without the threats of violence—constitute the most viable way to end the ongoing agony of the Afghan people.'[7]

The dramatic move was preceded by months of national consensus building, which found that Afghans overwhelmingly supported a negotiated end to the war. Ghani ignored the scepticism of some leading figures in his administration who argued that the insurgent leaders were too hardline and the Taliban too fragmented to make any such gambit worthwhile.

Meanwhile, there had been some indication of the Taliban, too, changing its take on peace talks. In February 2018, the militia published three statements calling for peace talks, including a direct letter addressed 'To the American people' in which was written, 'It must now be established by America and her allies that the Afghan issue cannot be solved militarily. America must henceforth focus on a peaceful strategy for Afghanistan instead of war.'[8]

The Taliban, however, maintained a deliberate ambiguity on Ghani's offer of peace talks. In the past, the Taliban had swiftly rejected any Afghan government calls for talks. The group had, since long, asserted its desire to speak exclusively to the US, which it regarded as its chief antagonist, not the Afghan government. This time, however, the insurgent leaders remained silent. While privately, Taliban officials dismissed the proposal as 'nothing new,' the movement stopped short of publicly spurning Ghani's offer. Taliban's continued silence was taken by the Kabul government as a sign that the movement was deliberating internally about whether to make a positive reply.

A major breakthrough came when the Kabul government and the Taliban agreed to a ceasefire over the Eid al-Fitr holiday in June 2018. Both sides ordered their respective forces to stand down during three days of festivities.[9] The brief truce witnessed some emotional scenes of Afghan troops and Taliban fighters embracing each other.

It was indeed a momentous event in the 17-year-long war when some 30,000 Taliban fighters, many of them carrying weapons, joined the Eid prayers and mingled openly with government soldiers in various cities of Afghanistan. The festivities and the joyous mood were illustrative of the public sentiment and support for peace and reconciliation. Most of the fighters had not seen life in town for a long time and were baffled by it.[10]

The truce, unprecedented since the Taliban's ouster from Kabul in 2001, saw a remarkable decline in levels of bloodshed and prompted celebrations across the country. The ceasefire had come amidst a major

Taliban offensive that helped the insurgent force expand its influence. Since the start of the summer offensive, the Taliban had overrun several districts, not only in central and western Afghanistan but also in the north. Taliban forces had been effectively active in 70 per cent of the war-torn country despite massive aerial bombing by the US forces that often caused civilian casualties.[11]

Not a single bullet was, however, fired during the ceasefire that also proved that the Taliban were fully united under a central command despite reports of division within its ranks. Yet the two bloody attacks carried out by the IS, during the ceasefire, that killed scores of people, including Taliban elements, also underlined the growing complexities of the Afghan crisis.

The bloodbath was meant to sabotage any move towards peace. The growing activities of the Middle East-based militant group had given a new and bloodier turn to the Afghan war. It was cause for concern for both the government in Kabul and for the Taliban. The expanding role of the IS had increased pressure on the two sides to counter the militant group that espoused a global terrorist agenda.

Not surprisingly, the Taliban fighters did not enter the non-Pashtun districts in northern Afghanistan during the ceasefire, despite their significant military successes in the region in recent months, for the simple reason that there was no expectation of the same kind of public response as witnessed in the Pashtun-dominated areas. That may also have been reflective of the reservations of the Afghan ruling elite regarding President Ghani's peace gesture towards the insurgents.

Yet the influx of Taliban fighters into the cities and their bonhomie with government officials during Eid had caused serious concern to the leaderships of both the Taliban and Kabul government. Fighters attending the reception given by senior government officials in Jalalabad and Kabul caused the most concern. Although almost all Taliban fighters reportedly returned to their posts before the end of the ceasefire, some chose to stay back. That worried the Taliban leadership and brought to the surface the fissures within.[12]

In a purported video message posted on social media, Mullah Mohammad Yaqoob, the son of Mullah Omar, castigated the Taliban commanders for being overly friendly with government officials. A major concern of some Taliban leaders was that the ceasefire and the close interaction with government forces could have affected the morale of the fighters.[13]

Similarly, for the Afghan government, the sight of thousands of insurgent fighters flooding the streets of the capital, Kabul, and other towns and being enthusiastically greeted by the people, was not a happy one either. Some Afghan leaders had expressed their scepticism over whether it was a wise decision to open the gates of the cities to insurgents. There was also fear that the fighters who had stayed back could be potential attackers.

A common theme in the ceasefire celebrations was the suspicion, shared on both sides, that outsiders had fuelled the war. Many soldiers and Taliban fighters, when asked why they fought if they evidently intermingled so easily, blamed either foreigners (by which government troops meant interlopers backing the Taliban, primarily Pakistanis) or 'Americans.' Not all politicians welcomed the ceasefire Eid celebrations, although only a few prominent figures said it out loud. Former Afghan intelligence chief, Amrullah Saleh, became a leading critic, warning of a 'Taliban Tet offensive' and of 'mass infiltration.' On the insurgent side, some Taliban commanders and ideologues condemned the fraternisation as a betrayal of thousands of martyrs, accusing foot soldiers of being too friendly during the ceasefire.[14]

These voices, while a minority, reflected divergent perspectives within the Taliban regarding their 'internal enemy,' the term they used to designate Afghan government forces. For many Taliban, Afghan soldiers were enemies primarily because they shielded foreign troops from attack; in other words, in the absence of a foreign presence, reconciliation was possible.

Insurgent hardliners, in contrast, viewed the Afghan army's affiliation with the government as sufficient reason for animosity, and thus considered mingling with them to be treachery. Overall, however, a majority on both sides expressed support for the ceasefire. Even Atta Mohammad Noor, an opposition politician and Tajik powerbroker, and a former Northern Alliance commander with a long history of battling the Taliban, backed the truce and called for its extension.

The Eid truce, however, proved to be only a fleeting respite, as fighting resumed shortly afterwards. The Taliban rejected Ghani's offer to extend the ceasefire and announced they would resume hostilities. The intensification of violence minimised the optimism generated by the truce. While the Taliban leadership may have demonstrated some flexibility in agreeing to a short ceasefire, perhaps at the persuasion of Pakistan and China, the militia would not accept President Ghani's offer for peace talks. However, the dynamics generated by the Eid ceasefire had opened a window of opportunity.[15]

There had been more positive signals coming from Kabul and Washington following the encouraging public response to the armistice. Besides the unilateral extension of the ceasefire, the Afghan president in a statement declared that the Kabul government was prepared to discuss the issue of foreign forces in talks with the Taliban. This went well beyond the initial offer made by President Ghani earlier, of releasing Taliban prisoners and the offer of peace talks.[16]

President Ghani's offer was backed by US Secretary of State, Mike Pompeo, who declared that the Trump administration was prepared to support, facilitate, and participate in these discussions. Earlier, General John Nicholson, commander US Forces Afghanistan and the 41-nation NATO-led Mission, had claimed that 'channels of dialogue' had opened with the Taliban.[17] However, there was a fly in the ointment; while the Taliban was willing to talk to the US, it refused to enter into any negotiations with the Kabul government. There was no indication of the insurgent leaders' showing any flexibility in their position on this matter.

In his Eid message, Mullah Hibatullah Akhundzada, the supreme leader of the Taliban, had reiterated his position of 'no talks' with the Kabul government. 'If the American officials truly believe in a peaceful end to the Afghan imbroglio then they must directly present themselves at the negotiation table so that this tragedy (invasion)—the destructive effects of which mainly harm the American and Afghan people—can be resolved through talks,' he declared.[18]

Recent military successes had intensified the Taliban's intransigence. Another factor boosting Taliban's confidence was that it was gaining greater international recognition. Not only Russia, but some other countries too, were now engaging with the Taliban at an official level. The increasing fragmentation of political power in Afghanistan had given further boost to the insurgents.

In July 2018, US officials secretly met Taliban members at the militia's political office in Doha. It was the first contact between Washington and the Taliban after the breakdown of talks between them in 2015.[19] Indeed, there was a growing realisation within the Trump administration that the war in Afghanistan could not be won through military means, and the only way out of the crisis was a negotiated political settlement. Yet, there was no clear strategy to start the peace talks.

Pakistan's role in getting Taliban back to the negotiating table had remained critical. Washington had repeatedly acknowledged Islamabad's importance in getting a political settlement and ending the war in Afghanistan. But there was nothing much left in the partnership wracked by allegations of 'double game' and 'deceit.' Nonetheless, a complete breakup was not an option for either side.

Events on the eve of a short visit to Islamabad in September 2018 by US Secretary of State, Mike Pompeo, and General Joseph Dunford, Chairman of the Joint Chiefs of Staff, had further vitiated the atmosphere. A telephone conversation between Mike Pompeo and Pakistan's newly elected Prime Minister Imran Khan had stirred up controversy, with Islamabad calling Washington's account of the discussion 'factually incorrect.' At one point, the dispute looked serious enough to impact the visit of Pompeo and Dunford who were scheduled to make a stopover in Islamabad on 5 September, while on their way to India for the first round of the India–US dialogue.[20]

The suspension of $300 million from the Coalition Support Fund to Pakistan and the controversy generated by the telephonic conversation between Pompeo and Imran Khan were symptomatic of the widening trust gap. The Secretary of State's short stopover in Islamabad en route to New Delhi, was the first face-to-face talks between the Trump administration and Pakistan's new government. President Trump had already laid down rules that required Pakistan to 'do more' in fighting terrorism on its soil. The visit was meant to 'reset' the relationship between the two countries and the main focus of the talks in Islamabad was the new US initiative to resume peace talks with the Taliban.[21]

President Trump had appointed Zalmay Khalilzad, a US citizen of Afghan origin, as a point man for talks with the Taliban in September 2018. Khalilzad, who had previously served as US ambassador in Kabul, had been closely involved in Afghan affairs since the US invasion of the country in 2001. He had been a member of the Republican national security elite for years and knew most of the players and influential figures in Washington and Kabul. He had also been a part of President Trump's foreign policy team of experts. His Pashtun–Afghan origin was seen as an advantage in the negotiations with Pashtun-dominated Taliban as there would be no language barrier.

With his well-known biases Khalilzad, in the past, had not gotten along well with Pakistani authorities and initially his appointment raised some eyebrows in Islamabad. But those reservations evaporated as he shuttled between Islamabad and Doha. He had a clear mandate from the Trump administration to get a peace deal with the Taliban before the 2020 US presidential elections. Pakistan's role was critical in the success of the talks. Khalilzad managed to develop a good rapport with the new Pakistani government as well as with the military leadership.[22]

Even as it seemed that the two estranged allies could still work together for a negotiated political solution to the Afghan crisis, President Trump fired yet another salvo of tweets against Pakistan in December 2018. The latest spat raised questions about the two countries maintaining even the illusion of meaningful alignment. It did not seem a spontaneous bout of rage that drove an impulsive US president to make such humiliating remarks; it was a well-thought-out move to increase the pressure on Islamabad.

The first volley of words came during an interview with *Fox News*, when out of nowhere Trump blasted Pakistan for not doing a 'damn thing' for the US, despite receiving billions of dollars in aid. He taunted Pakistan for sheltering Osama bin Laden and insinuated that the latter's presence in a high security zone was known to Pakistani officials.[23]

However, unlike the past when Pakistan ignored such invective from US officials, PM Imran Khan responded to President Trump's salvo with an equally harsh tweet: 'Instead of making Pakistan a scapegoat for their failures, the US should do a serious assessment of why, despite 140,000 NATO troops, plus 250,000 Afghan troops, and reportedly $1 trillion spent on the war in Afghanistan, the Taliban today are stronger than before.'[24]

President Trump, perhaps, did not expect such a retort from Pakistan's PM and his tenor got harsher in a spate of Twitter replies. The message was clear: the US would further toughen its stance towards Pakistan. But Trump's demand for unquestionable compliance was unacceptable to Pakistan.

The US policy of using pressure tactics to bring Pakistan to its knees had not worked, and the latest Twitter war between the two leaders further widened the trust deficit. Intriguingly, Trump chose to up the ante at a time when his administration was engaged in direct talks with the Taliban.[25]

Then, in an abrupt volte-face, just weeks after a toxic Twitter exchange, President Trump wrote a letter to Imran Khan seeking Islamabad's help in the Afghan peace negotiations. While the full text of his letter was not released, Trump's tenor appeared mellower. This blow-hot-blow-cold game had become the hallmark of the state of Pakistan–US relations.[26]

Ironically, while the Afghan war may have been the basic cause of tension between Pakistan and the US, it had also been a reason for the two estranged allies to stay together. More than ever, the US appeared serious in finding a political solution to the Afghan crisis. Trump's message came at a time when Zalmay Khalilzad had arrived in the region for his third round of shuttle diplomacy between Doha, Kabul, and Islamabad.[27]

However, despite all-out diplomatic efforts, the war had intensified, taking a huge toll on both sides. It was a classic war-war and talk-talk situation, making the reconciliation process extremely painstaking. Added to the mix was the internal Afghan political situation, and external factors, making the situation more complex, particularly as Afghanistan was now the centre of the new Great Game.

Khalilzad was engaged with the insurgents who appeared much stronger with their successes on the battlefield. The increasing diplomatic legitimacy had boosted their confidence. Declared as a terrorist group in the past, the Taliban was now recognised as an important military and political force in Afghanistan. Khalilzad had held two preliminary meetings with Taliban representatives in Doha in October and in November 2018. The talks were mainly focused on what the Taliban described as part of a 'trust-building process.' There had not been any statement from the US's side about the outcome of the two meetings.

Taliban reiterated their demand of official recognition for their office, scrapping of the UN black list, and release of Taliban prisoners as part of the confidence building measures. The Doha political office was critical for the insurgents to maintain contact with other countries. The Taliban had made it very clear from the outset that formal negotiations could not be started without US willing to discuss withdrawal of its military forces from Afghanistan. The US's decision to hold direct talks with the Taliban was indeed a step forward, but there was still no plan that could lead to a set of structured negotiations.[28]

One major challenge that Khalilzad faced was to get the Kabul government on board with the reconciliation process. While giving tacit support to direct US talks with the insurgents, President Ashraf Ghani had expressed his strong reservations over his government being kept away from the negotiating table. Addressing a conference on Afghanistan in Geneva in September 2018, Ghani stressed the need for an Afghan-owned, Afghan-led peace process as the only viable path to ending the long conflict.

He also declared that the upcoming presidential elections in September 2019 was critical for successful peace negotiations. He asserted that only an elected Afghan government would have the mandate to ratify and implement an agreement with the Taliban. The divide between the Kabul government and Washington over the modalities of the peace talks with insurgents was hard to bridge.[29]

Ghani insisted that any peace negotiations must include respect for Afghanistan's Constitution and its provisions with regard to women, and an end to foreign interference in his country's affairs. He believed that implementation of any peace deal would take at least five years.[30] This assertion seemed contrary to Khalilzad's mandate to expedite the reconciliation process.

As the Doha talks took off in September 2018, Islamabad released a number of high level Taliban prisoners, including the movement's co-founder, Mullah Abdul Ghani Baradar. These prisoner releases were a US-directed move aimed at assuring Taliban of Washington's seriousness about the talks. Mullah Baradar had been captured on 8 February 2010, in a joint CIA–ISI raid outside Karachi. The Obama administration had described the arrest of the Afghan Taliban's second-in-command as a 'turning point' in its war in Afghanistan.[31]

Mullah Baradar's detention became a major source of tension between Kabul and Islamabad. Karzai would demand his release in every meeting with Pakistani leaders. Interestingly, US officials would keep quiet whenever Afghan leaders asked for Baradar's release. But top US officials would later warn Pakistani leaders against his release. At one point, President Obama personally sent a message that Mullah Baradar should not be released. However, Pakistan refused to give US officials access to him.[32]

Mullah Baradar was initially dealt with very badly by Pakistani intelligence agencies after his arrest. But later he was treated with respect. Some Afghan officials were, however, taken to meet the detained Taliban leader that included Mohammad Umer Daudzai, the Afghan ambassador in Islamabad. But Mullah Baradar refused to talk to them. He refused to even look at Daudzai. 'We will meet when we both are free,' he told Daudzai, presenting him instead with a prayer mat and beads. 'Give it to your leader,' he told the ambassador.[33]

He remained in confinement as the Taliban insurgency swept across Afghanistan. A co-founder of the Afghan Taliban movement, he had a critical role to play in the effort to end the 17-year war. The long confinement had increased Baradar's respect among the Taliban commanders. After the death of Mullah Omar, he was considered the de facto leader of the movement.

Mullah Baradar's release showed the Trump administration's desperation to find a political solution to the Afghan crisis. The Americans now considered him as pivotal to the success of the talks. Following his release, Baradar had circulated an audiotape promising Taliban fighters that he would have a greater presence within the movement.

In the midst of the marathon Doha negotiations, the Taliban appointed Mullah Baradar as the chief negotiator. He was also elevated to second position in the Taliban hierarchy. His appointment manifested the seriousness the Taliban assigned to the peace negotiations. Another factor behind Mullah Baradar's elevation was believed to be the respect he commanded with, and his influence over, Taliban field commanders whose support would be critical to any peace agreement.[34]

A change in the Taliban negotiating team had also contributed to the breakthrough.

Mullah Baradar's presence and his heading the team certainly gave greater authority to the Taliban negotiators. His participation also meant that the Doha team would become more of a decision-making body than before. Before his arrest, he was already believed to be the most prominent Taliban leader in favour of finding a political settlement.

Although he seldom participated in the larger meetings between the two sides, his presence in Doha helped clear roadblocks. Whenever there was an indication of talks breaking down, Khalilzad would call on him and the problem would mostly be sorted out. But Baradar's health seemed to have suffered after spending nearly a decade in detention.[35]

In an interview, Khalilzad described Mullah Baradar as an 'Afghan patriot.'[36] In what could be termed as an irony of history, nearly 18 years after the US invasion of Afghanistan (and the ouster of the Taliban regime), Mullah Abdul Ghani Baradar sat across the negotiation table with US officials to discuss the timeline for the withdrawal of the occupation forces from his homeland. Among others, there were five former inmates of Guantánamo who were also part of the Taliban delegation, now engaged in peace talks in Doha with those who were their tormentors. They were released in 2014 in exchange for a US soldier held by the Taliban. Since then, they had been living in Doha. All of them had been close to Mullah Omar. All had held senior positions in the former Taliban government.

They included Mullah Khairkhwa who had served as a governor and acting minister of interior; Abdul Haq Wasiq, deputy minister of intelligence; Mullah Fazel Mazloom, a front-line commander who was also chief of the Taliban army. The other two were Mullah Norullah Noori and Mohammad Nabi Omari. Most of them were detained and sent to Guantánamo after they had surrendered—or even after they had started cooperating with the leadership of the new government the US had installed in Afghanistan.[37]

At the time of his arrest, Mullah Khairkhwa had returned to his home village, and had reached out to Hamid Karzai, who had been installed as president after the invasion. The former Taliban government deputy intelligence chief, Mullah Wasiq, had come to a meeting with CIA operatives to discuss cooperation with the US and Afghan officials when he and some of his associates, who had come along, were bound and taken away. Mullah Mazloom had surrendered to General Abdul Rashid Dostum, an Uzbek strongman in northern Afghanistan, whose militia had allied with US Special Operations forces.[38]

These five senior Taliban leaders came out of the shadows to join the negotiating team when the Trump administration decided to talk directly to the Taliban. Their inclusion in the team was also meant to send a message to Washington. Zalmay Khalilzad described their presence in the talks as 'more authoritative,' and tweeted that this could be 'a significant moment' in the talks.[39]

Thirteen years of imprisonment and torture had not diminished their resolve. And there was no sign of bitterness about what they had gone through. 'It's been a long war, with lots of casualties and destruction and loss. What gives me hope is that both teams are taking the issue seriously,' Mullah Khairkhwa told the *New York Times*. 'The two sides share a common interest, at least, in ending the war.'[40] The Americans were now sitting across the table with the same men who they had earlier incarcerated and declared terrorists. Each one of those representing the Taliban in the negotiations had a story of struggle, of being in power, and of a life in detention.

A further round of talks was held in Doha in February 2019 with Baradar leading the Taliban delegation. Khalilzad reported that this round of negotiations was 'more productive than they have been in the past' and that a draft version of a peace agreement had been agreed on. The negotiations had been slowed in part by the Taliban's need to ensure unity and cohesiveness within its ranks. The important thing for the Taliban leaders was to obtain a deal they could sell to their fighters.

The proposed deal involved the withdrawal of US and international troops from Afghanistan, and the Taliban not allowing other jihadist groups to operate within the country. The Taliban also announced that progress was being made in the negotiations. But the persistent Taliban refusal to negotiate with representatives from Ashraf Ghani's government remained a major stumbling block in taking the peace process forward.[41]

Exiting Afghanistan had become the biggest foreign policy challenge for the Trump administration. There was also increasing apprehension that the withdrawal of the US forces could further empower the Taliban and plunge Afghanistan into another round of civil war. America's desperation to pull out was itself seen as a victory for the Taliban who had gained greater international recognition over the years. The sight of Taliban leaders jet-setting around the region and given official protocol caused serious embarrassment to the Kabul government. It had also fuelled apprehension among other Afghan groups inside and outside the government. A major challenge for Khalilzad had been to take all those groups on board.

With the resumption of peace talks between the Taliban and US officials in Doha, Moscow ramped up its diplomatic efforts to stay in the game. The gathering in Moscow of disparate Afghan groups and regional players in March 2019 was indicative of the shifting sands of regional geopolitics. Described as the 'Moscow format,' the Russian initiative was a significant move to finding a regional solution to the protracted Afghan war. The spectacle of a former invading power hosting old foes was, indeed, remarkable.[42]

More significant was the fact that the insurgents shared the platform with Afghan delegates led by former Afghan president Hamid Karzai. The group consisted entirely of former officials, representatives of various Afghan political parties and warlords, many of them involved in the country's bloody civil war. There were only two women in the group.[43]

Sher Ali Istaknazai, the head of the Taliban political office in Doha, led the Taliban delegation. The conference represented the most significant contact between senior Afghan politicians and Taliban since the US occupation of Afghanistan in December 2001. The conference was held just a week after US officials and Taliban representatives ended six days of negotiations in Doha. Both sides had by then agreed, in principle, to a framework on two issues: a Taliban guarantee that Afghan soil would never again be used by terrorist groups like al-Qaeda, and a pledge from the US to withdraw its troops.

Absent from the talks, however, was representation from the Afghan government of President Ashraf Ghani, who had strongly criticised the meeting as an affront designed to undermine his office's authority and the Afghan state—he was in an impossible position.

While being at odds with his US backers, whom he accused of moving too quickly to reach a deal, he also found himself pitted against the country's political elite who were rallying around the US-led effort. 'What are they agreeing to, with whom? Where is their implementing power?' Ghani told a private Afghan TV channel, dismissing the talks. 'They could hold a hundred such meetings, but until the Afghan government, the Afghan Parliament, the legal institutions of Afghanistan approve it, it is just agreements on paper.'

Although the Kabul government did not officially participate in the talks, the presence of members of the High Peace Council, which oversaw peace efforts, and individual Afghan leaders, were highly significant. The conference may not have broken the stalemate, but it certainly melted some ice. It was, indeed, a diplomatic triumph for the Taliban. The Taliban representative tried to present a more moderate face, assuring the participants that they believed in women's rights, including provision of education and the right to work. But that would not satisfy the sceptics who had not forgotten the plight of women under the radical Islamic rule.[44]

Meanwhile, there was some sign of melting of ice between Washington and Islamabad as the peace talks between the US and Taliban made some tangible progress, raising hopes of reaching a formal peace agreement sooner. At the invitation of President Donald Trump, Prime Minister Imran Khan visited Washington D.C. in the third week of July 2019. It was a meeting between two unpredictable leaders, but they seemed to have struck a chord.

Putting behind the bitterness of the Twitter war that the two had engaged in previously, the Trump and Khan found some common ground to move forward. The summit talks in Washington had melted the ice, putting back on track a mainly transactional relationship between the two erstwhile allies. And, true to form, it was once again, the lingering Afghan crisis that had brought them together.

Predictably, the talks at the White House revolved around Afghanistan and regional security. It was quite significant that, for the first time, the military leadership of both sides participated in deliberations, reinforcing the perception that the relationship was mainly security-oriented.

It was an interesting development that the Trump administration now saw Pakistan more as a part of the solution than the cause of the problem in Afghanistan. And Pakistan was happy to cooperate in return for an assurance that its national security concerns would be addressed.

There was, indeed, a convergence of interests, notwithstanding the huge trust deficit between the two countries. For sure, relations between Washington and Islamabad, as Trump said, were 'much better now than before.' But it still remained tenuous given the existing strategic divergence. However, the silver lining to this turn of events was that there was no further 'do more' mantra from the US.

One of the reasons for the dramatic change in the environment was Pakistan's crackdown on militant groups, especially the arrest of Hafiz Muhammad Saeed, the founder of the Lashkar-e-Taiba (LeT) which had been accused of carrying out the 2008 attacks in Mumbai. Hafiz Saeed was arrested under terrorism laws on the eve of the Washington D.C. visit. The US had placed a $10 million bounty on the head of the founder of the banned LeT.[45]

Trump's remarks at the joint presser marked a welcome change from his earlier vitriolic statements that held Pakistan responsible for the worsening Afghan conflict. He now believed that Pakistan could save 'millions of lives in Afghanistan' because 'they have a power that other nations don't have with respect to Afghanistan.' In other words, the Trump administration needed Pakistan's support to extricate itself from a festering war that the US had not been able to win.[46]

Undoubtedly, Pakistan had played a very important role in facilitating peace negotiations between the US and the Taliban that had shown significant progress and the effort was duly acknowledged by the US president. But a major question was whether Pakistan could meet US expectations. Although Imran Khan had promised that he could persuade the Taliban to talk to the Kabul government in the coming days, there was still no indication of the insurgents softening their stance. US officials also wanted Pakistan to get the Taliban to agree to a ceasefire, but it was apparent that the Taliban were not willing to budge on the issue.

The resumption of US aid may not have been a major concern for PM Imran Khan; investment and economic cooperation figured more importantly in the meetings. President Trump, too, seemed interested in increasing US investment in, and expanding trade ties with, Pakistan. It was hoped that this approach could help broaden Pakistan–US relations beyond a purely security paradigm.

More importantly, Pakistan needed US help to stave off the looming threat of being blacklisted by the Paris-based terror-financing watchdog, Financial Action Task Force (FATF). In June 2018, Pakistan was placed on the grey list due to its 'strategic deficiencies' in the anti-money laundering and terrorism-financing regime pushed by the US.

Pakistan had missed its May 2019 deadline which required the country to keep terror-financing, and money laundering in check. Now Pakistan was required to swiftly implement its action plan by October 2019. The possibility of being blacklisted could have serious ramifications for Pakistan and would increase its isolation in the international community.

Although FATF did not have the power to impose sanctions, it could affect international transactions because it exposes states to greater scrutiny. Such restrictions would have disastrous implications for Pakistan's fragile economy. US support was critical to prevent such an action.[47]

Meanwhile, after a year-long, and nine rounds of intense negotiations, the US and the Taliban were close to sealing a historic deal that could pave the way for withdrawal of forces. 'We are at the threshold of an agreement that will reduce violence and open the door for Afghans to sit together to negotiate an honourable and sustainable peace,' tweeted Khalilzad after the end of the eighth and final day of the latest round of talks on 1 September 2019.

By the time Khalilzad left Doha he and his Taliban counterparts had finalised the text of the agreement to end the 18-year bloody war. Leaders of both teams 'initialled' their copies and handed them to their Qatari hosts and Khalilzad declared that the agreement document had been finalised 'in principle.' Before the end of the meeting, Khalilzad brought up the idea of a Taliban trip to Washington. Taliban leaders said they accepted the idea—as long as the visit came *after* the deal was announced.

Under the agreement the Taliban would give security guarantees in return for sharp reductions to the 13,000-strong US force in Afghanistan. The Taliban had also agreed to start direct negotiations with the Kabul government on the future political setup in Afghanistan once the agreement with the US was signed.

Khalilzad left Doha for Kabul with a sense of accomplishment to brief the Afghan leaders on the deal. Even as talks were wrapping up in Doha, the US ambassador to Afghanistan delivered an invitation to President Ghani to attend a meeting at Camp David, the presidential getaway, used for hosting presidents, prime ministers, and other notables. The idea was for Trump to hold separate meetings at Camp David with the Taliban and with Ghani, leading to a more global resolution.

President Trump wanted to be the dealmaker who would put the final parts together himself. He had been personally engaged with the developments in the Doha talks in the last few weeks. But just as the deal looked all sewn up, Trump abruptly called off the peace talks with Taliban. He announced his decision in a series of tweet messages on 2 September 2019.

He blamed a recent Taliban attack that killed one American soldier for his decision. But some reports suggested that it had more to do with Taliban's resistance to the US terms for a peace deal, and a rushed plan for a Camp David summit meeting. Talks that once seemed on the verge of a breakthrough had hit a wall over how the deal should be finalised and announced.[48]

President Trump's tweet calling off the talks was not just on a whim; it reflected strong reservation within his administration against the content of the proposed agreement that was seen as more favourable to the Taliban. A major objection was that there was no assurance from the Taliban to adhere to a permanent ceasefire. Among the most significant was a disagreement over the release of thousands of Taliban prisoners in Afghan prisons. There was also no firm commitment from the insurgents to agree to open direct talks with the Kabul government.

The Taliban responded strongly to the breakdown, warning that it would only have consequences for the US. In a statement, the group said that it had received an invitation in late August to visit the US, but had put off a decision until the deal was finalised.[49] Following breakdown of talks, the Taliban escalated their offensive. With no cessation in the Taliban violence there had been an escalation in air strikes by American forces, which had increased civilian casualties.

Amidst escalating violence, Afghanistan went into presidential elections at the end of September 2019. The threat of violence had led to a very low voter turnout and this, coupled with rigging allegations, made the election controversial. While the official result was delayed for months, the two main candidates—Ashraf Ghani and Abdullah Abdullah—had both (like the previous election) claimed victory. The controversial election intensified political polarisation in the country, making the prospect of a political solution to the Afghan crisis even more complex.

Both the Afghan presidential candidates were sceptical of the US talking directly to the Taliban. Not surprisingly therefore, they welcomed the breakdown of the US–Taliban negotiations. Regardless of their differences, what both Ghani and Abdullah agreed on was that the Taliban should talk directly to the Kabul government. That also cast a shadow over the peace process.

Despite the abrupt last-minute policy reversal, the Trump administration was still keen on a political settlement to end the unwinnable war. But any resumption of negotiations was predicated on the Taliban's softening their position on a permanent ceasefire and on holding direct talks with the Kabul government. It was not easy to remove these major stumbling blocks to reviving the stalled peace process.

However, a meeting between the Afghan Taliban leadership and Khalilzad in Islamabad in October 2019 paved the way for the resumption of peace talks. Mullah Baradar and other senior members from the Taliban's Doha political office were in Pakistan's capital to meet with Pakistan's civil and military leadership. The man who spent more than eight years in detention in Pakistan was now being received with a protocol reserved for a head of state.[50]

The presence in Islamabad of Khalilzad during the Taliban visit was no coincidence. Prime Minister Imran Khan had assured US officials during his meetings on the sidelines of the UN General Assembly session in New York in September that he would help in the resumption of the Afghan peace process. Which he did.

That may also have been the reason for the Trump administration to ignore Pakistan's grand diplomatic protocol awarded the Taliban leaders. The reception given to the insurgent group had angered President Ghani who publicly lashed out at Islamabad. His strong reaction was predictable as his government had been completely left out of the Afghan peace process.

Even the agenda at the Pakistan Foreign Office meeting in Islamabad reinforced the impression that the Taliban were being treated as a de facto government. And surprisingly, the US did not seem to have any problem with that. It marked a complete turnaround from Washington's past policy of threatening Pakistan over its links with the Taliban.

Although there had not been any official acknowledgement of the meeting between the US envoy and Mullah Baradar, the resumption of contacts between the two sides helped break the ice. Both sides appeared willing to pick up where they had left off. There was no formal statement on the recommencement of peace talks, but the Islamabad meeting did produce some positive results. While improving the possibility of the resumption of peace talks, it also led to the US and Taliban taking some significant confidence building measures, including a reduction in violence and exchange of prisoners.

The US had already released 11 Taliban detainees from Bagram prison in exchange for three Indian engineers. The Taliban agreed to release two American and Australian nationals in exchange for some other Taliban prisoners, including the brother of Sirajuddin Haqqani, who had been in a prison death cell in Kabul. Notwithstanding these positive signals, there were still roadblocks to navigate before any substantive talks between the US and Taliban could resume.

18 | The Endgame

The glittering ballroom at Hotel Sheraton in Doha that day was packed with representatives of several countries, and with Taliban delegates, witnessing a historic moment. Zalmay Khalilzad sat next to a solemn looking Mullah Abdul Ghani Baradar sporting his signature black turban at the ornate table. US Secretary of State Mike Pompeo, from the front row, watched the two men sign the historic peace agreement setting the stage to end the 19-year-long US war in Afghanistan.

The hall burst into cheer as a smiling Taliban chief negotiator stood up for handshakes with his American counterpart. Some Taliban present there joyfully shouted 'Allah-o-Akbar.' For them, the agreement that laid out the timetable for withdrawal of all US troops from Afghanistan was a victory.[1]

A Taliban spokesman described the peace agreement as a historic document proclaiming, 'the defeat of the arrogance of the White House in the face of the white turban.' It was humbling of the world's mightiest military power.

Khalilzad appeared somber: 'We must remember the lessons of history, and the darkness of conflict,' he remarked.[2]

In some ways, the Doha agreement revived memories of US military humiliation in Vietnam more than half a century ago. It may not have been a Saigon moment for the US forces, yet the deal with the Taliban, paving the way for withdrawal of all foreign troops from Afghanistan, was no less ignominious for Washington. It was not a document of surrender, but neither was it a declaration of victory for the most powerful military power on earth.

In what could be termed a remarkable twist of fate, US officials sat across the table, for more than 18 months, to negotiate peace with the very insurgent leaders who they had once declared as terrorists and sought to annihilate. Many of the officials in the Taliban negotiating team were former inmates of the infamous Guantánamo prison. The Donald Trump administration also faced an awkward reality of having to accept the Haqqani network, which it had listed as a terrorist group and pursued relentlessly with all its military might. The network's leader, Sirajuddin Haqqani, was the Taliban's deputy leader and military commander.

Such is the irony of history that yet another superpower was negotiating its exit from Afghanistan as the war-ravaged country observed the 31st anniversary of the withdrawal of the last Soviet soldier from its soil. While the Russian forces pulled out in 1989, a decade after invading Afghanistan, the Americans were mired in an unwinnable war there for two decades.[3]

Some of those Taliban with whom Americans negotiated the peace agreement, had also fought the Soviet forces with US support. Hailed at the time by the US as 'holy warriors,' they drove out the Red Army with the weapons supplied by the US. History took another turn when some of them turned their guns on their former patrons.

Regardless of who the adversary was at any point in time, two generations of Afghans have known only war and, despite the peace agreement between the US and Afghan Taliban, there was widespread scepticism whether the miseries of the Afghan people would end soon. Much of the peace negotiations took place in a year of record violence from both sides. In just the last quarter of 2019, the Taliban carried out 8,204 attacks, the highest for that period over the past decade. The US, in the meantime, dropped 7,423 bombs and missiles during the year, a record since the US Air Force began recording data in 2006.[4]

In the past five years alone, more than 50,000 members of the Afghan security forces have been killed, and tens of thousands wounded. The Taliban's losses were harder to verify, but their casualty rate was believed to be comparable. Out of about 3,550 NATO coalition deaths in Afghanistan, nearly 2,400 have been Americans.[5]

The US went into Afghanistan in 2001 out of a desire for revenge, following the 9/11 attacks on American soil, with little understanding of a land which has often been described as the 'graveyard of empires.' It was an unwinnable conflict from the beginning, but lies covered the failure. For almost two decades, the American people were deliberately misled by their leaders over a war that had gone terribly wrong.

A report titled 'The Afghanistan Papers' published in the *Washington Post* in December 2019 revealed how facts were distorted to hide the bleak reality of the battleground. Based on thousands of pages of government documents and confidential interviews, the report provides insightful detail into the lies and failures that were part of the US-led war in Afghanistan. It was a war that had gone wrong from the outset.[6]

The Afghanistan Papers (AP) had echoes of the Pentagon Papers, a report on the secret military history of the Vietnam War, that was leaked in 1971 and exposed fabrications of the government. Well, history is repeating itself with no lessons learnt. The AP contradict many public statements that were made by US presidents, military commanders, and diplomats, who kept on assuring their countrymen that the US war effort in Afghanistan was yielding dividends. Barack Obama even went as far as to declare the conflict a 'good war.'

The feeling of frustration and desperation expressed by the top officials, in confidential interviews, were in complete contrast to the public statements consistently trotted out by the American civil and military leadership. The lack of a clear strategy and conflicting objectives dogged the war from the outset. Although the failure of the US forces in Afghanistan had been evident for a long time, the magnitude of chaos and confusion in Washington over the Afghan war, exposed in the report, is very revealing.

How clueless the Americans were when they invaded Afghanistan in October 2001 to avenge the 9/11 attacks was well described by the three-star army general, Douglas Lute, the 'war czar' during the Bush and Obama administrations. 'We were devoid of a fundamental understanding of Afghanistan—we didn't know what we were doing,' General Lute told interviewers in 2015, as quoted in the *Washington Post* report. 'What are we trying to do here? We didn't have the foggiest notion of what we were undertaking.' Not surprisingly, the war dragged on, making it the longest the US has ever fought any war.[7]

The Taliban's resurgence was also aided by the strategic miscalculation made by the US when they decided to re-empower former strongmen and warlords, which caused old ethnic and tribal tensions to resurface. One of the biggest mistakes was failure of the West to avoid the perception that it was a party in the Afghan civil war.

It was indeed a quick victory for the US-led forces in 2001, in what Robert Grenier, the former CIA Station Chief in Pakistan, described as the 'first American-Afghan war' with the routing of the Taliban regime in December 2001. But the triumph was short-lived. Three years later, in 2004, the US found itself involved in its second Afghan war with thousands of coalition forces engaged in a fierce battle with the revitalised and regrouped Islamic insurgents. The revival of the Taliban as a powerful insurgent force should not have come as a surprise. In fact, the group was never really defeated.[8]

Tens of thousands of Afghans were killed in the war that cost close to a stunning trillion dollars. Since 2001, over 775,000 US troops had been deployed in Afghanistan. The distorted statistics made it appear that the US was winning the war when that was not the case. There were fundamental disagreements on the objectives of the US operation in Afghanistan within successive US administrations. While some officials wanted Afghanistan to become a political democracy, others wanted the war to change Afghan culture, including its views on women's rights.[9]

The US government's attempts to curtail runaway corruption, build a competent Afghan army and police force, and put a dent in Afghanistan's thriving opium trade never worked. Most of the US aid money was siphoned off by Afghan officials and warlords aligned with the US. Afghanistan became a narco (drug trafficking) state as a result of some very flawed policies. Despite spending billions of dollars on building and training the Afghan National Army and other security personnel, Afghan forces lacked the ability to fight the Afghan Taliban without American support. The casualty rate was much higher among Afghan soldiers than among the US and NATO forces.[10]

After fighting for nearly 19 years, the US seemed desperate to end an unwinnable war. All three American presidents since 2001—George W. Bush, Barack Obama, Donald Trump, and their respective military commanders—were not able to make good on their promises to win in Afghanistan. It is evident that there was bipartisan support in the US for withdrawal from a festering war.[11]

But a peace deal, paving the way for America's exit from Afghanistan, was seen as a major diplomatic victory for President Trump. Although the agreement, reached after protracted peace negotiations, raised hopes of bringing US soldiers back home there was still a long way to go before exit was possible.

The timeframe for the withdrawal of remaining foreign troops was linked to security guarantees by the Taliban, including a pledge that the country will not become a safe haven for terror groups. The insurgents were also required to ensure that international terrorist networks, such as al-Qaeda, will not be allowed to use Afghanistan as a base for attacks on US interests. The US troop withdrawal was to be completed in 16 months, from the signing of the agreement—provided the Taliban uphold their side of the bargain.[12]

Unfortunately, despite the signing of the US–Taliban peace agreement on 29 February 2020, the peace deal remained fragile with no cessation in fighting. Days after the Doha agreement, President Trump called Mullah Baradar to assure him that his administration was sincere in pulling out US troops. Trump later described his phone conversation with the Taliban second-in-command as very 'positive.' Baradar too assured the US president that Taliban would honour the peace agreement, and it all sounded very encouraging.[13]

However, hours after the historic telephonic contact, the US Air Force was back in action against Taliban fighters, who had launched a string of deadly attacks against the Afghan forces, bringing an end to a week-long truce. Since calling off the truce the insurgents carried out 43 attacks across 16 provinces killing dozens of Afghan soldiers. Taliban officials denied that there was any breach of the Doha peace agreement as they were only targeting Afghan troops and not foreign forces.[14]

While abiding by the peace agreement, the Taliban had stopped attacking US forces, but they intensified attacks on Afghan forces. The insurgents wanted to keep up the pressure on the Afghan government before intra-Afghan talks were held. A major reason for the Taliban not agreeing to a permanent ceasefire was that it would be hard to mobilise the fighters once they all went home.

Reduction in violence, and that too for a shorter period, still kept the fighters at the post. The situation had become more complex with the Taliban forces extending their control and influence over a large part of the country. It was a clear attempt to increase their leverage at the negotiating table.

Following the Doha agreement in February 2020, it was left to the Taliban and Afghan government to decide about the future political setup through negotiations. It was certainly not easy for the two warring sides to agree to an arrangement that could satisfy all Afghan factions. The two decades of foreign occupation and war had further intensified polarisation in the country.

Previously, the Taliban had refused to engage in direct talks with the Kabul government. It was only after the peace deal with the US had been inked that the insurgents agreed to intra-Afghan dialogue on the country's political future. With their battlefield victories and expanding territorial control, the insurgents had gained upper hand that had increased their confidence.

President Ashraf Ghani was not happy at being left out of the peace negotiations, but he had no choice but to accept the Doha agreement. His position had been further weakened after the controversial presidential elections in September 2019 that had led to the formation of a parallel administration by his rival Abdullah Abdullah. But, just as they did after the 2013 Afghan elections, the US arm-twisted Ashraf Ghani and Abdullah Abdullah to agree to a power-sharing arrangement, accompanied by threats to cut off a substantial part of aid to Afghanistan if the electoral dispute was not resolved.[15]

Zalmay Khalilzad finally succeeded in getting the squabbling Afghan political leadership together. The crisis over who would represent the Kabul government in the talks with the insurgents had also been resolved. The former chief executive, Abdullah Abdullah, was to head the government side in the negotiations, thus removing the ambiguity. It was extremely important this issue was resolved, as the Taliban leadership appeared much more unified and clear about its strategy than the Afghan government.[16]

While consolidating its military and diplomatic gains, the Taliban also sought to secure the support of communities it had fought in the past in order to present themselves as a national movement. The Taliban had traditionally relied on ethnic Pashtuns, but it had made a clear shift towards recruiting members of other ethnic groups with a view to expand their area of influence. Over the years, the insurgent group had made significant inroads in the non-Pashtun belt in northern Afghanistan and now had several Tajik and Uzbek commanders in its ranks, giving them more operational autonomy. The non-Pashtuns assumed important positions in the Taliban leadership and held key posts in provinces.[17]

The changing ethnic profile of the group was borne out by the fact that non-Pashtuns now constituted one-quarter of the Taliban Leadership Council and its various commissions. Members of ethnic minorities were also assigned important positions of provincial and district shadow governors and zonal commanders. By recruiting members of the Shia Hazara community, the Taliban tried to rebrand themselves as a multi-ethnic and multi-sectarian organisation in order to make themselves more politically acceptable.[18]

For the first time, the militia had appointed a Shia from the ethnic Hazara community as its shadow district chief. The surprise move came ahead of the intra-Afghan peace talks. The hardline Sunni militia had been previously blamed for persecuting the minority sectarian group during its stint in power. The Hazaras, who are of Mongolian descent, largely inhabit central Afghan provinces and have a significant presence in the capital Kabul. The Taliban tried to position themselves as a national movement capable of replacing the current Afghan government.[19]

Moreover, the Taliban also exploited the fractious ethnic landscape in northern Afghanistan to win over disgruntled tribal chiefs who felt marginalised by the Kabul government in terms of political representation. Some of them had joined the Taliban for protection since they could not rely on the Afghan security forces any more. The Taliban approach paid off, with an increasing number of minority ethnic groups joining the militant faction.[20]

The Taliban leveraged the peace deal with US to its advantage to woo regional warlords. With the withdrawal of US forces imminent, joining the Taliban had once again become a serious option for many people and groups in Afghanistan. While the electoral power struggle had further weakened the Kabul government's position, the Taliban had shown a greater degree of pragmatism. Increasing international recognition had given the militia greater confidence. Some warlords and power groups struck separate deals with the militia, which further weakened the Kabul government's position ahead of intra-Afghan peace talks.

It was not just the minority ethnic and sectarian groups that the Taliban sought to attract. Lamenting that Afghans had suffered enough in the relentless conflict, Taliban leaders tried to reassure the people that the militia would take all measures, in partnership with other Afghans, to make sure that the new Afghanistan was a bastion of stability where nobody felt threatened.

For many Afghans, however, the prospect of the return of Taliban rule was disconcerting. Notwithstanding its solemn pledges, the Taliban maintained a deliberate ambiguity about its political agenda, adding to a sense of confusion. There were some indications that the conservative Islamist movement would be willing to work within a pluralistic political system. Yet there was no clarity whether the group would be willing to work within a democratic political and constitutional setup.

In their informal interactions with various Afghan factions and delegations, the Taliban leaders had held out assurances that they acknowledged women's rights and would not oppose female education, but that had not helped remove the concerns about their actions after the withdrawal of foreign forces. In the past, the Taliban regime had completely banned women's education and rejected their right to work.

While the Taliban political leadership appeared more moderate and flexible in their views, there was no evidence that the commanders leading the fight would also be amenable to change. In an op-ed piece in *The New York Times* (NYT) on the eve of the signing of the peace agreement with the United States, Sirajuddin Haqqani, long considered an arch-enemy by the US, envisioned 'a new, inclusive political system in which the voice of every Afghan is reflected and where no Afghan feels excluded.'[21]

Taliban's second-in-command sounded more like a statesman and a peacenik rather than one of the most wanted 'terrorists' by the US, who had placed a bounty of millions of dollars on his head. Sirajuddin Haqqani, the most feared militant commander, leader of the Haqqani network, who had haunted American forces in Afghanistan for almost two decades, now appeared as the biggest proponent of peace. It was a well-crafted statement meant to allay fears of the Afghans, as well as of the international community, of the Taliban reverting to their old ways, and attempting to re-establish a tyrannical rule once the foreign forces withdrew.[22]

Perhaps the most significant point in the *NYT* op-ed piece was the recognition of the rights of women to education and to work. The issue had been a major concern for Afghan women and rights groups who feared that the Taliban would try to reverse the progress made in the field of female education in Afghanistan over the past two decades. Ironically, Sirajuddin Haqqani wanted the US, whose forces he had been fighting, to 'play a constructive role in the postwar development and construction of Afghanistan.'[23]

President Trump also suggested that the Taliban might be America's newfound allies. 'They will be killing terrorists. They will be killing some very bad people. They will keep that fight going,' the US president remarked at a news conference.[24]

Whether or not the solemn declaration in the *NYT* op-ed piece would satisfy its detractors, it did reflect a tangible shift in the thinking of the Islamist militia that previously rejected a pluralistic political process. Although such declarations might be seen as a good omen by the international community, for a large section of Afghans, it was not enough.[25]

Nonstop fighting between the Taliban and Afghan government's forces and delay in exchange of prisoners, as stipulated in the Doha agreement, remained a major obstacle. The escalation in violence, since the Doha agreement, had exacted dozens of civilian lives and had thrown the prospect of critical intra-Afghan dialogue into serious doubt. Many of those attacks were carried out by the so-called IS or Daesh. The rise of the terrorist group in parts of the country had worsened the Afghan situation.

It was not that the war-ravaged country had not seen this scale of violence before, but the assault on a maternity home in Kabul in the first week of May 2020 that killed mothers and babies was heart wrenching. It was not the first time that terrorists had targeted a hospital in Afghanistan, but the sheer brutality of the killing had shaken and outraged people.[26] The attack carried the hallmark of Daesh and sent a grim reminder of the prospect of the country falling deeper into chaos with the Trump administration indicating that the planned drawdown of US forces from Afghanistan could be expedited.

The radical faction, that had originated in the Middle East, managed to spread its tentacles in different parts of Afghanistan during the last few years and targeted civilian populations and minority religious sects with impunity. These bloody incidents had heightened fears that the militant group was trying to disrupt nascent peace process in the war-torn country. Daesh had launched several spectacular terrorist attacks in Kabul since the US and Taliban signed a peace agreement. The attacks had demonstrated the group's capacity to launch high profile attacks despite its recent battlefield setbacks at the hands of American forces and Taliban.

However, after weeks of intensifying insurgent attacks, the Kabul government blamed the Taliban for violence. Soon after the attacks, President Ashraf Ghani ordered Afghan security forces to abandon the 'active defense' posture they had been in since the signing of the US–Taliban agreement and return to offensive attacks against the insurgents. President Ghani even ignored the US exhortation that the Kabul government and Taliban should jointly combat Daesh rather than fighting each other.[27]

A major concern of the US was that the IS would gain ground in Afghanistan while the Afghan security forces and the Taliban were fighting each other. But furious over Taliban's rejection of his repeated offers for a ceasefire, in order to allow the Kabul government to focus on fighting the Covid-19 pandemic sweeping the country, President Ghani refused to heed US advice.[28]

Zalmay Khalilzad's shuttle diplomacy between Doha, Islamabad, and Kabul, delivered a major breakthrough in bringing the Taliban and Kabul government to agree on a three-day ceasefire during Eid ul Fitr starting from 24 May. The main aim was to resuscitate the US–Taliban peace deal. The ceasefire came just days after Hibatullah Akhundzada, the Taliban supreme leader, urged Washington 'not to waste' the opportunity offered by the Doha agreement.[29]

The three-day truce, short though it was, brought war-weary Afghans some respite from an unending chain of violence. It had only been the second ceasefire since the US invasion of Afghanistan in late 2001.[30] A similar three-day ceasefire was observed during Eid festivities in 2018. Successive events had also raised hopes of the elusive intra-Afghan dialogue finally taking off.

President Ghani's decision to free 2,000 Taliban prisoners had removed a major hurdle. The row over the exchange of prisoners had been a major roadblock to furthering the peace process. In the peace deal signed with the US, Taliban had set the release of prisoners as a precondition for the start of talks with the Kabul government. The fast-changing situation was yet another example of the shifting sands of Afghan politics. The Afghan peace depended entirely on the intra-Afghan talks.[31]

President Ashraf Ghani in mid-August passed an order to release the remaining batch of 400 Afghan Taliban prisoners thus clearing the final hurdle for the start of the negotiations between the two sides. While releasing most of the detainees, the government in Kabul was reluctant to free what it described as hardcore fighters; 156 of these prisoners had been sentenced to death.

The president's consent came after a consultative assembly or Loya Jirga, gave its approval. There was also American pressure behind the move. It's apparent that the Trump administration does not want any delay in its plan to withdraw US forces from Afghanistan.

The long-delayed negotiations between the Taliban and Afghan government finally began in Doha on 10 September 2020. It was indeed a historic moment when the two warring sides sat face to face for the first time since start of the war some two decades ago. It was the most critical phase of the Afghan peace process that began with the peace agreement between the US and Taliban.

On the eve of the talks, the Taliban announced some changes in their negotiating team bringing in Mullah Mohammad Yaqoob, the son of Mullah Omar, the late supreme leader of the militia. He had earlier been appointed to the pivotal post of chief of the Taliban's military operations. His rise in the Taliban hierarchy is seen as significant given his reputation as a hardliner.

Yaqoob emerged on Afghanistan's insurgent landscape some five years ago after it was confirmed that his father had died in 2013. The disclosure led to a fierce succession battle within the group and some powerful Taliban commanders backed Yaqoob to succeed his father. The bid failed, though he was made a member of the powerful leadership council. Two years later, he was appointed the deputy of Hibatullah Akhundzada, the new Taliban chief.

His rise from obscurity to one of the most senior positions in the Taliban hierarchy may owe to his bloodline since he is the eldest son of Mullah Mohammed Omar, the militia's founding father. Recent developments indicate, however, that the insurgent group is beginning to see him as a leader in his own right. Thirty-year-old Yaqoob was not just among the group's deputies but also its new military chief. His position as one of the most powerful militia members was further consolidated after his induction in the Taliban team for intra-Afghan negotiations, though the talks have been delayed since the group awaits the release of the last batch of its prisoners.

The new Taliban team also includes Anas Haqqani the younger brother of Sirajuddin Haqqani, deputy leader of the insurgent group. The Kabul government, a year ago, in exchange for two American and one Australian nationals held by the Taliban, released the younger Haqqani who was in a death cell in a Kabul prison.

Another significant addition to the team is the former chief justice in the ousted Taliban regime. Led by Taliban deputy leader Mullah Abdul Ghani Baradar, the rest are the same representatives who were there in the peace talks with the US. The changes in the Taliban negotiating team had made it more representative of the group's political and military leadership.

On the other side, while former chief executive Abdullah Abdullah directed the peace negotiations with the Taliban, the Afghan team in the talks was led by Masoom Stanekzai, a former head of the Afghan intelligence agency, NDS. He was forced to resign in 2019, following an extrajudicial killing of four Afghan civilians during a night raid carried out by the agency personnel in Jalalabad. Masoom Stanekzai had earlier served as secretary of the High Peace Council, which was set up by the Afghan government to talk to the Taliban in the past.

Although the talks opened on a positive note with both sides calling for peace and reconciliation, it was going to be a tricky path to end the war. Fighting raged on in different parts of the country as the two sides talked peace. In a situation where two sides had long been locked in war, it was never easy to negotiate peace and agree to a political transition.

Pakistan's role in facilitating the peace negotiations between the Taliban and US was crucial. For Pakistan, the Doha agreement was a vindication of its consistent position on the need for a negotiated political settlement of the Afghan crisis. This was also seen by Islamabad as the best way to neutralise Indian influence on the country's western border. A complete Taliban takeover was neither possible nor was it in the interest of Pakistan. Taliban's control across the Durand Line would give an immense boost to the Islamic militancy movement in Pakistan.

However, Pakistan's backing of the Taliban and the insurgent leadership operating from its soil had also been a major reason for strained relations with the Kabul government and other Afghan factions opposed to the Taliban. While its role in getting the Taliban to the negotiating table may have earned Pakistan appreciation from US, it drew ire from the Ghani government.

Pakistan's influence over the Taliban leadership had also waned over the years with the opening of its Doha office in 2013, and the growing international recognition of the insurgent group. Notwithstanding their close ties, the Taliban leadership also had misgivings over some of Pakistan's policies towards the insurgents. There was a limit to Pakistan's leverage over the group when it came to intra-Afghan talks.

With the Afghan endgame, the post-9/11 US–Pakistan relations came full circle. Originally touted as a strategic relationship, it morphed into a transactional one.

Perhaps the biggest confusion among various US departments had been over whether Pakistan was to be treated as a friend or as an adversary.

When Pakistan became America's key strategic partner in the so-called war on terror, it also went to war against itself. The implications of this internal struggle for Pakistan, for the US, and for the region, were huge. From the Pakistani vantage, the US embrace, difficult either to accept or to escape, pitted the nation against itself on many fronts: the military against the militants, the present against the past, a political partnership with the US versus a culture of jihadi radicalism.

The insurgent safe havens along Pakistan's western borders had provided the Taliban strategic depth in the country. That also gave impetus to Islamic militancy in Pakistan's tribal regions. The horizontal and vertical fragmentation of society along political, religious, and ethnic lines, which had intensified since 9/11, posed the most serious problem for Pakistan.

While cooperation was extremely critical in order to fight global terrorism, the US and Pakistani security agencies followed their divergent agendas in Afghanistan. That underlying tension cast a huge shadow over the US war against Taliban in Afghanistan. It was an association largely built on expediency and marked by mutual distrust. The two supposed allies could not figure out whether they were friends or enemies despite a nearly two decade-long partnership.

The post-9/11 relations between the two nations could best be described as 'frenemies'. While, on the one hand, Pakistan was accused of providing a base for the Afghan Taliban, its support was also deemed critical to enable the exit of American forces from Afghanistan. Ironically, while the Afghan war may have been the basic cause of tension between Pakistan and US, it had also been a reason for the two estranged allies to stay together. A complete breakup was not an option for either country. For the US, Pakistan's support was critical for its exit from Afghanistan. But it was also in Pakistan's interest to help stabilise the situation in Afghanistan.

Inevitably, the withdrawal of American forces from Afghanistan will have a huge impact on regional geopolitics. The country's strategic location has historically made it vulnerable to the involvement of outside powers and proxy battles. A major concern since the 2001 invasion has been that the American military withdrawal could lead Afghanistan to further descent into chaos fuelling a full-scale civil war, with India, Russia, and Iran backing different factions and dragging Pakistan into a protracted conflict. The spillover effects of spiraling instability and conflict in Afghanistan could be disastrous.

Realistically, however, there is still a long way to go before peace can return to the war-torn country. Decades of conflict had exacted a severe toll on the lives of millions of Afghans and wrought destruction that could not be ended easily even if the Afghan factions reached a power-sharing agreement. Complete withdrawal of foreign troops will have its own complications.

The long war has left the country divided. With their battlefield victories and expanding territorial control, the Taliban had gained an upper hand, thus creating a dangerous asymmetry of power as the Afghan endgame draws nearer. The Doha agreement, while laying down the timeframe of the foreign forces' withdrawal, offers both hope and fear to the Afghan people. The hope is that some kind of lasting peace could be reached. The fear is that the expansion of Taliban influence could lead to a resurgence of the tyrannical, medieval, rule which was the hallmark of the Taliban's first stint of power in Afghanistan. What will it be? Only time will tell.

Notes

Introduction

1. 'Remarks Following Discussions With President Pervez Musharraf of Pakistan and an Exchange With Reporters in New York City', 10 November 2001, *see*: https://www.presidency.ucsb.edu/documents/remarks-following-discussions-with-president-pervez-musharraf-pakistan-and-exchange-with.
2. Ibid.
3. *See* Chapter 3.
4. *See* Chapter 2.
5. R. L. Grenier, *88 Days to Kandahar*, Simon & Schuster, 2016, p. 8.
6. 'Afghanistan and India sign "strategic partnership"', *BBC News*, 4 October 2011, *see*: https://www.bbc.com/news/world-south-asia-15161776.
7. S. Yousufzai, 'Ten years of Afghan war: How the Taliban go on', *Newsweek*, 10 February 2011, *see*: https://www.newsweek.com/10-years-afghan-war-how-taliban-go-68223.
8. *See* Chapter 9.
9. *See* Chapter 10.
10. *See* Chapter 11.
11. *See* Chapter 12.

1 | History Starts Today!

1. Interview with Brigadier Mujtaba, former military attaché in Washington who was present in 13 September 2001 meeting at Langley.
2. Ibid.
3. J. Fitchett, 'Assassination of Massoud Removed a Potential Key Ally for U.S: Did bin Laden Kill Afghan Rebel?', *The New York Times*, 17 September 2001, *see*: https://www.nytimes.com/2001/09/17/news/assassination-of-massoud-removed-a-potential-key-ally-for-us-did-bin.html.
4. G. Tenet and B. Harlow, *At the Center of the Storm: My Years at the CIA,* Harper Collins, 2007, p. 141.
5. Ibid, p. 142.
6. Interview with Maleeha Lodhi, former ambassador to Washington from Pakistan.
7. Ibid.
8. Richard Armitage interview with PBS show *Frontline* on 19 April 2002, *see*: https://www.pbs.org/wgbh/pages/frontline/shows/campaign/interviews/armitage.html.
9. Ibid.
10. Author's interview with Lieutenant General (rtd) Tariq Ghazi, former corps commander Karachi.

11. P. Musharraf, *In the Line of Fire*, New York, Simon and Schuster, 2006, p. 201.
12. Ibid, p. 204.
13. B. Woodward, *Bush at War*, New York, Simon and Schuster, 2002, p. 59.
14. T. Hussain, 'U.S–Pakistan Engagement: The War on Terrorism and Beyond', *USIP, see:* https://www.usip.org/sites/default/files/sr145.pdf.
15. Z. Hussain, *Frontline Pakistan: The Struggle with Militant Islam*, I.B. Tauris, 2006, p. 28.
16. Mentioned in the 9/11 Commission Report on page no. 183. Also *see*: P. Musharraf, *In the Line of Fire*, New York, Simon and Schuster, 2006, p. 201.
17. Mentioned in the 9/11 Commission Report.
18. Ibid.
19. P. Musharraf, *In the Line of Fire*, Free Press, 2006, p. 211.
20. Ibid, p. 202.
21. A. Levy and C. Scott-Clark, *Deception*, 2007, p. 314. Pervez Musharraf is quoted telling his aid Sharifuddin Pirzada.
22. President Pervez Musharraf's interview with PBS show *Frontline* on 14 May 2002, *see*: https://presidentmusharraf.wordpress.com/2006/07/13/address-19-september-2001/.
23. Ibid.
24. Ibid.
25. Author's interview with two corps commander who attended the meeting that day.
26. Ibid.
27. Ibid.
28. Ibid.
29. Author's interview with Aziz Khan, Pakistan's former ambassador to Afghanistan.
30. Ibid.
31. Richard Armitage's interview with PBS show *Frontline* on 19 April 2002.
32. Z. Hussain, 'A general turn around', *Newsline*, February 2003.
33. P. Musharraf, *In the Line of Fire*, Free Press, 2006, p. 216.
34. R. Grenier, *88 Days to Kandahar: A CIA Diary*, 2015, p. 117–119.
35. Rahimullah Yusufzai narrated his discussion with Mullah Omar during a conversation.
36. Interview with a retired Lieutenant General and a former corps commander.
37. Ibid.
38. Richard Armitage's interview with PBS show *Frontline* on 19 April 2002.
39. Interview with Maleeha Lodhi.
40. General Shahid Aziz wrote in his memoirs published in Urdu, p. 244.

2 | The Original Sin

1. M. Fields and R. Ahmed, 'A Review of the 2001 Bonn Conference and Application to the Road Ahead in Afghanistan', *Institute for National Strategic Studies,* National Defense University, Washington, 1 November 2011.

2. President Musharraf and President Bush joint press conference in New York, *see*: https://georgewbush-hitehouse.archives.gov/news/releases/2001/11/20011110-6.html.

3. Z. Hussain, *Frontline Pakistan: The Struggle with Militant Islam*, I.B. Tauris, 2006, p. 48.

4. Ibid.

5. M. Fields and R. Ahmed, 'A Review of the 2001 Bonn Conference and Application to the Road Ahead in Afghanistan', *Institute for National Strategic Studies*, National Defense University, Washington, 1 November 2011.

6. Ibid.

7. In his remarks at a joint press conference with Colin Powell in Islamabad in October 2001, President Musharraf said: 'We agreed that a durable peace in Afghanistan would only be possible through the establishment of a broad based, multi-ethnic government representing the demographic contours of Afghanistan freely chosen by the Afghans without outside interference. Former King Zahir Shah, political leaders, moderate Taliban.' Press release US State Department. Also *see*: Z. Hussain, *Frontline Pakistan: The Struggle with Militant Islam*, I.B. Tauris, 2006.

8. Interview with Maleeha Lodhi, Pakistan's ambassador to Washington.

9. Ibid.

10. F. Vendrell, 'What Went Wrong after Bonn', 18 April 2012, *see*: https://www.mei.edu/publications/what-went-wrong-after-bonn.

11. M. Fields and R. Ahmed, 'A Review of the 2001 Bonn Conference and Application to the Road Ahead in Afghanistan', *Institute for National Strategic Studies*, National Defense University, Washington, 1 November 2011.

12. Ibid.

13. Ibid.

14. Ibid.

15. Interview with Aziz Ahmed Khan, former ambassador to Kabul.

16. *PBS*, Frontline show, 'Filling the vacuum', The Bonn Conference, *see*: https://www.pbs.org/wgbh/pages/frontline/shows/campaign/withus/cbonn.html.

17. Ibid.

18. Ibid.

19. S. Erlanger, 'After arm twisting, Afghan factions pick interim government and leader', *The New York Times*, 6 December 2001, *see*: https://www.nytimes.com/2001/12/06/world/nation-challenged- after-taliban-after-arm-twisting-afghan-factions-pick-interim.html.

20. *PBS*, Frontline, 'Filling the vacuum', The Bonn Conference, *see*: https://www.pbs.org/wgbh/pages/frontline/shows/campaign/withus/cbonn.html.

21. A. Levy and C. Scott-Clark, *The Exile*, Bloomsbury, 2017, p. 81.

22. Ibid.

23. M. Fields and R. Ahmed, 'A Review of the 2001 Bonn Conference and Application to the Road Ahead in Afghanistan', *Institute for National Strategic Studies*, National Defense University, Washington, 1 November 2011.

24. In that period Karzai would visit Islamabad and would often drop by to the Associated Press (AP) office. This conversation took place at a dinner.

25. F. Vendrell, 'What Went Wrong after Bonn', 18 April 2012, *see*: https://www.mei.edu/publications/what-went-wrong-after-bonn.

26. Ibid.

27. Ibid.

28. B. R. Rubin, 'Crafting a constitution for Afghanistan', Center on International Cooperation.

29. R. Grenier, *88 Days to Kandahar: A CIA Diary*, 2015.

30. M. Sack and C. Samii, 'Interview with Lakhdar Brahimi', *Journal of International Affairs*, vol. 58, Fall 2004. Also *see*: A Review of the 2001 Bonn Conference, NDU.

31. Ibid.

32. A. Rashid, *Taliban*, London, I.B.Tauris, 2000, pp. 186–7.

33. Ibid.

34. Z. Hussain, *Frontline Pakistan: The Struggle with Militant Islam*, I.B. Tauris, 2006, p. 30.

3 | The Fall and Rise of the Taliban

1. R. Grenier, *88 Days to Kandahar: A CIA Diary*, Simon and Schuster, 2016, p. 224.

2. Ibid, p. 230.

3. Ibid, p. 231.

4. Ibid, pp. 232-234.

5. B. Knowlton, 'Rumsfeld Rejects PlanTo Allow Mullah Omar To Live in Dignity: Taliban Fighters Agree to Surrender Kandahar', *The International Herald Tribune*, 7 December 2001.

6. Ibid.

7. Interview with Maleeha Lodhi, Pakistan's ambassador to Washington.

8. Ibid.

9. Interview with General Ehsanul Haq.

10. B. Knowlton, 'Rumsfeld Rejects Plan To Allow Mullah Omar 'To Live in Dignity': Taliban Fighters Agree to Surrender Kandahar', *The International Herald Tribune*, 7 December 2001.

11. Ibid.

12. A. Stric van Linschton and F. Kuehn, *Enemy We Created: The Myth of Taliban-Al Qaeda Merger in Afghanistan*, Hurst, 2012.

13. Z. Hussain, 'Taliban Question', *The Cairo Review of Global Affairs*, Fall 2014.

14. Ibid.

15. Ibid.

16. J. Page and Z. Hussain, 'A Friend and Foe: Warlord Who Thwarted the Russains Threatens NATO', London, *The Times*, 28 June 2010.

17. Z. Hussain, *The Scorpion's Tail*, New York, Simon and Schuster, 2010, p. 36.

18. Interview with General Ehsan ul Haq.
19. J. Solomon, 'Failed Courtship pf Warlord Trips Up US in Afghanistan Eager for Allies, Army Tries Turning Insurgents: Chaos Embroils Pakistan', *The Wall Street Journal*, 8 November 2007.
20. Z. Hussain, 'Taliban Question', *The Cairo Review of Global Affairs*, Fall 2014.
21. Z. Hussain, 'Taliban Question', *The Cairo Review of Global Affairs*, Fall 2014. Also *see*: A. Stric van Linschton and F. Kuehn, *Enemy We Created: The Myth of Taliban-Al Qaeda Merger in Afghanistan*, Hurst, 2012, p. 253.
22. Z. Hussain, *Frontline Pakistan: The Struggle with Militant Islam*, Columbia University Press, 2008, pp. 86-87.
23. Ibid.
24. Conversation with Agha Jan Motasim in Kabul in 2017. He is residing in Kabul now after he survived an assassination attempt in Karachi.
25. I interviewed President Karzai in Kabul in 2004 and it was published in the London *Times*.
26. Z. Hussain, 'Taliban Question', The Cairo Review of Global Affairs, Fall 2014. Also *see*:
27. Ibid.
28. Ibid.
29. Ibid.
30. A. Stric van Linschton and F. Kuehn, *Enemy We Created: The Myth of Taliban-Al Qaeda Merger in Afghanistan*, Hurst, 2012, p. 279.
31. Z. Hussain, 'Taliban Question', *The Cairo Review of Global Affairs*, Fall 2014. Also *see*: A. Stric van Linschton and F. Kuehn, *Enemy We Created: The Myth of Taliban-Al Qaeda Merger in Afghanistan*, Hurst, 2012, p. 257.
32. Ibid.
33. Ibid.
34. Ibid.
35. J. F. Burns, 'Afghan president escapes bullets; 25 killed by bomb', *The New York Times*, 6 September 2002, *see*: https://www.nytimes.com/2002/09/06/world/traces-terror-kandahar-kabul-afghan-president-escapes-bullets-25- killed-bomb.html. Also *see*: Z. Hussain, 'Taliban Question', *The Cairo Review of Global Affairs*, Fall 2014 and Z. Hussain, *The Scorpion's Tail*, New York, Simon and Schuster, 2010, p. 38.
36. Z. Hussain, 'Sources of Tenison in Afghanistan and Pakistan: A Regional Perspective', CIDOB, *Barcelona Centre for International Affairs*, December 2011.
37. S. Sengupta. 'US give India applause, Pakistan a pat on the back: President Bush's dealings with the two nuclear rivals illustrated the shifting balance of power in the region and the world', *The New York Times*, March 2006, *see*: https://www.nytimes.com/2006/03/05/world/asia/us-gives-india-applause-pakistan-a-pat-on-the-back.html.
38. C. Gall and E. Bumiller, 'Pakistan is tense as Bush arrives on a 24-hour visit', *The New York Times*, 4 March 2006, *see*: https://www.nytimes.com/2006/03/04/world/asia/pakistan-is-tense-as-bush-arrives-on-24hour-visit.html.

39. Z. Hussain, 'Sources of Tenison in Afghanistan and Pakistan: A Regional Perspective', CIDOB, *Barcelona Centre for International Affairs*, December 2011.

40. J. Boone, 'Musharraf: Pakistan and India's backing for 'proxies' in Afghanistan must stop', *The Guardian*, 13 February 2015.

41. Interview with Major General (retd) Mahmud Durrani who had served as Pakistan's ambassador to Washington.

42. Ibid.

43. S. Gay Stolberg, 'Bush Plays Chaperon for Awkward Encounter', *The New York Times*, 28 September 2006, *see*: https://www.nytimes.com/2006/09/28/world/asia/28prexy.html.

44. Interview with Major General Mahmud Durrani.

45. Ibid.

46. D. E. Sanger, 'Musharraf Defends Deal with Tribal Leaders', *The New York Times*, 22 September 2006, *see*: https://www.nytimes.com/2006/09/22/world/asia/2cnd-prexy.html.

47. Z. Hussain, *The Scorpion's Tail*, New York, Simon and Schuster, 2010.

48. *See*: www.washingtonpost.com/wp-dyn/content/article/2007/02/20/AR2007022001493.html. Also *see*: Z. Hussain, *The Scorpion's Tail*, New York, Simon and Schuster, 2010, pp. 90-91.

4 | The Great Escape

1. A. Hashim, 'Leaked Abbottabad Commission Report', *Al Jazeera*, 10 July 2013. Also *see*: Brigadier (retd) S. Qadir, *Operation Geronimo*, HA Publications, p. 15; A. Levy and C. Scott-Clark, *The Exile*, p. 184. Moreover, senior Pakistani security officials conformed to me the information.

2. I visited Martung village days after the 1 May 2011 US special forces raid in Abbottabad that killed Osama bin Laden. My report in Wall Street Journal: Z. Hussain, 'Investigators Track bin Laden's Couriers: Pakistan Identifies Two Key Aides', *The Wall Street Journal*, 1 June 2011.

3. Ibid.

4. A. Hashim, 'Leaked Abbottabad Commission Report', *Al Jazeera*, 10 July 2013. Also *see*: S. Qadir, *Operation Geronimo*, HA Publications, p. 14.

5. Ibid.

6. S. Qadir, *Operation Geronimo*, p. 14.

7. *Newsweek*, 'How Al Qaeda Slipped Away', 19 August 2002.

8. Ibid.

9. Z. Hussain, *Frontline Pakistan: The Struggle with Militant Islam*, Columbia University Press, 2008.

10. Ibid.

11. Z. Hussain, *Frontline Pakistan: The Struggle with Militant Islam*, Columbia University Press, 2008, p. 122. Also *see*: A. Levy and C. Scott-Clark, *The Exile*, p. 181.

12. A. Levy and C. Scott-Clark, *The Exile*, p. 181.

13. A. Hashim, 'Abbottabad Commission Report', *Al Jazeera*, 10 July 2013.
14. Ibid.
15. Z. Hussain, *Frontline Pakistan: The Struggle with Militant Islam*, Columbia University Press, 2008, p. 144.
16. Interview with General Ehsan ul Haq.
17. Ibid.
18. P. Musharraf, *In the Line of Fire*, Free Press, 2006, p. 265.
19. D. Filkins, 'Pakistanis Say Americans Joined Their Troops in Raids on Tribal Regions', *The New York Times*, 28 April 2002, *see*: https://www.nytimes.com/2002/04/28/world/nation-challenged-border-operations-pakistanis-say-americans-joined-their-troops.html.
20. Interview with General Ehsan ul Haq.
21. Z. Hussain, *Frontline Pakistan: The Struggle with Militant Islam*, Columbia University Press, 2008.
22. Ibid.
23. According to a senior Pakistani security official.
24. *Washington Post*, 'Raid netted top operative of al-Qaeda', 2 April 2002.
25. *Newsline*, 'Pistols at noon', Karachi, October 2002.
26. D. Johnston and D. Frantz, 'Arrests Raising Hopes in Hunt For Al Qaeda', *The New York Times*, 15 September 2002, *see*: https://www.nytimes.com/2002/09/15/world/threats-responses-investigation-arrests-raising-hopes- hunt-for-al-qaeda.html.
27. *See*: Abbottabad Commission Report.
28. *The New York Times*, 'Qaeda prisoner confesses to beheading of Daniel Pearl', 15 March 2007, *see*: https://www.nytimes.com/2007/03/15/world/americas/15iht-web-0315terrorupd.4921670.html.
29. E. Eckholm, 'Pakistan arrest Qaeda figure seen as planner of 9/11', *The New York Times*, 2 March 2003, *see*: https://www.nytimes.com/2003/03/02/world/threats-responses-terrorism-pakistanis-arrest-qaeda-figure-seen- planner-9-11.html.
30. D. Filkins, 'Khalid Sheikh Mohammed and the C.I.A', The New Yorker, 31 December 2014, *see*: https://www.newyorker.com/news/news-desk/khalid-sheikh-mohammed-cia.
31. *See*: Abbotabad Commission Report. Also *see*: S. Qadir, *Operation Geronimo*, p. 17.
32. Ibid.
33. Ibid.
34. 'President Bush Welcomes President Musharraf to Camp David', *see*: https://georgewbush- whitehouse.archives.gov/news/releases/2003/06/20030624-3.html.
35. D. Teather, 'New 'Bin Laden' videotape warns of real battle to come', *The Guardian*, 11 September 2003, *see*: https://www.theguardian.com/world/2003/sep/11/september11.alqaida. Also *see*: Z. Hussain, *The Scorpion's Tail*, p. 65.

36. R. Moreau and Z. Hussain, 'Bin Laden's back channel', *Newsweek*, 5 August 2004.
37. Ibid.
38. Z. Hussain, *The Scorpion's Tail*, New York, Simon and Schuster, 2010.
39. Ibid.
40. Z. Hussain, *The Scorpion's Tail*, New York, Simon and Schuster, 2010, p. 84.
41. S. Qadir, Operation Geronimo, p. 17. Also *see*: Z. Hussain and J. Page, 'Widow Says Home Was Base for 5 Years', *The Wall Street Journal*, 6 May 2011, *see*: https://www.wsj.com/articles/SB10001424052748704810504576305474289580168.
42. Ibid.
43. A. Hashim, 'Abbottabad Commission Report', *Al Jazeera*.
44. Z. Hussain and K. Johnson, 'Split Seen Between bin Laden, Deputy', *The Wall Street Journal*, 6 May 2011, *see*: https://www.wsj.com/articles/SB10001424052748704810504576305542986572646.

5 | Not-So-Invisible War

1. A senior former Pakistani official involved in the negotiations.
2. Wikileaks Cables: Before his election as president, Asif Ali Zardari had promised Patterson in August 2008 that he would pardon and give immunity to General Pervez Musharraf after he was elected President of Pakistan. The ambassador met Zardari on 23 August, PM Gilani on 21 August and with COAS Kayani on 20 August. In a cable sent to Washington after these meetings, Anne Patterson reported that Zardari had told her on 23 August that he was committed to give indemnity to Musharraf. The ambassador stressed that only the promise of indemnity had persuaded Musharraf to step down as president.
3. E. Schmitt and M. Mazzetti, 'Bush Said to Give Orders Allowing Raids in Pakistan', *The New York Times*, 10 September 2008, *see*: https://www.nytimes.com/2008/09/11/washington/11policy.html.
4. D. Walsh, 'US special forces working inside Pakistan WikiLeaks cables', *The Guardian*, 30 November 2010, *see*: https://www.theguardian.com/world/2010/nov/30/wikileaks-cables-us-forces-embedded-pakistan.
5. B. Woodward, *Obama's Wars*, Simon and Schuster, 2010, p. 26.
6. D. Walsh, 'WikiLeaks cables', *The Guardian*, 30 November 2010.
7. G. Miller and B. Woodward, 'Secret memos reveal explicit nature of U.S., Pakistan agreement on drones', *The Washington Post*, 23 October 2013, *see*: www.washingtonpost.com › world › 2013/10/23.
8. K. DeYoung, 'Secrecy defines Obama's drone war', *The Washington Post*, 19 December 2011.
9. Z. Hussain, *The Scorpion's Tail*, New York, Simon and Schuster, 2010.
10. Interview with Major General (retd) Mahmud Durrani.
11. Ibid.
12. Ibid.

13. A Peshawar-based reporter who worked for an English language national daily.

14. Interview with Major General (retd) Mahmud Durrani.

15. Z. Hussain, 'Pakistan spy chief replaced amid "double game" suspicions', *The Times*, 1 October 2008, *see*: https://www.thetimes.co.uk/article/pakistan-spy-chief-replaced-amid-double- game-suspicions-sf0bgck3p9d.

16. P. Zubair Shah, E. Schmitt, and J. Perlez, 'American Forces Attack Militants on Pakistani Soil', *The New York Times*, 3 September 2008, *see*: https://www.nytimes.com/2008/09/04/world/asia/04attack.html.

17. J. Perlez, 'Pakistan's Military Chief Criticizes U.S. Over a Raid', *The New York Times*, 10 September 2008, *see*: https://www.nytimes.com/2008/09/11/world/asia/11pstan.html.

18. Z. Hussain, 'Pakistan spy chief replaced amid "double game" suspicions', *The Times*, 1 October 2008.

19. S. Coll, 'Pakistan's new spy chief', *The New Yorker*, 30 September 2008, *see*: https://www.newyorker.com/news/steve-coll/pakistans-new-spy-chief.

20. A former senior ISI official who worked with Lt. General Pasha.

21. Ibid.

22. S. Coll, 'Pakistan's new spy chief', *The New Yorker*, 30 September 2008.

23. Ibid.

24. A senior ISI official told me in 2009.

25. C. Woods, 'CIA's Pakistan drone strikes carried out by regular US air force personnel Former drone operators claim in new documentary that CIA missions flown by USAF's 17th Reconnaissance Squadron', *The Guardian*, 14 April 2014, *see*: https://www.theguardian.com/world/2014/apr/14/cia-drones-pakistan-us-air-force-documentary.

26. T. Coghlan, J. Page, and Z. Hussain, 'Secrecy and denial as Pakistan lets CIA use airbase to strike militants', *The Times*, 17 February 2009.

27. J. Dao, 'The air war; 7 Marines killed in Pakistan crash', *The New York Times*, 10 January 2002, *see*: https://www.nytimes.com/2002/01/10/world/a-nation-challenged-the-air-war-7-marines-killed-in-pakistan- crash.html.

28. Z. Hussain, *Frontline Pakistan: The Struggle with Militant Islam*, Columbia University Press, 2008.

29. E. MacAskill, 'Barack Obama sets out new strategy for Afghanistan war: White House speech marks shift from Iraq to destroying the Taliban and al-Qaeda in Afghanistan and Pakistan', *The Guardian*, 27 March 2009, *see*: https://www.theguardian.com/world/2009/mar/27/obama-new-strategy-afghanistan-war.

30. Z. Hussain, 'Usama al Kini, head of al Qaeda in Pakistan, killed by US military', *The Times*, 9 January 2009, *see*: https://www.thetimes.co.uk/article/usama-al-kini-head-of-al-qaeda-in-pakistan- killed-by-us-military-qk579qkm0h7.

31. In 2009, in one of the many State Department cables Wikileaks disclosed Ambassador Anne Paterson confirmed that key player and Chief of Army Staff General Ashfaq Kayani directed his forces to aid those American drone strikes. Various US operations in the country's northern and tribal regions were, the

ambassador wrote, 'almost certainly (conducted) with the personal consent of... General Kayani.'

32. M. Mazzetti and D. E. Sanger, 'Obama Expands Missile Strikes Inside Pakistan', *The New York Times*, 20 February 2009, *see*: https://www.nytimes.com/2009/02/21/washington/21policy.html.

33. Z. Hussain, *The Scorpion's Tail*, New York, Simon and Schuster, 2010.

34. 'Pakistanis see US as biggest threat', *Gallup in Press and Web*, 2 August 2002.

35. C. Savage, 'U.N. Report Highly Critical of U.S. Drone Attacks', *The New York Times*, 2 June 2010, *see*: https://www.nytimes.com/2010/06/03/world/03drones.html.

36. Z. Hussain, 'The "secret" is out', *Dawn*, 15 May 2012.

37. Ibid.

38. 'UN expert criticizes "illegal" targeted killing policies and calls on the US to halt CIA drone killings', *reliefweb*, 2 June 2010, *see*: https://reliefweb.int/report/afghanistan/un-expert-criticizes-illegal-targeted-killing-policies-and- calls-us-halt-cia.

6 | Taming Pakistan: Shifting Sands in Washington

1. 'President Obama's Remarks on New Strategy for Afghanistan and Pakistan', *The New York Times*, 27 March 2009, *see*: https://www.nytimes.com/2009/03/27/us/politics/27obama-text.html.

2. T. Reid and Z. Hussain, 'U.S. Strategy for Pakistan and Afghanistan Barack Obama offers new strategy to tame Pakistan, *The Times London*, 28 March 2009, *see*: https://www.thetimes.co.uk/article/barack-obama-offers-new- strategy-to-tame-pakistan-0zrv3hd3ttl.

3. E. Schmitt, 'U.S. Envoy's Cables Show Worries on Afghan Plans', *The New York Times*, 25 January 2010, *see*: https://www.nytimes.com/2010/01/26/world/asia/26strategy.html.

4. T. Reid and Z. Hussain, 'U.S. Strategy for Pakistan and Afghanistan Barack Obama offers new strategy to tame Pakistan', *The Times London*, 28 March 2009.

5. Ibid.

6. Ibid.

7. 'President Obama's Remarks on New Strategy for Afghanistan and Pakistan', *The New York Times*, 27 March 2009.

8. J. Feffer and J. Prados, 'The AfPak Paradox.With its new unified approach, the Obama administration is trying to increase the U.S. focus on Afghanistan and Pakistan and simultaneously prepare for withdrawal', *Foreign Policy in Focus*, 1 April 2009, *see*: https://fpif.org/the_afpak_paradox/.

9. Z. Hussain, *The Scorpion's Tail*, New York, Simon and Schuster, 2010.

10. Ibid.

11. Z. Hussain, 'Taliban Move Closer to Islamabad', *The Wall Street Journal*, 23 April 2009.

12. Ibid.

13. 'Pakistan giving up to militants: Hillary', *Dawn*, 23 April 2009, *see*: https://www.dawn.com/news/459353.

14. J. Traub, 'Can Pakistan Be Governed?', *The New York Times*, 31 March 2009, *see*: https://www.nytimes.com/2009/04/05/magazine/05zardari-t.html.

15. H. Cooper, 'Emphasis on Al Qaeda at Three-Way Talks', *The New York Times*, 6 May 2009, see: https://www.nytimes.com/2009/05/07/world/asia/07prexy.html.

16. Ibid.

17. Ibid.

18. Ibid.

19. Interview with Nawaz Sharif in 2010 who was the then leader of the opposition.

20. Z. Hussain, *The Scorpion's Tail*, New York, Simon and Schuster, 2010.

21. Ibid.

22. Z. Hussain, *The Scorpion's Tail*, New York, Simon and Schuster, 2010.

23. Z. Hussain and T. Wright, 'Officials Probe Apparent Death of Pakistani Militant', *The Wall Street Journal*, 5 June 2011, *see*: https://www.wsj.com/articles/SB10001424052702303745304576365342674924296.

24. Z. Hussain, 'Death of Pakistan Taliban Leader Spawns Infighting', *The Wall Street Journal*, 10 August 2009, *see*: https://www.wsj.com/articles/SB124976257139816985.

25. Z. Hussain, *The Scorpion's Tail*, New York, Simon and Schuster, 2010. Also *see*: D. Walsh, 'Pakistani troops rescue hostages after militants attack military HQ', *The Guardian*, 11 October 2009, *see*: https://www.theguardian.com/world/2009/oct/11/pakistan-rawalpindi-militant-army-headquarters.

26. Z. Hussain, *The Scorpion's Tail*, New York, Simon and Schuster, 2010.

27. Ibid.

28. E. Schmitt and J. Perlez, 'U.S. Unit Secretly in Pakistan Lends Ally Support', *The New York Times*, 22 February 2009, *see*: https://www.nytimes.com/2009/02/23/world/asia/23terror.html.

29. D. Walsh, 'WikiLeaks cables: US special forces working inside Pakistan', *The Guardian*, 30 November 2010.

30. Ibid.

31. Ibid.

32. E. Schmitt and M. Mazzetti, 'U.S. Resumes Surveillance Flights Over Pakistan', *The New York Times*, 29 June 2009, *see*: https://www.nytimes.com/2009/06/30/world/asia/30drone.html.

33. Ibid.

34. A senior army officer narrated this to me when I visited South Waziristan, days after the area was cleared.

35. Z. Hussain, 'Suicide gunmen kill 40 at Pakistan army mosque', *The Times London*, 5 December 2009, *see*: https://www.thetimes.co.uk/article/suicide-gunmen-kill-40-at-pakistan-army-mosque-l3g5r9nm92s.

7 | Democracy versus National Security

1. 'WikiLeaks Wednesday, 07 October 2009, 13:31 S E C R E T SECTION 01 OF 03 ISLAMABAD 002427 EO 12958 DECL: 10/06/2019. SUBJECT: AMBASSADOR MEETS WITH KAYANI AND PASHA ABOUT KERRY-LUGAR. Classified By: Anne W. Patterson.' Some of the detail of the meeting was also shared to the author by a senior security official. Also *see*: J. Perlez and I. Khan, 'Aid Package From U.S. Jolts Army in Pakistan', *The New York Times*, 7 October 2009, *see*: https://www.nytimes.com/2009/10/08/world/asia/08pstan.html.

2. 'Wikileaks cables: Ambassador meets with Kayani and Pasha about Kerry-Lugar', classified by Anne W. Patterson.

3. Z. Hussain and M. Rosenberg, 'Pakistan Military Chief Tries to Mediate Standoff—As Unrest Grows, Gen. Kayani Pushes President to Yield to Demonstrators' Demands: Restore Judges', *The Wall Street Journal*, 14 March 2009, *see*: https://www.wsj.com/articles/SB123695719691520181.

4. 'Corps commanders express concern over Kerry–Lugar Bill', *Dawn*, 8 October 2009, *see*: https://www.dawn.com/news/855368.

5. Ibid.

6. K. Von Hippel and S. Shahid, 'The Politics of Aid: Controversy Surrounds the Pakistan Aid Bill', *Center for Strategic and International Studies (CSIS), United States*, 19 October 2009, *see*: https://www.csis.org/analysis/politics-aid-controversy-surrounds-pakistan-aid-bill.

7. Ibid.

8. In WikiLeaks. Mr Zardari is also quoted as telling the British Prime Minister Gordon Brown hat he feared a fresh army coup. He was reported in 2009 to have told that he feared General Kayani might 'take me out'.

9. In WikiLeaks. Also *see*: 'Move to work out joint strategy on WikiLeaks', *Dawn*, 2 December 2010, https://www.dawn.com/news/588158/defence-committee-meets-today-move-to-work-out-joint-strategy- on-wikileaks.

10. Z. Hussain, 'Pakistan's Struggle for Control of the ISI', *Newsweek*, 8 January 2008, *see*: https://www.newsweek.com/pakistans-struggle-control-isi-87743.

11. Ibid.

12. M. Mazzetti and E. Schmitt, 'Pakistanis Aided Attack in Kabul, U.S. Officials Say', *The New York Times*, 1 August 2008, *see*: https://www.nytimes.com/2008/08/01/world/asia/01pstan.html.

13. Ibid.

14. M. MacDonald, 'Zardari says ready to commit to no first use of nuclear weapons', Reuters, 22 November 2008, *see*: http://blogs.reuters.com/pakistan/2008/11/22/zardari-says-ready-to-commit-to-no-first-use-of- nuclear-weapons/. Zardari was speaking via satellite from Islamabad to a conference organised by the Hindustan Times when he was asked whether he was willing to make an assurance that Pakistan would not be the first to use nuclear weapons. 'Most certainly,' the newspaper quoted him as saying. 'I can assure you that Pakistan will not be the first country ever to use (nuclear weapons).'

15. In WikiLeaks. Also *see*: 'Move to work out joint strategy on WikiLeaks', *Dawn*, 2 December 2010.
16. WikiLeaks cables: American views on President Zardari. While far from perfect, the documents state, 'President Zardari is pro-American and anti-extremist; we believe he is our best ally in the government.' Also *see*: 'Wikileaks US diplomatic cables: Key Pakistan issues', *BBC News*, 1 December 2010, https://www.bbc.com/news/world-south-asia-11886512.
17. Interview with a retired corps commander.
18. Ambassador Anne Paterson's cable to Washington released by WikiLeaks.
19. WikiLeaks.
20. Ibid.
21. M. Landler, 'Clinton Suffers Barbs and Returns Jabs in Pakistan', *The New York Times*, 30 October 2009, *see*: https://www.nytimes.com/2009/10/31/world/asia/31clinton.html.
22. A former federal minister in the PPP government commented during an interview with the author.
23. The diplomatic cable, accessed by WikiLeaks, was sent by then US ambassador Anne W Patterson on 23 February 2010 about a meeting between President Zardari and US Senator John Kerry. It's also available on Dawn.com.
24. Ibid.
25. M. Landler and E. Schmitt, 'Meeting Pakistanis, U.S. Will Try to Fix Relations', *The New York Times*, 18 October 2010, *see*: https://www.nytimes.com/2010/10/19/world/asia/19diplo.html.
26. Ibid.
27. M. Jahangir, U.S. Department of State. Archive content: Interview with Hillary Rodham Clinton, *Express TV Group*, 22 March 2010, *see*: https://2009-2017.state.gov/secretary/20092013clinton/rm/2010/03/138928.htm.
28. U.S. Department of State, Archive content. Remarks Before the Senate Appropriations Subcommittee on State, Foreign Operations, and Related Programs, Testimony, Hillary Rodham Clinton, Secretary of State. Washington, D.C., 25 March 2010, *see*: https://2009-2017.state.gov/secretary/20092013clinton/rm/2010/03/139064.htm.
29. N. Rafique, '4th Pakistan-U.S. strategic dialogue—beyond the optics', *Institute of Strategic Studies*, *see*: http://issi.org.pk/wp-content/uploads/2014/06/1298972468_88995650.pdf.
30. Ibid.
31. Ibid.

8 | What's Your Plan for Afghanistan?

1. I had a series of conversation with General Kayani in 2017–18.
2. Ibid.

3. M. Landler, 'Short, Tense Deliberation, Then a General Is Gone', *The New York Times*, 23 June 2010, *see*: https://www.nytimes.com/2010/06/24/us/politics/24decide.html.

4. General Kayani.

5. Ibid. Also *see*: S. Coll, *Directorate S: The C.I.A. and America's Secret Wars in Afghanistan and Pakistan*, 2018.

6. V. Nasr, *The Dispensable Nation*, 2013, p. 11.

7. P. Baker, 'How Obama Came to Plan for 'Surge' in Afghanistan', *The New York Times*, 5 December 2009, *see*: https://www.nytimes.com/2009/12/06/world/asia/06reconstruct.html.

8. E. Schmitt, 'Obama Issues Order for More Troops in Afghanistan', *The New York Times*, 30 November 2009, *see*: https://www.nytimes.com/2009/12/01/world/asia/01orders.html.

9. V. Nasr, *The Dispensable Nation*, 2013.

10 General Kayani.

11. C. Fair, 'Obama's New "Af-Pak" Strategy: Can "Clear, Hold, Build, Transfer" Work?', The Centre for International Governance Innovation, *see*: https://www.cigionline.org/publications/obamas-new-af-pak-strategy-can-clear-hold-build-transfer-work.

12. V. Nasr, *The Dispensable Nation*, 2013, p. 11.

13. General Kayani.

14. V. Nasr, *The Dispensable Nation*, 2013, p. 12.

15. D. Filkins and M. Mazzetti, 'Karzai Aide in Corruption Inquiry Is Tied to C.I.A', *The New York Times*, 25 August 2010, *see*: https://www.nytimes.com/2010/08/26/world/asia/26kabul.html.

16. E. Schmitt, 'U.S. Envoy's Cables Show Worries on Afghan Plans', *The New York Times*, 25 January 2010, *see*: https://www.nytimes.com/2010/08/26/world/asia/26kabul.html. Also *see*: 'Text of Ambassador Eikenberry's Cables on U.S. Strategy in Afghanistan', *The New York Times*, *see*: https://www.nytimes.com/interactive/projects/documents/eikenberry-s-memos-on-the-strategy-in-afghanistan.

17. H. Cooper and M. Landler, 'U.S. Now Trying Softer Approach Toward Karzai', *The New York Times*, 9 April 2010, *see*: https://www.nytimes.com/2010/04/10/world/asia/10prexy.html.

18. J. Perlez, 'Pakistan Is Said to Pursue Role in U.S.-Afghan Talks', *The New York Times*, 9 February 2010, *see*: https://www.nytimes.com/2010/02/10/world/asia/10pstan.html.

19. 'Kayani spells out terms for regional stability', *Dawn*, 2 February 2010, *see*: https://www.dawn.com/news/852507/kayani-spells-out-terms-for-regional-stability.

20. J. Klein, 'A Bleeding Ulcer', *Time*, 24 May 2010.

21. 'The Meaning of Marjah. Hearing before the Committee on Foreign Relations United States Senate', 6 May 2010, *see*: https://www.foreign.senate.gov/download/hearing-transcript-050610. Also *see*: 'Losing hearts and minds in

Marjah?', *see*: https://afghanistan.blogs.cnn.com/2010/05/06/losing-hearts-and-minds-in-marjah/May 6th, 2010.

22. E. Schmitt, 'U.S. Envoy's Cables Show Worries on Afghan Plans', *The New York Times*, 25 January 2010, *see*: https://www.nytimes.com/2010/01/26/world/asia/26strategy.html.

23. T. Christian Miller, '$6 Billion Later, Afghan Cops Aren't Ready to Serve'. This story was co-published by ProPublica with Newsweek on 20 March 2010, *see*: https://www.propublica.org/article/six-billion-dollars-later-the-afghan-national-police-cant-begin-to-do.

24. Z. Hussain and G. Whittell, 'US Afghan strategy in peril as Pakistan refuses to take on key militant', *The Times London*, 16 December 2009, *see*: https://www.thetimes.co.uk/article/us-afghan-strategy-in-peril-as-pakistan-refuses-to-take-on-key-militant-52x0lf8bc2k.

25. General Kayani.

26. Ibid.

27. Ibid.

28. Ibid.

29. Ibid.

30. Ibid.

31. Z. Hussain, *The Scorpion's Tail*, New York, Simon and Schuster, 2010.

32. S. Gorman, A. Gopal, and Y. J. Dreazen, 'CIA Blast Blamed on Double Agent', *The Wall Street Journal*, 6 January 2010, *see*: https://www.wsj.com/articles/SB126264256099215443.

33. Z. Hussain, T. Wright, and K. Johnson, 'Suspect's Ties to Pakistan Taliban Probed', *WSJ*, 6 May 2010, *see*: https://www.wsj.com/articles/SB1000142405274870332220457522647282802644.

34. Z. Hussain. *The Scorpion's Tail*, 2010, p. 194. Also *see*: The White House, Office of the Press Secretary, 'Joint Pakistan-U.S. statement on the visit of National Security Advisor General James L. Jones and Director of Central Intelligence Agency Leon Panetta to Pakistan', 18–19 May 2010, *see*: https://www.hsdl.org/?abstract&did=24191.

35. A senior Pakistani official.

36. 'Severe consequences in case of Pakistan link: Clinton', *Reuters*, 8 May 2010, *see*: https://tribune.com.pk/story/11638/severe-consequences-in-case-of-pakistan-link-clinton.

37. S. Shane, 'C.I.A. to Expand Use of Drones in Pakistan', *The New York Times*, 3 December 2009, *see*: https://www.nytimes.com/2009/12/04/world/asia/04drones.html.

38. Z. Hussain, 'Pakistan Confirms Baradar's Capture', *WSJ*, 17 February 2010, *see*: https://www.wsj.com/articles/SB10001424052748703444804575071192027190492.

39. E. Bumiller, 'Taliban Leaders Unlikely to Accept Offer, Gates Says', *The New York Times*, 18 January 2010, *see*: https://www.nytimes.com/2010/01/19/world/asia/19military.html.

40. Z. Hussain, *The Scorpion's Tail*, 2010, p. 206.
41. Ambassador Patterson's cable to Washington revealed by WikiLeaks.
42. I have seen the thirteen points document that General Kayani presented to President Obama at the White House.
43. V. Nasr, *The Dispensable Nation*, 2013, p. 11.

9 | Enemies Now

1. *Dawn*, 'US official guns down two motorcyclists in Lahore', 27 January 2011, *see*: https://www.dawn.com/news/601997/us-official-guns-down-two-motorcyclists-in-lahore.
2. Ibid.
3. *Dawn*, 'Davis was assigned to protect CIA team tracking militants', 22 February 2011, *see*: https://www.dawn.com/news/608008.
4. J. Perlez, 'Pakistan Demands Data on C.I.A. Contractors', *The New York Times*, 25 February 2011, *see*: https://www.nytimes.com/2011/02/26/world/asia/26pakistan.html.
5. *The Nation*, '202 Blackwater personnel arrive', 4 November 2009, *see*: https://nation.com.pk/04-Nov-2009/202-blackwater-personnel-arrive.
6. Interview with a senior security official.
7. *Dawn*, 'Document reveals Gillani authorised Haqqani to issue visas to Americans', 24 March 2017, *see*: https://www.dawn.com/news/1322483.
8. A. Abbasi, 'Different authorities talk differently on CIA visa issue', Islamabad, *The News*, 25 March 2017, *see*: https://www.thenews.com.pk/print/194399-Different-authorities-talk-differently-on-CIA-visa-issue.
9. Interview with a senior security official.
10. Interview with General Shuja Pasha.
11. V. Nasr, *The Dispensable Nation*, 2013, p. 77.
12. Interview with General Pasha.
13. D. Walsh and E. MacAskil, 'Blackwater operating at CIA Pakistan base, ex-official says', *The Guardian*, 11 December 2009, *see*: https://www.theguardian.com/world/2009/dec/11/blackwater-in-cia-pakistan-base.
14. J. Scahill. 'Blackwater's Secret War in Pakistan', *The Nation*, 26 November 2009, *see*: https://nation.com.pk/26-Nov-2009/blackwaters-secret-war-in-pakistan.
15. WikiLeaks revealed this secret cable
16. M. Mazzetti et al., 'American Held in Pakistan Worked With C.I.A', *The New York Times*, 21 February 2011, *see*: https://www.nytimes.com/2011/02/22/world/asia/22pakistan.html.
17. *Express Tribune*, 'Cameron Munter: A short profile', 30 October 2010, *see*: https://tribune.com.pk/story/69823/a-short-profile.
18. G. Miller, 'After presiding over bin Laden raid, CIA chief in Pakistan came home suspecting he was poisoned by ISI', *The Washington Post*, 5 May 2016.

19. M. Mazzetti and S. Masood, 'Pakistani Role Is Suspected in Revealing U.S. Spy's Name', *The New York Times*, 17 December 2010, *see*: https://www.nytimes.com/2010/12/18/world/asia/18pstan.html.

20. Ibid.

21. G. Miller, 'After presiding over bin Laden raid, CIA chief in Pakistan came home suspecting he was poisoned by ISI', *The Washington Post*, 5 May 2016.

22. M. Mazzetti, 'How a Single Spy Helped Turn Pakistan Against the United States', *The New York Times*, 9 April 2013, *see*: https://www.nytimes.com/2013/04/14/magazine/raymond-davis-pakistan.html.

23. Interview with a senior Pakistani foreign ministry official.

24. M. Mazzetti, 'How a Single Spy Helped Turn Pakistan Against the United States', *The New York Times*, 9 April 2013.

25. Interviews with senior Pakistani civil and military officials familiar with the Davis affair.

26. A senior Pakistani foreign ministry official. Also *see*: M. Mazzetti, 'How a Single Spy Helped Turn Pakistan Against the United States', *The New York Times*, 9 April 2013.

27. G. Miller, 'After presiding over bin Laden raid, CIA chief in Pakistan came home suspecting he was poisoned by ISI', *The Washington Post*, 5 May 2016.

28. Z. Hussain and T. Wright, 'Pakistan to Charge Detained American With Murder', WSJ, 12 February 2011, *see*: https://www.wsj.com/articles/SB10001424052748703786804576137910853192954.

29. Interview with General Pasha.

30. Ibid.

31. *Dawn*, 'Davis issue may hit Afghanistan meeting', 9 February 2011.

32. J. Perlez, 'U.S. Postpones Meeting with Pakistan and Afghanistan', *The New York Times*, 13 February 2011, *see*: https://www.nytimes.com/2011/02/14/world/asia/14pakistan.html.

33. J. Tapper and L. Ferran, 'President Barack Obama: Pakistan Should Honor Immunity for "Our Diplomat"', Abc News, 26 January 2011, *see*: https://abcnews.go.com/Blotter/raymond-davis-case-president-barack-obama-urges-pakistan/story?id=12922282.

34. Interview with General Pasha.

35. Interview with Foreign Secretary Salman Bashir.

36. J. Rogin, 'Inside the secret U.S.-Pakistan meeting in Oman', *Foreignpolicy*, 24 February 2011, *see*: https://foreignpolicy.com/2011/02/24/inside-the-secret-u-s-pakistan-meeting-in-oman/.

37. Ibid.

38. Interview with a senior official who was present in the meeting.

39. Interview with General Pasha.

40. Interview with Salman Bashir.

41. Interview with Lt. General (retd) Asif Yasin.

42. M. Mazzetti, 'How a Single Spy Helped Turn Pakistan Against the United States', *The New York Times*, 9 April 2013.

43. Ibid.
44. G. Miller, 'After presiding over bin Laden raid, CIA chief in Pakistan came home suspecting he was poisoned by ISI', *The Washington Post*, 5 May 2016.

10 | Midnight Raid

1. I was one of the guests at the ambassador's dinner that night.
2. General Kayani's talk to a group of journalist days after the raid. Also *see*: Z. Hussain, M. Rosenberg, and J. Page, 'Slow Dawn After Midnight Raid', *WSJ*, 9 May 2011, *see*: https://www.wsj.com/articles/SB10001424052748704681904576311480146648792.
3. Ibid.
4. Abbottabad Commission Report leaked to Al Jazeera.
5. Interview with Foreign Secretary Salman Bashir.
6. From General Kayani's post-raid briefing to journalists. Also *see*: Z. Hussain, M. Rosenberg, and J. Page, 'Slow Dawn After Midnight Raid', *WSJ*, 9 May 2011, *see*: https://www.wsj.com/articles/SB10001424052748704681904576311480146648792.
7. Ibid.
8. My interviews with the residents of Bilal Colony hours after the incident. Also *see* my report in *The Wall Street Journal*: Z. Hussain and R. Mehsud, 'His "Waziristan Mansion" Was No Cave', *WSJ*, 3 May 2011, *see*: https://www.wsj.com/articles/SB10001424052748703703304576299320454078378
9. Ibid.
10. Major Amir's statement to the Abbottabad Commission.
11. Interview with a senior ISI officer.
12. Interview with Foreign Secretary Salman Bashir.
13. Ibid.
14. 'General Kayani says militants' back broken', *Reuters*, 23 April 2011, *see*: https://www.dawn.com/news/623236/newspaper/column.
15. *The White House*, 'Osama Bin Laden Dead', 2 May 2011, *see*: https://obamawhitehouse.archives.gov/blog/2011/05/02/osama-bin-laden-dead
16. 'Pakistan faces pressure after bin Laden killed near its capital', *Reuters*, 2 May 2011, *see*: https://www.dawn.com/news/625506
17. C. Gall, 'In Pakistani Statements, an Awkward Acceptance', *The New York Times*, 2 May 2011, *see*: https://www.nytimes.com/2011/05/03/world/asia/03denial.html.
18. A. Ali Zardari, 'Pakistan did its part', *The Washington Post*, May 2011.
19. J. Solomon et al., 'Pakistan's bin Laden Connection Is Probed', *WSJ*, 2 May 2011.
20. Ibid.
21. 'CIA director says agency ruled out working with Pakistan on bin Laden raid as it feared Islamabad "might alert targets"', *Al Jazeera*, 3 May 2011, *see*: https://www.aljazeera.com/news/asia/2011/05/20115381148250187.html.

22. Interview with a retired senior army officer who later held key government position.

23. Interview with a retired army officer who held a senior position during 2011.

24. I witnessed the proceeding at the NDU that day, from the guest gallery.

25. Ibid.

26. Interview with Salman Bashir.

27. T. Wright and M. Rosenberg, 'Pakistan Warns U.S. Against Raids', *WSJ*, 6 May 2011, *see*: https://www.wsj.com/articles/SB100014240527487048105045763050 33789955132.

28. Interviews with a senior federal minister and several lawmakers who attended the joint session of the parliament. Also *see*: Z. Hussain and J. E. Barnes, 'Pakistani General Under Fire', *WSJ*, 7 May 2011, *see*: https://www.wsj.com/articles/SB1 0001424052748704810504576307701926133030.

29. M. Rosenberg and Z. Hussain, 'Pakistan Spy Chief Offers Resignation', *WSJ*, 14 May 2011, *see*: https://www.wsj.com/articles/SB100014240527487038642 04576320130988406462.

30. Z. Hussain, 'Pakistan Arrests General Suspected of Radical Ties', *WSJ*, 21 June 2011, *see*: https://www.wsj.com/articles/SB100014240527023048879045 76399642200849186. Also *see*: 'Brig Ali Khan, four army officers convicted over Hizbut Tahrir links', *Dawn*, 3 Aug 2012, *see*: https://www.dawn.com/ news/739474/brig-ali-khan-four-other-officers-convicted-in-mutiny-case.

31. 'Kayani orders probe into intel failure, seeks cut in US personnel', *Dawn*, 5 May 2011, *see*: https://www.dawn.com/news/626467.

32. M. Rosenberg, T. Wright, and Z. Hussain, 'Pakistani Army Pleads for Respect', *WSJ*, 9 June 2011, *see*: https://www.wsj.com/articles/SB10001424052702304 43230457636944241687836.

33. 'Kayani orders probe into intel failure, seeks cut in US personnel' *Dawn*, 5 May 2011.

34. 'M. Rosenberg, T. Wright, and Z. Hussain, 'Pakistani Army Pleads for Respect', *WSJ*, 9 June 2011.

35. 'Pakistan knows more about Osama, al Qaeda', *Express Tribune*, 11 May 2010, *see*: https://tribune.com.pk/story/12292/'pakistan-knows-more-about-osama-al-qaeda'.

36. Interview with General Pasha. Also *see*: 'ISI official says Pakistan tipped off US on bin Laden: Report', *Agence France-Presse*, 28 April 2012.

37. 'How Umar Patek was captured', *Dawn*, 14 April 2011, *see*: https://www.dawn. com/news/620992/how-umar-patek-was-captured-2.

38. M. Rosenberg and T. Wright, 'Abbottabad, where bin Laden hid, had suspected safe houses in 2003; Pakistan says it shared intelligence with U.S', *WSJ*, 4 May 2011, *see*: https://www.wsj.com/articles/SB100014240527487043228045763 03240472777006.

39. S. Shah, 'CIA organised fake vaccination drive to get Osama bin Laden's family DNA', *The Guardian* 11 July 2011, *see*: https://www.theguardian.com/ world/2011/jul/11/cia-fake-vaccinations-osama-bin-ladens-dna.

40. Abbottabad Commission Report obtained by *Al Jazeera*.

41. 'Ibid.

42. S. Shah, 'CIA organised fake vaccination drive to get Osama bin Laden's family DNA', *The Guardian* 11 July 2011, *see*: https://www.theguardian.com/world/2011/jul/11/cia-fake-vaccinations-osama-bin-ladens-dna.

43. M. Mazzetti, 'Panetta Credits Pakistani Doctor in Bin Laden Raid', *The New York Times,* 28 January 2012, *see*: https://www.nytimes.com/2012/01/29/world/asia/panetta-credits-pakistani-doctor-in-bin-laden-raid.html.

44. 'Pakistan general gets life for spying', *BBC*, 31 May 2019, *see*: https://www.bbc.com/news/world-asia-48472238.

11 | Relations on a Slippery Slope

1. S. Lee Myers, 'In Tense Post-Bin Laden Trip to Pakistan, Clinton Seeks Firm Action on Extremists', *The New York Times*, 27 May 2011, *see*: https://www.nytimes.com/2011/05/28/world/asia/28diplo.html.

2. Ibid.

3. 'Clinton exonerates Pakistan over Osama Bin Laden', *BBC*, 27 May 2011, *see*: https://www.bbc.com/news/av/world-south-asia-13579463/clinton-exonerates-pakistan-over-osama-bin-laden.

4. A. J. Rubin, R. Rivera and J. Healy, 'U.S. Embassy and NATO Headquarters Attacked in Kabul', *The New York Times*, 13 September 2011, *see*: https://www.nytimes.com/2011/09/14/world/asia/14afghanistan.html.

5. A. J. Rubin, R. Rivera, and J. Healy, 'Pakistan's Spy Agency Is Tied to Attack on U.S. Embassy', *The New York Times*, 22 September 2011, *see*: https://www.nytimes.com/2011/09/23/world/asia/mullen-asserts-pakistani-role-in-attack-on-us-embassy.html.

6. Ibid.

7. 'Press Briefing by Press Secretary Jay Carney', 28 September 2011, *see*: https://obamawhitehouse.archives.gov/the-press-office/2011/09/28/press-briefing-press-secretary-jay-carney. Also *see*: E. Schmitt, 'U.S. Recalibrates Remarks About Pakistan', *The New York Times*, 28 September 2011, *see*: https://www.nytimes.com/2011/09/29/world/asia/us-recalibrates-mullens-remarks-about-pakistan.html.

8. Conversation with General Kayani.

9. Ibid.

10. Ibid.

11. S. Lee Myers, 'U.S. Officials Deliver Warning in Pakistan Over Extremists', *The New York Times*, 20 October 2011, *see*: https://www.nytimes.com/2011/10/21/world/asia/clinton-issues-blunt-warning-to-pakistan.html.

12. Interview with foreign secretary.

13. Ibid.

14. S. Lee Myers, 'Clinton Widens Audience in Pakistan, but Sticks to Tough Message', *The New York Times*, 21 October 2011, *see*: https://www.nytimes.

com/2011/10/22/world/asia/clinton-prods-pakistanis-again-though-more-gently.html.

15. 'Clinton warns Pakistan on insurgent havens', *The Washington Post*, 20 October 2011, *see*: www.washingtonpost.com › asia_pacific › 2011/10/20.

16. A. J. Rubin, 'Assassination Deals Blow to Peace Process in Afghanistan', *The New York Times*, 20 September 2011, *see*: https://www.nytimes.com/2011/09/21/world/asia/Burhanuddin-Rabbani-afghan-peace-council-leader-assassinated.html.

17. E. Schmitt and D. E. Sanger, 'U.S. Seeks Aid From Pakistan in Peace Effort', *The New York Times*, 30 October 2011, *see*: https://www.nytimes.com/2011/10/31/world/asia/united-states-seeks-pakistan-spy-agencys-help-for-afghan-talks.html.

18. Interviews with a senior Pakistani official engaged in the negotiations. Also *see*: E. Schmitt and D. E. Sanger, 'U.S. Seeks Aid From Pakistan in Peace Effort', *The New York Times*.

19. R. Nordland, '12 Americans Die as Blast Hits Bus in Afghanistan', *The New York Times*, 29 October 2011, *see*: https://www.nytimes.com/2011/10/30/world/asia/deadly-attack-strikes-nato-bus-in-kabul.html.

20. Interview with Maleeha Lodhi.

21. Ibid.

22. Ibid.

23. 'Clinton picks new US envoy to Afghanistan, Pakistan', *Reuters*, 15. February 2011 *see*: https://www.reuters.com/article/us-usa-afghanistan-envoy/clinton-picks-new-u-s-envoy-to-afghanistan-pakistan-idUSTRE71E0LN20110215.

24. D. E. Sanger, *Confront and conceal*, New York, Crown Publishers, pp. 7-9.

25. Ibid.

26. Ibid.

27. Conversation with General Kayani.

28. 'Pakistan outrage after Nato attack kills soldiers', *BBC*, 26 November 2011, *see*: https://www.bbc.com/news/world-asia-15901363.

29. I visited the area in 2009 after Pakistani forces cleared the area from the insurgents.

30. 'Pakistan voices "deep rage" over NATO attack, Foreign minister tells US secretary of state that incident that left 25 soldiers dead is "totally unacceptable"', *Al Jazeera*, 28 November 2011, *see*: https://www.aljazeera.com/news/asia/2011/11/2011112775817634246.html.

31. Interview with Salman Bashir.

32. Ibid.

33. Interview with Hina Rabbani Khar.

34. Ibid.

35. *See* Chapter 5.

36. S. Momand, 'Pakistan stops NATO supplies after deadly raid', *Reuters*, 26 November 2011, *see*: https://www.reuters.com/article/us-pakistan-nato-idUSTRE7AP03S20111126.

37. Ibid.

12 | Sorry, But 'No' Sorry

1. J. H. Cushman Jr., 'Obama Offers "Condolences" in Deaths of Pakistanis', *The New York Times*, 4 December 2011, *see*: https://www.nytimes.com/2011/12/05/world/asia/obama-offers-condolences-in-deaths-of-pakistani-troops.html.

2. J. Rogin, 'President Zardari suddenly leaves Pakistan—is he on the way out?', *Foreign Policy*, 6 December 2011, *see*: https://foreignpolicy.com/2011/12/06/president-zardari-suddenly-leaves-pakistan-is-he-on-the-way-out/. Also, senior members of the PPP government confirmed Zardari suffering from bipolar problem.

3. 'Memo offered to revamp Pakistan's security policy', *Dawn*, 19 Nov 2011, *see* https://www.dawn.com/news/674260/memo-offered-to-revamp-pakistans-security-policy.

4. 'Mansoor Ijaz: Fixer in Pakistan's "memogate" row', *BBC News*, 22 February 2012, *see*: https://www.bbc.com/news/world-asia-16649034.

5. 'ISI DG has all the evidence: Mansoor Ijaz', *Express Tribune*, 20 November 2011, *see*: https://tribune.com.pk/story/294898/dg-isi-pasha-has-forensically-tested-memo-evidence-mansoor-ijaz.

6. S. Shah, '"Memogate" scandal deepens as American accuser threatens to tell all', *The Guardian*, 12 January 2012, *see*: https://www.theguardian.com/world/2012/jan/12/memogate-scandal-pakistan-isi-haqqani.

7. J. Rogin, 'Mullen denies secret back channel in U.S.-Pakistan relationship', *Foreign Policy*, 8 November 2011, *see*: https://foreignpolicy.com/2011/11/08/exclusive-mullen-denies-secret-back-channel-in-u-s-pakistan-relationship/.

8. 'Pakistan US ambassador Haqqani resigns over "memogate"', *BBC News*, 22 November 2011, *see*: https://www.bbc.com/news/world-asia-15838839.

9. 'Haqqani bows out', *Dawn*, 23 November 2011, *see*: https://www.dawn.com/news/675305/haqqani-bows-out.

10. S. Masood and E. Schmitt, 'A Diplomat in a Gilded Cage, Feeling Trapped and Not Entirely Safe', *The New York Times*, 8 January 2012, *see*: https://www.nytimes.com/2012/01/09/world/asia/husain-haqqani-confined-in-pakistan-amid-legal-battle.html.

11. J. Rogin, 'President Zardari suddenly leaves Pakistan—is he on the way out?', *Foreign Policy*, 6 December 2011.

12. A member of the PPP government and a senior security official, who were present at the site confirmed the episode.

13. J. Rogin, 'President Zardari suddenly leaves Pakistan—is he on the way out? *Foreign Policy*, 6 December 2011.

14. 'Memogate case: Kayani, Pasha replies were illegal, implies PM Says they were not authorised by competent authority', *Express Tribune*, 9 January 2012, *see*: https://tribune.com.pk/story/319209/memogate-gilani-terms-kayani-pasha-sc-replies-unconstitutional.

15. 'Move afoot to bring down govt: Gilani', *Dawn*, 23 December 2011, *see*: https://www.dawn.com/news/682600. Also *see*: 'You're subservient, or you're

mistaken - PM tells military: Says if army believes it is a state within a state, it is unacceptable', *Express Tribune*, 23 December 2011, *see*: https://tribune.com. pk/story/310422/pm-gilani-fears-ouster.

16. Ibid.

17. 'Defence secretary Naeem Lodhi sacked', *Dawn*, 12 January 2012, *see*: https://www.dawn.com/news/687507/defence-secretary-naeem-lodhi-sacked.

18. 'Pakistan army warns PM Gilani over criticisms', *BBC News*, 11 January 2012, *see*: https://www.bbc.com/news/world-asia-16511826.

19. A. Gul, 'Pakistani Army Chief Dismisses Coup Rumors', *Voice of America*, 22 December 2011, *see*: https://www.voanews.com/east-asia/pakistani-army-chief-dismisses-coup-rumors.

20. Interview with Sherry Rehman.

21. Ibid.

22. Ibid.

23. Ibid.

24. Interview with a senior foreign ministry official familiar with the discussion between US Secretary of State and Pakistan's foreign minister in London conference. Also *see*: 'U.S. says Pakistan upbeat on eventual cooperation', *Reuters*, 23 February 2012, *see*: https://www.reuters.com/article/us-pakistan-usa/u-s-says-pakistan-upbeat-on-eventual-cooperation-idUSTRE81M15H20120223.

25. D. Walsh, E. Schmitt, and S. Lee Myers, 'United States Talks Fail as Pakistanis Seek Apology', *The New York Times*, 27 April 2012, *see*: https://www.nytimes.com/2012/04/28/world/asia/talks-between-us-and-pakistan-fail-over-airstrike-apology.html.

26. Ibid.

27. 'Shakil Afridi sentenced to 33 years in treason case', *Dawn*, 23 May 2012, *see*: https://www.dawn.com/news/720716/shakil-afridi-imprisoned-for-helping-cia-find-bin-laden.

28. I covered the NATO Summit in Chicago on 20 May 2012.

29. Ibid.

30. 'NATO sets "irreversible" but risky course to end Afghan war', *Reuters*, 21 May 2012, *see*: https://www.reuters.com/article/us-nato-summit/nato-sets-irreversible-but-risky-course-to-end-afghan-war-idUSBRE84J02C20120521.

31. D. Walsh, 'Notions of Honor Color High-Stakes Haggling Over NATO Supply Routes', *The New York Times*, 8 June 2012, *see*: https://www.nytimes.com/2012/06/09/world/asia/us-and-pakistan-in-high-stakes-haggle.html.

32. V. Nasr, *The Dispensable Nation*, 2013, p. 89.

33. J. Rogin 'Inside the U.S. "apology" to Pakistan', *Foreign Policy*, 3 July 2012, *see*: https://foreignpolicy.com/2012/07/03/inside-the-u-s-apology-to-pakistan/.

34. E. Schmitt, 'Clinton's "Sorry" to Pakistan Ends Barrier to NATO', *The New York Times*, 3 July 2012, *see*: https://www.nytimes.com/2012/07/04/world/asia/pakistan-opens-afghan-routes-to-nato-after-us-apology.html.

35. 'Salala air raid: United States says sorry – finally', *Express Tribune*, 3 July 2012, *see*: https://tribune.com.pk/story/403330/salala-air-raid-united-states-says-sorry--finally.

36. J. Rogin, 'Inside the U.S. "apology" to Pakistan', *Foreign Policy*, 3 July 2012.

37. S. Islam, 'Khar, Kayani in Brussels: Pakistan wins praise, but is it enough?', *Dawn*, 5 December 2012, *see*: https://www.dawn.com/news/768997/khar-kayani-in-brussels-pakistan-wins-praise-but-is-it-enough.

13 | Talking to the Taliban

1. 'Kerry visit casts Pakistan more as partner than pariah', *Christian Science Monitor*, 1 August 2013, *see*: https://www.csmonitor.com/World/Global-News/2013/0801/Kerry-visit-casts-Pakistan-more-as-partner-than-pariah.

2. Z. Hussain, 'The New Sharif era', *Dawn*, 21 May 2013, *see*: https://www.dawn.com/news/1012665.

3. General Kayani.

4. Ambassador Anne Patterson's cable to Washington in *WikiLeaks*.

5. Interview with former foreign secretary Jalil Abbas Jilani.

6. Ibid.

7. Ibid.

8. Ibid.

9. O. Waraich, 'The CIA and ISI: Are Pakistan and the U.S.'s Spy Agencies Starting to Get Along?', *Time.com*, 7 August 2012, *see*: https://world.time.com/2012/08/07/the-cia-and-isi-are-pakistan-and-the-u-s-s-spy-agencies-starting-to-get-along/.

10. Conversation with General Kayani.

11. D. Walsh and E. Schmitt, 'U.S. Blacklists Militant Haqqani Network', *The New York Times*, 7 September 2012, *see*: https://www.nytimes.com/2012/09/08/world/asia/state-department-blacklists-militant-haqqani-network.html.

12. V. Christoph Reuter, G. Schmitz, and H. Stark, 'Talking to the Enemy: How German Diplomats Opened Channel to Taliban', *Spiegel International*, 10 January 2012, *see*: https://www.spiegel.de/international/world/talking-to-the-enemy-how-german-diplomats-opened-channel-to-taliban-a-808068.html.

13. Ibid.

14. D. Nelson and B. Farmer, 'Secret peace talks between US and Taliban collapse over leaks', *The Daily Telegraph*, 10 August 2011, *see*: https://www.telegraph.co.uk/news/worldnews/asia/afghanistan/8693247/Secret-peace-talks-between-US-and-Taliban-collapse-over-leaks.html.

15. 'Clinton to Taliban: Dump al-Qaeda or "Face Consequences": US Sec. of State Hillary Clinton remembers Richard Holbrooke during address at Asia Society in New York', 18 February 2011, *see*: https://asiasociety.org/clinton-taliban-dump-al-qaeda-or-face-consequences.

16. M. Rosenberg, 'Taliban Opening Qatar Office, and Maybe Door to Talks', *The New York Times*, 3 January 2012, *see*: https://www.nytimes.com/2012/01/04/world/asia/taliban-to-open-qatar-office-in-step-toward-peace-talks.html.

17. Ibid.

18. 'How Qatar came to host the Taliban', *BBC News*, 22 June 2013, *see*: https://www.bbc.com/news/world-asia-23007401.

19. 'Afghan President Karzai to boycott talks with Taliban', *BBC News*, 19 June 2013, *see*: https://www.bbc.com/news/world-asia-22973111.

20. Author's interviews with senior Pakistan security and foreign ministry officials.

21. Author's conversation with Douglas Lute.

22. 'U.S. soldier charged with 17 murders in Afghan killings', *Reuters*, 24 March 2012, *see*: https://www.reuters.com/article/us-afghanistan-usa-charges/u-s-soldier-charged-with-17-murders-in-afghan-killings-idUSBRE82M0ZU20120324.

23. Author's interview with Foreign Secretary Jalil Abbas Jilani who was part of the Pakistani delegation in the trilateral meeting in Brussels. Also *see*: 'Kerry says Afghan-Pakistan talks productive', *Reuters*, 24 April 2013, *see*: https://in.reuters.com/article/us-afghanistan-talks-kerry-idUSBRE93N0VO20130424.

24. Jalil Abbas Jilani.

25. Ibid.

26. General Kayani.

27. Interview with senior Pakistani officials.

28. M. Rosenberg and A. J. Rubin, 'Taliban Step Toward Afghan Peace Talks Is Hailed by U.S.', *The New York Times*, 18 June 2013, *see*: https://www.nytimes.com/2013/06/19/world/asia/taliban-ready-for-peace-talks-to-end-afghan-war.html. Also *see*: 'Pakistan welcomes opening of Taliban office in Doha', *Dawn*, 19 June 2013, *see*: https://www.dawn.com/news/1019099.

29. Ibid.

30. 'Taliban's Qatar office stokes Karzai's ire. Afghan government is angry the Taliban raised their flag and vowed to continue fighting after opening their Doha centre', *Al Jazeera*, 21 June 2013, *see*: https://www.aljazeera.com/indepth/features/2013/06/2013620152934517697.html.

31. Z. Hussain, 'Afghanistan: a messy endgame', *Dawn*, 4 June 2014, *see*: https://www.dawn.com/news/1110343/afghanistan-a-messy-endgame.

32. Ibid. Also *see*: E. Schmitt and C. Savage and B. Bergdahl, 'American Soldier, Freed by Taliban in Prisoner Trade', *The New York Times*, 31 May 2014, *see*: https://www.nytimes.com/2014/06/01/us/bowe-bergdahl-american-soldier-is-freed-by-taliban.html.

33. Z. Hussain, 'The Taliban Question', *The Cairo Review of Global Affairs*, Fall 2014.

34. Z. Hussain, 'Afghanistan: a messy endgame', *Dawn*, 4 June 2014, *see*: https://www.dawn.com/news/1110343/afghanistan.

35. Z. Hussain, 'A flawed political transition', *Dawn*, 24 September 2014, *see*: https://www.dawn.com/news/1133907/a-flawed-political-transition.

36. Ibid.

14 | Storming the Witches' Brew!

1. Author's conversation with General Kayani few weeks before his retirement in November 2013.
2. Ibid.
3. Z. Hussain, 'New power balance', *Dawn*, 3 December 2013, *see*: https://www. dawn.com/news/1060152/new-power-balance.
4. Ibid.
5. 'Pakistan journalist Hamid Mir issues defiant statement', *BBC News*, 25 April 2014, *see*: https://www.bbc.com/news/world-asia-27153234.
6. Z. Hussain, 'Treason: the real test', *Dawn*, 28 December 2013, *see*: https://www. dawn.com/news/1076862/treason-the-real-test.
7. Z. Hussain, 'End of the charade?', *Dawn*, 19 February 2014, *see*: https://www. dawn.com/news/1087976/end-of-the-charade.
8. 'TTP tries to justify ruthless killing of 23 FC soldiers', *Dawn*, 18 February 2014, *see*: https://www.dawn.com/news/1087719.
9. 'Karachi airport attack signals tactical shift by Taliban', *Reuters*, 12 June 2014, *see*: https://www.reuters.com/article/us-pakistan-airport-attack-insight/karachi-airport-attack-signals-tactical-shift-by-taliban-idUSKBN0EN0ED20140612.
10. Z. Hussain, 'Inaction or capitulation?', *Dawn*, 11 June 2014, *see*: https://www. dawn.com/news/1111841/inaction-or-capitulation.
11. 'Pakistan army launches "major offensive" in North Waziristan', *BBC News*, 15 June 2014, *see*: https://www.bbc.com/news/world-asia-27858234.
12. Z. Hussain, 'Reclaiming North Waziristan', *Dawn*, 18 June 2014, *see*: https:// www.dawn.com/news/1113348/reclaiming-north-waziristan.
13. Ibid.
14. Ibid.
15. Interviews with senior security officials involved in North Waziristan operation.
16. 'Shaping a New Peace in Pakistan's Tribal Areas', *International Crisis Group (ICG)*, 20 August 2018, *see*: https://www.crisisgroup.org/asia/south-asia/ pakistan/b150-shaping-new-peace-pakistans-tribal-areas.
17. I have extensively covered all the operations in North Waziristan since 2004 and visited again in 2014 when most of the agency had been cleared. My eye witness account of the aftermath of 2014 operation was published in series of columns in Dawn newspaper.
18. Z. Hussain, 'Battleground North Waziristan', *Dawn*, 19 November 2014, *see*: https://www.dawn.com/news/1145359/battleground-north-waziristan.
19. Ibid. Also *see*: Z. Hussain, '2014: The iron hand', *Dawn*, 3 January 2015, *see*: https://www.dawn.com/news/1154834.
20. Ibid.
21. Ibid.
22. 'Pakistan: Imran Khan, Tahirul Qadri lead protest march', *BBC News*, 14 August 2014, *see*: https://www.bbc.com/news/world-asia-28770311.

23. 'PTI against the military operation in NW: Imran Khan', *Dawn*, 16 August 2012, *see*: https://www.dawn.com/news/742610/pti-against-the-military-operation-in-nw-imran-khan.

24. 'Pakistani protesters clash with police, soldiers secure state TV', *Reuters*, 1 September 2014, *see*: https://www.reuters.com/article/us-pakistan-crisis/pakistani-protesters-clash-with-police-soldiers-secure-state-tv-idUSKBN0GU0RT20140901.

25. Z. Hussain, 'Theatre of the absurd', *Dawn*, 27 August 2014, *see*: https://www.dawn.com/news/1127958/theatre-of-the-absurd.

26. Z. Hussain, 'The real battle', *Dawn*, 3 September 2014, *see*: https://www.dawn.com/news/1129484/the-real-battle.

27. 'Nawaz had "solid information" about former ISI chief's role in Dharna', *The News*, 25 July 2015, *see*: https://www.thenews.com.pk/print/13759-nawaz-had-solid-information-about-former-isi-chiefs-role-in-dharna. Also *see*: 'General (retd) Zaheerul Islam: The shadow warrior', *Herald*, 6 October 2015, *see*: http://herald.dawn.com/news/1153259.

28. Ibid.

29. 'Pakistan Taliban: Peshawar school attack leaves 141 dead', *BBC News*, 16 December 2014, *see*: https://www.bbc.com/news/world-asia-30491435.

30. Z. Hussain, 'Outsourcing policy', *Dawn*, 24 December 2014, *see*: https://www.dawn.com/news/1152765/outsourcing-policy.

31. Ibid.

32. Ibid.

33. Z. Hussain, 'Hard choice', *Dawn*, 7 January 2015, *see*: https://www.dawn.com/news/1155311/hard-choice.

34. Ibid.

35. Z. Hussain, 'Down a slippery slope', *Dawn*, 21 January 2015, *see*: https://www.dawn.com/news/1158315/down-a-slippery-slope.

36. Z. Hussain, 'Another Sharif in Washington', *Dawn*, 11 November 2015, *see*: https://www.dawn.com/news/1218827/another-sharif-in-washington.

15 | Death of Mullah Omar: Battle for Leadership

1. Interview with a senior Pakistani foreign ministry official who was present in the Murree meeting.

2. Ibid.

3. 'US welcomes Afghan-Taliban talks: White House', *Reuters*, 7 July 2015, *see*: https://tribune.com.pk/story/916787/us-welcomes-afghan-taliban-talks-white-house.

4. J. Boone, 'Ashraf Ghani visit may mark new chapter in Afghan-Pakistan relations', *The Guardian*, 14 November 2014, *see*: https://www.theguardian.com/world/2014/nov/14/ashraf-ghani-visit-pakistan-afghanistan.

5. 'Ghani dubs Pakistan "important pillar" of Afghanistan foreign policy', *Dawn*, 15 November 2914, *see*: https://www.dawn.com/news/1144677.

6. Z. Hussain, 'Analysis: Cautious optimism after Murree talks', *Dawn*, 9 July 2015, *see*: https://www.dawn.com/news/1193272/analysis-cautious-optimism-after-murree-talks.

7. Z. Hussain, 'Ghani's frustration', *Dawn*, 1 June 2015, *see*: https://www.dawn.com/news/1187178/ghanis-frustration.

8. Ibid.

9. Z. Hussain, 'Pakistan's Afghan predicament', *Dawn*, 5 May 2017, *see*: https://www.dawn.com/news/1211334/pakistans-afghan-predicament.

10. Ibid.

11. K. Johnson and M. Zahra-Malik, 'Taliban, Afghan officials hold peace talks, agree to meet again', *Reuters*, 8 July 2005, *see*: https://www.reuters.com/article/us-afghanistan-taliban/taliban-afghan-officials-hold-peace-talks-agree-to-meet-again-idUSKCN0PI0DX20150708.

12. Interviews with senior Pakistani officials.

13. K. Johnson and M. Zahra-Malik, 'Taliban, Afghan officials hold peace talks, agree to meet again', *Reuters*, 8 July 2015, *see*: https://www.reuters.com/article/us-afghanistan-taliban/taliban-afghan-officials-hold-peace-talks-agree-to-meet-again-idUSKCN0PI0DX20150708.

14. A. Siddique, 'Peace Overtures Showcase Iran's Deep Taliban Ties', *Gandhara*, 7 January 2019, *see*: https://gandhara.rferl.org/a/peace-overtures-showcase-iran-deep-taliban-ties/29696039.html.

15. 'Doubts and divisions among commanders as Taliban talk peace', *Express Tribune*, 13 July 2015, *see*: https://tribune.com.pk/story/919875/doubts-and-divisions-among-commanders-as-taliban-talk-peace.

16. A. Khan, 'Prospects of Peace in Afghanistan', *Institute of Strategic Studies (ISSI)*, *see*: http://issi.org.pk/wp-content/uploads/2016/07/2-Amina_Khan_SS_Vol_36_No.1_2016.pdf.

17. 'Taliban leaders biography attended Islamabad meeting', *Pajhwok Report*, 9 July 2015, *see*: https://www.pajhwok.com/en/2015/07/09/taliban-leaders-biography-attended-islamabad-meeting.

18. 'Taliban leader Mullah Omar backs Afghanistan peace talks', *BBC News*, 15 July 2015, *see*: https://www.bbc.com/news/world-asia-33535905.

19. 'Taliban leader Mullah Omar hails "legitimate" peace talks in Eid message', *DW*, *see*: https://www.dw.com/en/taliban-leader-mullah-omar-hails-legitimate-peace-talks-in-eid-message/a-18585594.

20. Z. Hussain, 'A paradigm shift', *Dawn*, 22 July 2015, *see*: https://www.dawn.com/news/1195527.

21. Ibid.

22. Ibid.

23. Ibid.

24. Z. Hussain, 'Daesh in Afghanistan', *Jinnah Institute*, 15 January 2018.

25. Ibid.

26. Ibid.

27. S. Engel Rasmussen, J. Boone, and E. Graham-Harrison, 'Taliban leader Mullah Omar is dead, says Afghan government', *The Guardian*, 29 July 2015, *see*: https://www.theguardian.com/world/2015/jul/29/taliban-leader-mullah-omar-dead-claims.

28. Ibid.

29. Z. Hussain, 'The death of a hermit', *Dawn*, 5 August 2015, *see*: https://www.dawn.com/news/1198412/the-death-of-a-hermit.

30. Ibid.

31. Z. Hussain, 'Delving deep into Mullah Omar's life in hiding', *Arab News*, 12 March 2019, *see*: https://www.arabnews.pk/node/1465466.

32. Ibid.

33. Ibid.

34. J. Goldstein, 'Taliban's New Leader Strengthens His Hold with Intrigue and Battlefield Victory', *The New York Times*, 4 October 2015, *see*: https://www.nytimes.com/2015/10/05/world/asia/kunduz-fall-validates-mullah-akhtar-muhammad-mansour-talibans-new-leader.html.

35. Ibid.

36. 'Taliban political chief in Qatar Tayyab Agha resigns', *BBC News*, 4 August 2015, *see*: https://www.bbc.com/news/world-asia-33770725.

37. Ibid.

38. M. Mashal, 'Taliban Envoy Breaks Silence to Urge Group to Reshape Itself and Consider Peace', *The New York Times*, 31 October 2016, *see*: https://www.nytimes.com/2016/11/01/world/asia/afghanistan-taliban-peace-talks.html.

39. Ibid.

40. 'New Taliban leader Mullah Akhtar Mansour calls for unity', *BBC News*, 1 August 2015, *see*: https://www.bbc.com/news/world-asia-33746487.

41. 'Afghan Taliban leader Mullah Mansour "open to talks"', *BBC News*, 22 September 2015, *see*: https://www.bbc.com/news/world-asia-34322125.

42. Z. Hussain, 'Talking the Afghan talks', *Dawn*, 2 March 2016, *see*: https://www.dawn.com/news/1242964/talking-the-afghan-talks.

43. Ibid.

44. Ibid.

45. Z. Hussain, 'The Taliban tightrope', *Dawn*, 25 May 2016, *see*: https://www.dawn.com/news/1260492/the-taliban-tightrope.

46. Ibid.

47. Z. Hussain, 'The Taliban tightrope', *Dawn*, 25 May 2016, *see*: https://www.dawn.com/news/1260492/the-taliban-tightrope.

48. Ibid. Also *see*: C. Gall and R. Khapalwak, 'Taliban Leader Feared Pakistan Before He Was Killed', *The New York Times*, 9 August 2017, *see*: https://www.nytimes.com/2017/08/09/world/asia/taliban-leader-feared-pakistan-before-he-was-killed.html.

49. D. Azami, 'Mawlawi Hibatullah: Taliban's new leader signals continuity', *BBC News*, 26 May 2016, *see*: https://www.bbc.com/news/world-asia-36381563. Also *see*: M. Mashal, T. Shah, and Z. Nader, 'Taliban Name Lesser-Known Cleric

as Their New Leader', *The New York Times*, 25 May 2016, *see*: https://www.nytimes.com/2016/05/26/world/asia/afghanistan-taliban-new-leader.html.

50. 'Profile: New Taliban chief Mawlawi Hibatullah Akhundzada', *BBC News*, 26 May 2016, *see*: https://www.bbc.com/news/world-asia-36377008.

16 | A Maverick in the White House

1. Z. Hussain, 'Russia getting into Afghan act', *Dawn*, 4 January 2017, *see*: https://www.dawn.com/news/1306197/russia-getting-into-afghan-act.

2. Ibid.

3. A. Khan, 'Russia-China-Pakistan Third Trilateral Dialogue on Afghanistan', *ISSI*, 17 January 2017.

4. M. Mashal and J. Sukhanyar, 'Afghanistan's Approach to Russian Diplomacy: Keep It in the Family', *The New York Times*, 27 February 2017, *see*: https://www.nytimes.com/2017/02/27/world/asia/afghanistan-moscow-putin-ghani-kochai.html.

5. 'Russia's interests coincide with Taliban's on fighting IS group', *FRANCE 24*, 23 December 2015, *see*: https://www.france24.com/en/20151223-russia-interest-coincide-taliban-fight-islamic-state-group-afghanistan.

6. Z. Hussain, 'Waiting for the Panama verdict', *Dawn*, 2 April 2017, *see*: https://www.dawn.com/news/1326468/waiting-for-the-panama-verdict.

7. Z. Hussain, 'Sharif under siege', *Dawn*, 26 October 2016, *see*: https://www.dawn.com/news/1292273/sharif-under-siege.

8. C. Almeida, 'Exclusive: Act against militants or face international isolation, civilians tell military', *Dawn*, 6 October 2016.

9. Ibid.

10. N. Najar, 'Gunmen Killed in Pathankot, India, Air Base Attack', *The New York Times*, 2 January 2016, *see*: https://www.nytimes.com/2016/01/03/world/asia/india-air-base-attack-pathankot.html.

11. A senior member of the Sharif government told me that there was a clear message from the military leadership that extension in the tenure of General Raheel Sharif could resolve the issue.

12. Z. Hussain, 'The general's legacy', *Dawn*, 14 January 2017, *see*: https://www.dawn.com/news/1298018.

13. Ibid.

14. Z. Hussain, 'Of civil and military relations', *Dawn*, 30 November 2016, *see*: https://www.dawn.com/news/1299464/of-civil-and-military-relations.

15. Ibid.

16. Z. Hussain, 'Tweeting defiance', *Dawn*, 3 May 2017, *see*: https://www.dawn.com/news/1330703/tweeting-defiance.

17. Z. Hussain, 'End of Sharif dynasty?', *Dawn*, 29 July 2017, *see*: https://www.dawn.com/news/1348319/end-of-sharif-dynasty.

18. M. Landler and M. R. Gordon, 'As U.S. Adds Troops in Afghanistan, Trump's Strategy Remains Undefined', *The New York Times*, 18 June 2017, *see*: https://www.nytimes.com/2017/06/18/world/asia/us-troops-afghanistan-trump.html.
19. Ibid.
20. J. Hirschfeld Davis and M. Landler, 'Trump Outlines New Afghanistan War Strategy with Few Details', *The New York Times*, 21 August 2017, *see*: https://www.nytimes.com/2017/08/21/world/asia/afghanistan-troops-trump.html.
21. Z. Hussain, 'America's flawed plan', *Dawn*, 23 August 2017, *see*: https://www.dawn.com/news/1353296/americas-flawed-plan.
22. Ibid.
23. J. Hirschfeld Davis, 'Trump Outlines New Afghanistan War Strategy With Few Details', *The New York Times*, 21 August 2017.
24. Z. Hussain, 'America's flawed plan', *Dawn*, 23 August 2017.
25. Ibid.
26. 'Trump attacks Pakistan "deceit" in first tweet of the year', *BBC News*, 1 January 2018, *see*: https://www.bbc.com/news/world-us-canada-42536209.
27. 'Trump has put Pakistan on notice, US VP Pence warns in surprise Kabul visit', *Dawn*, 22 December 2017, *see*: https://www.dawn.com/news/1378179.
28. Z. Hussain, 'America's flawed plan', *Dawn*, 23 August 2017.
29. Ibid.
30. Z. Hussain, 'China-Pakistan Economic Corridor and the New Regional Geopolitics', *Asiavision*, no. 94, June 2017.
31. Ibid.
32. D. S. Markey and J. West, 'Behind China's Gambit in Pakistan', *Council on Foreign Relations*, 12 May 2016.
33. M. K. Bhadrakumar, 'Chinese naval ships at Gwadar port call for a rethink of India's regional policy', *Dawn*, 28 November 2016.
34. F. Shah, 'Does the China-Pakistan economic corridor worry India?', *Al Jazeera*, 23 February 2017.
35. D. S. Markey, 'Behind China's Gambit in Pakistan', *Council on Foreign Relations (CFR)*, 12 May 2016.
36. Z. Hussain, 'Civil-military power matrix', *Dawn*, 19 September 2018, *see*: https://www.dawn.com/news/1433844/civil-military-power-matrix.

17 | Shifting Sands of Afghanistan

1. '2018 was the Afghan war's bloodiest year, according to UN', *SBS News*, 24 February 2019, *see*: https://www.sbs.com.au/news/2018-was-the-afghan-war-s-bloodiest-year-according-to-un.
2. Z. Hussain, 'Afghan war turns bloodier', *Dawn*, 13 January 2018, *see*: https://www.dawn.com/news/1386256/afghan-war-turns-bloodier.
3. 'Why Afghanistan is more dangerous than ever?', *BBC News*, 14 September 2018, *see*: https://www.bbc.com/news/world-asia-45507560.
4. Z. Hussain, 'Afghan war turns bloodier', *Dawn*, 13 January 2018.

5. 'Why Afghanistan is more dangerous than ever', *BBC News*, 14 September 2018, *see*: https://www.bbc.com/news/world-asia-45507560.

6. 'Afghanistan's Ghani offers talks with Taliban "without preconditions"', *Reuters*, 28 February 2018, *see*: https://www.reuters.com/article/us-afghanistan-taliban/afghanistans-ghani-offers-talks-with-taliban-without-preconditions-idUSKCN1GC0J0.

7. T. Khan, 'Tashkent Declaration' calls for Afghan govt-Taliban direct talks', *The Daily Times*, 28 March 2018, *see*: https://dailytimes.com.pk/220609/tashkent-declaration-calls-for-afghan-govt-taliban-direct-talks/.

8. M. Barker and J. Borger, 'Taliban publish letter calling on US to start Afghan peace talks', *The Guardian*, 14 February 2018, *see*: https://www.theguardian.com/world/2018/feb/14/taliban-publish-letter-calling-us-start-afghan-peace-talks.

9. M. Mashal, 'Afghan Sides Agree to Rare Cease-Fire During Eid al-Fitr', *The New York Times*, 24 May 2020, *see*: https://www.nytimes.com/2020/05/24/world/asia/afghanistan-taliban-cease-fire-eid.html.

10. Z. Hussain, 'A window of opportunity?', *Dawn*, 20 June 2018, *see*: https://www.dawn.com/news/1414907/a-window-of-opportunity.

11. 'Taliban threaten 70% of Afghanistan, BBC finds', *BBC News*, 31 January 2018, *see*: https://www.bbc.com/news/world-asia-42863116.

12. Z. Hussain, 'A window of opportunity?', *Dawn*, 20 June 2018.

13. Ibid.

14. B. Osman, 'As New U.S. Envoy Appointed, Turbulent Afghanistan's Hopes of Peace Persist', *International Crisis Group (ICG)*, 5 September 2018, *see*: https://www.crisisgroup.org/asia/south-asia/afghanistan/new-us-envoy-appointed-turbulent-afghanistans-hopes-peace-persist.

15. Z. Hussain, 'A window of opportunity?', *Dawn*, 20 June 2018.

16. Ibid.

17. E. Mitchell, 'Top Afghanistan general: Some Taliban involved in 'secret' talks to end war', *The Hill*, 30 May 2018, *see*: https://thehill.com/policy/defense/389937-top-afghanistan-general-some-taliban-involved-in-secret-talks-to-end-war.

18. A. Gul, 'Afghan Taliban Chief Renews Call for Direct Talks with America Voice of America', *VOA News*, 12 June 2018, *see*: https://www.voanews.com/south-central-asia/afghan-taliban-chief-renews-call-direct-talks-america.

19. P. Constable, 'U.S. talks with the Taliban could be a breakthrough in the Afghan war', *The Washington Post*, 1 August 2018.

20. Z. Hussain, 'Total breakup is not an option', *Dawn*, 5 September 2018, *see*: https://www.dawn.com/news/1431051/total-breakup-is-not-an-option.

21. Ibid.

22. Interview with a senior Pakistani foreign ministry official.

23. 'Trump blasts Pakistan as "fools," charging the country let bin Laden hide there', *Fox News*, 19 November 2018, *see*: https://www.foxnews.com/politics/

trump-blasts-pakistan-as-fools-charging-the-country-let-bin-laden-hide-there-despite-receiving-us.

24. 'PM hits back at "false assertions" by US president, who accused Islamabad of not doing "a damn thing" for Washington', *Al Jazeera*, 20 November 2018, *see*: https://www.aljazeera.com/news/2018/11/imran-khan-hits-trump-tirade-pakistan-181119174825408.html.

25. Z. Hussain, 'A toxic Twitter war', *Dawn*, 3 December 2018, *see*: https://www.dawn.com/news/1446901.

26. Z. Hussain, 'Into the Afghan labyrinth', *Dawn*, 5 December 2018, *see*: https://www.dawn.com/news/1449570/into-the-afghan-labyrinth.

27. Ibid.

28. Ibid.

29. 'Afghanistan's Ghani Presents "Road Map" For Peace Talks At UN Conference', 28 November 2018, *see*: https://www.rferl.org/a/afghanistan-ghani-roadmap-peace-talks-un-conference-/29626218.html.

30. Ibid.

31. Z. Hussain, 'Ironies of the Afghan war', *Dawn*, 30 March 2019, *see*: https://www.dawn.com/news/1472565.

32. Interview with senior Pakistan security and foreign ministry officials.

33. Ibid.

34. Z. Hussain, 'Ironies of the Afghan war', *Dawn*, 30 March 2019.

35. M. Mashal, 'U.S. and Taliban Begin Highest-Level Talks Yet on Ending Afghan War', *The New York Times*, 25 February 2019, *see*: https://www.nytimes.com/2019/02/25/world/asia/us-taliban-talks-afghanistan-qatar-baradar.html.

36. M. Mashal and L. Jakes, 'At Center of Taliban Deal, a U.S. Envoy Who Made It Personal', *The New York Times*, 1 March 2020, *see*: https://www.nytimes.com/2020/03/01/world/asia/zalmay-khalilzad-afghanistan-taliban.html.

37. M. Mashal, 'Once Jailed in Guantánamo, 5 Taliban Now Face U.S. at Peace Talks', *The New York Times*, 26 March 2019, *see*: https://www.nytimes.com/2019/03/26/world/asia/taliban-guantanamo-afghanistan-peace-talks.html.

38. Ibid. Also *see*: Z. Hussain, 'Ironies of the Afghan war', *Dawn*, 30 March 2019.

39. Ibid.

40. Ibid.

41. 'Afghan peace talks: Taliban co-founder meets top White House envoy', *BBC News*, 25 February 2019, *see*: https://www.bbc.com/news/world-asia-47351369.

42. Z. Hussain, 'The "Moscow format"', *Dawn*, 14 November 2018, *see*: https://www.dawn.com/news/1445504.

43. Ibid. Also *see*: A. Higgins and M. Mashal, 'In Moscow, Afghan Peace Talks Without the Afghan Government', *The New York Times*, 4 February 2019, *see*: https://www.nytimes.com/2019/02/04/world/asia/afghanistan-taliban-russia-talks-russia.html.

44. Z. Hussain, 'The "Moscow format"', *Dawn*, 14 November 2018.

45. Z. Hussain, 'Moving forward', *Dawn*, 9 August 2019, *see*: https://www.dawn.com/news/1495910/moving-forward.

46. 'Remarks by President Trump and Prime Minister Khan of the Islamic Republic of Pakistan Before Bilateral Meeting', *Oval Office*, 22 July 2019, *see*: https://www.whitehouse.gov/briefings-statements/remarks-president-trump-prime-minister-khan-islamic-republic-pakistan-bilateral-meeting/.

47. Z. Hussain, 'Moving forward', *Dawn*, 9 August 2019.

48. M. Crowley, L. Jakes, and M. Mashal, 'Trump Says He's Called Off Negotiations With Taliban After Afghanistan Bombing', *The New York Times*, 10 September 2019, *see*: https://www.nytimes.com/2019/09/07/us/politics/trump-taliban-afghanistan.html.

49. M. Mashal, 'Taliban Talks Hit a Wall Over Deeper Disagreements, Officials Say', *The New York Times*, 8 September 2019, *see*: https://www.nytimes.com/2019/09/08/world/asia/afghanistan-taliban-camp-david.html.

50. Z. Hussain, 'Back to Afghan peace talks?', *Dawn*, 16 October 2019, *see*: https://www.dawn.com/news/1511080/back-to-afghan-peace-talks.

18 | The Endgame

1. M. Mashal, 'Taliban and U.S. Strike Deal to Withdraw American Troops From Afghanistan', *The New York Times*, 29 February 2020, *see*: https://www.nytimes.com/2020/02/29/world/asia/us-taliban-deal.html.

2. Ibid.

3. Z. Hussain, 'A long way to Afghan peace', *Dawn*, 19 February 2020, *see*: https://www.dawn.com/news/1535381/a-long-way-to-afghan-peace.

4. T. Gibbons-Neff, 'Taliban's Continued Attacks Show Limits of U.S. Strategy in Afghanistan', *The New York Times*, 31 January 2020, *see*: https://www.nytimes.com/2020/01/31/world/asia/afghanistan-violence-taliban.html.

5. Ibid.

6. 'The Afghanistan Papers—Washington Post', 9 December 2019, *see*: https://www.washingtonpost.com/graphics/2019/investigations/afghanistan-papers/documents-database/.

7. Ibid.

8. R. L. Grenier, *88 Days to Kandahar: A CIA Diary*, Simon and Schuster, 2016, p. 8.

9. 'How 775,000 U.S. troops fought in one war: Afghanistan military deployments by the numbers', *The Washington Post*, 11 September 2019.

10. 'The Afghanistan Papers - Washington Post', 9 December 2019, *see*: https://www.washingtonpost.com/graphics/2019/investigations/afghanistan-papers/documents-database/.

11. Z. Hussain, 'War, lies and failure', *Dawn*, 11 December 2019, *see*: https://www.dawn.com/news/1521633/war-lies-and-failure.

12. L. Maizland, 'U.S.-Taliban Peace Deal: What to Know', *Council on Foreign Relations*, 2 March 2020, *see*: https://www.cfr.org/backgrounder/us-taliban-peace-deal-agreement-afghanistan-war.

13. Z. Hussain, 'President Trump's phone call and what next for Afghan peace process', *Arab News*, 6 March 2020, *see*: https://www.arabnews.pk/node/1637621.

14. Ibid.

15. Z. Hussain, 'Afghanistan's shifting sands', *Dawn*, 27 May 2020, *see*: https://www.dawn.com/news/1559649/afghanistans-shifting-sands.

16. Ibid.

17. Z. Hussain, 'Taliban woo minority groups ahead of intra-Afghan peace talks', *Arab News*, 9 May 2020, *see*: https://www.arabnews.pk/node/1672261.

18. F. Bezhan, 'Ethnic Minorities Are Fuelling the Taliban's Expansion in Afghanistan', *Foreign Policy*, 15 June 2016, *see*: https://foreignpolicy.com/2016/06/15/ethnic-minorities-are-fuelling-the-talibans-expansion-in-afghanistan/.

19. R. Kumar, 'Taliban attempts to woo Afghanistan's Hazara community with new appointment', *The National*, 28 April 2020, *see*: https://www.thenational.ae/world/asia/taliban-attempts-to-woo-afghanistan-s-hazara-community-with-new-appointment-1.1011775.

20. F. Bezhan, 'Ethnic Minorities Are Fuelling the Taliban's Expansion in Afghanistan', *Foreign Policy*, 15 June 2016, *see*: https://foreignpolicy.com/2016/06/15/ethnic-minorities-are-fuelling-the-talibans-expansion-in-afghanistan/.

21. S. Haqqani, 'What We, the Taliban, Want', *The New York Times*, 20 February 2020, *see*: https://www.nytimes.com/2020/02/20/opinion/taliban-afghanistan-war-haqqani.html.

22. Z. Hussain, 'Coming full circle', *Dawn*, 26 February 2020, *see*: https://www.dawn.com/news/1536695/coming-full-circle.

23. S. Haqqani, 'What We, the Taliban, Want', *The New York Times*, 20 February 2020.

24. 'In Trump's Words: Praise for the Taliban and Optimism About the Coronavirus', *The New York Times*, 29 February 2020, *see*: https://www.nytimes.com/2020/02/29/us/trump-coronavirus-hoax-taliban.html.

25. Z. Hussain, 'Coming full circle', *Dawn*, 26 February 2020.

26. M. Mashal and F. Abed, 'From Maternity Ward to Cemetery, a Morning of Murder in Afghanistan', *The New York Times*, 12 May 2020, *see*: https://www.nytimes.com/2020/05/12/world/asia/afghanistan-violence-kabul-nangarhar.html.

27. 'Afghan leaders blame Taliban for vicious attack on maternity ward', *CBS News*, 14 May 2020, *see*: https://www.cbsnews.com/news/afghanistan-war-taliban-kabul-hospital-attack-maternity-ward-test-us-peace-deal-today-2020-05-14/.

28. 'Afghanistan: Taliban rejects call for ceasefire during Ramadan', *Al Jazeera*, 24 April 2020, *see*: https://www.aljazeera.com/news/2020/04/afghanistan-taliban-rejects-call-ceasefire-ramadan-200424104202456.html.

29. K. Gannon, 'Taliban to halt military operations over 3-day Eid holiday', *Associated Press (AP)*, 29 July 2020, *see*: https://apnews.com/6890a0305b82b a39ce4c25415090f938.

30. H. Noori, 'Eid ceasefire between Taliban and government gives respite to weary Afghans', *The National*, 3 August 2020, *see*: https://www.thenational.ae/world/ asia/eid-ceasefire-between-taliban-and-government-gives-respite-to-weary-afghans-1.1058507.

31. 'Afghan president pledges to release up to 2,000 Taliban prisoners', *Al Jazeera*, 5 May 2020, *see*: https://www.aljazeera.com/news/2020/05/afghan-president-pledges-release-2000-taliban-prisoners-200525053352382.html.

Index